A WOMAN'S LIFE IS A HUMAN LIFE

Also by Felicia Kornbluh

Ensuring Poverty:
Welfare Reform in Feminist Perspective
(with Gwendolyn Mink)

The Battle for Welfare Rights:
Politics and Poverty in Modern America

FELICIA KORNBLUH

A WOMAN'S LIFE IS A HUMAN LIFE

My Mother, Our Neighbor, and the Journey from Reproductive Rights to Reproductive Justice

Grove Press
New York

FIRST EDITION

Published simultaneously in Canada
Printed in the United States of America

This book is typeset in 13-pt. Centaur by Alpha Design & Composition in Pittsfield, NH.

First Grove Atlantic hardcover edition: January 2023

Library of Congress Cataloging-in-Publication data is available for this title.

ISBN 978-0-8021-6068-3
eISBN 978-0-8021-6069-0

Grove Press
an imprint of Grove Atlantic
154 West 14th Street
New York, NY 10011

Distributed by Publishers Group West

groveatlantic.com

23 24 25 26   10 9 8 7 6 5 4 3 2 1

A firm hand falls enthusiastically on my shoulder. "Daughter," she says back on her own ground, "next time, I won't wait for you to invite me."

When we are leaving the car, I lock her suitcase into the trunk but take along with me the manuscript on which I have been working. She raises her eyebrows, whispering, as if we were conspirators. "Our book?" she asks.

— Kim Chernin, In My Mother's House

There are so many roots to the tree of anger
that sometimes the branches shatter
before they bear.

Sitting in Nedicks
the women rally before they march
discussing the problematic girls
they hire to make them free.
An almost white counterman passes
a waiting brother to serve them first
and the ladies neither notice nor reject
the slighter pleasures of their slavery.
But I who am bound by my mirror
as well as my bed
see causes in colour
as well as sex

and sit here wondering
which me will survive
all these liberations.

—Audre Lorde,
"Who Said It Was Simple"

To my three sisters

and

To the memory of Susan E. Davis and Meredith Tax

CONTENTS

A WOMAN'S LIFE IS A HUMAN LIFE

Prologue

THE MORNING after the cerebral hemorrhage that would take my mother's life, I was with my closest family members, all of us in our Saturday best, trying to compose ourselves as an audience for my nephew Eli's bar mitzvah. My mind wandered to the scene in synagogue about thirteen hours earlier: Eli, insouciant in his suit, my sister Rebecca and me returning to our seats after lighting Sabbath candles—that pointedly female responsibility in Jewish practice that we did only awkwardly, mumbling the Hebrew prayer. My mother, Beatrice, leaned over to kiss my sister. Then her face went slack, her words blurred, and we made a desperate call for an ambulance. It was too late.

By early Saturday morning, my mother was on life support, her brain mostly washed away like a cheap but utterly irreplaceable hard drive. My spouse and brother-in-law were at her side, not expecting a miracle. We wondered if the bar mitzvah should continue, but the rabbi and cantor told us to proceed. Apparently, in Jewish law, if a wedding and funeral party meet at a crossroads, the funeral steps aside for the wedding to pass: joy wins. The future over the past.

Karen, my older sister, leaned across to ask my father a question: "What's that organization Mom was part of? The one that legalized abortion in New York? The Professional Women's Caucus?" My father, who was not having the best morning of his life, was game, nonetheless, to talk politics. "I think that was what it was called." I stared, first at Karen, then at Dad: *What were they talking about?* I am a professional historian. I teach and write about women and gender, law, and movements for social change. *What* Professional Women's Caucus that legalized abortion in New York? On top of my hollow grief, I couldn't believe that I had never learned about this part of her life. And for about twelve hours it had been decisively too late to ask.

Alongside the sharpness of regret, this all crashed on me as a cosmic joke. Mom and I had a close, loving, relationship for the decade or so before she died. But I had spent years fighting with her, working to distinguish myself from her and succeed on my own. Cosmic joke, yes, and my mother's last laugh. Her rejoinder, in every one of those terrible arguments, was some version of "You think you're so smart. Your old mother knows more than you think she does." Well, she got that right.

The conversation my sister Karen started that morning in synagogue set this project in motion. I determined to learn everything I could about the abortion law campaign my mother and other activists pursued, although not, as far as I can tell, through the Professional Women's Caucus—whose most distinguished member, according to an ancient contact list marked up in my mother's distinctive scribble, was a New York law professor named Ruth Bader Ginsburg. I learned that the leaders in this campaign were the National Organization for Women (NOW), Planned Parenthood, the National Association for the Repeal of Abortion Laws (NARAL, today NARAL Pro-Choice America), and, at the very end of the 1960s, smaller groups from the self-named radical wing of the women's movement. I learned that New York was the national leader in liberalizing abortion law, leapfrogging over other states and setting the stage for the Supreme Court to act in *Roe v. Wade*. And I learned that this was in fact the real story of how abortion ceased to be a crime in the United States: not a march through the federal courts by well-trained lawyers making erudite arguments, but a contested call-and-response between grassroots activists and officials at the local and state levels, who were for over one hundred years the ones who made public policy on abortion. Only at the end of a long process of change did activist lawyers take to the federal courts and advocate before the U.S. Supreme Court.

As I studied the history of reproductive rights, I stumbled onto the story of a second woman I knew: my family's neighbor for nearly a decade, on the other side of the hall in our Manhattan high-rise, Dr. Helen Rodríguez-Trías. Rodríguez-Trías was an effective activist, a female Puerto Rican physician at a time when that made her an extreme outlier, and eventually the first Latina head of the American Public Health Association (APHA). She represented APHA at a historic United Nations conference in Egypt that repudiated post–World War II policies of "population control," which tried to entice or coerce poor people into having fewer children as a way to reduce their poverty, while not endorsing other policies that could reduce poverty right away. She built the foundation for this work in New York in the 1970s, when she cofounded the Committee to End Sterilization Abuse (CESA).

Dr. Helen Rodríguez-Trías saw sterilization abuse as an invidious form of population control that was happening every day in the United States, targeting Puerto Ricans who were U.S. colonial subjects, as well as Black women, Latinas, and Native Americans on the U.S. mainland. Women's health, she argued, was endangered most of all by "poverty, violence, joblessness, homelessness, lack of control over our lives or those of our children." A political agenda that included legal abortion and birth control, which let people refrain from having children but didn't enable people to have children and raise them safely, was necessary but incomplete. Rodríguez-Trías and the organizations she founded or inspired are nearly absent from scholarship and journalism about American history.

The more I learned about Dr. Rodríguez-Trías, the more I saw her story as a complement to the one my mother led me to about how abortion in America ceased to be a crime. That's because of who I am: From the profile of my interests (feminism, activism, law), it's pretty obvious that my apple did not fall far from the maternal tree. But after it fell, it rolled a few feet away. While I researched changes in abortion law, my day job was talking with students about the history of feminism, including the challenges many women of color and left-of-center whites have posed to the movement's privileging of abortion rights and not, say, high-quality health care for all or policies that reduce economic inequality. A distinctive movement for reproductive justice has been offering these challenges since the 1990s, when women of color met to plan for that same conference on population that Rodríguez-Trías attended in Cairo and wound up naming a new feminist demand. The reproductive justice movement wants legal abortion and much more, to create conditions that let all people choose whether and when to bear and raise children. Around the time my mother died, I started serving on the board of trustees of my regional Planned Parenthood chapter. I joined a lively and sometimes excruciating effort within the board to incorporate reproductive justice into our work.

I started to think of Rodríguez-Trías as much more than my neighbor, more than an important New Yorker and woman doctor. CESA, her organization, led a campaign against coercive sterilization rooted in the right to have children as well as to avoid doing so. The most influential opponents of CESA's efforts were the organizations with which my mother identified most closely: the national office of NOW and Planned Parenthood at the local and national levels. The debate between them centered on a rigorous consent procedure and waiting period for sterilization, which CESA proposed as a response to reports that doctors in New York City hospitals were pushing clients to agree to sterilization, sometimes without explaining that the procedure was usually irreversible. To the officers of NOW and Planned Parenthood, any barriers in the way of an option like sterilization would themselves deprive people of their reproductive rights. Also important were Planned Parenthood's allies in the Association for Voluntary Sterilization, a pro-sterilization advocacy organization.

While I could draw a straight line from my mother's politics to those of reproductive rights advocates today, Rodríguez-Trías was starting to seem like a critical precursor to the reproductive justice movement. I started to see her, too, as laying groundwork for a global effort to overturn the mid-twentieth-century policy consensus around population control, a consensus that had even shaped the campaign to decriminalize abortion.

The tension I found between the worldview of the woman in apartment 8B, my mother the abortion advocate, and the woman three or four yards away in 8A, Rodríguez-Trías, who helped lay track for the reproductive justice movement, captures in miniature long-standing tensions in liberalism and feminism. The only partially overlapping histories of the movements that inspired Mom and Helen speak to big, persistent questions: How do we form coalitions to make genuine change? How can progressives fight what seems like overwhelming opposition without letting our agendas default to a racially skewed or class-biased lowest-common denominator? How can movements for gender and sexual rights champion all people's freedom while continuing to fight the many battles that go into preserving access to birth control and abortion? Finally (and this one is, obviously, personal for me), how do all of us navigate our personal politics, respecting the views of those we love and those who came before us, even when we know there was much they failed to understand?

Six months before she died, I spent hours interviewing my mother about her life as a lawyer. I learned about her experiences at Brooklyn Law School in the early 1950s, one of four women in her class. She faced the odds and graduated *cum laude*, well before Ruth Bader Ginsburg blew everyone away at Harvard and Columbia Law Schools. I learned about her first marriage to an academic named Otto, whose professional challenges helped explain my mother's persistent anxiety about my own vocational choices. And I reviewed the details of her career, from early jobs with small independent law firms and trade unions to the late 1950s and early 1960s, when Mom went to work in Washington, D.C., as assistant to a board member of the government's National Labor Relations Board (NLRB). After that, I knew, she met my father at a convention of the liberal standard-bearer Americans for Democratic Action, moved to New York City, and made a career in the NLRB's office in Brooklyn Heights. Already in her midthirties and eager to be a mother, she had three children in fairly rapid course: Karen in 1963 and "the twins," Rebecca and me, in 1966.

With the narcissism of a child toward her parents, the sense that their stories end when we show up, I barely asked about later parts of her story—even though I knew my mother joined the New York City chapter of NOW shortly after its founding, and I had once seen a document indicating that she'd been part of a lawyers' network that was the precursor to the NOW Legal Defense and Education Fund (later, Legal Momentum). She and Dad were members of a "reform," or progressive alternative, Democratic Party group called the Hudson Independent Democrats, which met above Hanratty's restaurant on a then-sketchy corner of 96th Street and Amsterdam Avenue. For me, club meetings meant playing for hours with the Freedman girls across the street, in the rec room of their huge building, while their parents and mine sorted out their views on the war in Vietnam.

It was only after I lost her that I realized how much I had failed to learn from my mother. Why was she so passionate about reproductive rights? At her memorial service, I heard for the first time, from the initial Democratic cosponsor of the law that decriminalized abortion in New York, that Mom was the one who had persuaded him to lead that fight. Their work together, retired New York state senator Franz Leichter said, was "perhaps only a footnote in history, but one that should be read." That helped explain why, whenever I raised the subject of abortion, Mom would say with what I remember as clenched fists and a flushed face: "You don't understand, Felicia! They"—the illegal abortionists—"were butchers! Butchers!" On occasions too numerous to catalog, she interrupted conversations about health care with a warning to "never go to a Catholic hospital! All they care about is the fetus," she railed, "never the mother!" She would say this if my sisters, each of whom has two children, were talking about birthing options. And she would say it if any of us mentioned appendectomy or setting a fractured bone: in my mother's understanding, what she believed was a preference for fetuses over adult women signaled a general lack of trustworthiness, perhaps to the point of medical incompetence. It likely also implied to her that Catholic hospitals were per se anti-woman and therefore objectionable, and should be boycotted on principle. My mother was big on principle. She supported Planned Parenthood for decades, going so far, after her retirement and her Los Angeleno third husband's passing, to serve the organization as a volunteer sex educator in Southern California public schools.

Legal abortion and birth control were matters of principle for my mother. But those principles were products of the life she lived. She was raised by a working-class but aspiring immigrant single mother, my grandmother Miriam, who fled the former Russian empire as a teenager in 1917 amid the confusion of the Soviet revolution and World War I. Finances were tight in my mother's Depression-era childhood. She remembered digging into her own piggy bank to help Miriam make it through the month. To save money and get into the workforce as soon as possible, Mom went to law school after only two years of college, selling gloves at Macy's during the winter holidays to pay her way. But a J.D. with honors only qualified this young, female, Jewish attorney for jobs a half step up from the "pink collar" clerical ghetto.

Far from abstract or rooted in formal constitutional ideas, my mother's reproductive politics grew from a hard-won, dirt-under-the-fingernails understanding of sex inequality and the treacherous clamber upward that social mobility required. Without some degree of control over her reproduction, how could a woman get through school? Or fight the hostility she was almost certain to encounter when she tried to join an elite profession like law? Or make the case to employers that she was a dependable hire for the long term?

There was trauma behind my mother's principles, too. Miriam and my mother's father, Nathan, had a troubled marriage. They divorced at a time when divorce was rare. The only explanation I ever heard was that he tried to control Miriam's money when the two of them worked similar manufacturing jobs during World War II and she wouldn't stand for it. Mom had her own unsuccessful first marriage, to the scholar. Once, and only once, and only to me, my mother said that after her divorce from Otto, when she was a seemingly happy career gal in the nation's capital, she was raped by a man she met at a party.

Several months after she died, I found a letter in which my mother joyously announced the birth of "the twins," including premature, colicky Felicia. She also listed a stream of ills in the prior two years that included a "D&C." Dilation and curettage, or D&C, was the most common method of abortion in the 1960s, and the phrase "D&C," was a common shorthand or euphemism for an abortion. Dilation and curettage also was, and is, a medical procedure doctors use in cases of miscarriage and to treat other conditions. I don't know if my mother had an illegal or legal abortion, or a miscarriage, or something else. All I know is that it was something she understood as bad and as important enough to mention to two close friends, albeit friends who lived in Washington, D.C., and were unlikely to mention the incident to any of their mutual acquaintances.

I never got to interview Dr. Helen Rodríguez-Trías, who died in 2001. Luckily, though, I was able to talk to several of her friends and two of her children, Jo Ellen Brainin-Rodríguez, her eldest, and Daniel Curet-Rodríguez, her youngest and the only one who lived for a while in the apartment across the hall. Thanks to her late husband, the labor organizer and professor Eddie González, Rodríguez-Trías's papers have been gathered into an archival collection that includes frank assessments she made of her life and career.

Rodríguez-Trías was born in New York City in 1929, a year later than my mother. Like my mother, she was a child of the Great Depression and of migration. She, too, had a father who was rarely in her life after a young age, perhaps planting seeds for her commitment to the economic well-being of women with or without male partners. Her parents, businessman Damian Rodríguez and teacher Josefa Trías, relocated to Puerto Rico when she was an infant. A decade later, her mother left her alcoholic father behind and returned to New York with Helen. They lived in the Washington Heights neighborhood, later a haven for Spanish-speaking people from the Caribbean but at this time filled mostly with immigrants from Eastern and Southern Europe. School administrators must have been wearing biased blinders, because they tried to assign this brilliant woman to a "slow" class, from which a perspicacious teacher rescued her.

By deciding to leave New York again after high school, Rodríguez-Trías escaped the racism toward Puerto Ricans on the U.S. mainland. But she couldn't escape the fact that Puerto Rico was a colonial possession of the United States. She enrolled at the University of Puerto Rico. As she wrote: "The year of my return to Puerto Rico, 1947, was highly charged politically. University authorities refused to allow Nationalist Party leader [and independence activist] Pedro Albizu Campos, just released from federal prison, to speak on campus. Students struck and the university shut down. I was peripheral to the student movement but began to identify with the political struggles of the island." Her brother, whose financial help made it possible for her to study full-time, responded by cutting off support. She dropped out of school, joined a leftist organization, and was back in New York City by the summer of 1948.

Rodríguez-Trías, nineteen years old, met David Brainin, twenty-three, in the offices of a newspaper he edited. They married six months later,

"as suited two young leftists . . . in a nontraditional ceremony." David
and Helen—an Eastern European Jew and a light-skinned Puerto Rican
with friends of many hues—were harassed by neighbors, who tried
to get them evicted. They asked Representative Vito Marcantonio to
intercede on their behalf; this was the kind of constituent service around
which the socialist from East Harlem had built his career.

Although they shared political commitments, Rodríguez-Trías's
and Brainin's union did not last. At the time they separated, she was
achingly lonely, with three young children at home and a husband
who had relocated them to Ohio and taken a job in a factory so that
he could organize its workers. She wanted to live close to her mother,
who was on her way to Puerto Rico for breast cancer treatment. Jo
Ellen was three; a second daughter, Laura, just under two; and baby
David, five months old. In 1955, Rodríguez-Trías remarried. With
her new husband's financial support, she enrolled once again at the
University of Puerto Rico. In 1960, she graduated first in her class
from the University of Puerto Rico School of Medicine, six months
pregnant with her second son, Daniel. With her husband taking on
most of the at-home parenting, she completed her residency in pediatrics and started a promising medical career.

As was true with my mother's, Helen's feminism grew from her life
experiences as well as her personal ideology. Some of those experiences
were bitter ones. Of course, she was sensitized to the workings of
hierarchy by mainland racism and the independence struggle in Puerto
Rico. Her considered response to these circumstances was to affiliate
with anti-imperialists and socialists. But it wasn't until she departed
Puerto Rico once more, after her second marriage dissolved and she
came to serve as head of the pediatrics department at New York's
Lincoln Hospital, that Rodríguez-Trías became an active feminist:
Jo Ellen told her mother that the stepfather who had once seemed so
supportive molested her and Laura while Rodríguez-Trías was at the
hospital. This "revelation," she recalled, "made the women's movement
a personal matter of survival for me."

Rodríguez-Trías became part of the effort to decriminalize abortion and of the women's health movement that emerged from the push for women's liberation. Then she cofounded a new kind of reproductive rights movement, which fought controls on bodily freedom and family decision-making that affected Puerto Ricans, other Latinas, Black and Indigenous women, and only a fraction of white women. In 1974–75, with *Roe v. Wade* not yet two years old, a group of about ten women including Rodríguez-Trías, Puerto Rican Socialist Party member Maritza Arrastía, lawyer Nancy Stearns, and white activists Carol Marsh and Karen Stamm, started meeting as CESA. In 1977, as the U.S. government implemented the Hyde Amendment, which forbade states from using their federal Medicaid health insurance dollars to fund abortions, Rodríguez-Trías helped found a new organization, the Committee for Abortion Rights and Against Sterilization Abuse (CARASA). CARASA joined with CESA in lobbying for regulations that limited sterilization abuse and against restrictions on abortion access for people who used the federal Medicaid health insurance program and others with low incomes.

As she became more prominent in the fields of pediatrics and public health over the coming decades, Rodríguez-Trías remained a leader in the politics of gender and reproduction. She advocated new sterilization guidelines internationally and called for domestic violence and HIV/AIDS to be considered public health crises. With the endorsement of Manhattan borough president David Dinkins, she cofounded the New York Latino Commission on AIDS and, in the late 1980s, left hospital administration to head the New York State AIDS Institute. She and González left New York in the middle 1990s, and from 1996 to 1999, she codirected the Pacific Institute for Women's Health in California.

In January 2001, Rodríguez-Trías, her children, and grandchildren flew to Washington, D.C. She finally received national recognition when President Clinton awarded her the Presidential Citizens Medal just weeks before he left office. The White House didn't quite capture her significance but pointed in its direction. Clinton lauded her commitment to "better patient care, for better treatment and prevention of AIDS, for women's health rights" and generally for "fighting the good fight . . . mostly among poor people that are too often forgotten by others." She shared the dais with the first Black female federal judge, Constance Baker Motley; sports greats Hank Aaron and Muhammad Ali; and actress Elizabeth Taylor.

Less than a year after that high point, Rodríguez-Trías, a heavy smoker in her youth, was felled by lung cancer. Oldest daughter Jo Ellen acknowledged her mother for teaching the political lesson "that the struggle matters, even when your chance of success is slim. Struggle creates hope and possibility." Rodríguez-Trías was, she said, "a complex and multi-dimensional woman, and her contributions in the social arena were many. But the things I will miss are her touch, her voice, her scent, her laugh and her embracing love."

Dr. Helen Rodríguez-Trías and Beatrice Kornbluh Braun were not friends. They were not really allies. When I search for language to describe what they were to each other, what bubbles up is a phrase from the old comedy duo Mike Nichols and Elaine May: "There was proximity, but no relating." Mom and Helen may not even have known the different roles each played in the foundational chapters of modern reproductive politics. One of my few memories of their spending time together is my mother's confused shaking of her head after returning from a fundraiser across the hall. The meeting was about conditions in Puerto Rico. "What was that all about?" she asked. My mother didn't understand why a reproductive-rights die-hard such as herself would have been supposed to care about the general well-being of people who had been colonized by the United States, their policies on women's rights, like all their policies, subject to approval by a mainland U.S. Congress they did not elect. I also remember her description of Rodríguez-Trías on more than one occasion as a "high type" Puerto Rican. Even as a teenager, I winced at the ugliness of Mom's implicit belief that most Puerto Ricans were impoverished and undereducated, whereas our neighbor was a well-off, sophisticated professional. But it was only when reading for this project that I heard in my mother's phrase an echo of early- and middle-twentieth-century eugenics, which categorized people into higher and lower "types" based on their biology, supposedly revealed through instruments like intelligence tests.

This history takes its inspiration from a pair of neighbors on the eighth floor of 800 West End Avenue, New York City. The branches of the reproductive rights movement in which Beatrice (Cogan Riedl) Kornbluh Braun, Esq., and Dr. Helen Rodríguez-Trías participated were rooted in their respective backgrounds and political philosophies. The modern incarnations of these movements still build from the distinctive life experiences and ideologies of their members. When they work together, as they did in the push to decriminalize abortion in New York, they can be incredibly powerful allies. Where they diverge, they leave participants, as with Mom and Helen, in the kind of propinquity that might as well be miles of distance across arid terrain: no relating.

I hope my mother's history and that of her allies in NOW , Planned Parenthood, and NARAL remind the partisans of those organizations that the will of a majority that favors keeping abortion legal can find ways to express itself despite a hostile federal judiciary—indeed, despite a hostile popular minority that controls most of the levers of political power. I hope Helen Rodríguez-Trías's story and that of CESA and the organizations that came after it give solace and a few organizing tips to people who do the extraordinary work of seeking reproductive justice. Last, I hope that by being honest about Mom's and Helen's arid proximity, I can help everyone who cares about these issues find ways to rebuild, to open our minds, to broaden our sense of the possible, to relate.

Introduction

Both Sides

I T WAS 1963, and Karen Stamm was unmarried, pregnant, eighteen years old, and eager for an abortion. A bright woman from a lower-middle-class family, she was finishing her education and in no way interested in having a child. Her home state of New York had treated abortion as a crime since the early nineteenth century. Before then, the common law, a body of law that originated in England, governed abortion policy. Under common law, abortion before "quickening," the time when a woman could feel the fetus kick in her womb, usually between sixteen and twenty weeks into a pregnancy, was no crime at all. Authorities rarely prosecuted even women who terminated pregnancies fairly late on, since the concept of quickening relied on a woman's interpretation of what was happening in her own body, and she was unlikely to say that she had broken the law.

From the beginning, New York led the country in making explicit in legislation what had been unstated in the common law. Starting in 1830, state law defined a carve-out or exception to the blanket illegality; it allowed a doctor to perform an abortion if he (and they were virtually all "he") judged it necessary to save a woman's life. By the 1960s, this was known as "therapeutic" abortion. Its availability varied based on doctors' caprice and their fear of legal repercussions.

For a small number of people who sought abortions, nearly all fairly wealthy white women, doctors interpreted the word "life" to mean something like quality of life. Utilizing the power the law gave them over the therapeutic exception, doctors performed abortions for women who could argue successfully that an unwanted pregnancy would damage their mental health—and with whom the doctors were sympathetic. Stamm received approval on this kind of mental health basis. It helped that she could prove that she had seen a therapist. But the doctors still could have rejected her request: "The committee which interviewed me," Stamm remembered, "was, I think, only 1 or 2 people (docs), who seemed most interested in my grades. I interpreted that as I was worth going out on a limb for since I was a good student. Otherwise, who knows what they would have done."

Just before the procedure, at Montefiore Hospital in her natal borough of the Bronx, she recalled, "I was handed a consent form. It was a one-page consent form for the abortion. I read it, I signed it, I turned it over. The other side of it was a consent form for sterilization. And during the time I was there, I was approached by one of the staff doctors who told me that since I was so irresponsible, he was sure it"—pregnancy outside the bounds of marriage—"was going to happen again, and why didn't I just turn the paper over and sign the other side and get it over with?" The doctor persuaded her mother to join the chorus. In effect, he told Stamm that the same factors making her unable or unwilling to raise a child in her late teens, or the abortion itself, or the sexual activity that led to her pregnancy, or all three, made her permanently unfit for motherhood. Later, she learned that what had happened to her was fairly common. Many doctors who performed "therapeutic" abortions pressed unmarried pregnant women to agree to sterilization.

Despite the pressure, Stamm refused to sign the sterilization-consent page. "After that I made a commitment to myself, which was that if ever there arose a situation in which I could do something about this, I would do it. But in 1963, there was no discussion. There was no political discussion about abortion, about sterilization, about women's rights, about something beyond the elemental notion of free sex, I mean, which we had all sort of adopted . . . somewhat anyway as a way of life." That commitment led her to become a reproductive rights activist in the 1970s, first as member of a group called the Women's National Abortion Action Coalition and then as a leader of the Committee to End Sterilization Abuse (CESA). Stamm joined Dr. Helen Rodríguez-Trías in arguing that, much as laws that criminalized abortion violated women's rights by interfering with their ability to end a pregnancy, sterilization abuse violated their rights by keeping women from becoming parents. Sterilization abuse and the right to be a parent were literally the other side of the page from abortion restrictions and the right to avoid parenting when one chose to do so.

What happened to Karen Stamm was the result of two big flaws in state abortion laws in the years that preceded the first major efforts to reform them. First, while a small number of women could access legal abortions because their doctors believed they were psychologically unfit to carry unwanted pregnancies to term, the doctors might by the same logic push them toward sterilization: if one pregnancy was impossible on mental health grounds, doctors could use those same grounds to justify their sense that women who aborted should never become mothers. Second, the whole idea of therapeutic abortion was that the procedure should be accessible only when medically appropriate. And only a trained, credentialed physician was empowered to decide when a patient's symptoms added up to what in official parlance were the "indications" for abortion. All power rested with the doctors, who may have been sympathetic to a young white woman with some economic means, like Karen Stamm. But even when approving therapeutic abortions for women like Stamm, some doctors appear to have believed that pregnancy, abortion, and then sterilization were the wages of sin. Rather than have a sexually active unmarried woman return for a second abortion, or let her pass "promiscuous" genes to future generations, the doctor would perform a surgery on her and shape her future.

The two sides of reproduction, the right to it and the right to control or resist it, comingled in a different way for Loretta Ross than they did for Karen Stamm. Because of a malfunctioning birth control device, Ross lost the ability to get pregnant in 1973. It was the year of *Roe v. Wade*, supposedly a banner time for reproductive liberty. Ross was twenty-three years old and recently a student at Howard University, cream of the historically Black college and university (HBCU) system. A self-described military brat who reveled in the sophistication she developed from living all over the United States and briefly in Germany, Ross's sophistication didn't save her from being raped at eleven, becoming pregnant at fourteen as a result of a relationship with a twenty-seven-year-old cousin, or experiencing the full brunt of America's restrictive reproductive policies. She became a mother at fifteen, reneging on a promise to the staff at a Salvation Army home for unwed mothers that she would let them place her son for adoption, and became pregnant a second time because she needed parental consent for birth control. Her mother recommended celibacy instead. Ross aborted that pregnancy—legally, thanks to a federal court case that had liberalized the law in Washington, D.C.

Loretta Ross would eventually work with Dr. Helen Rodríguez-Trías and become a preeminent reproductive justice advocate and theorist. But that was long in the future: as a student whose third pregnancy occurred while taking (and occasionally forgetting to take) the pill, Ross asked at the university health center for an easier-to-manage form of birth control. The student medical clinic at Howard offered, free of charge, a long-acting, difficult-to-remove intrauterine device (IUD) called the Dalkon Shield. "And of course it was a defective IUD that ended up causing acute pelvic inflammatory disease, [which traveled up] the fallopian tubes" and went undiagnosed for months while she was under the care of a doctor who chaired the Department of Obstetrics and Gynecology of a major teaching hospital. Although she did not experience the kind of pressure applied to Stamm, Ross wound up with a full hysterectomy and considers herself a victim of sterilization abuse. She remembered with a lilt of irony: "To be told at twenty-three that one shall not have any more children, it has a way of getting your attention." As she sees it, the Dalkon Shield was the kind of long-acting birth control method that was "very attractive to people who are making decisions about the fertility of vulnerable women." Ross "didn't get any information on contraindications" or potential risks, she remembers, not from Howard and not from her esteemed physician—although published research indicated that this form of reliable contraception was apt to cause exactly the problems that led to Ross's hysterectomy.

After her experience, Ross became an activist. First, she sued the company that made the malfunctioning IUD, A.H. Robins. "So it was in that moment that I'm conscious of becoming a reproductive rights activist, because I was pissed off. I was like, whatever—all this that has happened to me shouldn't happen to nobody else. This is just ridiculous. And so I entered the movement feeling that I'd been the victim of sterilization abuse." She realized, too, that she was hardly the only Black woman she knew who had been sterilized through one means or another.

While thinking through the implications of her experiences, Ross joined a Black Marxist-Leninist reading group called the D.C. Study Group. From there, she volunteered with the D.C. Rape Crisis Center, a women-of-color-led shelter and advocacy group, and became its director in 1979. She left the Rape Crisis Center in the mid-1980s to bring her perspectives to the national feminist movement as director of Women of Color Programs for the National Organization for Women. As a NOW official, she organized the first-ever conference on Women of Color and Reproductive Rights. After years more work, linking people who were passionate about abortion rights with those who cared about sterilization abuse, and reproductive rights activists with anti-violence service providers, Ross co-convened a meeting of women of color in the movement in 1994. The group coined a new term to describe their agenda, a broader understanding of reproductive rights: "Reproductive Justice."

Listening to Stamm and Ross, and thinking about my mother and Helen Rodríguez-Trías, I had to conclude that abortion rights were just a small part of reproductive politics, necessary but insufficient. The knock-down, drag-out battle to decriminalize abortion and, since 1973, to preserve the principles embodied in *Roe v. Wade*, has been an incomplete proxy for reproductive or sexual liberation.

This book chronicles the work of two social movements for reproductive rights. One decriminalized abortion in New York and then nationally, and then became a movement to defend abortion rights. The other created new health-care guidelines to avert sterilization abuse. When it broadened in the late 1970s, this movement worked toward what activists at that time called "Reproductive Freedom," an agenda much like the later one for reproductive justice, which encompassed everything from fighting for abortion rights to opposing sterilization abuse, advocating universal childcare, battling police violence, and trying to ensure that parents had enough income to raise their children in safety and dignity.

In the era just before and after *Roe v. Wade*, the movement for decriminalization and then for abortion rights was the stronger and more mainstream of the two. It nonetheless faced powerful opposition from conservative religious forces and, more and more as the decade of the 1970s progressed, from a third social movement, for the "right to life"—a movement that is itself a vital presence in this story, although I do not chronicle it fully. The missed connections and at times open conflict between the movement for abortion rights and the movement against sterilization abuse and for reproductive freedom occurred for two reasons. One was a genuine difference of philosophy: a belief on the part of sterilization-abuse opponents in the need for strict regulations to prevent abuse, and an equally strong belief on the part of some advocates of abortion rights that such regulations themselves threatened people's reproductive autonomy. Second was a sense on the part of many proponents of abortion rights that they could not afford the risk involved in expanding their mandate to include new issues when they were in a hard fight to preserve the legality and accessibility of abortion.

It seems in hindsight that the movement for abortion rights might have been stronger if it had embraced those risks instead of shying away from them. Of course, opposition to legal abortion has been forceful and persistent. However, politics that have started and ended with defending abortion have proved vulnerable to attack in ways that a broader agenda that included opposition to sterilization abuse and a defense of all people's right to parent might not have been. An abortion-centered approach created opportunities for conservatives to pursue their agenda of remaking the Republican Party, vanquishing its liberal wing, and marrying economic policies that favor the wealthy with sexual and reproductive policies that appeal to a supposedly moral majority. Feminists who defended the right to choose abortion but rarely spoke about the challenges people faced in making other reproductive choices became perfect foils for conservative Catholics and their unlikely allies among Evangelical Protestants, who became the most reliable Republican voters after the 1980s. I can imagine an alternative history in which liberals and feminists in the mainstream of the reproductive rights movement chose to fight intensively for the right to parent as well as the right to avoid parenting, for controls on coercive sterilization as well as for unrestricted access to abortion. They wouldn't have won any friends in the top reaches of Catholic hierarchy, but they might have stanched the exodus of lay Catholics from the Democratic Party. After all, the views of lay Catholics on abortion policy were not settled in the 1960s and 1970s. Catholic voters who rejected the push to decriminalize abortion were also repelled by mass sterilization, and at least a portion of them might have joined mainline (that is, not evangelical) Protestants, atheists, and Jews under a political banner that recognized the importance of supporting parents in their efforts to have and raise children. It is impossible to know for sure, but history might have been different, indeed, if advocates had embraced reproductive rights on both sides of the page.

In addition to what appears in retrospect to have been an inaccurate assessment of risk, leaders in reproductive rights organizations were weakened by limitations in perspective that came from their whiteness and unconscious participation in white privilege. I take "white privilege" to mean a system of unearned advantages experienced by those who are understood to be white and denied to people who are read as nonwhite. White privilege has shaped economic arrangements, public policies, and political ideologies in the modern United States. Whiteness has reached, historian Nell Irvin Painter writes, "into concepts of labor, gender and class." White privilege shapes public life and "private" lives, including families, friendships, and beliefs. Among the characteristics of privilege that white people carry—in an "invisible knapsack," according to gender studies scholar Peggy McIntosh—is a capacity to be ignorant about the experiences and perspectives of people of color without suffering any consequences for that ignorance in white-dominant culture. This is a kind of opposite to W.E.B. DuBois's "second-sight" and "double-consciousness," the privilege of supposing that there is "one main piece of cultural turf; it [is] my own turf."

White privilege and the lack of it structured women's experiences of sex and reproduction. The white women in CESA, an interracial organization devoted to solving a problem that affected more women of color than white women, were surely not perfect. But they had, as activists in later generations might have put it, "done the work" so that their whiteness did not block the progress they wanted to make. However, most whites in the movement to decriminalize abortion, my beloved mother included, did not examine their white privilege, and so racial bias affected their "vision as does a faulty lens," in the words of Rodríguez-Trías, "constantly distorting the 'others' and their reality."

Mom and white women like her believed that ensuring access to birth control and abortion was the most significant, perhaps the only meaningful, reproductive rights claim to make. This was a match for their own experiences and assumptions about how the world worked. Mom never considered the ways that coercive sterilization impinged upon the rights of Latinas, Black women, Indigenous women, some poor or unmarried whites, and queer or disabled people, because she neither shared their experiences nor extended herself to understand those experiences. She did not learn from or work with people whose lives and understandings differed profoundly from hers.

Activists like my mother could have fought for legal abortion and for a long list of other things that would have secured reproductive autonomy to all people. But the fight to decriminalize abortion was by itself a vital and historic one. As feminist legal thinkers started to argue in the period covered by this book, the criminalization of abortion was part and parcel of a legal regime that demeaned and diminished all women. Laws that forbade doctors from performing abortions or women from obtaining them never kept abortions from occurring. They did make it difficult, expensive, perilous, and sometimes deadly to obtain what had the potential to be a fairly safe medical procedure. The laws communicated to all women about their marginal status in a society that treated their most typical bodily, sexual, romantic, and medical experiences as matters of shame and punishment. Laws that criminalized abortion were products of all-male or mostly all-male legislatures; medical practices that deprived women of access to abortion emerged from an overwhelmingly male medical profession; and the moral opprobrium that met abortion seekers and informed the laws was the work of clergymen who could make women feel terrible about their choices even if they could not keep them from making those choices.

These laws in theory affected everyone equally but in fact harmed Black women, Latinas, young and unmarried women, and working-class or poor women the most. For this reason, many of the important, although rarely remembered, leaders of the movement to decriminalize abortion in New York were Black people who were committed to Black freedom and equality as well as to women's rights. Harlem's assemblyman Percy Sutton, for example, introduced the first bill in the state's modern history to liberalize the abortion laws. Labor leader and public administrator Dorothy "Dollie" Lowther Robinson proposed an amendment to the state's constitution that would have codified equality on the basis of sex and made access to abortion a component of that equality. Activist attorney Florynce "Flo" Kennedy helped put the issue of abortion decriminalization before the membership of the National Organization for Women and later served as one of four co-counsels in the first federal case that made women, not doctors, the subjects of abortion litigation.

The most significant contribution of the movement to decriminalize abortion was its forceful recognition of women's personhood. By insisting on women's rights to obtain safe, legal, and affordable abortion care, the decriminalization movement said in effect that women's lives—their physical lives and their future lives after the point at which they either were or were not able to terminate their pregnancies—mattered, not because of their capacity to bear children or to be partners to men but in themselves. This was especially true of the explicitly feminist iteration of the movement for abortion decriminalization, which emerged from the New York branch of the National Organization for Women and became a centerpiece of NOW's program for women's civil rights. A short time later, it became the most concrete demand of a self-described "radical" branch of the women's movement, which saw the abortion laws as stigmatizing women's sexuality and expressing men's dominance.

My mother's particular contribution, as a member of NOW in New York, was to outline legislation that would have removed abortion fully from the state legal code. Weeks after she shared her draft, it was a bill, the first proposal for full decriminalization of abortion introduced into any state legislature in the country. Although that bill would be modified on its way to passage, it was a landmark because it encapsulated what had become by the late 1960s the position of most feminists—that rather than *reform* the old laws as some lawyers and doctors wanted to do, by loosening the criteria under which a physician could grant his patient an abortion, government must *repeal* all controls on abortion and allow women to decide for themselves when it was right to terminate a pregnancy. My mother's draft expressed in legislative terms the insistence of Florynce Kennedy and thousands of others that abortion shouldn't be regulated any more than appendectomy should.

The role my mother played in New York's legislative decriminalization of abortion may have been relatively minor, but the statute she helped pass was far more than the "footnote in history" that the retired state legislator called it. By eliminating criminal sanctions for doctors and patients before the twenty-fourth week of a pregnancy, and imposing no residency requirement on people who sought abortions, New York became the most liberal abortion jurisdiction in the United States above the municipal level—according to one expert, the most liberal in the world.

After implementation of the statute in July 1970, pregnant people from across the country and the globe found their way to doctors in New York, often with the assistance of the Clergy Consultation Service (CCS) headquartered in Greenwich Village's Judson Memorial Church, and other referral services whose members risked prosecution for helping patients locate safe and affordable procedures. The data from New York were unambiguous: women from out of state arrived in this outlier jurisdiction by the thousands, testifying to their need and to the lingering inequality between those who could and those who could not get to New York. The cost of abortion declined. Maternal mortality dropped dramatically, especially for Latinas and Black women, who had accounted for virtually all the deaths from illegal abortion in the years just before the New York law changed.

Decriminalization in New York was not everything, but it was a very big thing, a shift in formal legal text that changed many people's experiences of law before the Supreme Court ruled on the constitutionality of Texas's abortion law in *Roe v. Wade*. Stanley Katz, a former law professor and American Civil Liberties Union (ACLU) lawyer and an alumnus of feminist battles in Illinois, has said that in the movement for decriminalization of abortion, "we all looked to New York" for a model of how to change the law. "We never expected the Supreme Court to bail us out." The enormous grassroots effort that had gone into changing the law in New York, and the law itself (including its tortured road to implementation) were significant in themselves, and they laid the foundation for what the U.S. Supreme Court did in 1973 when it decided *Roe v. Wade*.

To Dr. Helen Rodríguez-Trías, Karen Stamm, and Loretta Ross, there was plenty of evidence that neither New York's decriminalization nor *Roe v. Wade* fully guaranteed reproductive rights to all Americans. If nothing else, people who identified with the civil rights movement, as all three of them did, knew that the great leader Fannie Lou Hamer had been made infertile by a white doctor who performed a hysterectomy on her, without her knowledge or consent, when she was in the hospital for the removal of a noncancerous tumor. The involuntary sterilization of Black women was common enough to be known popularly as the "Mississippi appendectomy." As Hamer put it, "In the North Sunflower County Hospital" in the Mississippi Delta, "I would say about six out of the 10 Negro women that go to the hospital are sterilized with the tubes tied."

Revelations in the late 1960s and early 1970s made activists aware that an unsafe early version of the birth control pill, with what one participant in the study called "too many side reactions to be accepted generally," had been tested first on women in Puerto Rico—on medical students whose grades were held back until they completed participation in the drug trial, and later among residents of a public housing project. The leader of the study attempted to enroll women in it without informing them of the potential side effects. Despite mixed results, the research team submitted data from the Puerto Rico experiments to the Food and Drug Administration. In 1960, the agency approved the pill for sale across the United States.

In the same period, disabled people, their loved ones, and their allies publicized the ways people were treated in institutions. Involuntary or coerced sterilization was just one on a long list of practices that made "Close the Institutions" a slogan of the disability rights movement of the 1970s.

These scandals revealed that traces of the pseudoscience known as eugenics, based on the racist and ableist idea that the "unfit" should bear fewer children, and at its height early in the twentieth century, were still present after World War II. Beginning with Indiana in 1907, more than thirty U.S. states had authorized forced sterilizations to ensure that those considered "socially inadequate" did not pass on what eugenicists considered bad, heritable traits. Because of these laws, more than sixty-five thousand people in the United States had been subject to forced sterilization by the 1960s. In 1927, Justice Oliver Wendell Holmes, Jr., wrote a majority opinion for the U.S. Supreme Court that found Virginia's law allowing involuntary sterilization of "mental defectives" constitutionally permissible. Affirming the legality of the sterilization of Carrie Buck, who was in fact of normal intelligence and had become pregnant as a result of sexual assault, the justice wrote: "It is better for all the world if, instead of waiting to execute degenerate offspring for crime or to let them starve for their imbecility, society can prevent those who are manifestly unfit from continuing their kind. . . . Three generations of imbeciles are enough."

In the postwar period, the example of involuntary sterilization and mass murder under the Nazis caused policies that promoted sterilization in the United States to change but not disappear. The targets of these policies were not completely different after the war than before, but their emphases shifted—from forcible sterilization to coercive or semi-voluntary sterilization, from sterilizing men to sterilizing women, and from focusing on poor white people like Carrie Buck and immigrants from Eastern and Southern Europe, to focusing on Latinas and Black people, especially those who received government financial aid. Disabled people continued to be at risk of involuntary or semi-involuntary sterilization. However, as greater numbers were able to live outside of institutions, their portion of the total declined.

A new ideology or belief system emerged, called "population control." The ideology of population control was widely shared by social scientists, wealthy individuals, and policy makers in the middle and late twentieth century. Advocates of population control did not usually speak in terms that were explicitly racist or ableist; they were not like the Nazis, who turned their ideas about racial hierarchy into a program of mass extermination. However, they believed that it was essential to shape people's reproductive behavior in order to improve a society. Population control became a primary mode of U.S. policy. The drive to reduce global population shaped the work of government agencies and of private entities backed by U.S. philanthropists and ordinary taxpayers working in Asia, Africa, and Latin America. The idea that population control meant progress was woven into efforts to reduce poverty and promote modernization, to enhance democracy, to improve women's status, and to reduce pressure on the world's resources, including on its natural environment. As Thomas Shapiro, a sociologist who wrote one of the first books on population control (and who got interested in the issue because he belonged to a group in St. Louis that allied with CESA), explained: "The prevailing idea was that nations would handicap their economic 'take-off' because population growth would constantly erode economic growth. Since 'overpopulation' was said to exacerbate social unrest, diminishing the number of potentially dissatisfied people could minimize the possibilities of political instability."

In a narrow sense, population control advocates were right. A family or community with a finite amount of money or food would find that the resources went further with fewer people to share them. Fewer people meant fewer individual acts of environmental destruction. However, these advocates placed too much emphasis on population, separated from all other factors that produced wealth, poverty, and well-being in a community or a society. They placed too little faith in the residents of those communities or societies to arrive at their own solutions to their problems. Population control ideology treated as untouchable the distribution of resources between the United States and Europe and countries in the rest of the world, some of the resources of which had been extracted when they were colonial possessions. Population control focused only on how lowering population might make a particular country less poor. Population control policies gave people the tools to lower their birth rates but did not emphasize the importance of high-quality basic health-care systems that would in themselves improve people's well-being and could offer a range of contraceptive options so that people could choose for themselves whether and when to have children. The environmental argument for population control, which was most closely associated with the organization Zero Population Growth, founded in 1968, overemphasized individual contributions to environmental harm and missed the greater impact of industrial polluters and government entities.

The elite consensus around population control was far-reaching. It even shaped the thinking of some proponents of decriminalizing abortion in the years before the New York law change and *Roe v. Wade*. Ruth Cusack, for example, onetime chair of the abortion committee of NOW's New York chapter, advocated abortion decriminalization in two separate ways. For her, transforming the abortion law seems to have meant opportunity, liberty, and equality when she thought about people like herself, white women with advanced educations who were heading into careers that could be derailed by an unplanned pregnancy. But she veered into population-control thinking when, in letters to legislators, she conjured the specter of "the unwanted child" and overwhelmed mother, and the costs in institutionalization and incarceration she believed society would have to pay to sustain them.

A similar complexity appears in the history of Planned Parenthood, whose leader, Margaret Sanger, had made alliances with eugenicists and sometimes made eugenicist arguments herself, and was also deeply committed to women's autonomy, including the autonomy of working-class women. After World War II, internationally oriented affiliates of Planned Parenthood were deeply involved in population control policies—not policies of involuntary sterilization but others designed to encourage poor people to lower their fertility. Sanger and others in the organization did not resolve the tension between their passion for increasing women's reproductive choices and freedom, and their participation in international projects that aimed to lower the birth rates of people who were Black, brown, and poor. Within the United States, Planned Parenthood played a critical role in promoting abortion law reform, starting with a conference of its medical committee in the late 1950s that helped inspire the first legislative efforts to loosen the laws.

In one instance I have studied, the roots of post–World War II population control grew directly from the soil of prewar eugenics. The Sterilization League of New Jersey, originally the project of a committee of the Princeton League of Women Voters and dedicated to the eugenic sterilization of those designated disabled or mentally ill, had by the 1970s transformed into the Association for Voluntary Sterilization, an organization dedicated to promoting permanent, voluntary sterilization as a fail-safe form of contraception. Ruth Proskauer Smith served as executive director of the organization for nine years, before helping lead the first dedicated abortion-law advocacy group in the United States, New York's Association for the Study of Abortion (ASA). A board member credited her with "somewhat single-handedly" making the Association for Voluntary Sterilization successful in the context of postwar concerns about poverty and population. The New York abortion law reformer who headed Planned Parenthood after Sanger's death, Dr. Alan Guttmacher, wrote articles in favor of population control—again, without racist or ableist language and not promoting involuntary measures. He served at one time as chair of the Association for Voluntary Sterilization's medical committee.

Individuals who led the efforts to reform or repeal abortion laws also believed in population control. Lawrence Lader, for example, the leading journalist advocating legal abortion in the 1960s and the person in whose apartment plans were hatched for the National Association to Repeal Abortion Laws (NARAL), produced a book celebrating population control while he was helping to pass the New York abortion law and found NARAL. He titled it *Breeding Ourselves to Death*. In a later book, he invited readers to stop denying "the function of abortion in population control." Nelson Rockefeller, the governor who signed the abortion decriminalization law in New York in 1970 and vetoed its repeal two years later, was a multimillionaire member of a family that did more than any other to promote the cause of population control around the world. At the height of the battle over abortion in New York, his older brother, John D. Rockefeller III, chaired the Nixon administration's Commission on Population Growth and the American Future, which "concluded that no substantial benefits would result from continued growth of the nation's population." Assemblywoman Constance Cook, the legislative strategist most responsible for passing the New York law, believed that Rockefeller was "influenced particularly by his brother" in coming to support transformative abortion legislation.

Part of the reason that Dr. Helen Rodríguez-Trías arrived at the issue of sterilization abuse sooner and with greater urgency than other feminists was that she had spent much of her life in Puerto Rico. An imperial possession of the United States, Puerto Rico was not only the locus of a morally troubling large-scale study of the birth control pill. It was also the first place in the world with mass population control via sterilization. Puerto Rico suffered from being outside the United States in the sense that some philanthropists and policy makers didn't consider Puerto Ricans real Americans, but inside the United States in that the Puerto Rican government was subordinate to the U.S. government. The Puerto Rican island was, in the words of a famous Supreme Court opinion, "foreign in a domestic sense" to the mainland United States.

Sterilization in Puerto Rico resulted from partnerships between government and private funders, and a meeting between families' desires for birth control and the limited options they were offered. It also resulted from an artificial separation between sterilization and abortion, with one becoming legal and popular and the other criminalized. The birth control movement in Puerto Rico predated the rise in sterilizations. In the 1920s, legalizing birth control was a Socialist Party cause, and Puerto Rican nurses and social workers opened the island's first birth control clinic in the 1930s. In 1935, the New Deal government of Franklin D. Roosevelt assumed management of the birth control program on the island. Staff of the program did home visits to evaluate people's needs and share information about contraceptive methods like the diaphragm.

From the perspective of policy makers in Washington, D.C., this birth control program became problematic when opposition to it arose from Puerto Rican nationalists who treated it as an example of imperialist policy. Fearful that Catholics who heard about their dissent would desert the Democratic Party, the administration of Franklin D. Roosevelt withdrew its support from the program. A scion of the Procter & Gamble Company fortune and population control enthusiast named Clarence Gamble became the program's main backer. He financed private clinics and a Maternal and Child Association (Asociación pro Salud Maternal e Infantil) whose main purpose was to provide contraceptives and gather data about their effectiveness—as distinct from supporting the overall health and well-being of Puerto Rican citizens. He advocated the decriminalization of birth control, which occurred in 1937, the same year that the Puerto

Rican government legalized sterilization and created a eugenic sterilization board to hear professionals' assessments of various people's (supposedly) biological endowments and, based on this information, to make decisions about mandating involuntary sterilizations.

Thousands of Puerto Rican women, who faced limited access to basic medical care, rural and urban poverty, and all the circumstances that also led women on the mainland to use birth control, eagerly became patients of these clinics. In the Puerto Rican legislation of the late 1930s, sterilization was allowed for "health reasons," which came eventually to cover all reasons for all people of childbearing age who sought sterilization. Unfortunately, many of the non-sterilization birth control methods Puerto Ricans were offered were experimental ones, provided by rich inventors like Gamble and representatives of major pharmaceutical companies. They believed that most Puerto Ricans couldn't effectively use condoms or diaphragms, and they seized the opportunity Puerto Rico presented to test products that could make them millions in the U.S. market. Some of the things they tried were rankly ineffective. Others, like the early generations of long-acting intrauterine devices (even before the faulty IUD that harmed Loretta Ross) and of the highly effective birth control pill, could be downright dangerous.

Sterilizations, not those mandated by the eugenics board but the ones that were ostensibly voluntary, became an ever more popular contraceptive option. This helped give Puerto Rico the lowest level of population growth in the Caribbean by 1955 and the highest national sterilization rate in the world, at over 35 percent, by the end of the 1960s. Two-thirds of those sterilized were in their twenties. This was shocking to the people who founded CESA and the activists on the U.S. mainland who paid attention to the anti-imperial struggle in Puerto Rico. But sterilization was an attractive option for many Puerto Rican women because it was reliable and long-term. A woman who used sterilization as birth control avoided other problematic options, such as IUDs and the pill, which many may have thought were dangerous even after results from the experimental trials led to improvements; and abortion, which remained illegal and stigmatized in Puerto Rico before *Roe v. Wade*.

In the overwhelming majority of cases, neither the U.S. nor Puerto Rican governments forced women into sterilization. At the same time, as Rodríguez-Trías argued, and sociologist Iris López and others underline, the language of "reproductive choice" was hardly accurate in describing Puerto Rican women's very high rates of sterilization. In fact, it doesn't match the decisions most people make about whether, when, and how to have children. Puerto Ricans asked for or consented to sterilization as they sorted out their lives—lives shaped by, among many other factors, imperialism, racism, economic opportunity, economic inequality, for-profit health care and drug development, sexism, and migration away from family networks. People sometimes "chose" sterilization on the basis of faulty information, including suggestions that it was not permanent, and that one's tubes, once tied, could be untied later.

One last set of circumstances that made this issue complicated when Rodríguez-Trías, Stamm, and other CESA members encountered it was the way sterilization was experienced on the U.S. mainland. Just as there was a long history of Black, brown, disabled, and poor people being compelled or persuaded into sterilization, people who were native-born, white, able-bodied and -minded, and relatively well-off were unable to become sterilized when they wanted to. This was consistent with other policies in the twentieth century, which were shaped by race, class, and gender. Beginning at the turn of the twentieth century, public figures like Theodore Roosevelt complained about the too-low birth rates of native-born white people, creating pressure for anti-abortion policies and crackdowns on people like Margaret Sanger, who provided information to others about birth control. At the same time, they complained about what they believed were hordes of immigrants, people of color, and so-called imbeciles overpopulating the United States. The second concern built support for mandatory or coercive sterilization.

Despite the efforts of the Association for Voluntary Sterilization, surgical sterilization was a relatively tough sell during and immediately after the encounter with fascism in World War II. Regardless, many doctors in the 1950s prevented people they considered good procreative material from opting for sterilization. Medical professionals typically used a rule of 120: a woman's age multiplied by the number of children she had borne had to total 120 or more before they would accede to her sterilization request. This meant that a woman of thirty would not be sterilized unless she had four or more children. The American Medical Association and American College of Obstetricians and Gynecologists endorsed this 120 rule, as did many hospitals. Such policies had real power although they were not written into legislation. They changed only after they were challenged openly, and even then did not change completely.

Decades of pro-sterilization public education by the Association for Voluntary Sterilization, and a relaxing of medical guidance, led to a flurry of court cases in the early 1970s. These cases were brought with the help of the American Civil Liberties Union and the more radical Center for Constitutional Rights. People who wanted to stop getting pregnant sued hospitals for the right to be sterilized—and hospitals resisted, because their leaders were uncomfortable with sterilization (especially of nondisabled white people with private insurance) and unsure of its legal status.

The Committee to End Sterilization Abuse emerged against this background. CESA members focused on controlling the internationally imperialist and domestically racist and class-based dimensions of population policy. They sought to ensure that poor, working-class, and nonwhite U.S. citizens, and all other people, had the reproductive right to bear and raise children when they choose to do so—free, at least, from involuntary sterilization, or coerced or uninformed consent to the ending of their reproductive capacity. Struggles over reproductive health care were part and parcel of struggles over health care itself. In New York, they mixed with efforts by Black and Puerto

Rican community groups to make public hospitals responsive to their needs, and with initiatives by many activists in the 1970s to replace the U.S. health-care system with a nationally universal one.

The CESA version of reproductive rights was upside down to that of the Supreme Court majority in *Roe v. Wade.* The Puerto Rican, Black, and leftist white feminists in the group argued that racist doctors were pressuring their clients, shielding vital information, performing unnecessary surgeries, and removing women's ability to parent no matter their desires. By contrast, Justice Harry Blackmun wrote the *Roe* opinion as though the interests of doctors and their patients were virtually identical.

A Woman's Life Is a Human Life has two purposes. The first, occupying about two-thirds of the narrative, is to tell the complex story of how a diverse group, mostly of women activists, revolutionized abortion law. In 1967, New York feminists believed they might have to pass an amendment to their state constitution, or even the U.S. Constitution, to change the laws that made abortions inaccessible, unsafe, and grossly expensive for most people who sought them. However, working with risk-taking ministers, rabbis, doctors, and lawyers, they compelled the state legislature to pass the most liberal abortion law in the country just three years later. Three years after that, the Supreme Court learned from their victory in New York and decided *Roe v. Wade.*

This story is obviously relevant at a time when states are destined to be once more, as they were for over a century, the main arbiters of abortion policy. It shows how effective a political coalition can be when it throws everything it has at its chosen problem—from disruptive civil disobedience, to demonstrations of commitment by people of faith, to tireless lobbying that holds fence-sitters "on the pan" until they feel the heat of their constituents' dissatisfaction, as Assemblywoman Constance Cook, cosponsor of the liberalizing law in New York, described her method of rounding up votes for a bill.

It is also relevant at a moment when democracy is increasingly imperiled. New Yorkers like my mother were hardly alone in fighting for changes in their state abortion law. From 1965, when Assembly-man Sutton introduced his abortion law reform bill, until 1970, when a version of the bill my mother outlined passed into law, the democratic system seemed to work. Across the country, public opinion gradually turned against the old, highly restrictive laws. One state after another passed reform legislation. New York's was the most liberal, and Washington State's, approved by referendum in that November's elections, the last.

After the Washington referendum, the trend stopped. Public accep-tance of abortion continued to advance but state-by-state legislative reform did not. Largely in response to the New York law, the Catholic hierarchy and a smaller number of Protestant and Orthodox Jewish abortion opponents built political machinery that kept state legisla-tures from reflecting people's changing views. It wasn't that difficult: feminists and other pro-liberalization advocates were exhausted after years of fighting sexism, as well as the silence and stigma that sur-rounded abortion, and ambivalence about what sociologist Alice Rossi called "recreative" versus "procreative" sexuality. (They also fought one another.) Abortion opponents found it easy to raise funds and to organize activists from Sunday pulpits. Everything that made it difficult for women to talk about their experiences of sex, pregnancy, and abortion likewise kept most legislators from discussing legal abortion as a positive good. In New York itself, the 1970 law faced immediate threats. In 1972, only a gubernatorial veto saved it. Anti-abortion activists were on the verge of a third repeal campaign in 1973 when the U.S. Supreme Court ruled. Against this background, the Supreme Court in Roe v. Wade, which has often been accused of overturning the democratic will of state legislatures, may be seen instead as an agent of democracy.

This book's second purpose is to explain how a separate but related reproductive rights movement built on, and critiqued, the movement that had decriminalized abortion. After Roe, Dr. Helen Rodríguez-Trías and other members of the Committee to End Sterilization

Abuse soured on a politics that treated access to abortion as the be-all and end-all of women's reproductive needs. In 1976, they organized successfully for a New York City law (passed by a vote of 38–0, with three abstentions) to eliminate sterilization abuse. In 1978, CESA and the newer Committee for Abortion Rights and Against Sterilization Abuse organized nationally to get the federal Department of Health, Education, and Welfare to mirror the New York City law in regulations that applied to all health-care institutions that received funding from the department. In both cases, their unlikely opponents included Planned Parenthood and the national leaders of the National Organization for Women.

Like the story of how activists changed the law of abortion, the chronicle of the fight against sterilization abuse is one of legal change that occurred not from the courts down but from the grassroots up. However, CESA and CARASA won their victories with different political coalitions than the more mainstream feminist and reproductive rights organizations had done. In New York City, for example, Rodríguez-Trías and her comrades met with members of the city council in interracial teams that were passionate about the cause but not experienced lobbyists or well-heeled insiders. They stumped for endorsements from feminists, civil libertarians, Black and Puerto Rican movement groups, and progressive doctors, but not from doctors in the mainstream of their profession or experts in population science. Mexican American and Indigenous women, who were battling sterilization abuse in their own communities, joined the coalition when it went national.

The politics of CESA and CARASA led to new ideas. Rodríguez-Trías learned from her experience at Lincoln Hospital—which, shortly before she arrived, was occupied by the Puerto Rican nationalist group the Young Lords, demanding better and more responsive health care for all the hospital's patients—that reproductive rights were inseparable from every other aspect of people's health. She and the other CESA founders took on the problem of sterilization abuse because it was a crisis on both the island of Puerto Rico and the U.S. mainland. But they did not only battle an evil. They also outlined an ambitious and forward-looking political program: What, they started to ask, would it mean for people to have the right to parent, as well as the right to choose not to parent via contraception and abortion? CARASA members encapsulated this program in the term "Reproductive Freedom," meaning women's "possibility of controlling for themselves, in a real and practical way—that is, free from economic, social, or legal coercion—whether, and under what conditions, they will have children."

Notes on Language

I have struggled with some of the language used in this book. In discussing pregnancy and biological parenting, I generally wrote of "women" and "mothers" as the relevant parties and only infrequently used more gender-fluid phrases like "pregnant person" or "people with the capacity to get pregnant." I leaned toward the former for two reasons: First, it was the language of the period and people this book is about: liberals, radicals, and feminists who believed that restrictive reproductive policies were part of a larger skein of sexist law that had to be undone. It was also the language of the medical, legal, and religious institutions with which the patients and activists at the heart of the book interacted. The phrase in the book's title, "A Woman's Life Is a Human Life," is historical, taken from the Reagan-era battle against the effort to enshrine fetal rights in a constitutional amendment. In using it, I do not mean to suggest that people who do not identify as women are unharmed by policies that violate reproductive rights and justice, or lack standing in these debates. Second, sexist law is still with us. We must acknowledge the transgender and nonbinary people who can bear children and recognize their subordination. I think it is also important to acknowledge the ongoing presence of (cisgender, heterosexual) male dominance in our institutions. Laws that narrow access to contraception and abortion, or that permit the compulsory or coercive sterilization of people who have the capacity to get pregnant, are unthinkable apart from that dominance. Similarly, I generally (except in this introduction) eschewed the term "Latinx," which was unknown in the period this book covers, in favor of "Latina" and "Latino"—although I more often wrote more specifically about Puerto Ricans in New York and Mexican Americans in California. Please note, too, that some of the data on which I relied to assess both the pre-legalization and post-legalization situation in New York did not capture the experiences of Latinx people other than Puerto Ricans. These were New York City figures, and they calculated outcomes for only three categories: of white people, Black people, and Puerto Ricans.

Following current parlance at the time of writing, I referred to people of African descent as Black. This was tricky when writing about Puerto Ricans, many of whom have African heritage. Since I did not know precisely how each person discussed in the book self-identified, I relied on their political affiliations; if someone joined organizations devoted to Puerto Rican independence, for example, and I had no other information about their identity, I called them Latina/o, even though they may well have had African heritage and identified as both Puerto Rican and Black. I referred to people descended from the original human settlers in North America as either Native American or Indigenous. And I used the term "disabled" in reference to people whose physical and cognitive characteristics have been considered disabling in the modern United States. I also utilized its opposites, "able-bodied" and "able-minded," as well as the political term "ableist," meaning a system of belief that places people who are categorized as not disabled above those categorized as disabled.

Chapter One

Reformers and Reform

"**I**was in college," Carol Marsh, then Carol Rosenberg, remembers. "I was twenty-one. I thought I was using protection. I had a boyfriend then and I got pregnant. And there must have been a hole in the diaphragm or something like that. But anyway, I immediately felt desperate. And I didn't know what to do. I mean, I knew that I had to end the pregnancy, that there was no way. I was twenty-one, but I was a very young twenty-one, and there was no way I could raise a child. And to go through a pregnancy and then give it up for adoption . . . I would have to leave school. It seemed so cruel. And I didn't feel like I could go to my parents. I thought my father would have a heart attack and die and my mother would freak out."

It was 1966. Marsh, a student at Adelphi University, didn't know where to turn. Her best friend from high school was Karen Stamm, who'd had a legal abortion three years earlier. But Marsh couldn't do what her friend had done. She asked her doctor about qualifying for a so-called therapeutic abortion, granted on grounds of danger to a pregnant person's health, including sometimes their mental health, "and he said they're not very favorable toward it right now and by the time, if it did get approved, it would be too late." Stamm asked people she knew at City College and found a dermatologist in New York City who would do the procedure for her friend. Marsh borrowed money and had the abortion without anesthesia—twice, since the doctor was not particularly skilled and didn't succeed the first time. "And so it was about a couple of days later, I started just gushing, and it just didn't stop and I was really terrified. So I called Karen, and she said, 'You have to come to the emergency room with me.' . . . And like an idiot, she said to her mother, 'I have to go take Carol to the emergency room.' And so [her] mother, no dummy, calls my parents."

Marsh needed a dilation and curettage, or D&C, to clean out an infection that had developed in her womb. She spent two nights in the hospital, with what she remembers as hostile care from nurses who disapproved of what she had done. "And the resident came in and asked me to give him the name of the doctor and I refused." Her parents, secular Jews who had no particular religious or philosophical objections to abortion, nonetheless reacted badly to the incontrovertible evidence that their daughter was sexually active. Marsh recalls her mother walking "into the bathroom while I was taking a bath and she said to me, 'How do you decide who you sleep with?'" Later, when Marsh was ready to return to college, her father "drove me back out to school and he said, 'You broke my heart.' So between the two of them, you can see why I didn't tell them."

Carol Marsh's experience with the dermatologist happened the same year the New York State legislature held its first hearings in eighty years to consider a major reform to its law criminalizing abortion. The hearing was called to consider an abortion law reform bill introduced by Harlem Democratic assemblyman Percy Sutton. Sutton's bill marked the start of the most successful legislative campaign in the country, pre–*Roe v. Wade*, to change the law so that no one would ever again have to go through what Marsh went through.

The criminal abortion laws produced despair and death for decades before the Sutton bill and a small number of similar bills in other states started changing public policy. Why then and not earlier—or later? Credit is owed, first of all, to Carol Marsh and thousands like her. They took enormous risks to end their pregnancies despite the fact that most abortions were illegal. They faced the stigma that surrounded both abortion and female sexuality, especially the sexuality of unmarried women. Unorganized but unstoppable, they engaged in a kind of grassroots mass action that forced powerful people and institutions to change. By persistently showing up in doctors' offices asking for help, and taking themselves to hospital emergency rooms demanding medical intervention, pregnant people forced health care professionals to deal with the consequences of the laws that governed abortion access. The cynical and often hypocritical system of enforcement had turned doctors, often unhappily, into legal informants and made them vulnerable to prosecution for performing or recommending abortion. This produced a crackdown on access to therapeutic abortion between Karen Stamm's in 1963 and Carol Marsh being denied one three years later. And it produced the bizarre scene in which a medical resident, who was trained to attend to Marsh's health, asked her to give up her abortionist for criminal prosecution. Many lawyers didn't like the enforcement regime any more than medical professionals did: it was a notorious tool in the hands of headline-seeking district attorneys and other local officials who sought to burnish their reputations for morality. Enforcement was haphazard and grossly unfair, with effects that weighed most heavily—sometimes fatally—on people of color and whites who lacked private insurance.

Some in the legal and medical professions heeded this grassroots action. Doctors affiliated with the Planned Parenthood Federation of America met in 1956 under the auspices of Dr. Mary Steichen Calderone, the organization's medical director and daughter of modernist photographer Edward Steichen. In 1958, Steichen Calderone published an edited collection of remarks from the conference, which spread news of medical dissent from the long-standing consensus on abortion beyond a small circle of doctors and Planned Parenthood staff and supporters. In 1959, the American Law Institute, an elite group of attorneys and legal intellectuals, proposed a new model criminal law for the states that included a reformed approach to abortion: it would still be a crime in most cases but would be permissible on the grounds of danger to a pregnant person's physical and mental health, loosely defined, as well as serious fetal anomalies revealed in prenatal testing, or if the pregnancy was the result of rape or incest.

Shifts in professional opinion were important. But they didn't change the laws. The model criminal code was influential but merely a suggestion. Most legislators simply chose not to follow it. But after the American Law Institute published its recommendations, New Yorkers and Californians formed advocacy groups focused on abortion law reform. The advocates met two more changes that ultimately turned the abortion law reform cause from an aspiration to a reality: the rise of a new liberalism, especially within the Democratic Party, and the rise of a new feminist movement whose members came to understand legal abortion as a load-bearing wall in the structure of emancipation they were trying to build.

The feminism of the 1960s and a new spirit in the Democratic Party ultimately did much to carry the inchoate movement for abortion law reform to success. These two trends were closely related to each other. Many of the important players in the history of changing abortion laws started out as liberals who wanted the Democratic Party to be as good as its history and ideals. Only later did they start to think of themselves as feminists—after the founding of the key civil rights organization the National Organization for Women, created in 1966 by the famous author Betty Friedan in conjunction with women professionals and labor movement leaders.

Although my mother was not a famous or charter member of NOW, she joined the organization's New York City chapter in 1967, shortly after its creation. Hers was one path people took to NOW and to seeing abortion as a fundament of women's rights. Beatrice Kornbluh, Esq., was a Democrat who was inspired by the liberalism of the New Deal period of President Franklin D. Roosevelt and First Lady Eleanor Roosevelt. Before joining NOW, she was a local leader of Americans for Democratic Action, a group sponsored by Eleanor Roosevelt and other New Deal stalwarts to keep the liberal flame alive in a generally conservative time. Americans for Democratic Action favored Black civil rights and foreign policy internationalism while opposing communism abroad and within the United States.

From the time her first marriage ended onward, my mother spent her entire career with the National Labor Relations Board, an agency the Roosevelt New Deal created to regularize and legalize trade union representation for employees. She was not alone among professional women, in the years between World War II and the emergence of 1960s feminism, in gaining a foothold in the middle class through white-collar government work and thinking of herself as a political liberal. It might be more accurate to describe women like my mother as feminist liberals, rather than as they're usually known, liberal feminists, since post–New Deal liberalism came first, chronologically, in their politics.

My mother was a post–World War II liberal in that she was comfortably anti-communist. Nonetheless, she supported Americans for Democratic Action in its opposition to the way anti-communism was weaponized during the two decades after the war. In fact, she was a veteran of a loyalty investigation before she started her federal job, and had to defend herself in a hearing at which she was not at all sure she would prevail. It was the raging anti-communist late 1950s and it was part of Mom's record that she had joined a student chapter of the left-leaning National Lawyers Guild while at Brooklyn Law School. The Guild was in the crosshairs of the FBI and the predatorily anti-communist House Un-American Activities Committee, because its attorneys defended suspected communists and because they argued that the FBI itself threatened Americans' rights. As she told the story:

> When I got my job with the government, they did, they had security checks. And I was called in for a security check because I had been a member of the National Lawyers Guild. I was fit to be tied, really. I mean they made me go through a hearing. And by— And luckily my

boss who was no liberal, he was very supportive . . . at a time [when he] could easily have been not . . . So it was really, I mean I was genuinely anti-communist, it was funny. But they were ready to condemn me I guess for that. But then they, I passed, thank goodness, and went on from there and was able to go on and stay. But it was very sad. This other guy claimed that all he had ever done was sign some petitions. He had not even been a member of anything, he just signed some petitions. And because of that he lost his government job . . . Strange and awful time. Strange and awful time.

In New York, my liberal parents affiliated with what was called the "reform" wing of the Democratic Party, basically a local version of Americans for Democratic Action that worked to make the party more progressive. The reformers took as their opposition the "regular Democrats," known also as "machine Democrats" or loyalists to "Tammany Hall," an archaic term for a patronage-oriented political operation that was more interested in sustaining itself than in changing the system.

My parents' neighborhood, the Upper West Side of Manhattan, was one of two main centers of reform Democratic ferment in New York. The other was Harlem, often considered the heart of Black New York or even the capital of Black America. One of Harlem's representatives in the New York State legislature was Percy Sutton, a child of the Jim Crow South who had been beaten by a white policeman for passing out civil rights leaflets when he was only thirteen years old. He was arrested for being a Freedom Rider in the early 1960s. As an attorney, he represented Betty Shabazz and bravely helped her arrange the funeral of her husband, Malcom X, in 1965.

The Upper West Side was the home of State Senator Manfred Ohrenstein, who introduced Sutton's abortion reform bill into his legislative chamber. Ohrenstein, a Jewish refugee from Nazi Germany, initially won his seat in 1960 by challenging a machine Democrat in a primary in the manner of the twenty-first-century politician

Alexandria Ocasio-Cortez—a battle in which he benefited from a personal endorsement by Eleanor Roosevelt. He may have leaned toward the reform end of the political spectrum because of his own formative experience of race-based persecution. His neighborhood (and my parents') was slightly down-at-the-heels, thanks to the wave of federally funded, racially specific suburbanization that led thousands of Eastern European Jews and other whites to flee the city. Those who remained were overwhelmingly liberal. The Upper West Side's reform Democrat in the state assembly was Al Blumenthal, first elected in 1962. When Percy Sutton left the legislature for higher political office, Blumenthal picked up the baton on the abortion issue.

NOW cofounder Betty Friedan did not start out as a liberal but as more of a socialist, even a "fellow traveler" to communists. However, by the middle 1960s she ran in circles that were similar to my parents'. Friedan was a pro at reinvention. In her bestselling book, *The Feminine Mystique*, she made herself seem conventional and all-American. This effaced her religious and ethnic roots and the origins of her feminism in the political left and mid-twentieth-century labor movement.

At her birth in Peoria, Illinois, the woman the world would know as Betty Friedan was named Bettye Goldstein. Harry, her father, was an immigrant from Ukraine, unlike her mother, Miriam, whose family had come to the United States a generation earlier from Hungary. Harry Goldstein owned a jewelry store that did well until the Great Depression, and so the family was relatively wealthy, even as they also suffered discrimination and social segregation. They attended a Reform Jewish synagogue and celebrated Christmas. Bettye Goldstein dropped the extra "e" in her first name upon graduation from elite, WASPy, intellectually serious Smith College. She took the name of her husband, Carl Friedan, upon marriage.

In *The Feminine Mystique*, Friedan suggested that she had personally experienced the boredom and professional limitations described in the book. This was a distortion. In fact, Friedan had never been strictly a stay-at-home suburban mother, even while living a commuter train ride away from New York City and raising young children. After moving to Long Island and having her second child, she worked as a freelance journalist. Moreover, her background in college and after graduation was in the American left. She opposed U.S. entry into World War II during the period of the "Nazi-Soviet pact" and even after the Nazis invaded the USSR and communists started urging the Roosevelt administration to get involved. This left her in a tiny political corner shared only by pacifists and some members of the Socialist Party. She finally supported war against Hitler after the Japanese attacked Pearl Harbor. From 1943 to 1946, she worked for a news service affiliated with the labor movement, and from 1946 to 1953 as an in-house writer for the United Electrical, Radio, and Machine Workers of America (UE). The UE in this period has been described as "the largest communist-led institution of any kind in the United States." It was also notoriously forward-looking on women's issues, thanks in part to one of Friedan's interviewees from the 1940s, Ruth Young, the first woman to serve on the union's executive board. In 1952, Friedan herself penned an influential pamphlet for her union about sex-based inequality, *UE Fights for Women Workers*.

The Feminine Mystique made Friedan a celebrity. The book analyzed what she termed the "problem that has no name" of female discontent in the midst of American plenty and global power. She argued by way of explanation that the post–World War II prosperous American suburbs were like "comfortable concentration camps" for women who spent their adult lives in them. Friedan didn't acknowledge that the ability to live, howsoever sufferingly, in that suburban environment was a terrific racial and class privilege. She did later back off from the offensive reference to the Holocaust.

Liberalism and labor feminism had come together a few years before Beatrice Kornbluh, Esq., and Betty Friedan both became members of NOW. This happened in 1963, in the same season that Friedan's book exploded into white suburbia, with the publication of a book called *American Women*, the product of two years' work by the President's

Commission on the Status of Women. The commission, a product of agitation by labor union women, was appointed by John F. Kennedy early in his presidency. It capped off what was by then a decades-long effort by activists in and around the labor movement to transform the way women workers were treated in public policy. It also recognized Kennedy's debt to the women voters who had helped elect him.

The immediate launching point for NOW was a great liberal achievement, the Civil Rights Act of 1964, which President Lyndon Johnson maneuvered to passage after his predecessor was murdered. Title VII of the act, which covers civil rights in the workplace, was the law's only section that forbade discrimination on the basis of sex as well as race, color, religion, and national origin. Title VII also established a new federal agency to implement and enforce the law, the Equal Employment Opportunity Commission (EEOC). Despite the plain text of the statute, the leadership of the new agency, including its chair, Franklin D. Roosevelt, Jr., didn't really believe that Congress had put the kibosh on sex-based employment practices. But many working women did. In the first fiscal year of the new equal-employment office, about 37 percent of the complaints it received were about sex discrimination.

It fell to the new agency, the EEOC, to treat the law against sex discrimination as either an unenforceable fluke or as a serious mandate for government action. Aileen Clarke Hernandez was the only woman President Johnson included among the appointed commissioners of the agency. Hernandez's father, Charles Henry Clarke, was a follower of the Black nationalist Marcus Garvey. He and her mother, both immigrants to New York City from Jamaica, taught her never to back down from a racist—or sexist—fight. She remembered: "I arrive at my first political science class—the teacher looks down at me and then he says, 'If you are not prepared to do all of the work that we're talking about, I would suggest that you leave now and sign up for home economics.' And I look around and for the first time I discover I'm the only girl in the room. I would not move because I knew my mother would never forgive me if I did." Hernandez had

been involved in the Black civil rights movement, with her friend Pauli
Murray, since her student days at Howard University. She worked
for nearly a decade for the International Ladies Garment Workers
Union. Before President Johnson appointed her to the EEOC, she
had served as second in command at the California Division of Fair
Employment Practices. Hernandez had her eye on the anti-sex discrimination provision in Title VII. She pushed unsuccessfully to see
that it was enforced, and she resigned in frustration from the agency
just sixteen months after being appointed.

Within the staff of the EEOC, a leader in the effort to breathe life
into the sex discrimination portion of the law was Sonia "Sonny"
Pressman, a friend of my mother's from when she worked in Washington, D.C., before meeting my father. Sonny was the first woman
lawyer in the EEOC general counsel's office. She became what she
called a "sex maniac," who fought to get the nation's legal apparatus
into the game of fighting sex discrimination. Pressman described
the sense of destiny that drove her work: "I had been born only
because my mother's favored abortionist was out of the country, my
immediate family and I had escaped the Holocaust [by emigrating
from Germany and moving to the United States in the early 1930s],
and I was bright. To me, that meant that I had been saved to make a
contribution to the world."

Despite Hernandez's and Pressman's efforts, the federal equal-
employment office failed to take aggressive action in response to women's
cries against discrimination. Some of their colleagues kept right on
believing that fighting sexism was an unimportant also-ran to the serious
task of fighting racial discrimination—as though one had to choose, as
though no one experienced both racial and sex-based discrimination.
After trying to make the bureaucracy work from the inside, Pressman
shared tales about the situation—"with tears in my eyes"—to journalist Betty Friedan, who knew that something woman-related and
controversial was afoot and wanted to include it in her second book.
Pressman remembers telling Friedan that the time had come for "an

organization to fight for women like" the National Association for the Advancement of Colored People (NAACP), which won *Brown v. Board of Education* before the Supreme Court, "fought for African Americans."

It was clear that the federal government wasn't going to counter sex discrimination just because it was part of its apparent legal mandate to do so. Activist women inside and outside the government decided to stand and fight over this one big issue. In 1965, Justice Department attorney Mary O. Eastwood and Hernandez's friend Pauli Murray, veterans of the Civil and Political Rights Committee of the President's Commission on the Status of Women, took their concerns public by publishing an article about the need for government action against employers' treatment of women workers. Murray had been thinking about what the two called "Jane Crow," systematic and legally enforced discrimination between the sexes, comparable to the "Jim Crow" system of racial discrimination, for two decades before cowriting the essay. Murray started theorizing it as a student at Howard University School of Law, the renowned training ground for civil rights attorneys. It was at Howard, surrounded by Black people in positions of power, that the difference between Murray's treatment and that of the male majority stood out in a way it had not when Murray was in the Black minority among powerful whites. In a letter kept for her files and later shared with Friedan, Murray had complained, "at the risk of appearing presumptuous," to the head of the law fraternity at Howard, who had excluded women from a meeting. Murray identified herself as a member of a "minority group," women, that faced unequal treatment that could affect their career prospects.

Murray and Eastwood's essay, "Jane Crow and the Law," went beyond the immediate issue of the dereliction of duty by the EEOC. It made the first sustained argument in print for the existence of systematic sex discrimination in U.S. law. Murray and Eastwood built from fundamentals: legalized sex discrimination exists and is a violation of human rights comparable to the violations enabled by Jim Crow racial segregation. "The addition of 'sex' to Title VII of the Civil Rights Act," they wrote, "represents an important step toward implementation of our commitment to human rights." They countered the EEOC staff who refused Hernandez's and Pressman's entreaties, on the grounds that the Civil Rights Act was intended to address racial and not sex-based discrimination, with a reminder about Black women, who suffered from both. Ultimately, they argued for the same thing that Ruth Bader Ginsburg would fight for years later, treating discrimination that subordinated women as a violation of the constitutional promise of "equal protection of the laws."

Women in activist networks around the unions were just as attuned as Murray and Eastwood, and Pressman's friends in the federal bureaucracy, to inaction at the EEOC. They saw this one federal agency that Congress had tasked with fighting sexism punt on cases of everyday discrimination at work and fail to bring the hammer down on newspaper publishers who were still listing job-wanted ads under "Help Wanted—Male" and "Help Wanted—Female." It didn't take a sex discrimination maniac or theorist of Jane Crow to find that a violation of Title VII, or so it would seem. Labor activists took their fury about the EEOC to the third National Conference of State Commissions on the Status of Women. Despite the best efforts of the woman chairing the proceedings, who was trying to avoid public rebuke of a Democratic administration, "that night a group of women"—including Hernandez and Murray—"jammed into Betty Friedan's hotel room." They decided to push for a strong resolution denouncing the EEOC for inaction on Title VII enforcement and demand that the agency treat sex discrimination seriously. The next day, the conference chair ruled their proposals out of order. The women "gathered at a table during lunch and, under the nose of the luncheon speaker, formulated their plans for 'an NAACP for women,'" an idea that seems to have been proposed by the Black labor activist Dollie Lowther Robinson as well as by Sonny Pressman.

And so the work began. Friedan and her labor and professional women colleagues, including Murray and Pressman, met to found the

National Organization for Women in October 1966. "The purpose of NOW ," read the statement adopted at that meeting, "is to take action to bring women into full participation in the mainstream of American society now, exercising all the privileges and responsibilities thereof in truly equal partnership with men." By "the mainstream of American society," the new group meant education, including higher education and advanced professional training; work outside the hyper-segregated jobs that were already readily available to women; and active participation in the major political parties. The NOW statement called out the government for failing to enforce the sex equality provision of Title VII and pointed to federal and state governments that failed to follow through on the recommendations of the Commission on the Status of Women and its sister commissions in the states. "There is no civil rights movement to speak for women, as there has been for Negroes and other victims of discrimination," it read. "The National Organization for Women must therefore begin to speak." There was no mention of abortion.

Meanwhile, back in New York, the abortion law reform movement in medicine and law was starting to get some traction from reformers in the Democratic Party. In 1964, a Westchester, New York, couple named Sylvia and Dan Bloom had joined with a friend from the Ethical Culture Society to agitate for a change in the abortion laws. They asked "lawyers, doctors, and other professionals" to join their advisory board. Building on the change in medical opinion represented by the Planned Parenthood conference and the effort among lawyers that produced the American Law Institute's model abortion law, their recruitment effort was a success. Their group, initially called the Committee for a Humane Abortion Law and soon renamed the Association for the Study of Abortion, was, in the words of legal scholar David Garrow, "America's first notably active abortion action organization."

The ASA included people like Dr. Alan Guttmacher, the New York City–based president of the Planned Parenthood Federation of America. Originally from Baltimore, Guttmacher had chaired the combined Department of Obstetrics and Gynecology at Mount Sinai Hospital in Manhattan for a decade before succeeding founder Margaret Sanger in the top leadership position in Planned Parenthood. ASA's founding executive director was Ruth Proskauer Smith, a former employee of the Human Betterment Association for Voluntary Sterilization (later, the Association for Voluntary Sterilization) whose personal wealth allowed ASA to thrive.

Members of the Association for the Study of Abortion started by sponsoring showings of films about the issue, circulating printed material with information about the current law and its consequences, and writing letters to medical personnel in New York–area departments of obstetrics. They surveyed obstetricians to take their temperature on the possibility of a law-reform initiative. Spokespeople Guttmacher and Harriet Pilpel, an attorney for both Planned Parenthood and the ACLU, called for court cases that might provoke federal judges to apply the U.S. Constitution to questions about abortion access—as the Supreme Court was just then applying it to the issue of contraception for married couples in the case *Griswold v. Connecticut* (1965). A legislative campaign was not part of their thinking until representatives of the group happened to participate in a forum on abortion sponsored by a neighborhood political club on the East Side of Manhattan, the Yorkville Democrats. A surprisingly positive reception led to a new strategy.

Assemblyman Sutton was only in his first term as a state legislator, but he was willing to take risks. Changing the abortion laws was a way to address an ongoing crisis for Black and Puerto Rican women in New York, including his constituents, who suffered vastly more deaths from illegal abortion than did white women. In New York City, which had the best data in the country but was probably seeing the same trends as other big cities, deaths from abortion increased in the 1950s and 1960s, even as medical technology advanced and childbirth overall became safer. A report in the *American Journal of Public Health* found with alarm an increase in maternal mortality between 1954 and 1962 that was especially marked at the height of U.S. wealth and power in the early 1960s. The researchers also found stark racial and ethnic differences: a remarkable one-quarter of deaths to pregnant white women in New York City between 1951 and 1962 were due to poorly performed abortions, but an even more astounding *one half* of Black and Puerto Rican maternal deaths were abortion-related. Sutton himself remembered the origin point of his bill as the experience of a friend whose wife had died in the 1940s from a poorly performed illegal abortion. "This background," he said years later, "demanded that I take some action when I had the opportunity."

The overall numbers and the disparity had the same causes. As historian Leslie Reagan has proved, a relatively permissive climate around abortion during the Depression-era 1930s swung hard during and after World War II in the opposite direction. Local police departments, sometimes provoked by crusading district attorneys, increased their prosecutions of illegal practitioners. This included, in a change of practice, working to shut down abortion providers whose services were safe and reliable—as opposed to the late-nineteenth- and early-twentieth-century pattern of prosecuting only those whose patients had died. In a parallel development, the availability of legal so-called therapeutic abortions declined. In New York City, there was a "consistent downward trend" in legal abortions from 1943 to 1962.

Although state legislatures did not rewrite their laws, practices changed dramatically. When the reputation of abortion declined and the pace of prosecutions increased, doctors retreated from serving their patients. At Manhattan's Mount Sinai Hospital, for example, Dr. Guttmacher created a committee of doctors to consider each abortion request (and generally to lower the number of procedures) because he did not want his institution to be known for having a liberal approach to abortion. There was no legal mandate to create such a committee. However, Guttmacher, who admitted that he found the restrictive state law "outmoded," nonetheless saw the committee system as a way to signal to authorities that Mount Sinai was "cleaving closely to the letter of the law" and should therefore be left alone.

While the systems for approving legal abortions varied from institution to institution, the committee structure became common at U.S. hospitals. The Mount Sinai committee had five members, all senior physicians from different hospital departments, and its decisions had to be unanimous if a pregnancy termination was to be approved. "No case is considered," Guttmacher reported, "unless the staff obstetrician-gynecologist desiring to perform the abortion presents affirmative letters from two consultants in the medical field involved. Five copies of the letters must be filed at least 48 hours in advance of the Committee's meeting, so that each member may have an opportunity to study the problem." Unsurprisingly, he found that such a system, in concert with off-the-record conversations with colleagues in which he often discouraged them from bringing cases before the committee, produced "a material reduction in the number of requests for therapeutic interruption."

Disparities in access to legal abortion were inseparable from inequality in health care overall. Decades before legislation such as the Emergency Medical Treatment and Labor Act (1986), expectations for health-care equity were low, and distinctions by economic status were pervasive. In New York City, there were two levels of distinction: First was the difference between patients at publicly managed, municipal hospitals and those at private hospitals (nonprofit, or "voluntary," institutions, or for-profit ones). Women seeking abortions or other health care at the municipal hospitals paid on a sliding scale and were disproportionately poor, Black, Puerto Rican, and/or recent migrants to the city. Second were distinctions within the private hospitals, between "private" patients—those with good private-sector health insurance—and so-called ward patients, who relied on charity medicine or, after the creation of the public insurance programs Medicaid and Medicare in 1965, on those federal programs. Lawrence Lader, the journalist and advocate who participated in national and

New York abortion politics, reported that in 1960–61 the private hospitals in New York City performed one abortion for every 250 total pregnant patients, and the public hospitals one for every 10,000. At one hospital in particular, Metropolitan Hospital in East Harlem, the figure was one in 13,000. Of women who sought legal abortions from hospital committees, five white women were approved for every Black woman, thirty whites for every Puerto Rican.

Assemblyman Sutton enlisted the help of Dr. Guttmacher. When Sutton's bill was introduced in 1965, it instantly made him a leader on the issue among state legislators across the United States. A companion bill introduced by Senator Ohrenstein was a mirror of the assembly bill. Both proposed laws followed the criteria outlined in the Model Penal Code the American Law Institute had proposed. They would have decriminalized abortion in case of rape, incest, fetal anomalies, or danger to a pregnant woman's health. Sutton and Ohrenstein proposed to do this straight-ahead, through explicit mention in the statute, instead of leaving it up to doctors to judge for themselves when the medical indications made it appropriate to recommend a therapeutic abortion.

In 1966, Sutton supported his legislative initiative with a series of articles in the *New York Amsterdam News*, a Harlem newspaper with a national Black readership. His series carried the clickbait title (well before "clicks") "Is Abortion Ever Right?" The articles were a second prong in the battle Sutton and other reform-minded Democrats were waging to change public opinion on the way to changing the law. His arguments might seem cautious today. In their time, they were very bold given that it had been more than three-quarters of a century since the New York legislature had entertained a major abortion bill, and not a single state in the country had yet liberalized the restrictive abortion laws they passed in the nineteenth or early-twentieth centuries.

Sutton started with the kind of melodrama that had suffused decades of sensational anti-abortion news reports: "For a price running from Fifty to Fifteen Hundred Dollars, and upwards," he wrote, "a pregnant woman can buy death." But then he pivoted and started to build the case for reform. He explained that even the Catholic Church, which believed in the "right to be born," permitted certain life-saving surgeries that incidentally destroyed fetuses, "and many Protestants feel that more birth control education and more lenient abortion laws are preferable to the present situation in which women are often forced to risk their lives in aborting an unwanted child." He let experts and on-the-street interviews with Harlemites and other Black New Yorkers stand in for his own perspectives. He asked a doctor in Harlem: "Is abortion ever right?" Sutton happily recorded the answer: "'Don't be ridiculous,' answered Doctor D. 'OF COURSE THERE ARE TIMES WHEN ABORTION IS RIGHT!'" He got an even more enthusiastic answer from Doctor D's pastor, to the effect that "in some cases THE FAILURE TO ABORT IS WRONG!" The minister added that it was immoral to disallow abortion in a case in which pregnancy or childbirth would harm the mother or when the fetus was likely to become what he called a "vegetable," with profound disabilities.

Assemblyman Sutton's articles provoked an active reader response. It reached the point where he felt the need to tell readers he was "opposed to abortions, except under very strict, hygienic hospital conditions." His final article in the series made the case for a change in law by reiterating the range of self-harmful things women were known to do in order to abort: "Humiliation, agony and the risk of death, do not deter New York women from abortions," he concluded. He conducted a straw poll on the streets of Black neighborhoods in the city and found that only one in twenty-two women who had terminated a pregnancy regretted her decision (and that one, not for moral reasons). Sutton declaimed: "Some abortions are legal! More abortions should be legal!"

The newspaper columns were only the beginning. The leadership of Assemblyman Sutton's own political party, those "regular" Democrats who opposed the reform faction with which he identified, did not allow his bill in the assembly or Ohrenstein's in the senate to be considered for very long. The draft laws languished in committee and didn't make it to votes on the floor of their respective legislative houses. But they represented a start toward greater public education and understanding of the issue.

While his abortion bill was dying on the vine, Sutton was chosen by the city council to become Manhattan borough president. The position had recently been vacated by attorney Constance Baker Motley when President Johnson appointed her as the first Black woman ever to hold a federal judgeship. Assemblyman Al Blumenthal, who chaired the Committee on Health, pledged to introduce a new abortion law reform bill in the next session.

Blumenthal was good to his word. His bill closely resembled Sutton's. It drew, similarly, on the model law circulated by the American Law Institute, which had also started to provoke legislative change campaigns in North Carolina, California, and Colorado. In addition to Sutton's emphasis on hospital-based abortions—a requirement that would have limited access but might have helped recruit more doctors to the cause of changing the law—Blumenthal added an additional limiting requirement, a provision that each procedure would have to be approved by a committee of doctors before it could proceed. This restriction potentially made it as hard to access abortion after the law passed as it was before, or even harder, since writing the committee standard into statute would give doctors less flexibility than they had previously.

Agitation by the Association for the Study of Abortion and other groups outside the legislature helped give the debate more gravitas in 1967 than it had two years earlier. The New York State Catholic Conference, for example, had barely bothered to fight the Sutton bill, because its leaders thought the legislation had so little chance of moving. But Blumenthal was a more senior Democrat than Sutton, and the popular climate around abortion had begun to shift. The Catholic religious hierarchy and lobbying apparatus swung into force. With Cardinal Francis Spellman of New York in the lead, all eight of the state's bishops signed a letter urging Catholics, "with all their power," to fight the Blumenthal bill. They told priests in all 1,700 of the state's Catholic churches to read the letter as part of their Sunday services on February 12, 1967. "The opposition concentrated its wrath on Assemblyman Blumenthal," Lawrence Lader remembered. With a hint of antisemitism and an echo of arguments used to condemn left-wing political regimes around the world, the opponents "consistently linked abortion with godlessness."

Reform-minded Democrats and their allies did their best to pass Blumenthal's bill. They were lucky in that they included in their ranks Senator Basil Paterson, a Black Harlem Democrat close to Sutton who was also Catholic. Paterson's involvement helped to mute claims that abortion was racist and that all Catholics opposed liberalizing the law. Blumenthal compromised in an effort to get his bill out of the various committees reviewing it, so that it could go to the floor of the assembly and get a vote of the whole body. Media coverage of a legislative floor debate would be another big step toward taking abortion out of the netherworld of shameful practice. Even if the bill failed, the publicity might move the needle on public understanding. But the compromise was devastating for the potential positive impact of the law, limiting the mental health grounds for abortion so that only someone who was severely mentally ill could qualify.

Outside groups supported the effort to get the Blumenthal bill out of committee. The range of organizations reflected the powerful impact that people like Carol Marsh, who sought abortion care no matter the proscriptions against it, had on professionals who knew what happened to many women like her. The roster of organizations did not yet include any single-issue groups focused on women's rights, autonomy, or citizenship. No one in the coalition supporting the bill argued for abortion on the basis of the pregnant person's need for freedom or self-ownership, for abortion as a way to narrow inequality between the sexes, or as a matter of racial and economic justice. The people who led a petition drive in support of the Blumenthal bill were doctors, lawyers, and progressive clergy—members of the New York Obstetrical Society, New York County Medical Society, New York State Council of Churches (mainline Protestants), United Synagogue of America (Conservative Jews), New York Civil Liberties Union, and New York Bar Association Committee on Public Health. Despite these efforts, Blumenthal's bill went down to defeat in committee—not in the health committee but in the powerful Assembly Codes Committee, which was stocked with mainstream Democrats and Republicans unfriendly to abortion law reform. The vote was 15–3. In the midst of the debate, the Speaker of the Assembly stripped Blumenthal of a leadership position as a member of the Democratic Advisory Committee. He was the only reform Democrat on that committee.

Individual abortion seekers like Carol Marsh and the professionals whose opinions they shaped had done their best. So had the reform Democrats. But the politics of abortion law reform had hit a stalemate. Something had to change.

Chapter Two

Change the Law NOW

AS THE delegates to the New York State Constitutional Convention of 1967, almost all men, gathered warm and snug inside, writer and activist Betty Friedan marched outside the New York State Capitol in the freezing rain with a hardy band of feminists. They demonstrated in support of a resolution by the Black labor leader and feminist Dollie Lowther Robinson, a delegate to the convention. Lowther Robinson's resolution would make opposition to discrimination based on sex part of the state's constitution for the first time in history. As part of her stand for women's rights, Lowther Robinson included language announcing that "the right to terminate a pregnancy under medical supervision" would henceforth be a "civil right of every female person."

The New York State Constitutional Convention was a slightly desperate answer to gridlock and disarray, a political crisis caused by divisions between Democrats and Republicans and by a civil war within the Democratic Party. The Democratic Party's progressive and more conservative wings, the so-called reform and regular factions, were so divided that they hadn't been able to agree on who would lead either legislative house for the first five weeks of the 1965–66 session, although they had majorities in both. It was in the midst of this turmoil that the first two abortion law reform proposals in eighty years had been introduced into the legislature by reform Democrats and had fallen to ignominious defeats. New York's Constitution, one of fifty state constitutions that differ significantly from the U.S. Constitution, had last been revised in the late 1930s. It had not been taken down to its studs and rebuilt since 1894.

The rain-soaked feminists carried protest signs from their new organization, the National Organization for Women. They had just created the first local chapter of the group, in New York City. It was the first organization in the history of the modern women's movement, perhaps in all U.S. history, to claim access to abortion as integral to civil rights. The person who carried their demand into the councils of power, Dollie Lowther Robinson, was both representative of the early membership of NOW and extraordinary: She had come to labor leaders' attention by leading a strike in 1937 of the three hundred women who worked with her at the Colonial Laundry, where they made six dollars for every seventy-two-hour workweek. By the late 1960s, she had spent decades agitating for labor and women's rights as a union leader and an official in the federal and New York State governments. To boot, she was the cofounder, with novelist Ann Petry, of a group called Negro Women Incorporated, and during World War II had been an adviser to the NAACP and to the important Black labor leader A. Philip Randolph.

Just as they sought equality on the basis of sex in every corner of public life, from the workplace to the classroom, the voting booth to the loan office, these feminists sought access to abortion as a reproductive right that was part of the infrastructure that enabled all other rights. Their demand was that the state's Bill of Rights be retired and replaced with one that, unlike the U.S. Constitution's, specifically guaranteed equal rights on the basis of sex. And that the text specify, as Lowther Robinson's proposal put it, that being able to choose the option of abortion was part and parcel of equal rights.

Dollie Lowther Robinson, Betty Friedan, and their protesting comrades were loosely affiliated with the Democratic Party reformers. But they had their own complaints and constitutional aspirations that other liberal Democrats didn't necessarily share. If the constitution was to be rewritten, then they wanted it to make explicit mention of women's rights and to grant them a win on abortion law that they feared they might never gain through the divided, dysfunctional legislature. They marched to demand that the constitutional convention bypass a system that seemed immune to change despite shifting social values.

Today, historians sometimes remember the National Organization for Women in its formative years as a center of moderate feminism, full of people who were content to work within the system instead of demanding its radical transformation. However, in reality, NOW was a big tent that contained people (mostly women) with multitudinous approaches to sexual and gender-based rights. The organization became a haven for those who were deeply political but disaffected, activists in the making who had nowhere else to go with their passion for women's emancipation or their desire to do something about their own frustrated ambitions.

In its first years and months, the people who found their way to NOW included opponents of legal abortion and those who personally favored decriminalization but wanted to keep abortion out of the women's civil rights agenda. However, once NOW identified itself with the issue, beginning just prior to New York's constitutional convention and ending with the passage of a national NOW resolution on reproductive rights in 1968, those opponents left. A portion of them formed an alternative feminist civil rights group, the Women's Equity Action League.

When first created, the National Organization for Women was more of a decentralized movement than a top-down membership organization. This helped account for the range of people, views, and tactics that found shelter under its big tent. Several New York members were more tactically daring and politically far-reaching than Friedan and other national leaders. In NOW's formative period, that was okay. Within the New York chapter, the range ran from labor feminists like Dollie Lowther Robinson to wealthy, white professionals like the advertising executive Muriel Fox. The chapter made room, initially, for Florynce Kennedy, the activist attorney and public intellectual who wanted to synthesize Black Power and woman power, and for the white intellectual and activist Ti-Grace Atkinson, who apprenticed herself to Kennedy to learn about radical politics.

In New York and then nationally, NOW began to smash the framework of abortion law reform that had been established by members of the medical and legal professions and adopted by New York's Democratic state legislators Percy Sutton, Manfred Ohrenstein, and Al Blumenthal. That framework shaped bills across the country that would have liberalized abortion law. But critically, it was a *reform* and not a transformation of the old system of therapeutic abortion—a system in which individual doctors or committees of doctors got to decide whether a particular situation qualified one for this safe and fairly common medical procedure. NOW members pushed for an approach that to many outside the group, and some inside it, seemed distinctly out-there in the context of its times: full *repeal* of all restrictions, redoing the law to free pregnant people seeking abortions and the practitioners who served them from all criminal sanctions.

NOW staked out one of the most ambitious positions on abortion law of any national organization in the United States and placed a unique feminist stamp on the issue. NOW cofounder Betty Friedan was not in the vanguard of this change, but she got with the program after the New York chapter voted to include abortion decriminalization in its agenda. "Don't talk to me about abortion reform," she wrote in a speech that remembered the constitutional convention protest in New York. "Abortion reform is something dreamed up by men, maybe good-hearted men, but they can only think from their male point of view. For them, women are the passive objects that somehow must be regulated. . . . [But what] right have they to say? What right has any man to say to any woman—you must bear this child? What right has any state to say?"

Critics argue that NOW's mostly white, middle-class members didn't understand the ways race and class fractured women's experiences, so they could never do what they claimed, which was to represent the interests and needs of all women. Indeed, activists and scholars argue that there's no such thing as a single agenda that can capture the interests and needs of all women (think Mom and Helen, yards from each other and light-years away). The critics aren't wrong. NOW's chief tactics, of lobbying, bringing lawsuits, and orderly demonstrations like the one Friedan led during the constitutional convention, were more moderate than the confrontational moves of some later feminists. The group's agenda failed to cover all the issues that were important to communities of color and sometimes even opposed them, as it did right away when Florynce Kennedy tried to build bridges between NOW and Black Power. But Black women, including Kennedy, Lowther Robinson, and Aileen Clarke Hernandez, were active members and played pivotal roles in forming NOW's agenda. Arguably, Pauli Murray had played the most formative role when she theorized "Jane Crow" segregation in a way that helped Friedan and others imagine what a national organization for women might do.

NOW's position on abortion spoke to the ways race and class shaped access to this pillar of reproductive rights. Advocates had good reasons to suppose that gaps in access to abortion care between wealthier whites and less wealthy women of color would become *more* extreme if the law were reformed as Democratic Party mavericks were trying to do in New York. Abortion law reform, a bold departure from over a century of harsh criminal codes, was at the same time kind of conservative. A reform approach like Percy Sutton's or Al Blumenthal's would have increased the power of doctors to recommend abortion for their patients. It would not have increased the power of pregnant people themselves to assess their needs for abortion and act on their assessments.

Abortion law reform essentially extended the regime of therapeutic abortion, lengthening the list of so-called medical indications for abortion. Private physicians who knew their patients' circumstances, and were sympathetic to them, would likely use this flexibility to help the patients secure safe, legal abortions. Doctors in public hospitals, and others serving poor and nonwhite patients, were less likely to have ongoing relationships with them. They were far less likely to use the flexibility they gained from a reformed law to help the patients they saw. One Philadelphia-area physician, for example, referred about twelve women a year to a nurse who was a skillful abortionist. But 100 percent of these were his private patients, not the "ward patients" in the hospital with which he was affiliated. "Every doctor I knew well," he said, "had someone. Now, it was something you didn't talk about, even with your best friends. But when doctors' families . . . let's say a doctor would come to you and say, 'Look, my daughter . . .' Well, you had to have someplace that you could send people that you wanted to help."

Betty Friedan had soared home from the first national NOW meeting in fall 1966 on the high of having cofounded—at last!—an organization she hoped would create a movement for women's rights. Then, on a forbiddingly cold night in February 1967, the famous writer chaired a meeting at Muriel Fox's apartment near Fifth Avenue. The meeting's purpose was to create the first local chapter of the National Organization for Women, the New York–area chapter. Nationally, nearly 114 of the roughly 600 total NOW members were New Yorkers. In attendance were the pioneering women's historian Gerda Lerner, as much an alum of left-of-center midcentury politics as Friedan herself; sociology graduate student Cynthia (Fuchs) Epstein; Atkinson, an art critic and student; Fox, who was a close Friedan confidante and already a leader of NOW at the national level; and Kennedy, who was at the time helping to organize the first national Black Power Conference, scheduled for July in close-by Newark, New Jersey.

The first question Friedan suggested the meeting take up was how NOW should participate in the effort to rewrite the New York State Constitution. "She felt this offered a great opportunity for NOW to set the pattern for the rest of the country and to press for amendment of Article I, Section 2, of the present Constitution to include a clause prohibiting all discrimination based on sex." The group agreed unanimously. The cochair of a committee to plan next steps, appointed in her absence because the bad weather had kept her from attending in person, was New York State's senior Republican assemblywoman, Constance Cook. Fox told the assembled about some of the campaigns NOW had initiated at the national level, including fighting for full enforcement of the anti-sex-discrimination provision of Title VII of the Civil Rights Act by the Equal Employment Opportunity Commission; advocating for federally funded childcare, "not as part of relief or poverty programs but as a recognized right of working parents"; and demanding full equality in jury service irrespective of sex.

The assembled did not agree on all points. As Kennedy remembered it, when she talked about the fact that women should oppose the war in Vietnam, Friedan and Fox "went bonkers." When she suggested that women use their consumer dollars to pressure media that depicted women in sexist ways (and that supported the war), Fox in particular, one of the very few women who held a senior position in a major advertising agency, "almost had a nervous breakdown." Atkinson remembered, "[Kennedy] kept putting up her hand and making suggestions that just sounded like she was from Mars to me, but the way she handled herself, the way she would propose things as a motion, the way she seemed to take it so well if it didn't pass and she just kept doing what she thought should be done—she didn't let anybody step on her. I thought, 'Wow.'" One of Kennedy's proposals was for the new women's movement to get behind the movement for Black Power. The overwhelmingly white group was in no rush to follow through on the suggestion.

Some of the members were not sure about abortion. They started discussing New York's laws on marriage and divorce, which, like those on abortion, were scandalously out of step with popular opinion and practice; in 1967, adultery was the only legally acceptable basis for divorce, a standard that had essentially not changed since 1813. When the conversation turned to abortion, Friedan reminded the group that NOW at the national level had no policy on the issue. But several members present—with Kennedy, who had published an article calling for liberalization of the abortion laws as early as 1964, no doubt in the lead—insisted on addressing abortion as a civil rights issue, in line with the effort to elevate women's rights generally by lobbying for new language in the state constitution. They rejected the hint from Friedan that they should wait for NOW's national board to sort out its views and called instead for the national organization to follow *their* lead. In the end, the vote was overwhelming, with just one dissent and two abstentions, "to recommend that the national Board open discussion of abortion as a civil right of women."

As Friedan focused on building NOW nationally, local leadership fell to Jean Faust, one of the less well-known people in attendance at that first meeting. Faust was a white North Carolinian transplant to New York City and a former English teacher who entered politics through her participation in the Democratic Party's liberal reform movement. In the local Democratic club she joined, however, the sexist habits of male politicos had not been reformed. "All the work of the club," she remembered, "especially mailings, was done by the women while the men stood around talking." She established a committee on women's rights in her club. Despite the sexism, the reform movement changed Faust's life. After she volunteered for his campaign, Representative William F. Ryan, one of the few reform Democrats in the U.S. House of Representatives, hired Faust as a staff member. Four years later, she was in on the ground floor of NOW in New York: "I don't know how I was on the list, but I got a postcard for the first meeting of NOW in NYC and couldn't wait to attend. It was a small group and we were asked to stand, give our names and occupations. Probably because I worked for the congressman, I was asked after that meeting to form the first chapter in NYC and act as first president."

A few weeks after Jean Faust started organizing NOW in New York City, the state constitutional convention began in the state capitol. Representatives to the convention were welcomed on the first day of the proceedings, April 4, 1967, with a benediction from the chief opponent of abortion decriminalization in New York, His Eminence Cardinal Francis Spellman. The convention proceeded in parallel with the debate over Assemblyman Blumenthal's bill, with the likely outcome from both being zero change in the law but a jump in public awareness of the issue. The overwhelmingly male and elite delegates to the convention spent far more time discussing a proposal to repeal the state constitution's education amendment, called the Blaine Amendment, which forbade public funding to parochial schools, than it did discussing women's civil rights. Parochial-school funding was the top priority of the New York Catholic leadership—perhaps a reason that Spellman and the bishops did not get even more vocally involved in the abortion debate.

Dollie Lowther Robinson's proposal for women's equality, with abortion as essential to that equality, was discussed as part of a potential new state bill of rights. The leading politicians who set the agenda for the convention lumped her amendment in with initiatives to limit government wiretapping, to control the levels of bail demanded of criminal defendants, and to impose gun control and sustain gun rights. It was also considered alongside an initiative from political allies of the state's Catholic hierarchy that defined fetal personhood as existing from the moment of conception and would have therefore led to even more restrictions on abortion access than already existed.

Although they may not have expected much in the way of an immediate response, members of the National Organization for Women, Chapter I, followed through on the initiative from their first meeting. They actively supported Lowther Robinson's ambitious resolution to repeal Article I of the state constitution and replace it with a provision forbidding discrimination on the basis of sex, as well as other characteristics—and to specify that this nondiscrimination protection included guaranteeing that the *"right to terminate a pregnancy under medical supervision"* not be *"denied nor abridged by the state or any agency or subdivision of the state."* Jean Faust wrote on behalf of New York NOW to the chair of the convention's Committee on the Bill of Rights and Suffrage in support of the proposal. She worked hard to get the NOW-endorsed proposal in front of all the convention delegates, pulling together "mailings on NOW proposals for [the] New York State Constitutional Convention (up to 10 pages, 200 packets—no copying equipment, no Xerox machine) to all delegates—about six times."

Kennedy, Friedan, Fox, Atkinson, and Faust may have felt like they were part of a tiny band of advocates. But the proposals they endorsed hit a chord with women outside New York City, who also demanded that the constitutional convention take their rights seriously and treat access to abortion as one of those rights. One well-informed writer to the chair of the convention's Judiciary Committee asked for help figuring out, a few days ahead, when the proposal to "make abortion the civil right of every female" was to be considered, so that she could be there to observe the debate. She added that the treatment of Blumenthal's bill by the assembly "was a most bitter blow to me, so you can understand my present desire to attend." Mrs. A. Weissenfels argued for the Lowther Robinson/NOW proposal on the grounds that it accorded "women the respect due them as contributing members of society." She styled legal or constitutional arguments in its favor: the proposal was important because it acknowledged people's "right to marital privacy," she wrote, drawing on the recent Supreme Court decision in the birth control case *Griswold v. Connecticut*. She added that abortion as a constitutional right would allow women to follow the dictates of their own religion, in line with the U.S. Constitution's First Amendment. And she quoted the Eighth Amendment to the U.S. Constitution in claiming the provision would prevent the "cruel and unusual punishment" imposed on a woman when she had to carry an unwanted pregnancy to term.

These testimonials in support of abortion rights by women outside New York City, suburbanites who were mostly white, reveal troubling currents in the movement to transform abortion laws. They mixed arguments for women's legal and constitutional rights with others that were right out of the period's obsession with "population control"—a fear that the number of people would outstrip the world's resources, which led to policies to reduce birth rates of people in relatively poor countries or relatively poor and racialized communities in wealthy countries. Population control was a top-down effort rather than one that came from the bottom up, and so they argued in effect that *some* women deserved freedom, autonomy, and rights while the government should encourage others to have fewer children for the sake of the social good.

These advocates of loosening abortion laws brought population control into the debate in two ways. They expressed concern for the ability of individual families to care for their children and concern for the social costs of what they believed was excess population, the tax dollars that went to cash welfare, incarceration, and the institutionalization of people with physical, psychological, and cognitive disabilities. Although rarely explicit, these arguments were suffused with assumptions based on race and class and unexamined biases about disability: Why did some large families trip alarm bells more than others? Why assume that the children of poor people and those who were Black, Latino, or Native American would need welfare or commit crimes? And if they were poor or committed crimes, wasn't this likely a result of discrimination and the failure of the American promise of social mobility rather than a population problem? Why, in making the case for reproductive rights, did some advocates take it as given that a disabled child was an unwanted child?

In the 1960s, these arguments gained force from two particular risks to healthy pregnancies. The first was a major outbreak of "German measles," or rubella, in the United States, from 1964 to 1965, which produced eleven thousand miscarriages and twenty thousand babies born with rubella-related conditions ranging from cataracts to deafness and heart defects. The second was a global scare about the drug thalidomide, which was never approved for use in the United States but which some women nonetheless took for pregnancy-related nausea. A woman named Sherri Finkbine, the Phoenix-based host of the television show *Romper Room*, received thalidomide from her husband when he returned from a trip to London. After West German authorities reported a large incidence of birth defects among infants whose mothers had taken the drug, Finkbine sought a therapeutic abortion. When her local hospital at first agreed to perform the procedure and then reneged because her identity had been leaked to the media and the hospital did not want to become known for providing abortions, she publicized her situation and inspired a national debate about parental decision-making about abortion. Finkbine flew to Sweden to terminate her pregnancy.

Population control, unspoken assumptions, and the era's particular pregnancy fears appeared in several of the letters to New York constitutional convention delegates. Lillith Lehner from Carle Place, New York, for example, inveighed against the nineteenth-century abortion law still on the statute books because it failed to "take into consideration the population explosion and the consequent need to plan families sensibly and, at all costs, to avoid unwanted children." She wrote in a melodramatic mode: "The unwanted children: what becomes of them and the glorious chance to live that has been given them? They fill the children's wards in public hospitals; they vegetate in homes, waiting for adoption; they wander the streets and join the ranks of the hopelessly delinquent. The fact that they are unwanted robs them, from the beginning, of a decent chance in life." Sylvia Burgman from Bethpage, Long Island, regretted that the best argument for a liberalized abortion law was "the fact that more and more men realize the need for population control because of economic necessity"—but she didn't refuse population control as an argument for abortion access. She was moved by the fear that one might have "a deformed or retarded child" if one had had German measles early in pregnancy or had taken thalidomide. But she ended with a ringing plea for freedom in the realm of reproduction, expressed in constitutional terms: "Our federal constitution guarantees us the right to 'life, liberty, and the pursuit of happiness,'" she wrote, quoting the Declaration of Independence rather than the U.S. Constitution. "The latter phrase will not truly apply to women until the day comes when a woman has the choice of bearing, or not bearing, a child."

The rising feminist movement had an impact on the state constitution that was drafted that spring and summer, although not on its political fate. Thanks to Dollie Lowther Robinson, the advocacy and activism of the New York members, and of their allies, the proposed Bill of Rights for New York State included landmark language forbidding sexist discrimination. "No person," it read, "shall be denied the equal protection of the laws. No person shall, because of race, color, creed, religion, national origin, age, *sex* or physical or mental handicap, be subjected to any discrimination in his [*sic*] civil rights by the state or any subdivision, agency or instrumentality thereof or by any person, corporation or unincorporated association, public or private. The legislature shall provide that no public money shall be given or loaned to or invested with any person or entity, public or private, violating this provision." The draft constitution made no mention of abortion as a woman's civil right. Nor did it mention the civil rights of fetuses.

For members of NOW, women's and abortion rights were the most important part of the constitution-writing process. But they were only a brief scene in the drama staged around the state constitutional convention. The draft constitution that emerged from the convention gave Cardinal Spellman what he wanted most. This was language about the separation of church and state that followed the language of the First Amendment to the U.S. Constitution—and would therefore, consistent with the latest federal jurisprudence, permit some taxpayer funds to flow to Catholic private schools. A majority of representatives to the convention favored respecting citizens' privacy, although not in the sexual realm; the draft constitution included a long section detailing the "right of the people to be secure against unreasonable interception of telephone, telegraph and other electronic communications." It was a potentially transformative document. But it was subject to approval of the people of the state via a public referendum, and there it failed. By a two-to-one margin, New Yorkers, who were understandably unsure what all the changes would actually mean in practice, responded to the opportunity to transform the state's constitution with a resounding "no."

By the fall of 1967, New York seemed like a laggard on the abortion issue and not the leader it had promised to be two years earlier, when Assemblyman Sutton had introduced the first reform bill in the state's modern history. Legislators and advocates in Colorado, North Carolina, and California had accomplished what reform Democrats in the New York legislature and even a constitutional convention had failed to do: they changed policy by walking through the gauntlet of opposition and parliamentary debate to pass laws their governors were willing to sign. In each case, they based their bills on the model code that the American Law Institute had formulated.

New York was not only no longer seeming like a leader; it no longer seemed particularly exceptional. Proposals to liberalize abortion laws were introduced in twenty-eight state legislatures in 1967. There was wind at the back of this movement, expressed in the flurry of bills that responded to the demands of reform-minded doctors, lawyers, and pregnant (or potentially pregnant) citizens. Advocates who followed the issue closely realized that the new laws in California, Colorado, and North Carolina opened the window only slightly on legal abortion, raising to about 5 percent the portion of women seeking the procedure who were actually able to get it. But compared with the ash heap that the earliest legal-change efforts had produced, the state legislative victories in 1967 surprised and delighted the feminists who wanted to transform the nation's abortion laws.

The rising visibility of the issue provoked change in the nascent women's civil rights movement. After they mobilized around the constitutional convention in their home state, members of New York NOW decided to take the abortion issue to their colleagues in the national organization. Faust remembered helping organize a strong New York "chapter push" when the new civil rights group met in Washington, D.C., for the second time, in November, 1967. The focus of national NOW's attention was still on other matters—employment discrimination and the fight against it, the need for childcare to support parents who worked outside the homes, media representations of women, and strategies for participating actively in the coming presidential elections. But following the New York example, many arrived at the second national conference ready to put abortion on the group's agenda.

Sociologist Alice Rossi, chair of national NOW's Temporary Committee on Family, drafted a proposal around which other members rallied. She was a founding member and original board member of NOW, a New Yorker by birth who was teaching at Johns Hopkins University in Baltimore at the time of the conference. She had earned her Ph.D. in 1957 and was in her forties before she found feminism. In 1964, she had appeared with Dr. Alan Guttmacher on a New York television program advocating liberalization of the restrictive abortion laws—an occasion that had led Florynce Kennedy, in reaction, to publish her first meditation on the issue. In that same year, Rossi published the groundbreaking article "Equality Between the Sexes: An Immodest Proposal." As she remembered: "My theme was simple enough. I wrote that motherhood had become a full-time occupation for [wealthy] women, and motherhood was not enough. For the psychological and physical health of mother and child, and for the progress of society, equality between men and women was essential and inevitable." The essay garnered a fierce reaction: "I was considered by some a monster, an unnatural woman, and an unfit mother. My husband, also a sociologist, received an anonymous condolence card lamenting the death of his wife." The Association for the Study of Abortion had funded Rossi in 1965 to analyze opinion research on abortion. She found that 71 percent of Americans surveyed supported moderating the laws so that a woman could abort if her health was seriously at risk from completing a pregnancy.

In the policy paper circulated before the national NOW meeting, Rossi called for either an amendment to the U.S. Constitution or a raft of new state laws that would establish the right to access abortion. Passing a national constitutional amendment in favor of abortion rights was a very tall order indeed—even taller than the order to amend the New York Constitution had been, and that experience had not inspired much faith in the strategy. So the real way forward, as Rossi described it, was a state legislative approach that followed the semi-victories in California, North Carolina, and Colorado, and the thought-provoking failures in states like New York, with new state bills that went much further in the direction of securing abortion rights.

Rossi's committee circulated a model state law that was more ambitious than the ones crafted by the American Law Institute or the bills then circulating in state capitols. It would have repealed existing criminal penalties on abortion and given abortion seekers the ability to sue anyone who interfered with the exercise of their right. Existing laws could "be replaced with statutes which give a pregnant woman a right of *civil* action against any government official who requires or attempts to require her to have an abortion or who prevents or attempts to prevent her from having an abortion. In other words, the statute would recognize her civil right to determine her own reproductive process."

Writing in her own name, and not on behalf of the committee, Rossi made a range of arguments in favor of abortion as a basic right of women. She participated in the tendency of well-off white women in this period to bolster their claims with overwrought references to the tragedy of the unwanted child, and to abortion as a salve to the supposed global population crisis. At the same time, she situated abortion within the general mission of NOW to transform women's lives. Abortion regulation was in her view one component of a three-part system of sexual inequality, and free access to abortion an integral part of a three-tiered demand for sexual freedom:

1. The right to decide and the means to achieve it, when and with whom a woman shall engage in sexual intercourse.
2. The right to decide and the means to achieve it, whether and when sexual intercourse shall be recreative or procreative.
3. The right to decide and the means to achieve it, when a given pregnancy shall be brought to term or not.

To respect these rights, the correct approach required, at the very least, removing abortion "from the penal code entirely."

In the lead-up to the national NOW conference, Rossi and her committee members were joined by New York's Ti-Grace Atkinson in weighing in on the abortion issue. Atkinson issued a robust response to "A Statement on Abortion and Birth Control from the Catholic Viewpoint," by E.J. [Elizabeth] Farians, also a veteran of the first New York chapter meeting, for consideration at the conference. Farians argued that a proscription of abortion "rests on the basic justice of all of society." Atkinson countered by insisting that access to abortion rested on the human rights of adults, who were certainly alive, and not fetuses, which were not. "An abortion is an act that interrupts the reproductive process," she wrote. "This act cannot take human life because there is no human life as a component of the process. A particular human life does not begin until a particular reproductive process, of which the embryo or fetus is a component, is ended."

The same pre-national-conference packet that had contained the proposals from Rossi's committee also contained a report Friedan submitted as NOW's president. Friedan proposed a NOW agenda for 1968 that included "the right of women to full sexual equality with men and to the dignity and privacy of their own person." What this meant practically, she explained, was a demand to remove birth control and abortion from state criminal codes and to legalize abortion through an act of Congress—legislation at the national level that would be a capstone to the legislative work that reformers in New York and other states had begun.

The idea that abortion access could be secured through national legislation may have started with Friedan and a small number of other NOW leaders, but in the years before Roe v. Wade, it was picked up by others as well. In 1972, for example, Representative Bella Abzug sponsored the Abortion Rights Act in the U.S. House of Representatives. The Women's National Abortion Action Coalition, the reproductive rights group that gave Karen Stamm her first opportunity to work on these issues, helped Abzug draft the law and circulated petitions supporting it. Its existence is a good reminder of how distant Supreme Court intervention appeared even to people who were fully invested in the cause of liberalizing abortion access, and how willing they were to try other paths to changing the laws. It is also a reminder that legislative efforts like the national Women's Health Protection Act in the twenty-first century are not unprecedented: Legislators introduced the act to Congress in 2013, in response to threats to Roe and state-level restrictions on reproductive rights. They reintroduced the draft law to every Congress thereafter until the U.S.

House of Representatives (but not the Senate) finally approved it in September 2021.

When the members of NOW convened for a weekend in the late fall of 1967, it did not take them long to start debating abortion. On the first day of the meeting, they participated in an "all-conference discussion" of two contentious issues, the Equal Rights Amendment (ERA) and abortion. The assembled voted unanimously to include a demand for the ERA in the statement of purpose of their still-new organization. Then they discussed Rossi's abortion proposal. A heated back-and-forth ended with no decision, so the members of Rossi's committee spent the dinner hour in an intense huddle to come up with language that could satisfy a majority of members. Rossi introduced the final motion: "NOW endorses the principle that it is a basic right of every woman to control her reproductive life, and therefore, NOW supports the furthering of the sexual revolution of our century by pressing for widespread sex education, provision of birth control information and contraceptives, and urges that all laws penalizing abortion be repealed." It passed.

A revolution had begun in the debate over abortion, law, and sexual equality. The abortion reform laws in just a few states expanded access a bit, pushing at the edges of the old legal framework without trans-forming it. But the new approach approved by New York's chapter of the National Organization for Women, and then by the national NOW conference, was something else again.

Various bids for abortion law *reform* treated women as victims of circumstance. They positioned doctors granting therapeutic proce-dures to an ever-larger group of supplicants as the main subjects of a liberalized legal code. The NOW approach, on the contrary, saw women as civil and political agents and treated them as subjects of a changed law. Thanks to Dollie Lowther Robinson, among others, this approach had its first major test in the contretemps over the New York State Constitutional Convention. It didn't win there, but after what happened in New York, abortion law reform wasn't really an option within NOW. What might have seemed a delusional goal just two years earlier was now the position of a majority of members of the women's civil rights movement: not *reform* but full *repeal* of the criminal abortion codes, possibly enabled by a federal constitutional amendment or statute passed by the U.S. Congress. NOW member Alice Rossi would have gone even further: to secure abortion rights with legislation that enabled women to sue anyone who got in the way of exercising their reproductive rights. In New York, the effort to change the law was still stuck in the maw of complicated state politics. A rising movement for sexual equality wouldn't let it stay there for long.

Chapter Three

Want an Abortion?
Ask Your Minister—or Your Rabbi

REVEREND HOWARD Moody, the Baptist minister of Judson Memorial Church in New York City's Greenwich Village, sat down one day early in 1967 with an irascible journalist and two Episcopal priests to talk about abortion. It was the same season in which the women's civil rights movement started boiling over with demands for a radical new approach to sexual equality. The clergy had watched with dismay as the campaign for the liberalization of New York State's abortion law stalled. They knew only too well about the failure of the earliest bills for abortion law reform. At the time they met, reform Democratic assemblyman Al Blumenthal had introduced the second major bill to moderate the standards for legal abortion. Moody and the priests were worried—with good reason—that this proposal, too, would fail. If that happened, then the nineteenth-century law would remain on the books, and desperate people would keep showing up in their offices, begging for help.

The journalist at Reverend Moody's meeting was Lawrence Lader, who had recently published the first mass-market book arguing for a major reform in abortion laws. Lader was incensed at the cost women were paying for illegal abortion, financially and in terms of their lives. He knew that state abortion laws created sharp inequalities: "The fairly well-off women could usually get someone reasonably decent" to perform their procedures "for fifteen hundred or two thousand dollars," he remembered later. "That was a hell of a lot of money. But the poor were using the fifty-dollar local hack with terrible, terrible results." He arrived with a radical proposal: Moody and the priests could start a movement among clergy to counsel pregnant women who had what were euphemistically termed "problem pregnancies." They could help those who chose abortion find safe, reliable doctors.

The four men who met that day knew that even the act of referring someone for an abortion could be prosecuted as a crime. Despite the risk, they convinced a few of their clerical colleagues to gather with them at Washington Square Church in Greenwich Village after "the final blow" of legislative leaders refusing even to let Blumenthal's bill out of committee for discussion by the full state assembly. "It seemed to us ironical," remembered Moody and the Judson Memorial Church administrator Arlene Carmen, who did much of the day-to-day work of the referral service, "that the legislators who refused even to talk about reforming the law were all men who had never been pregnant, and the group of persons preparing to give aid and counsel to the women were clergy (mostly men) who belonged to an institution that was more responsible than most for the law staying on the books."

The Clergy Consultation Service, a faith-driven abortion underground, reprised some of the moral spirit of the nineteenth-century movement for the abolition of slavery. As with abolition and the Black civil rights movement, the voices of activist clergy and other people of faith were central to the service's legitimacy and its underlying argument. In taking on an issue so close to the fight against sexual inequality, one that inevitably pointed to failures in the normal workings of both medicine and law, the Clergy Consultation Service represented something new in the history of American reform. Working alongside other efforts—such as Jane, Chicago's smaller but in later years better-known feminist referral service and eventually provider of illegal abortions—the clergy changed the politics of abortion.

From the time of the restrictive nineteenth-century abortion statutes through New York's law change in 1970 and *Roe v. Wade* in 1973,
midwives, doctors, and skilled (or not-so-skilled) laypeople performed
abortions. Covert information networks, mostly of female relatives
or friends, made it possible for patients to find these practitioners.
But there was no public center of information on how to obtain
safe abortion care. The Clergy Consultation Service came to serve
as such a center. Unlike Jane and other projects that emerged from
the women's movement, it was national in scope. The clergy service
advertised its existence and operated aboveboard despite the legal risks.
It shepherded thousands of women to doctors who were capable of
performing safe abortions.

For years, the most visible religious presence on the issue of abortion had been that of conservative Catholic hierarchy and clergy, who
claimed it was immoral. These conservative Catholics had enormous
influence on legislators in state capitols across the country, including
in New York. Reverend Moody's Protestants and the Jews who joined
them insisted that there was another side to the argument. The moral
wrong, they claimed, lay with an outmoded law, which drove pregnant
people to desperate acts and made it impossible for clergy to provide
the solace and guidance that were their mission. The clergy understood abortion referral as pastoral service, a necessary response to
women's distress and to unsafe abortions as a risk to pregnant people's
lives. Lader and other instigators of the service also understood it as
political strategy. They hoped that an abortion-referral organization
helmed by religious leaders would force the criminalization regime to
crumble from within. Would local police really arrest scores of clergy
or hundreds of women whose abortions were the result of referrals
from spiritual leaders? If they did, how would the public react? And
if they didn't, wasn't that tantamount to acknowledging that abortion
criminalization had failed?

While clergy were in the lead in this manifestation of the referral
movement, it's important to remember that the actions of individual

abortion seekers were its provocation and heart. Much as pregnant women demanding access to abortion care had driven some doctors and lawyers to change their views in the late 1950s, they forced clergy to confront the limits of their ability to offer moral counsel while following the letter of the law. Lader approached Reverend Moody about instigating this experiment in religious civil disobedience only after scores of women wrote to him with appeals for help when they read his 1966 book on abortion. One writer couldn't come close to meeting the need by referring them, one by one, to the few decent abortion providers whose contact information he happened to have. Moreover, Lader understood that religious leaders could lend respectability to the issue of abortion, long a subject of shame, whispers, and stigma, and only slowly becoming a subject of mainstream political debate.

The clergy referral service demonstrated that sometimes the best way to change a law is to leave it alone. The centerpiece of this project was the kind of grassroots direct action for which the Black civil rights movement was best known, the kind many white Protestant and Jewish clergy had learned from supporting that movement. Reverend Moody, Arlene Carmen, and the clergy they recruited hoped to serve people who were in immediate need while at the same time applying pressure for a shift in policy by defying what they saw as immoral laws—and accepting the consequences if the laws were enforced against them.

The founders of the Clergy Consultation Service on Abortion were enmeshed in the same grassroots effort to pull the Democratic Party in a progressive direction that my parents and many of the early activists in the National Organization for Women were, too. Reverend Howard Moody, who had a particularly expansive view of his role as a spiritual leader, was the first president of the liberal Democratic club in his neighborhood, the Village Independent Democrats. At the time, Greenwich Village was contested territory between traditional Democrats and the upstarts who saw their mission as reviving the left-liberal spirit of the Roosevelt New Deal within their party—even doing the New Deal one better by making Democrats the party of Black civil rights and women's rights.

Moody and his church, Judson Memorial, represented one version of Greenwich Village. This was the historic home of twentieth-century political, cultural, and artistic revolutions. Early in the century, the Village made room for experiments in socialist politics and "free" love. It was home to the birth control theorist and anarchist Emma Goldman, and onetime socialist and Planned Parenthood founder Margaret Sanger. After World War II, it fostered subversions inspired by the Beat poetry movement of writers Allen Ginsberg, Diane di Prima, and Jack Kerouac. In "The Beatitude of the Beat Generation," Moody wrote that beyond the youthful rebellion that emerged in lower Manhattan after the Holocaust and Hiroshima was a serious critique of "carefully planned nuclear annihilation and the violence of adults who allowed two hot wars and continue a cold one," as well as an "almost obsessive craving to believe," which people of faith ought to respect. Following the Beat generation, the Village's unscrubbed low-scale buildings housed the creators of experimental off-off-Broadway theater, ardent liberals, and cultural dissidents who demanded new approaches to feminism and gay rights.

Another Greenwich Village had prevailed despite several generations of artistic and political ferment. The residents of this Village were Italian American working- and middle-class families, who tended to support the Democratic machine—and, not incidentally, to oppose turning abortion law reform into a signal Democratic issue. For years, their local political leader was Carmine DeSapio, who until the early 1960s was also the acknowledged leader of the statewide Democratic Party. In 1963, a young reformer named Ed Koch dealt a blow, if not a knockout punch, to the machine by defeating DeSapio for the role of Democratic district leader. With the Village Independent Democrats and the whole Democratic reform movement behind him, Koch won rematches against DeSapio in 1964 and 1965.

Reverend Moody and Arlene Carmen at Judson Memorial Church cut their political teeth on these battles. Carmen knew Reverend Moody from her first political experience, as a volunteer with Village Independent Democrats in the quest to defeat DeSapio. She became "heavily involved in reform politics" in New York—although was ultimately turned off by the ambition and political turnabouts of former standard-bearers for the progressive Democrats like Koch. Beyond his leadership of Village Independent Democrats, Reverend Moody opposed the war in Vietnam, joining the mass movement against it after 1965, when Democratic president Lyndon Johnson sent thousands of U.S. ground troops into the maw of the conflict. He was one of the white clergy in New York City who allied with Reverend Milton Galamison, a Black Presbyterian minister from Brooklyn who headed the long-running and long-frustrated campaign to desegregate the city's schools.

Other clergy who gave their names to the referral service were similarly political. They were mostly Moody's allies from prior battles, including the ones over race and education in the nation's leading liberal city. Reverend Finley Schaef, also a Greenwich Village pastor, was a lifelong progressive who became aware of abortion as a serious issue when a woman asked him for help locating one for her teenage daughter, a victim of incest. Schaef was the first colleague Moody talked to about organizing clergy around the abortion issue. Like Moody, Schaef was anti-war and pro–civil rights. Later in the 1960s, he made his church a sanctuary for young men evading the draft to Vietnam, let members of the Black Panther Party speak from the church's pulpit, and led his congregation in becoming the first in the United States to respond positively (with $15,000) to civil rights leader James Forman's "Black Manifesto" demanding reparations from white Christians to the movement for Black emancipation.

Rabbi Israel Margolies, of Beth Am, the People's Temple, in Washington Heights, had been a founding member of the New Jersey chapter of the Committee for a Sane Nuclear Policy in the 1950s. He marched beside Reverend Dr. Martin Luther King, Jr., against segregation in Englewood, New Jersey. Five years before they cofounded the Clergy Consultation Service, Rabbi Margolies and Reverend Moody had been among a very small group of U.S. clergy who spoke on behalf of Sherri Finkbine when she sought an abortion after using thalidomide. Margolies gave a sermon supporting Finkbine and opposing laws that kept parents from terminating pregnancies that were likely to produce profoundly disabled infants. He argued in terms that were common in the period, assuming that disabled children's lives were of little value: "The truly civilized mind," he commented, "would be hard put to devise a greater sin than to condemn a helpless infant to the twilight world of living death, or to sentence two innocent parents to caring for, yes, and loving a creature who is a grotesque mockery of God's image." Responses to the Finkbine case became an early demarcation line between mainline Protestant and non-Orthodox Jewish, versus Catholic, approaches to public policy on abortion. A pollster found that 56 percent of Protestants thought Finkbine was in the right about terminating a pregnancy when it seemed likely that her fetus had been badly damaged by thalidomide, while 33 percent of Catholics supported her choice.

For Moody and others in the clergy service, there was little daylight between politics and pastoral mission. Following the model in Reverend Dr. King's "Letter from Birmingham Jail," they prayerfully courted responses from authorities—up to and including arrests of religious leaders—that might incense the public into demanding a change in policy. The clergy were willing to risk arrest in large part because of their experiences with the Black civil rights movement. A minister named Bob Pierce, who had worked alongside Moody and Galamison to desegregate New York City schools, called illegality "a threshold for all" of the participants in the service. "We all did counseling all the time, but we hadn't been asked to step across a threshold. Well, we had in the civil rights movement, we'd had a lot of experience stepping across that kind of threshold, so this didn't seem like a big deal. Sure it was illegal and all that, but we'd done that."

There wasn't much daylight between politics and religion at Judson, either. Under the ministry of Moody and his predecessor, Robert Spike, the church developed into "a faith-based institution that responds to the societal issues of its time and place by working and advocating for progressive change—with special attention to the needs of people that many mainstream churches tended to overlook or find 'undeserving,'" like drug addicts, prostitutes, and pregnant women seeking abortions at a time of legal proscription and cultural shaming. Arlene Carmen couldn't remember one moment of controversy at the church over supporting the clergy service, even when that meant donating Moody's and Carmen's time to it, absorbing its budget into the church's budget, and, near the end of the criminal abortion era in New York, potentially housing an abortion clinic on the church's grounds. "The congregation" of Judson Memorial Church, she said, was "a very strange mixture of people," including frustrated staff members of Protestant denominational headquarters, adult children of clergy who had drifted away from organized religion because they found it irrelevant or hypocritical, and even a few otherwise secular Jews, like Carmen. They wanted "this church to do what they believe the church," writ large, "was meant to do."

Participating clergy were also moved to act by the changed and changing views of abortion by Protestants within so-called mainline denominations and Reform, Conservative, Reconstructionist, and unaffiliated Jews. By the time Moody, Lader, and the others met to create their abortion referral service, the Episcopal Church, the United Church of Christ, the United Methodist Church, and the United Presbyterian Church had liberalized their positions on abortion. These denominations built on a statement in 1961 by the National Council of Churches, which represented all the mainline denominations, decrying most abortions but describing abortion as an acceptable choice if a woman's life or health was endangered by carrying her pregnancy to term. This was a significant step forward from the New York law, which allowed abortion only when it was a matter of preserving a woman's life (although, as was the case with Karen Stamm's legal abortion, doctors sometimes interpreted "life" broadly). In May 1967, as the clergy service was organizing, the American Baptist Convention came out in support of an abortion law reform similar to the one that Assemblymen Blumenthal and Sutton and Senator Ohrenstein had advocated. Reverend Moody and other activist clergy spoke and, more importantly, acted on behalf of those Protestants, Jews, and Catholics who wanted to make sure that conservative religious leaders, such as Cardinal Spellman of New York, weren't the only religious or moral ones who were active on this issue.

Even Catholic views on abortion were in flux in the last years of the 1960s. Cardinal Spellman aside, this was true among some clergy and to a great extent among the laity. Few were deeply invested, immediately following the call to participate in the modern world that emerged from the Second Vatican Council ("Vatican II," 1962–65), in fighting hard to preserve nineteenth-century abortion laws. Even Catholic leaders who involved themselves in debates over abortion policy were not unified in opposing a change in the laws. Dr. Robert F. Drinan, S.J., for example, an influential Catholic legal intellectual, dean of the Boston College Law School, and later a U.S. congressman, vociferously opposed the kinds of laws introduced by reform Democrats in New York, based on the model code designed by the American Law Institute, but was open to a seemingly more liberal approach that would remove government from the issue.

Drinan believed that the right of a fetus to develop into a human being was inviolate and so he opposed abortion. But crucially, like many lay Catholics, what he found most repellent was the insertion of legislators and physicians into debates over which fetuses would live and die. If the options were having the state regulate abortions and removing the state entirely from sanctioning or denying abortions, Drinan preferred to keep abortions out of the legal code entirely, a radical alternative at the time. "Abortion on request—or an absence of law with respect to abortion—has at least," he argued, "the merit of not involving the law and society in the business of selecting those persons whose lives may be legally terminated. A system of permitting abortion on request has the undeniable virtue of neutralizing the law so that, while the law does not forbid abortion, it does not on the other hand sanction it—even on a presumably restricted basis." Drinan's overall stance on abortion made him an unlikely ally for the decriminalization movement, but his deep-seated belief in fetuses' right to life manifested as a rejection of any state interference in abortion, positive or negative.

Jewish views on abortion changed in the early decades after World War II as well. Across the Jewish denominational and legal spectrum, there was wide agreement that abortion was justified to save the life of a pregnant person. According to most interpretations of the key verse in the Hebrew Bible, *Exodus* 21:22, the life of a pregnant woman trumps the life, or potential life, she carries: As one expert paraphrases many of the sages' take-home lesson from this passage, "The woman is a living person, a *nefesh* [thing with a soul], and anyone who harms her body or kills her must pay in kind. The fetus is not a person in this sense. Destroying it through causing an abortion is not a capital crime and carries no capital punishment."

As early as 1958, in response to a query about abortion in the case of a mother's German measles, the Conservative Central Conference of American Rabbis issued a "responsa" (legal and scholarly opinion) that affirmed the primacy of the woman's well-being. The rabbis concluded that given the "strong preponderance of medical opinion that the child will be born imperfect physically, and even mentally, then for the mother's sake (i.e., her mental anguish now and in the future) she may sacrifice this part of herself"—much as the Jewish legal consensus held that one could cut off a limb if it housed disease and endangered one's life. In November, 1967, the Union of American Hebrew Congregations, representing the Reform Jewish movement, published a resolution on the "moral imperative to modernize abortion legislation." The resolution decried gaps in abortion access on the basis of wealth and asked state legislatures to "permit abortions under such circumstances as threatened disease or deformity of the embryo or fetus, threats to the physical and mental health of the mother, rape and incest and the social, economic and psychological factors that might warrant therapeutic termination of pregnancy."

The widely accepted Jewish legal approach to abortion, and liberalizing views of its Reform and Conservative branches, may have helped produce an overrepresentation of Jewish women, my mother included, among abortion activists. Beatrice Cogan Kornbluh did not have much of a Jewish education. In fact, my grandma Miriam was so far in flight from the heavy hand of her Old World rabbi father that she raised my mother with virtually no religious training—despite a persistent cultural sense of the family's Jewishness. But my mother's views on abortion mirrored the one in *Exodus* and those of the Conservative and Reform rabbis: The quasi-life of a fetus was less important than the life of the mother carrying it. *That's* why her daughters were never, ever, to patronize a Catholic hospital, where, she believed, doctors were bound to save the fetus first.

Many other Jewish women played important roles in this history, in part, no doubt, because its center was New York City. National Organization for Women co-founder Betty Friedan, for example, would soon sponsor the Women's Strike for Equality with Jewish feminists Gloria Steinem and U.S. representative Bella Abzug. The ranks of activists in New York included novelist Alix Kates Shulman and theorist Shulamith Firestone, whose Orthodox parents refused to speak to her, much less acknowledge her contributions to abortion law reform, since she had chosen a mostly secular life. They also included Ellen Willis, a die-hard fighter for sexual liberty. One of Willis's most personal essays concerns a years-long debate with her religiously observant brother over his decision to leave the U.S. for Israel. Karen Stamm and Carol Rosenberg Marsh, close friends

from their heavily Jewish neighborhood and the Bronx High School
of Science, were activists both for abortion decriminalization and
against sterilization abuse. Historian Atina Grossmann was raised in
Manhattan by refugees from Nazi Europe. She was active in civil rights
and the political left before joining feminist campaigns for accessible
abortion and against sterilization abuse. The late Justice Ruth Bader
Ginsburg herself tried unsuccessfully, as part of the work of her
ACLU Women's Rights Project, to get a reproductive rights opinion
based in women's constitutional equality out of the U.S. Supreme
Court. Perhaps, like my mother, these advocates and activists learned
or intuited a Jewish legal preference for the mother's life over that of
the fetus. They likely felt the immediacy of challenges to reproductive
autonomy as a result of Nazism, an object lesson in what can happen
when ideas about good and bad bodies, including reproductive bodies,
are weaponized by an intrusive and powerful state.

After Moody had recruited his colleagues to join him in the Clergy
Consultation Service, they got practical about how to set up the
project. A crack legal team briefed them on the legal risks involved.
Aryeh Neier, head of the New York Civil Liberties Union and later
a national and international leader in civil liberties and human rights
law, was involved in the project from the beginning. Ephraim London,
a volunteer attorney with the New York Civil Liberties Union, and
Cyril Means, Jr., a pro-decriminalization law professor, filled them
in on what might happen if they skirted the criminal abortion law.
     London, the main lawyer for the clergy service, looked like Abe Lin-
coln, "tall and willowy and sixty seven years old or thereabouts." He told
Carmen and the clergy how to think about what they were doing and
never to describe it as illegal. In his professional opinion, it wasn't—or
at least he could make a credible legal argument that it wasn't. Nonetheless, he advised that they should create the counseling service with the
law in mind: To avoid prosecution, members of the clergy would meet
in person with women who had "problem pregnancies," listen to them,

offer whatever guidance was requested, and let them know the options. If the women wanted to abort, then the clergy would make referrals to doctors they knew to be willing and safe. Staff member Carmen was the only one who dealt directly with the abortion providers, and she remembered, "I never counseled or made referrals." In addition, all of the doctors to whom they referred—and they were always licensed physicians—practiced outside New York State. "That was the other protection, because it meant that several states would have to agree to prosecute." The inefficiency built into the localized American system of criminal enforcement would work in their favor.

In May 1967, an article on the front page of the *New York Times* baptized this new religious movement for changing abortion laws. "Clergymen Offer Abortion Advice" was the provocative headline for a story that put the Clergy Consultation Service on Abortion officially on the map. Members of this new network lagged behind NOW's members in their understanding of what was at stake in changing the abortion laws: They did not yet speak the language of sex equality or advocate full repeal of abortion restrictions. Their founding statement described abortion seekers as "helpless victims," not adults with rights. But they established a moral framework for the issue—a framework that ultimately led Moody and other clergy to fight for repealing *all* controls on a pregnant person's ability to access abortion. They insisted that "higher laws and moral obligations transcending legal codes" compelled them to oppose the existing regime.

Out of their shared commitment to the effort, and a sense of both danger and solidarity, the clergy agreed to a "procedural covenant" that they never committed to paper. While each clergyperson would counsel women in their customary way, "the way in which a woman would be referred and to whom she would be referred would be agreed upon and cleared by the group. In this area there would be no room for individual preferences"—at pain of expulsion from the Clergy Consultation Service.

Carmen believed that one of the most important aspects of the service was the total lack of personal or profit motive in it. This was essential to her own feeling of comfort, even as she was becoming increasingly turned off by the grasping ambition of some Democrats she knew. She thought it also made all the difference with the public, and in the relative safety of participants in the project from prosecution. "There was no suggestion of personal profit, or self-aggrandizement" in the clergy service, she remembered. The fact that no money ever passed through her hands, or those of the clergy, was a hedge against charges in court or the media that the service was an "abortion ring," in the terminology of the time, or a conspiracy to profit by breaking the law. Any district attorney who tried to score points by appearing to crack down on the "vice" of illegal abortion would have found the morally serious, generally low-paid clergy, and the hardworking church administrator, pretty unpromising targets. (It was a lot easier to go after supposedly unscrupulous "abortionists," especially those without medical licenses and those who were female, immigrants, and/or not white, as had been the pattern in the periodic crackdowns on this illegal but common trade since the middle nineteenth century.)

Armed with information about the legal risks and in agreement about some fundamental rules for how they would work together, Moody, the other clergy, and Carmen established Judson Memorial Church as the headquarters for the Clergy Consultation Service. All it required was a bit of publicity (thank you, *New York Times*), word-of-mouth sharing among women, an answering machine (an innovative piece of technology then), and Carmen's ability to schedule a group of clergy to serve one week each per month. At the start of each week, Carmen recorded an outgoing message that let the caller know she had reached the Clergy Consultation Service and offered phone numbers for two Protestant ministers and one rabbi from which she could choose for a follow-up call. She insisted that it was not a difficult assignment, although an additional ingredient that made the project take off was her diligence and organizational élan.

More difficult than setting up the consulting rotation was locating doctors outside New York State who were competent and willing to skate around state laws. Carmen and Moody concluded that without the names of good physicians, "we were of no value to women." The counseling effort started with the few names participating clergy had acquired over the years, when they were advising their own congregants and others who approached them quietly. They then culled names from women who came for counseling, who had no way to know whether a recommended abortionist was skilled. "Any gas station attendant who was an abortionist, you know, moonlighting somewhere in New Jersey doing abortions, was not exactly ideal. That didn't make it any better for the woman. What we were trying to do was to improve that whole experience," Carmen remembered. And so, at the urging of the clergy service's medical advisers, she went undercover, posing as a pregnant woman in distress to find out which doctors were okay.

The great value-add of the clergy service became its role as a clear-inghouse of contacts to good doctors. Carmen, Moody, and company were not the only ones doing referrals in the last years before New York decriminalized abortion. But they were the best-organized and best-known group with the longest list of potential practitioners. Acting like a "girl reporter" of yore, Carmen took moderate risks so that the pregnant women who came to the service wouldn't have to take greater ones. "Often," she recalled, "I never got [too] far, because something about the situation was so appalling," whether that was the doctor's demeanor, the condition of their office, the price they charged (including unanticipated "extras" some practitioners sprang upon their patients only in person), or the medical procedure they proposed to use. "The procedure itself was to be only a D and C [dilation and curettage] and that was to be performed under local anesthetic or without anesthetic." As terrible as an abortion without anesthetic sounds, and no doubt was, the medical advisers to the service had insisted that they not refer to any doctor who performed abortions under general anesthetic because these too commonly ended in harm to the patient. Carmen's undercover operation ultimately had her interviewing two dozen or more doctors. "After a while," she recalled nonchalantly, "the novelty and the fear of it wore off, and then it became just routine; it was just a part of what I was doing."

The doctors who joined the clergy's list were a diverse lot. Some were outside the U.S. mainland, including in Puerto Rico. When my New York City neighbor Dr. Helen Rodríguez-Trías remembered her early medical career in Puerto Rico, she was bitter about the hypocritical enforcement of the commonwealth's criminal abortion law, which prevented most rural and poor women from getting the care they desired but made it fairly safe for wealthy women from the mainland. But from the perspective of the clergy service, this hypocrisy was a kind of godsend: "Over the years," Arlene Carmen remembered, "we always had somebody in Puerto Rico" willing to provide safe abortions for a fee. Farther afield, the clergy service helped women with the greatest resources in terms of time and money get to Japan or Sweden, which had liberalized their laws before the service began, or to England, after a major legislative reform in the spring of 1968.

Despite their professional training to "do no harm," the vast majority of licensed physicians in the United States managed to live with the fact that perhaps one million women each year sought out unlicensed and potentially dangerous practitioners for abortions. Carmen and Moody had to locate and build relationships with the tiny minority who were willing to provide abortion care at the edges of or in defiance of the law.

Although some doctors appeared to have been interested in abortion as a lucrative source of business, others on the clergy service's referral list had political commitments that matched Reverend Moody's and Arlene Carmen's. One of the most well known was the saintly seeming Dr. Henekh "Henry" Morgentaler in Montreal. Morgentaler, a childhood survivor of the Lódz ghetto and both Dachau and

Auschwitz concentration camps, lost almost all his family to the Nazis. He provided scores of abortions to women referred by the Clergy Consultation Service. A Jewish secular humanist and political leftist, he also became an advocate for legal change. "The image I had," he remembered, "was that if you had a person drowning in the lake, and you were there, able to help that person just by extending your arm, everyone would do that, right?" A 1969 reform of the Canadian law, which allowed for abortion on account of danger to a mother's life or health, as defined by a committee of doctors, did little to ease Morgentaler's legal exposure. He served eighteen months in prison for the crime of performing abortions. The lawsuit that finally ruled Canada's criminal abortion law unconstitutional—in *1988*—bears his name.

Another renowned doctor, Lawrence Lader's go-to practitioner, was "a brusque and iconoclastic Serbian-born physician in Washington, D.C.," named Milan Vuitch. "Women cry for help and doctors just chase them away," complained Vuitch, who performed thousands of abortions, spoke openly about them, and was the object of near-constant police harassment. The clergy service stopped preferring Vuitch to many other doctors only when he was arrested in 1968. Dr. Vuitch gained partial immunity from prosecution when a federal appeals court threw out his criminal conviction on the grounds that the District of Columbia's abortion statute was unconstitutionally vague and a form of discrimination against the poor. The U.S. Supreme Court overruled that decision, upholding the law, which allowed abortion in case of threats to a woman's life or health, but interpreting "health" broadly enough to cover the grounds on which Vuitch had performed this particular abortion. However, the ruling applied only to Vuitch's work in Washington, D.C., and not to work at his clinics in Maryland and Virginia. He was prosecuted successfully in Maryland and given a one-year jail term, which his attorney appealed from the Maryland Supreme Court into the federal courts, while also filing a *habeas corpus* petition that kept Vuitch at liberty. His conviction was still under appeal until a judge in a federal district court overturned it just months before *Roe v. Wade*.

For all the heroism in the clergy service, Arlene Carmen was clear about its limitations. The case of Puerto Rico, haven in a sexist world for non–Puerto Rican women with significant financial means and no haven at all for local abortion seekers, is the most glaring. But even in New York City, the clergy service helped only people who could raise what was then a remarkable sum—for a medical exam, often, in New York City, at the Margaret Sanger Bureau operated by Planned Parenthood, prior to meeting with a participating clergyperson; for the abortion itself; for travel abroad, or to Puerto Rico, or at least to a jurisdiction outside New York State; to subsidize an absence from work and care for one's other children; and perhaps for overnight lodging and travel costs for a romantic partner or other friend to accompany them.

After the first wave of work required to get the service up and running, Carmen and other leaders went to work on lowering the cost of the abortion itself. They built on the relationships she had developed with doctors after visiting them in her role as a woman seeking an abortion to start conversations about enabling more women to afford safe procedures. At first, abortions cost at least $500 to $600 ($4,208 to $5,050 in 2022 dollars), plus travel costs, in the United States, and $800 ($6,734 in 2022) if the patient flew to Great Britain. The staff of the service, who knew they provided a steady and lucrative stream of business for doctors on their list, learned to haggle effectively, although "it wasn't easy coming," Carmen said. They were increasingly able to get doctors to adhere to their standards—down to $300 by 1970 and, after New York State dramatically liberalized its law, to $125 for an abortion in New York City. Whatever the price, the clergy service didn't offer any financial aid, and people who couldn't raise the money had to make their own accommodations.

Beyond the sheer financial obstacles were cultural and informational ones. The people who showed up requesting aid were inside the information networks Carmen, Moody, and their colleagues reached with their public relations efforts or via word of mouth, when the mouths were nearly all those of white mainline Protestants and Jews from European backgrounds. Even if they knew about the service, people would come only if they were comfortable talking privately about their sexual and medical lives with white pastors, or Reform, Conservative, or Reconstructionist rabbis. Few Black clergyman participated in the service. Carmen, who made the week-by-week schedules, said there were "never" Black clergy available for clients in New York City who wanted to consult them—probably, she thought, because Black clergy had their hands full with other political battles, and because some Black Protestants saw abortion as paving the road to racial genocide. "It didn't take long to realize," she remembered, "that we were a white middle-class service."

Data the Judson staff gathered in June 1970, told the story of the success and failure of the clergy at serving people in need. Interestingly, the doctrinal origins and leanings of the service do not seem to have been major barriers. Roughly matching the population of the state of New York, 34 percent of the patients who reported any religious identification described themselves as Protestant. An equal percentage said they were Catholic. Twenty-three percent described themselves as Jewish. A lopsided number of the people who sought out the clergy service—5,326 out of 6,319—were white. Only 12 percent of the total were Black, and a negligible percentage (less than 2 percent) Puerto Rican. The networks that led people to the service help explain the racial and class tilt of the clientele: nearly a third got to the clergy service through their M.D.s or psychiatrists, and nearly another third got there with the help of friends. The initial circle of whites who knew about the service built upon itself.

When New York decriminalized abortion through the twenty-fourth week of a pregnancy in 1970, the city became a sanctuary for many people who needed abortions from elsewhere in the United States and the world. But racial and class-based obstacles persisted.

The Black feminist health activist and founder of the National Black Women's Health Project, Byllye Avery, remembered making a presentation in Gainesville, Florida, about abortion in the early 1970s and getting a reputation thereafter as someone who could help people find safe doctors. After a panicked call from a white woman, she remembered, Avery and some feminist friends "located Clergy Consultation [Service] up in New York and talked about how she could come to New York and get the abortion. They gave the woman the information. We're done." But it was different for Black women without financial means: One woman refused even to take the clergy service's phone number because "she said she didn't need no telephone number in New York. She didn't know nobody in New York. She didn't have any way to get to New York, you know. She didn't have no money for New York and all. And that woman died from a self-induced abortion."

Even with these severe limitations, the Clergy Consultation Service had to expand in order to meet the need. Within months of opening, Carmen, Moody, and the participating ministers and rabbis were inundated with requests for help. The affiliated clergy were counseling dozens of pregnant people every day, sending them to the vetted providers in the mainland United States, in Puerto Rico, and elsewhere around the world. Arlene Carmen estimated that by the time New York State reformed its abortion law in 1970, the participating ministers, priests, and rabbis were seeing ten thousand or more pregnant people per year. The New York City operation, managed from Judson Memorial's tiny administrative offices, couldn't possibly serve everyone.

It turned out that they didn't have to. As Carmen and Reverend Moody reflected a few years later: "Ignorant of the national dimensions of the problem of unwanted pregnancies, we intended to tackle the problem of an unjust law in New York State and never thought as we began that the New York CCS would be duplicated elsewhere in the country." However, their model was one that others both wanted to and could replicate, in part because it was so inexpensive to manage.

Inspired by the work of the clergy service, individual clergy contacted Moody about setting up their own operations, and women's groups around the country recruited clergy to set up local referral services. The first affiliate organization started in California, where the state's reform law from 1967 promised to ease some of the barriers to finding reliable, safe abortion providers. Reverend J. Hugh Anwyl from the Mount Hollywood Congregational Church, working with the California Committee for Therapeutic Abortion, made his way to the Village and learned the ins and outs of the service from Carmen and Moody. He opened the Los Angeles Clergy Consultation Service on Problem Pregnancies in the spring of 1968. Thanks to the greater latitude clergy and doctors enjoyed in California because of the new state law, the Los Angeles service was soon the busiest in the country.

The team at Judson Memorial Church worked actively to expand beyond New York City. Moody pressed his progressive clergy colleagues, especially those who were sending women to New York City for referrals, to build their own operations. Reverend Alan Hinand in Pennsylvania, for example, received a call from Moody saying that "starting in about two months I'm going to tell" the women from Philadelphia who were streaming to Judson Memorial Church "to call you!" Hinand recruited fellow Baptist ministers, three rabbis, and ministers from Presbyterian, United Church of Christ, and Episcopal congregations. He also located women volunteers who agreed to perform much of the work needed to establish the group. Together, they founded the Pennsylvania Clergy Consultation Service on Problem Pregnancies in November 1968.

Most of the affiliates followed the New York model closely. In Cleveland, for example, a Presbyterian minister named Robert Hare helped establish one of the earliest referral services after New York's. As at Judson, the Cleveland group had little infrastructure other than a telephone number, an answering machine, and a church administrator who coordinated clergy schedules. People who were interested in counseling, or simply wanted referrals to safe abortions, "would call the number, listen to the tape stating that the following three or four persons were available for counseling this week." As in New York, lawyers for the Cleveland clergy said they were not breaking the law but advised them nonetheless to separate counseling and referral from one another and told clergy never to contact doctors directly. When Reverend Hare "became satisfied that having the pregnancy terminated was indeed what the counselee intended to do, I would say to the counselee, 'I know there's a clinic near the Heathrow Airport in London, if you have that kind of money or want to do it in England where there are no legal inhibitions'. Or, I know of Dr. So-and-so in this place or Dr. So-and-so in that place, who are bona fide physicians." He gave the pregnant "counselee" the information that was appropriate to their circumstances and let them make their own arrangements.

The national clergy network grew quickly. Its center was always Arlene Carmen's office in Greenwich Village. By the time Carmen and Moody published the first newsletter of the National Clergy Consultation Service on Abortion, in February 1970, there were ten state-level affiliates, from Connecticut to Hawaii, plus a regional one in upstate New York. In addition, there were so many individual clergy counseling women who might want abortions that the staff at Judson couldn't keep track of them all. By November 1970, there were clergy referral operations in twenty states, with local chapters in cities like Reverend Hare's Cleveland. By July of the following year, the number of state affiliates was up to twenty-six, including Tennessee, Texas, Indiana, and Alabama, and the local groups included those in Gainesville, Jacksonville, and Tampa, Florida. In May 1972, just over half a year before the Supreme Court decided *Roe v. Wade*, there were state-level clergy referral networks in thirty of the fifty states, including former holdouts Virginia, Louisiana, and New Hampshire.

For the most part, Carmen's and Moody's lawyers were right about participating clergy being safe from prosecution. The leaders of the Clergy Consultation Service in New York believed that members of the police force and politicians looked the other way at their activities or even silently condoned them, although they were also certain that their phones were tapped. They saw their relative immunity from legal consequences as partly owing to the cultural power of the clergy, but they also believed that many of the men in charge of enforcing the criminal abortion statute had daughters, wives, friends, and lovers who themselves needed referrals to safe, reliable abortion providers. They told the story of Reverend Lyle Guttu, who said a married couple visited him after the wife's abortion. The husband said Guttu should "feel free to call him if he could ever be of help in his line of work. Asked what his line of work was, he replied that he was a captain in the New York City Police Department." In addition, Carmen thought, even without a personal connection to someone seeking an abortion, "they knew that we were sending women to very safe places, so that the women wouldn't come back here to New York and wind up in the hospitals with botched abortions." The New York County (Manhattan) district attorney, Frank Hogan, who had participated early in his career in a raid on one of Margaret Sanger's original birth control clinics, and who would have been the most natural antagonist for the Manhattan-based service, never lifted a finger against the Clergy Consultation Service.

There were exceptions to the general rule that participating clergy were safe from prosecution. Religious leaders were almost never the main targets of prosecutorial ire: those were doctors, who were accused, as abortion providers had been periodically by grandstanding local politicians since the nineteenth century, of making millions at the expense of young girls and decent matrons in distress. However, because of the pace of clergy referrals, especially to the most qualified and well known of the medically licensed abortion providers, several clergy ran into legal trouble. Rabbi Max Ticktin, for example, of the University of Chicago student Hillel, was charged along with the Detroit-area doctor to whom he had referred a policewoman posing as a pregnant abortion seeker. Rabbi Ticktin, who had served with his wife, Esther, as a fighter with the pre-Israeli-state military force, the Haganah, and had begun to lay the groundwork for a new, counterculture-inspired approach to Jewish worship known as the *chavurah* movement, never complied with the demand that he give evidence against the doctor. Although they confiscated some of his files, authorities learned little from them since they were written in Hebrew or in code to obscure sensitive information. Rabbi Ticktin endured a long legal ordeal, which ended with the *Roe* opinion from the Supreme Court.

Reverend Robert Hare in Cleveland was charged in Massachusetts as part of the prosecution of a local doctor who performed abortions. Under pressure, a patient that doctor had seen, whom Hare had counseled, fingered them both. Rather than face extradition to Massachusetts, Hare went of his own accord. "We hammed it up a little bit I guess," he remembered. "I put on liturgical garb for going to court—this was a form of liturgy—and the poor judge, and the bailiff and the prosecutor and the prosecutor's assistant just didn't know what to do with this. Here I was, standing there in a black suit and white collar in Cambridge, Massachusetts—a predominantly Catholic territory—answering an indictment on abortion. This was inconceivable." Hare, too, had to wait for the court's decision in *Roe* to know that he could no longer be prosecuted.

The legal action with the most potential to disrupt the clergy service began in the New York City borough of the Bronx in May 1969. After months of surveillance, Burton Roberts, the Bronx district attorney, ordered a raid on an abortion clinic in the Riverdale neighborhood that Lawrence Lader described as the busiest on the East Coast. When police arrived, they found a doctor from the Dominican Republic (who later revealed he lacked a license to practice medicine in New York) performing an abortion on a seventeen-year-old, and two other women recovering from their procedures. District Attorney Roberts worked both sides of abortion politics: He represented himself as a defender of morality and law, and played to the anti-authority and anti-Protestant views of some of his constituents, by underlining the fact that many of the clinics' patients were referred to it by "prominent individuals, including clergymen." At the same time, he argued that the raid—or rather, the legal situation that enabled the raid—was itself evidence of an outmoded law.

Roberts called sixty witnesses before a grand jury, ensuring days of headlines. His witnesses included Lader himself, Reverend Moody, Moody's close ally Reverend Finley Schaef, and Reverend Jesse Lyons, an original member of the clergy service and senior pastor of Riverside Church, the interdenominational uptown Manhattan landmark where Reverend Dr. Martin Luther King, Jr., had preached the anti-war sermon "Beyond Vietnam," in 1967. Lyons had withdrawn from the Clergy Consultation Service because he refused to follow its cardinal rule of referring pregnant women exclusively to clinics out of state, which he believed made it too burdensome for most to access abortion. Unlike Moody and Finley, he had referred women to the location in Riverdale, and so was potentially more vulnerable than they were.

The Bronx district attorney was eager to prosecute the clinic staff but not, it turned out, for a legal face-off with activist clergy. On the advice of Ephraim London, Moody and Schaef continued their long-standing policy: admit no guilt, continue to operate the referral service aboveboard, and explain honestly that they had never referred women to the Riverdale clinic or profited from abortion referral. They cooperated with the grand jury investigation and answered the questions put to them. Reverend Lyons took a different approach on the advice of his counsel, Cyril Means, Jr. He told Roberts's office that he would offer no testimony to the grand jury. The criminal abortion statute, he argued, was unconstitutional "on its face," for reasons Means and legal theorist Roy Lucas had outlined in recently published work. In addition, Lyons argued that the state's abortion law and the grand jury inquiry itself chilled his "right to the free exercise of my profession as a minister of the Gospel under the First Amendment in that it interferes with my counselling of women" regarding their reproductive choices. The two different strategies, Moody and Schaef's and Lyons's, produced the same result: after reams of publicity, the district attorney let the clergy alone. Even the clinic staff escaped with only misdemeanor convictions and fines.

The Clergy Consultation Service changed the politics of abortion in the United States. It was constrained by the fact that it was forced to operate in a legal gray area, reaching the people who needed its help through quiet, informal channels and relying on the tiny number of doctors who were willing to put their careers, even their liberty, at risk. While counseling thousands, first in New York and then around the United States, participating clergy still met only a fraction of the need and duplicated the class-based inequality that already existed in abortion practice. At the same time, the clergy service made indelible contributions to the fast-developing politics of abortion law reform: in their daily counseling sessions and referrals, participating clergy embodied a moral argument for abortion access to which most Americans had never before been exposed.

Participants in the Clergy Consultation Service reaffirmed the theology of Dr. King and other religious leaders of the Black civil rights movement. They saw a tension between moral law and secular law; they adhered to the former and accepted the consequences of defying the latter. The priority they placed on women's lives grounded a demand for policy change just as firmly as the belief in fetal human rights anchored policy arguments by conservative Catholics. The clergy and staff of the service worked alongside the nascent feminist mass movement to demonstrate the vast need for abortion services, and to help people understand the issue anew in spiritual terms.

The clergy service changed the abortion debate. Its great success lay in the fact that scores of people were able to have the safe abortions they desired after being counseled by members of the network. Because of the work of Arlene Carmen, and staff like her throughout the United States, the clergy service referred women only to skilled physicians. The experiences of these patients proved that doctors, operating in their offices, could provide safe, reliable abortions day after day and week after week. For over a hundred years, sensational news stories about the dangers of abortion had titillated readers and supported restrictive laws. The experiences of those who were counseled by the clergy service worked to untie the issue of abortion from the specter of injury and death—much as they worked to delink abortion from sexual scandal and shadowy immorality.

Chapter Four

Repeal Gets a Hearing

A FEW days before Thanksgiving in 1968, a hardworking lawyer took time away from her job and three children to address her newly elected state representative. "Dear Franz," my mother wrote to our Austrian-born and reform-minded assemblyman-elect, Franz Leichter. "Enclosed is an abortion repeal law."

And so she walked onto the historical stage. The law my mother outlined that day would be the first in U.S. history introduced to a legislature promising free and unencumbered access to abortion for all who wanted it. It may have been the first such law introduced to a legislative body anywhere in the modern West. As of September 2021, only four U.S. states, plus the District of Columbia, had managed to make abortion as accessible as my mother wanted it to be in New York more than a half century earlier. This draft law was of much more than local interest: once it was introduced, supporters and opponents around the country and the world followed its career. Its existence galvanized what had been a tiny and unorganized sentiment for abortion law repeal, a fringe on what was already a fairly marginal political movement, to do something about the injustices generated by restrictive abortion laws. It also galvanized anti-abortion forces. The bill that mirrored the outline my mother sent to Franz Leichter inspired similar efforts in other states. It was an early focus of the National Association for the Repeal of Abortion Laws (NARAL), created in the spring of 1969. Feminist organizing for abortion law repeal, in New York and nationally, created the momentum behind the Supreme Court's decision in *Roe v. Wade*. This organizing is on a short list of the most significant things the post–World War II feminist renaissance ever accomplished.

At the request of the abortion committee of the National Organization for Women, New York chapter, of which she was a member, my mother had combed the state legal code (in hard copy, without a good law library) to find every mention of abortion so that it could be deleted. Assemblywoman Constance Cook, the upstate New York Republican recruited to the cause of repeal by the chair of the NOW committee, had asked the feminist advocates to write the bill for her. As the only lawyer in the group, my mother made this her task. By the time she was done, the committee had recruited Leichter, a Democrat, to join Cook as a lead cosponsor of this almost unthinkably ambitious legislation.

My mother did not act alone. Coordinating this statewide effort, which embodied some of feminism's most searching claims, was a fanatic for abortion law repeal named Ruth Cusack. Before moving to Long Island, New York, in the late 1960s, Cusack had been part of a small group in California that criticized abortion law reform on the model proposed by the elite American Law Institute—not because they thought it was too liberal but because they found it too restrictive. Cusack and the activists Lena Phelan and Patricia Maginnis thought such reforms were not only inadequate but also a dangerous distraction from the real goal of full and unfettered access to this form of medical care.

Two shifts at the very end of the 1960s turned what had been a stalemate over abortion law reform in New York into success for the most liberal abortion law in the country. Both originated outside the conventional political process. First was the push for abortion law repeal by Cusack, my mother, other NOW members, and the people they persuaded to join them. Second was the growth of a new sub-movement within the movement for women's emancipation, a self-described radical feminism whose style and demands New York NOW at first awkwardly accommodated and ultimately couldn't contain. Abortion law reform of the kind that the liberal Democratic legislator Al Blumenthal championed, which would have given doctors and hospital committees greater latitude to choose who deserved abortions, did not inspire mass action. But the call to get government out of the abortion business altogether inspired thousands of people, from professionals in skirt suits and pantyhose to anti-establishment college students in bell-bottom jeans.

The two changes were interwoven with each other. Cusack remembered the effort for repeal as primarily one of "middle-class, middle-age" advocates like herself, whose style was conventional but whose priority was a groundbreaking new law. I'm sure my mother saw it similarly, and thought that a version of her bill ultimately passed thanks to patient lobbying with key legislators by middle-class marrieds and mold-breaking woman professionals. However, Cusack's and Mom's relatively quiet tactics won the day thanks to a reframing of the abortion issue by feminists with a different style. "There is no need for any legislation on abortion just as there is no need for legislation on an appendectomy," Florynce Kennedy said at a mass demonstration for abortion law repeal—over a year after Kennedy resigned in frustration from NOW. Lucinda Cisler, a leader of the statewide coalition New Yorkers for Abortion Law Repeal (NYALR), left NOW, separated from many of her former allies, and even opposed the New York bill in its final form because legislators had compromised with their squeamish colleagues in order to get it passed. "This is the measure of our present oppression," she wrote. A "chain of aluminum," in the form of legislation that compromised in any way with the principle of full repeal, "*does* feel lighter around our necks than one made of iron, but it's still a chain, and our task is still to burst entirely free."

Advocates from NOW saw legal abortion as a foundation of sexual equality. It would enable women to pursue their educations and career aspirations, to avoid or alleviate poverty, and to access medical care much as men did, without legal barriers. The new feminists added a few twists to these arguments. "All women are oppressed by the present abortion laws," Cisler wrote. She and other radical feminists thought tearing up the abortion laws was a big step toward undoing women's status as a subordinated class. Men as a group oppressed women, they thought, much as white people oppressed Black people, and the rich oppressed people who were poor or working-class. State laws that restricted access to abortion were prime examples of how the system worked. Under pressure from NOW members *and* feminists who demanded not equality with men but women's liberation from this systematic subordination, public opinion and legislative calculation both changed. Finally, repeal could gain a hearing.

Ruth Cusack, who chaired the NOW abortion committee and the statewide coalition to pass a repeal bill, is hardly a model of twenty-first-century progressive reproductive politics. She is, instead, an example of the general idea that the coalition that favored decriminalizing abortion was diverse and included some middle-class white professionals whose views were informed by both a genuine hunger for women's equal status and racial, class, and anti-disabled biases.

Before she moved to New York, Cusack lived in Northern California, where she joined the first organized campaign for abortion law repeal in the country. She originally learned that it was possible for people with information and money to find safe abortions in the early 1960s, as a graduate student at the University of California, Berkeley. This astounded her because she "was the generation where your life is ruined by the fact you have sex, you're going to have a baby, you don't have sex, you get married first. This whole thing," she remembered, "it affected my life, it affected all my friends." It enraged her that this feature of life for women was unnecessary, and yet "nobody is doing anything about it."

In the spring of 1964, Cusack heard a lecture on the Berkeley campus by Garrett Hardin. Hardin was a professor at the University of California at Santa Barbara, a trained biologist and advocate of population control who would become most famous for his essay "The Tragedy of the Commons," which claimed that unrestricted population growth "in a welfare state" led inevitably to negative social outcomes. "How," he asked, "shall we deal with the family, the religion, the race, or the class . . . that adopts overbreeding as a policy to secure its own aggrandizement?" In a book published a few years after Cusack heard him speak, Hardin claimed that unrestricted abortion access was one way to reduce human population and end what he believed, echoing arguments economist Thomas Malthus made at the close of the eighteenth century, were unsustainable demands on natural resources. Cusack did not immediately detect what later generations of readers would perceive as racist and elitist dimensions of Hardin's philosophy. She contacted him to learn more about changing the abortion laws, and he put her in touch with Northern California activist Pat Maginnis, who, like Hardin, favored repealing all the legal controls that stood in the way of women's access to abortion.

When interviewed thirty years after these events, Cusack distanced herself slightly from Hardin, a founder of NARAL whose views on population control and later publications on race and immigration caused the Southern Poverty Law Center to label his ideology "white nationalist" and his policy prescriptions "fascist." Although not overtly racist or anti-immigrant herself, Cusack argued in two different modes for abortion rights: On the one hand, she spoke movingly of the need for laws to respect women's dignity and autonomy by letting them make their own choices about what to do when they had unwanted pregnancies. On the other, she lobbied legislators on abortion law repeal by invoking stereotypes about people who were not wealthy or white. She suggested that liberty and dignity were for the kinds of white, professional-class women she knew at Berkeley, while a policy that encouraged contraception and made abortion easy to access would save other women from becoming overwhelmed by their circumstances and save society from the consequences of their mistakes.

Before she started lobbying with NOW in New York, Cusack had involved herself in legislative advocacy in California. In 1965, she wrote to Assemblyman John T. Knox, the first to sponsor an abortion law reform measure in California, arguing for full repeal. In this instance, she confined herself to arguments for legal abortion as a source of women's liberty. She warned that passing a reform measure (such as the one that would soon become law in California, thanks to a signature by Governor Ronald Reagan) might "lead to complacency" and impede efforts "to arrive at the only decent solution to the matter of abortion, which is the repeal of any laws whatsoever which prevent any woman who wants one from obtaining an abortion." In her view, reform laws with limited—if liberalized—criteria that someone other than the pregnant person had power to evaluate conflicted with "the right of a woman to own her own body, the right to decide for herself if and when she is to bear a child."

When she moved to New York, Ruth Cusack built the campaign for abortion law repeal from the liberal religious networks that also supported the Clergy Consultation Service on Abortion, and from one corner of the big tent that the National Organization for Women had become by the late 1960s. In December 1967, she built on a national Unitarian resolution in favor of abortion law reform, the first such statement from a major religious denomination, and started organizing from the narrow institutional base of the Social Responsibility Committee of the Unitarian Fellowship of the Three Villages on Long Island. She mailed every Unitarian congregation in the state asking members to contact their representatives about supporting repeal, not reform, and invited their recommendations for possible legislative sponsors of a repeal bill. "Abortion reform bills do not solve the problems created by the present laws," she insisted. "Criminal abortions will be eliminated only when any woman who wants an abortion can get it from a qualified physician."

Before she joined NOW , Cusack was a nearly one-woman band playing the tune of full legislative repeal. When she showed up to speak before a local meeting of the state Democratic Party, she met her first ally, another Long Islander named Gloria Nelson. Nelson, she remembered, "was just sort of like me—a little individual trying to get something going," via a tiny group called Legalize Abortion for Women (LAW). Cusack wrote to Al Blumenthal, the legislator most identified with the issue in New York; to him, she played a mournful song decrying the "disastrous" consequences of abortion bans, including "bitter mothers, neglected children, overworked fathers, families in name only. Almost any personal or social ill," she claimed, "can be attributed to that sorry condition that exists when an unwanted child is born." Cusack also wrote the first of many letters to Perry Duryea, a Republican assemblyman from her area, who was then minority leader of the chamber. She argued that abortion law repeal would provide "obvious benefits to society," by granting women "dignity and respect" while also preventing the births of "unwanted children." She communicated with the Democratic assembly Speaker and used his qualified okay to a floor vote on abortion law repeal as a basis for urging all of the state's legislators to favor repeal.

Capping her nearly solo effort, Cusack testified at a public hearing of the Governor's Commission to Review New York's Abortion Law. Republican Governor Nelson Rockefeller had created the commission in January, 1968, to exert pressure on the legislature to advance a reform bill after the Democrats' efforts had failed the previous year. Rockefeller directed the commission "to review the State's abortion law, and to recommend appropriate changes in time for action by the current session of the Legislature." The group had to work fast; fewer than three months elapsed from the start of deliberations to publication of its final report. However, the time frame may not have been too burdensome, since most of the commission's members had been immersed in debates over abortion for years. Rockefeller appointed Dr. Alan Guttmacher from Planned Parenthood and Mount Sinai Hospital; Cyril Means, Jr., the law professor who had advised the Clergy Consultation Service at its founding and whose contribution to the commission's findings was a legal history of abortion in New York that must have been in preparation before he joined the commission; a law professor from Fordham named Robert M. Byrn, already a seasoned anti-abortion advocate; and religious leaders Reverend Monsignor William F. McManus for the Catholic hierarchy's view and Dr. Louis Finkelstein, head of the Conservative movement's Jewish Theological Seminary. The only women in this esteemed company were identified by their husbands' names: Mrs. Marc Hughes Fisher, director of Region 1 of the National Council of Negro Women, and Mrs. Charles Hayden, "also known as Phyllis McGinley, poet and author, winner of the 1961 Pulitzer Prize in American Poetry"—whose work the Poetry Foundation later described as full of "affectionate portrayals of life in the suburbs" and "the virtues of being a housewife."

The hearing convened by the Governor's Commission in New York City was the occasion of Ruth Cusack's introduction to leaders of the National Organization for Women. Betty Friedan and Ti-Grace Atkinson, the latter who was by then chair of NOW's New York City chapter, testified in favor of repealing the abortion laws. Friedan called for removing abortion from the penal code as a matter of women's civil rights *and* claimed it was good public policy vis-à-vis "those women who are unable to have children and bring them up properly."

Cusack met briefly with Atkinson, the white writer whom Florynce Kennedy had mentored and who had been present at the very first meeting of NOW's New York local chapter. Atkinson would resign from NOW six months later, complaining that Friedan and other leaders did not seem to grasp "the inextricable relationship between caste and class" and seemed to believe the goal of feminism was for women to assume positions of power. By contrast, Atkinson thought the point was to smash existing structures of power. In testimony to the commission, Atkinson insisted that she spoke only for herself, presumably because her stance was more militant than that of other NOW officers. She favored repeal and thought that in the meantime women should break the law:

MISS ATKINSON: Women, of course, are going against the law. All women, I think, have helped someone at some time get a recommendation or reference to someone who is an abortionist. . . . But I resent very much having to give it on my knees, to have to feel I am forced to break a law, which to me is immoral and exploitive of women. . . . I am convinced repeal will come. But many women will die before that. I think this is something that states are going to have to face, whether they will eventually have to arrest women for helping other women publicly.

"Frankly," Cusack offered later to her California ally Pat Maginnis, "Betty Friedan turns me off. However, they [NOW members] are probably one of the best means of getting something done on abortion repeal in New York."

Cusack was right about the significance of having NOW as a base from which to agitate for repeal. Despite messy internal politics and conflicts with the national organization, New York NOW opened the doors of more legislators than her Unitarian social action committee had. At Atkinson's invitation, Cusack attended a meeting of the New York NOW Committee on Sex Education, Contraception, and Abortion. She left the meeting as the committee's chair. Soon afterward, Cusack noticed that the letterhead of NOW–New York listed as a vice president one member of the state legislature, Assemblywoman Constance Cook.

Writing on behalf of a small coalition that included NOW, the Clergy Consultation Service on Abortion, and the American Civil Liberties Union, Cusack asked Assemblywoman Cook to sponsor a bill that would fully repeal abortion restrictions. Cook was on the verge of winning her third election to represent Ithaca, joining just two other women serving in the legislature. "Repeal," Cusack wrote, "will give women the dignity of deciding if and when their bodies will be used for reproduction," unlike the kind of reform that liberal Democrats had been supporting since 1965. And simply by Cook's introducing a bill, Cusack predicted, people who had supported reform would switch their position, "since that is what many of them wanted anyway." By mid-August 1968, Cusack had her reply: the assemblywoman from Ithaca would sponsor the bill. When they spoke on the phone, Cook "said it wouldn't pass" but might pave the way for a reform bill to pass as a kind of compromise position. Regardless, Cusack pretended that Cook was as much of a true believer as she was and "told everybody to write to her" and thank her for supporting this historic bill.

As it turned out, the repeal movement could not have asked for a better point person in Albany than this particular NOW vice president. Constance Cook, a woman attorney who had earned both undergraduate and law degrees from Cornell over a decade before my mother graduated from Brooklyn Law School, was a pattern-breaker who did not make much of a fuss about her accomplishments. She was well respected in the state capitol, having worked there for years before her election as Ithaca's representative to the assembly. Cook was also in the governor's favor because they were both what she called "old-fashioned liberal Republicans," and so it was easy for her to vote with him without compromising her own principles. Despite reservations about its future, Cook committed herself to the abortion law repeal bill and asked New York's NOW chapter to draft it for her. In response, Cusack asked for help from NOW at the national level. Receiving none, Cusack tried drafting it on her own. When my mother joined her committee, Cusack asked Mom to finish the work.

Cook and the liberal Republicans alone could not mount a credible push for abortion law repeal. They needed some Democrats on their team. However, in response to the letter from Cusack, the Democrat who was most closely associated with the issue, Assemblyman Blumenthal, argued that "the only feasible approach" was a moderate reform. He insisted that "a majority is not now obtainable for" repeal. Senator Manfred Ohrenstein told Cusack that he would support abortion law repeal if an advocacy group wrote to him and formally requested his aid. He did not volunteer to sponsor repeal legislation. A member of Cusack's committee of New York NOW, Irene Duvall, then wrote to all the neighborhood-level Democratic political clubs in Manhattan seeking legislative sponsors. At the same time, my father, David, a low-level Democratic officeholder, approached Franz Leichter, who had just won a primary for the state assembly district in their shared neighborhood—a neighborhood in which winning a Democratic primary was as good as being elected, since it was home to fewer Republican voters than bodegas that sold Caribbean-style café con leche, or bakeries that offered hamantaschen, the pastry associated with the Jewish holiday Purim, year-round.

Leichter credits my mother with persuading him to become the lead Democratic sponsor of this historic legislation. "I met with your mother, Bea," he told me a few months after speaking at her memorial service, "and she made a very compelling case that the approach shouldn't be the one proposed by Al Blumenthal of really sort of an incremental approach . . . but that abortion should become the choice of a woman and become a regular medical procedure. And I just thought it made a lot of sense."

Although I don't think my mother knew this, Leichter may have been an unusually easy sell for this particular request. He was a Jewish refugee from wartime Vienna, where his mother, Dr. Kathë Leichter, a sociologist trained by Max Weber, had been a leading socialist feminist. When the Nazis took Austria, Franz, his brother, and his father escaped to the United States. The regime arrested Kathë as a political enemy, and a Jew, and interned her at the women's concentration camp at Ravensbrück. She continued to organize the women until the Nazis murdered her at a "T4" center, created for the assassination of people considered disabled or unfit. The Austrian government has remembered her with an annual prize for an Austrian woman historian of exceptional achievement.

In addition to believing that the choice of abortion "should be left to the woman," Franz Leichter had a sense that repeal might be politically easier to achieve than the kind of reform for which some of his colleagues had been fighting. Rather than getting "embroiled in all of the arguments that came up in opposition to the approach around Blumenthal of requiring certification by two doctors, what is medical necessity, is it mental, is it economic problems, and so on," he thought "that we would be just better off in a sense completely eliminating the punitive approach, the penal approach to abortion." Without quibbles over the criteria under which abortion would be allowed, it might be easier for a majority of legislators to reach agreement. Following the line of thought proposed by the Catholic legal scholar Father Robert Drinan, it might even be possible for some Catholic voters to accept a complete withdrawal of government from the decision to end a pregnancy. Reform proposals that picked and chose among the many grounds for abortion offered a kind of state sanction to abortion. They also offended many people by including "fetal anomalies" among the permissible grounds, suggesting to some that policy makers believed some embryos or fetuses—potential lives—were more worthy than others.

After Leichter announced his willingness to sponsor the bill, NOW members got very interested in him. He started to retreat from the idea of decriminalizing abortion for the whole nine months of a pregnancy. This was proof of the out-of-the-box, unfamiliar nature of what these feminists wanted; even a very liberal incoming member of the state legislature, who was probably eager to make his name by sponsoring a bold bill, seems to have gotten a little queasy at the idea

of eliminating restrictions on reproductive decision-making completely. In the months that followed, Leichter's qualms were mirrored
by other legislators in this roughly one-third Catholic state, even as
the legislators came under zealous pressure to strike the nineteenth-
century criminal abortion law from the state code.

Ruth Cusack wrote in October to acknowledge Leichter's promised
assistance and pledge help with his general election campaign—not
realizing that his Republican opponent had little to no chance of
winning. (She was still new to New York City politics.) A letter from
my mother followed: In response to the legislator's idea of stopping
unrestricted abortion access at twenty-four weeks, which my mother
had heard about from Cusack, she argued that to include any time limit
was to concede "the Catholic viewpoint that abortion of any fetus
is murder. We believe," she added, "that there are certain Catholics
we will never persuade, but that there are many to whom repeal of
criminal penalties will appeal where 'reform' will not." In addition, by
once again anointing doctors the judges and juries of who deserved
an abortion, a law with a time limit would echo the therapeutic abortion regime. As in the case of hospital abortion committees under
then-current law, she wrote, "because hospitals do not wish to appear
to be abortion 'mills,' hospital boards will not permit more than a
self-imposed quota number of abortions which are not illegal even
under current law."

My mother and Ruth Cusack overcame Assemblyman Leichter's
concerns. It's always treacherous to wonder about what didn't happen in history, but Cusack at least thought that the whole repeal
effort "would never have gone" without Leichter's co-sponsorship—
without, that is, the combined leadership of a well-respected Republican woman and reform-minded male Democrat.

When Assemblywoman Cook came to New York City early in
December, 1968, she saw my mother's draft bill and she met Leichter
for the first time. Cook "reiterated her desire for complete repeal—no
time limits." She and Leichter met with a group from NOW (although

not with my mother, who was no doubt at work). They decided to announce the bill at a press conference before Christmas and to steam forward even though they were its only sponsors in the assembly and not a single state senator had yet joined them. Cook pre-filed the bill before the start of the legislative session, before Leichter had even been seated as a legislator.

On a parallel track with this effort was an advocacy effort to support the nascent bill. From her perch as chair of the NOW abortion committee, Cusack led the drive to create a coalition that would move it forward. One of her first contacts was Arlene Carmen, coordinator of the Clergy Consultation Service. Carmen, Reverend Moody, and the other members of the clergy service became dependable allies for the legislators working for repeal.

New York legislators started to consider the bill for abortion law repeal in 1969. It probably wouldn't have been credible a decade, or even a year, earlier. U.S. politics were as radical in 1969 as they ever have been. It was four years after ground troops arrived officially in Vietnam to prop up an unpopular anti-communist government. In despair over what seemed like a never-ending war, the protest group Students for a Democratic Society dissolved into the terrorist Weather Underground and tried to foment revolution. The Black Panther Party for Self-Defense, a militant response to stalled progress on civil rights, reached its high point in 1969—before surveillance, arrests, and the police killing of Chicago leader Fred Hampton pushed it back on the ropes. It was the year of the Stonewall Riots, days' worth of battles in the streets of New York City between police and gay, lesbian, and transgender people who were tired of third-class treatment.

There was a similar spirit in feminism. The National Organization for Women was no longer the only game in town. Self-described radical feminists had organized their first small discussion groups in New York City in 1967. Two years later, the thinkers and activists Shulamith Firestone and Ellen Willis cofounded a group called

Redstockings. By calling themselves Redstockings, Firestone and Willis identified with the women intellectuals known as Bluestockings in the late nineteenth and early twentieth centuries, as well as with red as a color of revolution.

In *The Dialectic of Sex*, a groundbreaking treatise and declaration of independence from male-dominated political traditions, written in 1969, Firestone described her kind of feminism as a "struggle to break free from the oppressive power structures" promoted by biology and reinforced by social structures. In their Redstockings manifesto, Firestone and Willis set themselves apart from male-dominated protest politics and NOW, with its emphasis on equality between the sexes and civil rights gains without fundamental social change. "*All men* receive economic, sexual, and psychological benefits from male supremacy," they wrote. "*All men* have oppressed women." Although they generally responded tepidly to proposals for new legislation, since they believed that legislation couldn't transform society, Redstockings and some of the other radical feminist cells in New York City committed themselves to abortion law repeal.

Thanks to Redstockings and their comrades, as well as to Ruth Cusack's committee, the energy for abortion law repeal started to gather in New York and nationally. The members of Cusack's committee spun their efforts off from NOW, which was bogged down in internal fights; the New York chapter was the focal point within NOW for fights over ideology and strategy, which tore the group apart and led Ti-Grace Atkinson and Florynce Kennedy to resign. After Assemblywoman Cook filed the repeal bill, Cusack herself stepped down as committee chair and founded a local pro-repeal group in her part of Long Island. Two of Cusack's former committee members, Arlene Emery and Emily Moore, became leaders of a new entity called New Yorkers for Abortion Law Repeal. They were joined in this new group by Ruth Proskauer Smith, recently executive director of the Association for the Study of Abortion—an organization so out of step with the rising spirit of the times that its leader, physician

Robert Hall, refused NOW members observer status at its 1968 abortion conference because they were not "truly expert in abortion in a professional rather than a personal sense." The group included, too, the stalwart for abortion law liberalization, Manhattan borough president Percy Sutton, and the energetic younger feminists Lucinda Cisler and James Clapp.

In the most literal possible manifestation of "inside" and "outside" strategies to push for change, both Redstockings and New Yorkers for Abortion Law Repeal organized protests on February 13, 1969. That was the day on which state legislators arrived in New York City for hearings on the abortion law reform proposals championed by Assemblyman Blumenthal. The witness list was by invitation only. Redstockings chose to disrupt the proceedings from inside the room where they were happening. New Yorkers for Abortion Law Repeal demonstrated for repeal, not reform, on the sidewalk outside and planned to keep picketing until the hearings were over. Despite their different styles, the two groups shared demands: No more debate! And rapid passage of the Cook-Leichter bill—in other words, full repeal, with no restrictions and no middlemen or gatekeepers decid-ing who would receive abortion care and who would not. As a radical feminist flyer, unsigned but written by Ellen Willis, put it, in terms on which both feminist camps could agree: "LET THE EXPERTS TESTIFY. SUPPORT CONSTANCE COOK'S BILL—REPEAL *ALL* ABORTION LAWS."

Willis, whose day job was as a rock and roll critic for the *New Yorker* magazine, not only wrote the flyer for it but also participated in the Redstockings protest. She also wrote a piece the *New Yorker* published anonymously in its "Talk of the Town" section on activist efforts to support what she called the Cook bill. This "repeal bill," she wrote, "has received little public attention. Newspapers that mention it at all tend to treat it as a quixotic oddity. Most people do not know that the Cook bill exists, and some legislators, when asked for their support, have professed not to have heard of it." She added: "Whatever their ideological differences, feminists have united on the abortion issue," and on the Cook-Leichter approach to it. "They oppose Blumenthal's reforms—or any reforms—and demand total repeal. Abortion legislation, they assert, is class legislation, imposed on women by a male-supremacist society, and deprives women of control over their bodies. They argue that women should not have to petition doctors (mostly male) to grant them as a privilege what is really a fundamental right, and that only the pregnant woman herself can know whether she is physically and emotionally prepared to bear a child."

The story Willis filed included both protests. She noticed the New Yorkers for Abortion Law Repeal picketing outside the building, near city hall at Worth Street. "About thirty women, including City Councilman [sic] Carol Greitzer, came to the hearings to demonstrate against reform and for repeal, against more hearings and for immediate action." Then she chronicled the more unprecedented action inside the hearing room, evidence of how the forces behind changing the law had been emboldened since Percy Sutton introduced the original reform bill in 1965.

The "expert" witnesses invited to speak at the hearing included fourteen men and only one woman, a nun. First up was the chairman of Governor Rockefeller's Commission to Review New York State's Abortion Law, a retired judge. He explained that a majority of the commission's members supported a reform measure like Blumenthal's. "Suddenly," Willis reported, "a young, neatly dressed woman seated near the front stood up. 'O.K., folks,' she said. 'Now it's time to hear from the real experts. I don't mean the public opinion you're so uninterested in. I mean concrete evidence from the people who really know—women. I can tell you the psychological and sociological effect the law has had on me—it's made me angry! It's made me think about things like forcing doctors to operate at gunpoint.'" When the chair tried to restore order to the proceedings, other women started shouting: "Where are the women on your panel?" one said. "I had an abortion when I was seventeen. You don't know what that's like," said another. "Men don't get pregnant. Men don't rear children. They just make the laws." One state senator upbraided the demonstrators: "What have you accomplished? There are people here who want to do something for you!" Willis quoted the response: "We're tired of being done for! We want to do, for a change!"

Political journalist Gloria Steinem also covered the hearings. Her piece, briefer than the one by Willis, claimed that police attempting to restore order "resorted to the rather feminine tactic of hair-pulling" to get the protesters out of the room. Florynce Kennedy, "at whose name strong white men shake," Steinem added, offered a suggestion for resolving the abortion law logjam: "Listen," Kennedy reportedly said, "why don't we shoot a New York state legislator for every woman who dies from an abortion?"

The hearings, and the relatively polite protest outside them, may have been news under any circumstances. But activism inside the hearing room made for headlines. Redstockings, Florynce Kennedy, and the radicals who rallied with them earned the kind of publicity that made their perspectives hard to ignore. Even the backlash against their action must have made women who were reading the papers think anew—as when the chairman of the hearings called their insistence on a right to speak "disgraceful conduct," and a Democratic state senator "quipped, 'I would bet that all those ladies (the demonstrators) are mentally disturbed and shouldn't be allowed to have a baby.'"

In the same season as Redstockings' inaugural action, the cause of abortion law repeal became a national one with the creation of a cross-country network that built on the foundations created in New York and also helped the New Yorkers move their bill forward. The first steps toward creating the National Association for the Repeal of Abortion Laws had been made by Lawrence Lader, the journalist who had helped instigate the Clergy Consultation Service, and a few others, who met in Lader's apartment starting in August 1968. They helped plan a national

conference at Chicago's Drake Hotel on February 14–16, 1969, the
main work of which was to launch NARAL.

The conference gathered veterans of the abortion wars in New York
and other states so that they could forward the cause of repeal. Its
individual sponsors included Friedan; Shirley Chisholm, the first Black
woman in Congress, representing Brooklyn, and a New York NOW
vice president; Alice Rossi, the sociologist and author of the abortion
paper discussed at the second NOW convention; Howard Moody and
Finley Schaef, the ministers leading the Clergy Consultation Service;
Rabbi Israel Margolies from Washington Heights; CCS legal advisers
Aryeh Neier of the ACLU and Cyril Means, Jr.; Percy Sutton; Ruth
Proskauer Smith; and Estelle Griswold, the Connecticut Planned Parenthood leader who helped change the nation's birth control laws and
give rise to the modern idea of sexual privacy in *Griswold v. Connecticut.*

A variety of political perspectives was represented at the conference.
They ranged from Garrett Hardin's belief in abortion as a means of
reducing population and pressure on ecological resources, to Moody's
and Margolies's faith that free abortion access was a solution to moral
wrongs, to the feminism of Ruth Cusack, also shaped by biased ideas
about good and bad parents. Participants heard from a pre-conference
planning committee of Lader, Hardin, and activist physician Lonny
Myers from Chicago. Helping to lead workshops were Cusack, Reverend Moody, and lawyer Means.

One highlight of the conference was Betty Friedan's keynote
address. From the perspective of later decades, her framing might seem
obvious, even trite. But it was in fact an invention of the movement
whose embers Friedan had helped breathe into flame since *The Feminine
Mystique* appeared in 1963. She channeled progressive currents within
NOW, and borrowed arguments from the radical move for women's
liberation that NOW could no longer contain. Friedan described
a "very basic part" of the drive for women's equality, dignity, and
freedom as "control over our own bodies, over our own reproductive
process"—for its own sake, not as a means to the end of economic

or political parity with men. Only with their voices and perspectives at the center of discussion, she wrote, would "women move out of their enforced passivity, their enforced denigration, their definition as sex objects, as things, to human personhood, to self-determination, to human dignity." In summarizing her position, Friedan echoed Willis and other Redstockings members at the hearing protests in lower Manhattan: "I am no expert on abortion," she said, "but I am the only kind of expert that there needs to be now."

Before the delegates went home, they elected a twelve-person planning committee for the new entity that would stitch together local repeal efforts, the National Association for the Repeal of Abortion Laws. Half the committee's members were New Yorkers with close ties to the repeal campaign: Lader (chairman), Ruth Proskauer Smith (vice chair), Ruth Cusack (secretary), Betty Friedan, Percy Sutton, and the only doctor in New York who would admit that he provided illegal abortions, Bernard Nathanson.

After the national conference, the repeal effort in New York continued to be intertwined with the rise of NARAL. The introduction of Cook and Leichter's bill to the state assembly in time for the legislative session in 1969 was, according to Lader, a critical boost to the national group-in-formation. "If we were going to create a national movement," he wrote, "we needed a political symbol around which our forces could gather. We had to make a break with the past" of abortion law reform on the old American Law Institute model. New York's draft law (as outlined initially by my mother) became that symbol. New York was, according to Lader, a "pivotal state" for testing the viability of repeal as a political and policy demand.

Radical feminists who probably didn't know about the Chicago conference, and had little regard for Betty Friedan, kept working for abortion law repeal in their own way. Five weeks after they disrupted the state legislative hearings in New York City, Redstockings and other radical feminists staged an abortion hearing of sorts, titled like an off-off-Broadway theater performance. "Abortion: Tell It like It Is" appeared in the sanctuary of Washington Square Methodist Church, home of CCS minister Finley Schaef.

Alix Kates Shulman was in the audience that night. Shulman, who would soon write *Memoirs of an Ex-Prom Queen*, the first bestselling novel from the movement, had joined a small radical feminist group in 1967. She participated in an iconic 1968 demonstration against the Miss America Pageant, at which cosmetics and other symbols of conventional femininity were tossed into a "Freedom Trash Can." She then stepped away from radical feminism for a few months. In 1969, other alumnae of the Miss America protest invited her to join a new group called, tongue in feminist cheek, Women's International Terrorist Conspiracy from Hell (WITCH). As she walked across a street in the East Village, she ran into a friend "who had also been part of the planning group of Miss America. And she said, 'What are you doing here?' And I said, 'I'm going to my WITCH meeting there.' And she said, 'Oh don't go there, come here,' which was right across the street. She said come to our meeting. It's Redstockings.'"

The event in the church basement was what the radical feminists called a "speak-out," and it was the first speak-out ever organized. At the moment Shulman joined, Redstockings was engaged in extensive "consciousness-raising about sex." The speak-out was a more public version of consciousness-raising, a practice particular to radical feminism that embodied the movement's idea that (as Carol Hanisch put it), "The Personal Is Political." By sharing what was considered strictly private, even shameful, with other women and learning that many had had similar experiences, one learned that many of the worst obstacles one faced were not the results of one's own faults or bad luck but were structural in nature, products not of a single woman's life trajectory but of a system that systematically advantaged men and disadvantaged women.

Although by then she had had three illegal abortions before her two children, Shulman did not testify at the speak-out. But she wasn't going to miss it, no matter what. On the night of what came to be known as the world's first public testimonials of women's abortion experiences, Shulman, the radical feminist, said to her husband, "I'm going across the park to this abortion speak-out." He didn't want her to go, but she left the house anyway, "an act of defiance. You can't even imagine that one would have to be defiant to one's husband in order to do anything. I'm sure you can't imagine it. But that's the way it was then."

Activist and writer Susan Brownmiller, who had been part of New York's very first radical feminist group, reported on the event in the unimprovably named breakout feminist essay "Everywoman's Abortions: 'The Oppressor Is Man.'" "For three hours," and for the first time in history, she wrote, women "testified from their own experiences with unwanted pregnancy and illegal abortion." Rosalyn Baxandall was the first of a dozen who told their stories: "I thought I was sophisticated," she joked. "My boyfriend told me if he came a second time, the sperm would wash away, and I believed him." A woman named Judy Gabree tied the risks of restrictive abortion laws with the threat of sterilization. "I went to eleven hospitals searching for a therapeutic abortion," she told the rapt crowd. "At the tenth, they offered me a deal. They'd do it if I agreed to get sterilized. I was twenty years old." In a story recovered fifty years later by Nona Willis Aronowitz from a recording of the event, a woman said of the hoops through which one had to jump to be granted a legal abortion on the grounds of mental health: "You couldn't just casually threaten suicide—you had to sound like you meant it. You have to go and bring a razor, or whatever: 'If you don't tell me I'm going to have an abortion right now, I'm going to go out and jump off the Verrazzano Bridge.'"

Gloria Steinem covered the event for *New York Magazine*. She was already something of an "it" girl, or woman, of the downtown Manhattan scene. But Steinem had a secret. She'd had an abortion in Europe when she was a college student studying abroad—legal but still shameful, or so she thought. The world's first speak-out was also the moment of her feminist awakening: "It was the first time in my life," Steinem told an interviewer decades later, in a cascade of excited clauses, that she "ever heard women in public stand up and tell the truth about their lives, parts of their lives that were unacceptable, and just telling the stories, the individual true stories of what it had been like to go out and try to enter a criminal underworld, to endanger yourself, to seek an illegal abortion, all the particular circumstances of each woman. I was just so transformed by that, that what happened only to women could be taken seriously even though it only happened to women; that there were other women who were telling the truth about this." An article on women's liberation that she published shortly after the event argued "that if these new, small radical groups of women could come together in some way" with groups like NOW, "there could be a crucial movement."

In the annals of feminism, the Redstockings speak-out has become legendary. It was the precedent for the "Manifesto of the 343" French women, including Simone de Beauvoir, who declared that they had had abortions despite their illegality. The New York speak-out and French protest also inspired the publication of a two-page-long list of Americans, including Steinem, who declared the same in the preview issue of the feminist magazine *Ms.* Steinem founded the magazine with her public speaking partner, the Black feminist and community organizer Dorothy Pitman Hughes, and others, in response to gendered and racial biases in media representations of the women's movement(s). Declaring without sensationalism that they had had abortions was precisely what they wanted to do in *Ms.* and wouldn't have been able to do in any other large-readership publication.

The impact of the Redstockings abortion speak-out has been felt far beyond the movement innovations of the late 1960s and early 1970s. It inspired feminist attorneys, who have repeatedly submitted briefs to the federal courts that build on individual women's abortion experiences to ground arguments about the deprivations of rights and undue burdens states have created with blocks to abortion access. It

modeled the confessional yet impatiently confrontational mode of
politics that defined the anti-rape movement from the 1970s onward,
and still shapes annual "Take Back the Night" rallies on campuses and
in cities across the United States. And it paved the way for repeated
Twitter waves in the twenty-first century that have come under the
hashtag #ShoutYourAbortion.

What's been nearly forgotten about this remarkable political
moment is its legislative context. Radical feminists in 1969 weren't
just speaking their truth for the sake of speaking their truth. They
were trying to pass a law. Their efforts, combined with those of liberals in state government and tactically moderate feminists like Betty
Friedan and Beatrice Kornbluh, helped put an amended version of
the Cook-Leichter bill over the top within a year.

Chapter Five

Into the Courts!

I S ACCESS to abortion a civil right, a woman's right, a constitutional right?

These questions were left unanswered after feminists redefined the goal of policy change, from reforming state abortion laws to simply repealing every part of the legal code that mentioned abortion. For NOW leaders like Betty Friedan and New Yorkers Ruth Cusack and my mother, answering those questions was easy enough. Accessing abortion was an essential right because, without a degree of control over her reproduction, a woman could not pursue higher education or training, employment, property ownership, or even political participation equally with men. If she was always pregnant, or raising more children than she felt she could manage, a woman could not gain any of those things—even if government and private businesses removed the overtly discriminatory bars that had kept them out of reach for decades. An unwelcome pregnancy was a kind of trump card against women's advancement.

For feminists outside NOW, the answer was the same, but the reasoning was a little different. They continued to argue, as the Redstockings members had done when they disrupted the legislative hearings, that women were the "true experts" on their bodies. They shared a sense with more moderate feminists that restrictive abortion laws caused what legal scholar Reva B. Siegel has called "dignitary harm."

Was there anything more undignified than making women beg for abortions on narrow legal or medical grounds—or treating their lives as valuable only because they might bear children? But radical feminists who gave the movement new life as the 1960s were closing, such as Ellen Willis and Shulamith Firestone, departed from Friedan and NOW when they argued that the legal situation surrounding abortion proved their theory that women were unified by experiences they had in common, that they were a "sex-class" with shared interests and a shared enemy. At the same time, they came to understand that the abortion laws demonstrated that within the sex-class were subclasses. In other words, they learned over time that women in the United States had diverse experiences of privilege and subordination, based most of all on their wealth and racial background.

New York feminists from both NOW and the radical wing of the movement pressed to undo the legal regime around abortion in order to make the American promises of equality and freedom more real to women. They moved in two directions at once. The first was legislative: They kept working to pass a version of the Cook-Leichter bill, as originally outlined by my mother. At the same time, they worked to change the law by bringing cases in the federal courts. This trend started in the federal District Court for the Southern District of New York, a.k.a. New York City. Then it went national and crested with the Texas case *Roe v. Wade*.

Leading the charge with the New York case *Abramowicz v. Lefkowitz* was Nancy Stearns, an attorney whose inspiration was the alliance between law and activism in the southern civil rights movement. She was joined by a legal team that included Florynce Kennedy, who had quit NOW, which she found "boring and scared," just before the organization's New York chapter had persuaded Cook and Leichter to introduce their abortion law repeal bill. But Kennedy didn't give up on feminism or on the cause of undoing restrictive laws. Less than a year after resigning from NOW, she and the attorneys Carol Lefcourt, Diane Schulder, and Ann Garfinkle worked with Stearns to bring the spirit of mass action from civil rights, Black Power, and the abortion speak-out into the federal courts.

In *Abramowicz v. Lefkowitz*, which would likely have made it to the Supreme Court before *Roe v. Wade* if the strategy to rewrite New York's abortion legislation had failed, the five-woman legal team represented over two hundred women. These included writers Grace Paley, Alix Kates Shulman, and Elinor Langer, radical feminist leader Robin Morgan, leftist militant Jane Alpert (soon to go underground after participating in bombing government buildings), and feminist historian of medicine Judith Walzer Leavitt. This large group served as a stand-in for women as a class of persons whose lives were constrained by laws that made abortion illegal, inaccessible, gratuitously expensive, and unsafe. The plaintiffs and their lawyers took the bold step of claiming that New York's highly restrictive law had to fall because it violated the U.S. Constitution. At a time when even Ruth Bader Ginsburg, as an advocate for legal equality, had not yet asked the federal courts to apply the Constitution's promise of "equal protection of the laws" to distinctions between women and men, the *Abramowicz* team demanded exactly that—an understanding of constitutional equality on the basis of sex that would invalidate New York's abortion law because of the specific burdens it imposed on women.

This nearly forgotten case forms a vital chapter in the history of reproductive rights and justice, even though it did not wind up changing abortion law. This is because it was the first federal case that treated women, not doctors, clergy, or other professionals, as the citizens whose rights counted in evaluating public policy in this critical area. The people who had the capacity to get pregnant, and who would either be able to secure abortions or would not be able to, charged the government of the State of New York with a kind of malfeasance for violating their constitutional rights.

The trajectory of this case, a would-be landmark in the legal and constitutional saga of women's rights, had everything to do with the trajectory of the legislative campaign for abortion law repeal. And both had everything to do with challenges to old patterns of sex-based subordination that came from the grassroots. The effort to change legislation, and change-oriented litigation, were different but complementary strategies for rewriting the law. By late 1969, when the *Abramowicz* case came together, the forces promoting abortion law repeal, from Betty Friedan to Ellen Willis, had succeeded to a degree that would have been nearly unthinkable three or four years earlier. They had drafted a bill and gotten legislators to sponsor it, and built both a statewide and a national network (NARAL). They had brought NOW and its defectors together on this one demand, and they had led public demonstrations that changed public opinion and pressured influential professionals to join the movement.

The lawyers and plaintiffs who brought the *Abramowicz* case may have thought to do so only because the diverse group demanding legislative repeal put the injustice of abortion restrictions on their radar. But they also pursued the new court-based strategy because the legislative campaign seemed stuck. Months after New York assembly members Constance Cook and Franz Leichter introduced the nation's first repeal bill, that historic legislation was, to all appearances, in a logjam from which the feminist grassroots alone seemed unable to rescue it.

Linda Greenhouse, a young staff writer for the *New York Times* who faced her own battles against sexism in the newsroom, wrote a prescient article on the *Abramowicz* case and three others filed with it. Greenhouse thought these cases had the potential to overturn state abortion laws across the country within a year. "A legal and constitutional 'right to abortion,'" she commented, "at first hearing, sounds fantastic, illusory." Greenhouse continued, "The very phrase rings of the rhetoric of a Women's Liberation meeting." To attorneys whose friends and allies had put women's liberation on the national agenda and helped transform the abortion decriminalization movement into one for full repeal, this idea didn't seem "fantastic." It seemed worth fighting for, and possibly within their grasp. This was especially because the justices of the California Supreme Court, in September 1969, invalidated the conviction of a doctor who performed abortions. The California court found the state's abortion law (the old statute from before the legislature reformed it in 1967) too vague and indirectly related to the purposes legislators claimed it served. Before the end of the year, there was also a "wholly unexpected" first-time win for abortion access in the federal courts: Judge Gerhard Gesell of the U.S. District Court for the District of Columbia invalidated a more liberal but still restrictive law that applied only to the district. Judge Gesell vacated the conviction of Milan Vuitch, the doctor who was a stalwart on the referral list of the Clergy Consultation Service.

The case brought by Stearns, Kennedy, Schulder, Garfinkle, and Lefcourt built on the ideas of both NOW and the radical feminists of the late 1960s. The heart of the case was a class action by over two hundred women who were or might get pregnant, representing themselves and "all others similarly situated"—a legal move that jibed with the idea that women were, as radical feminist theory had it, a sex-class that was oppressed in common by men.

Abramowicz v. Lefkowitz went by the name of its first named plaintiff, Helen Abramowicz, M.D. However, the lawyers only included Dr. Abramowicz and other professionals among their plaintiffs because— believe it or not—the idea of an abortion case in the name of women who sought or might one day seek abortions was so extraordinary. Stearns's project from the start was to move away from an emphasis on doctors' rights to perform abortions and emphasize instead the rights of "ordinary" women as citizens with their own relationships to the Constitution. The legal team worried that this approach simply would not fly in the federal courts, and so they added plaintiffs whose rights they thought judges could more easily understand, including clergy members who were referring people to safe abortions and nonprofit advocacy groups working to change the laws. Dr. Abramowicz just happened to be near the start of the alphabet, the head of a long list whose largest subgroup was of women whose interest in the case was simply that they were "female citizens of the United States and of the State of New York." Ti-Grace Atkinson, former head of New York NOW , headed the ranks of these "female citizens" who volunteered as plaintiffs in *Abramowicz v. Lefkowitz*. A woman named Maryann Zilboorg was last in a literal *A–Z* collection of women who were married or unmarried, parenting or childless, who'd had abortions in New York or elsewhere in the United States or abroad, or who hadn't had abortions when they wanted and felt they needed them—because they could not afford them, or because they had the means but state law still made it impossible for them to end a pregnancy when that was what they thought made the most sense in their lives.

The lead defendant, a stand-in for the whole legal apparatus that enforced the criminal abortion law, was Louis Lefkowitz, attorney general of New York State. He was joined by Frank Hogan, the district attorney for New York City, the same one who had allowed the Clergy Consultation Service to do its work unmolested. The last defendant was Burton Roberts, district attorney from the Bronx, who *had* prosecuted members of the clergy service for their referral work.

For the attorneys, the roots of *Abramowicz v. Lefkowitz* grew in the same soil that nurtured all the social change campaigns of the 1960s and 1970s. This was especially true for Florynce Kennedy and Nancy Stearns. Raised in "a very tacky little frame house" in a segregated pocket of an integrated neighborhood in Kansas City, Missouri, Kennedy remembered learning "about white people" as a child when the Klan threatened her father, a Pullman porter, waiter, and business owner. "When Daddy came out, they told him, 'You have to get out of here by tomorrow.'" He responded by getting a gun and threatening to shoot any Klan member who walked onto the front step of his house. "They went away and they never came back." She graduated Columbia Law School in 1951, already disillusioned with conventional legal ways of thinking ("They want an almost mathematical mind, the kind of person who can walk past a pool of blood and think, 'what a beautiful shade of red.'") Her worst suspicions were confirmed when she attempted to make the system work for her clients, including the performers Billie Holiday and Charlie Parker—or at least to preserve some of the resources in their estates for their heirs after each died, young, of drug-related causes.

Florynce Kennedy got involved in Black Power at the same time that she joined NOW. This was also roughly the same time when she started thinking deeply about the role of media in all the things she didn't like about the United States. With a group of other Black feminists, white labor leaders, and left-wing white women, Kennedy created an organization called the Media Workshop to fight "Jim Crow advertising and the segregated media." She became a different kind of lawyer from the one Columbia had trained her to be: From the summer of 1967 to the spring of 1968, she served as co-counsel, with the flamboyantly radical attorney William Kunstler, for Black Power leader H. Rap Brown, who had been charged with inciting a riot in Cambridge, Maryland. Kennedy and Kunstler fought for Brown's freedom in the media as much as in court. Kennedy got northern whites who identified with "the movement," including NOW feminists, to contribute to his defense fund. She then became a legal adviser to Valerie Solanas, the woman who wrote a militant feminist protest piece (performance piece?) called *SCUM Manifesto*. Solanas was tried for an alleged attempt to kill the artist Andy Warhol. Although she insisted on representing herself in court, Kennedy advised her and defended her in the court of public opinion. Kennedy and Ti-Grace Atkinson held a press conference at which they described Solanas as a feminist with ideas that deserved to be heard.

At the time of the *Abramowicz* case, Nancy Stearns had had a shorter career than Kennedy, but it was one of total political engagement. After college and a stint in graduate school, she moved to Atlanta to work for the Student Nonviolent Coordinating Committee, the uncompromising, youth-run organization fighting Jim Crow segregation and subordination in the South. Stearns was still there in the spring of 1964, when white supremacists in cahoots with the local sheriff's office murdered the young civil rights organizers James Chaney, Andrew Goodman, and Michael Schwerner. She stayed with the movement through that summer, when a flock of other young white Northerners came south to fight for voting rights and against racial violence in the project known as Freedom Summer.

After nearly a year of participating as she could in the movement, Stearns decided she "needed a skill" to contribute more meaningfully to the kind of social change she wanted to see in the world. She met Arthur Kinoy, an attorney whose progressive résumé included serving as counsel to the United Electrical, Radio, and Machine Workers of America, the same union for which Betty Friedan had been a staff member, and defending Julius and Ethel Rosenberg when they were accused of being spies for the Soviet Union. Kinoy had come south from New York as a volunteer lawyer for the southern civil rights movement. He urged Stearns to get a law degree.

Stearns took Kinoy's advice. She also stayed in communication with him, and spent a summer working at his firm, the number one left-of-center, activist, private law firm in the country, Kunstler, Kunstler, and Kinoy. The other partners were William Kunstler and his brother Michael. By the time Stearns received her law degree, Kinoy, William Kunstler, and two other attorneys had founded the Center for Constitutional Rights, a nonprofit designed to assist the civil rights movement and other movements of the day. Stearns's first job after law school was with Kinoy, fighting subpoenas that had been issued by the communist-hunting House Un-American Activities Committee of the U.S. Congress. When she finished that work, she joined the staff of the Center for Constitutional Rights.

In 1969 Stearns, unlike Kennedy, did not identify with the feminist movement. She remembered having been briefly part of "a women's group that was just talking," which made her "miserable." She started conceptualizing the *Abramowicz* case after meeting members of the Women's Health Collective, a breakaway faction of the left-of-center health-care analysis group Health/PAC, and an early manifestation of what would soon be a robust women's health movement. She remembered: "What I did with the people from the Women's Health Collective was, before we started the litigation we went around the city to the different boroughs and different parts of Manhattan and we had meetings where we would have women come, and one of us would talk about the medical aspects of abortion, another one would talk about abortion as a political issue and women's relationship to the medical system in general, and to the way doctors treat women as patients. And I would talk about the legal aspect. And then we would see if the women wanted to talk about their own experiences with the healthcare system, and if they wanted to talk about abortions they'd had, or had tried to get, or anything. And then we would see if they wanted to be part of a lawsuit challenging the law. And when we first started doing this it wasn't necessarily that we even thought the law would be struck down, even though we thought it should be struck down." Stearns had lots of ideas about why restrictive abortion laws were unconstitutional, but there were no precedents for feminist, social-change-oriented legal work of this kind, and so it took her a while to imagine the *Abramowicz* case into being.

After talking to progressive women around New York City about abortion, Stearns realized that she might be able to change women's status by using the kind of lawyering she learned from Kinoy, and had started to practice at the Center for Constitutional Rights. She was less interested than Florynce Kennedy and William Kunstler were in their work for H. Rap Brown, Valerie Solanas, and the Chicago Seven, in using legal proceedings as a kind of theater in which oppressive social structures could be placed on display, and could reach a mass public through the media. Her focus was on creating a court case that could help build the social movement for women's liberation, much as Kinoy and other activist attorneys had gone to court in support of the civil rights movement in the South.

Legally and strategically, the key change that Stearns made as she began the *Abramowicz* case was from a defensive posture to what lawyers working on behalf of the civil rights movement had come to call an "affirmative" one. This was a brand-new approach for the women's movement of the 1960s, and closely related to the switch from having abortion providers or other professionals be the subjects of litigation to having people who wanted abortions, or might one day want them, be the subjects. "When laws had been struck down up until then in other states," Stearns explained, "they had uniformly been where a doctor or an abortion counselor had been prosecuted and it was a defense to a criminal prosecution. So we were the beginning of the affirmative challenge, and that was part of the approach that Kinoy and Kunstler . . . had used in the South also, affirmatively challenging laws that had been used to try to shut down the civil rights movement." Affirmative litigation gave its architects power to choose the plaintiffs in whose name it would be brought, and to some degree gave them the power to shape a case so that it would raise the questions they saw as most significant. In *Abramowicz*, Stearns and the other attorneys argued implicitly that the rights of "female citizens" were at the crux of legal questions about abortion, simply by recruiting a large group of those citizens to participate in the case. When Stearns took the idea of bringing affirmative litigation to the movement against restrictive state abortion laws to her colleagues at the Center for Constitutional Rights, they gave her the go-ahead.

Abramowicz v. Lefkowitz was an ambitious piece of legal stagecraft. Before filing it with the federal district court, and after traveling around New York City with members of the Women's Health Collective, Stearns recruited help from Lefcourt, Garfinkle, and Schulder, all young feminist attorneys. Schulder introduced her to Kennedy.

When the five lawyers started working together, they made the case even more ambitious than Stearns had originally imagined it to be. As a hedge against the possibility that a federal court would simply throw out their innovative approach, in which "ordinary" women were the main plaintiffs, they added four other concatenations of plaintiffs. First was a group of New Yorkers whose stake in the matter was their "deep concern for the health and welfare of women who suffer unwanted pregnancies and are not able physically, psychologically or financially to raise the child." This group included Reverend Finley Schaef of the Clergy Consultation Service. Second was New Yorkers for Abortion Law Repeal, the statewide network that had grown from the NOW Committee on Sex Education, Contraception, and Abortion. Third were doctors, starting with Helen Abramowicz, M.D., who were allegedly "chilled and deterred" from practicing ethically because the statute left them unsure about whether it was legal to refer patients to abortion providers, or to terminate pregnancies themselves. Last was the Medical Committee for Human Rights, a progressive doctors' organization that supported the southern civil rights movement at the time of Freedom Summer and then expanded its mission to become what member Fitzhugh Mullan called "the New Left in medicine."

The first stop for the feminist legal team was the courtroom of Judge Edward Weinfeld of the federal District Court for the Southern District of New York. They had to convince Weinfeld that the challenge they were making to New York's law raised significant questions about whether the state was violating the U.S. Constitution. If he decided it did, then the case would go to a panel of three federal judges. And when those judges ruled, the losing side could appeal for a final judgment directly to the U.S. Supreme Court.

Stearns and her co-counsels argued for abortion rights in stark terms. They emphasized the ways existing laws were implemented differently depending on a woman's race and class. The "statement of facts" they submitted in a memorandum of law for the court began with the claim that the New York laws regulating abortion access "yearly send Black and Puerto Rican women to their deaths, force countless thousands of other women from all walks of life to endure the ignominy, degradation, danger, and pain of an illegal abortion," and burden everyone who cares about these women. The laws represented "invidious discrimination, and direct invasion of privacy."

The legal team in *Abramowicz* had to address "standing," that is, whether, in this novel piece of legal craftwork, women as women were legitimate parties to the suit. In this, the lawyers echoed all the feminists who fought for abortion law repeal by insisting that women were the "true experts" on the issue. "There is no person," the attorneys argued, "with a greater personal stake in the question of the constitutionality of the New York Abortion Laws than any fertile woman of childbearing age." This was so, they continued, because of the many ways an unwanted pregnancy, or an unsafe or illegal abortion, might shape her life. She also had standing because of her vulnerability to legal enforcement: "Every woman," the attorneys claimed, is "in the position of a criminal for the very fact of attempting to control her own body."

Stearns, Kennedy, Schulder, Lefcourt, and Garfinkle made a series of claims about women and the Constitution. They argued that a woman who had to carry a pregnancy to term because the law placed a safe abortion out of her reach suffered "cruel and unusual punishment." They also asserted that the state kept women from exercising rights guaranteed by the First Amendment, like the right to *hear* important and medically accurate information (the flip side, according to a handwritten note on Kennedy's copy of the document, of freedom of speech). They insisted that New York's abortion laws violated women's rights to "personal privacy," free association, and "life and liberty guaranteed by the Fourteenth Amendment."

The feminist attorneys got their wish. Judge Weinfeld decided that the case did indeed raise important constitutional questions. New York State would have to answer for its laws before a three-judge federal panel. The *Abramowicz* case got simpler at this point, although the overall effort to undo New York's abortion laws did not. The district court combined the *Abramowicz* case with three others, all designed to overturn the New York law. Probably all the attorneys involved hoped that, within a few months, they would be arguing for abortion rights before the U.S. Supreme Court. As Stearns explained, of the four cases that were ultimately argued together, "one was basically abortion counselors [clergy]. One was basically doctors. One was basically low-income women . . . and then ours." Although the *Abramowicz* case itself had started out with several different batches of plaintiffs, combining it with the other cases gave the legal team what Stearns called "the luxury" of "focusing on the legal issues and the strategy and the tactics with respect to women."

Of the other cases, the most significant was the doctors' case. This case, *Hall v. Lefkowitz*, had more elite clients than did the *Abramowicz* case—more renowned and established doctors, and no plaintiffs who were not titled professionals. The arguments it relied on were more conservative than the ones Stearns, Kennedy, Schulder, Lefcourt, and Garfinkle were forwarding in that they didn't start from a recognition of racial and class difference or women's subordination. But *Hall v. Lefkowitz* was the first federal case in U.S. history to argue that the same sexual privacy rights that the U.S. Supreme Court recognized in *Griswold v. Connecticut* applied to abortion. The lead attorney was Roy Lucas, a theorist and strategist recently graduated, like Stearns, from NYU Law School. Lucas's paper on sexual liberty, privacy, and abortion, written originally for a law school class and then hurriedly published in the *North Carolina Law Review*, had passed from hand to hand among abortion repeal activists and lawyers. Lucas's team, including ACLU attorneys Norman Dorsen and Harriet Pilpel, filed *Hall v. Lefkowitz* slightly before the feminist team filed their case. Their case was a serious piece of activist lawyering, designed to change the law and not just to keep people from getting cut on its sharpest edges.

In addition to the multiple cases that were now moving as one, the other factor that made the litigation more complicated was that abortion opponents made formal requests to join the case. (Their presence and arguments are worth remembering the next time someone suggests that abortion was uncontroversial before the Supreme Court decided

Roe v. Wade.) The first group of potential joiners, known in legal terms as "interveners," were doctors. They claimed a special interest in the public policy of abortion and in the "welfare of the child in utero." They also claimed that there was a risk to their ability to practice, or advance in, their profession because they opposed abortion. Success by the repeal side in the case "would," the doctors' advocate wrote, "place a heavy burden on their belief that the unborn child is entitled to protection against all adversaries—including even its mother."

A second anti-abortion sally was made by an attorney who wanted the court to appoint him the "next friend," or stand-in for the interests of, the fetus of one of the plaintiffs in the low-income parents' case that had been combined with *Abramowicz*. George Eaton and his attorneys argued on the basis of fetal constitutional rights, over a decade before the anti-abortion movement made this a centerpiece of their strategy. They claimed that "the unborn infant [was] a person entitled to the same rights, privileges and protections afforded by the Constitutions and laws of the United States and State of New York as are afforded to persons already born." In support of this position, a biologist argued that the fetus's "existence, although parasitic" on its mother, was nonetheless separate from hers. It was, he claimed, a being with rights, with enough agency while gestating to support "its own life and growth on nourishment acquired from the mother."

The district court rejected the application to intervene by the man who wanted to serve as guardian of the fetus. However, Weinfeld and his brethren accepted the application of the doctors, who made fetal rights arguments along with other arguments. The feminist attorneys came to call them and their attorney the "friends of the fetus," a term Schulder and Kennedy attributed to Ti-Grace Atkinson.

The team went into high gear to prepare for a trial date in February 1970. The three federal court judges who were to hear the case "really didn't want to hear testimony," Stearns believed, "because they didn't want to hear a bunch of women, I think. Because you've got to think back to what the judiciary looked like in those days. It was all white men. They didn't want to hear these awkward things about sex, and pregnancy, and abortion, and et cetera, et cetera. So they said what we should do is take depositions and then do everything on paper." This disappointed Kennedy, Stearns, Lefcourt, Schulder, and Garfinkle, who wanted a trial in which they could do the kind of public education Kennedy had done during the trials of H. Rap Brown and Valerie Solanas, the kind William Kunstler did in the trial of the Chicago Seven, the activists who had been charged with rioting during the 1968 Democratic National Convention. Yet they warmed to the idea of submitting written depositions instead of having a trial when they remembered that civil rights activists in the South had, on at least one occasion, used the public taking of depositions as a movement strategy. They decided that they could use the tactic to their advantage.

The legal team then had to decide who would actually offer depositions for the court's consideration. Dozens were willing to tell their stories, to serve as the "real experts" on abortion. Florynce Kennedy and Diane Schulder had primary responsibility for taking depositions. So, as they put it, "people who wanted to testify would come to Flo Kennedy's place" for pre-deposition interviews in one of the two rooms of her apartment/office.

Stearns, Kennedy, Schulder, Lefcourt, and Garfinkle decided to keep the number of depositions small, for fear of losing the judges' attention and of spending more money on the case than they had. They selected a group that was entirely middle-class and white, since they believed they were obliged to protect people whose lives could not withstand any economic or other reprisals they might suffer for their role in the case. This led the lawyers to leave out Black women such as Florence Rice, a friend of Kennedy's and leader of the Harlem Consumer Education Council. Rice had had two illegal abortions, one of which led to an infection and hospitalization. Although Rice told her story at Kennedy's apartment and was willing to tell it publicly,

Kennedy and Schulder did not want to be responsible for her losing the job at which she made her living, as a cleaner for wealthy white people.

Once they chose the people who would share their stories, the attorneys convened a kind of deposition speak-out. They planned to take depositions on the ground floor of Washington Square Methodist Church, which was Reverend Schaef's church and the very church in which Redstockings had held the world's first speak-out. (They would have used the basement space at the church, the very room in which the speak-out had occurred, but a play by the Black radical playwright LeRoi Jones (Amiri Baraka) was being staged in that space at the time.) Their idea was similar to the idea behind feminist "consciousness-raising": rather than treating abortion as a private matter, shrouded in shame and secrecy, they wanted to go public, in order to reveal that everything about women's abortion experiences was political. "And it was a very large room," Stearns remembered, "and we had lots and lots of women there just to listen, to be part of the crowd."

The lawyers representing the attorney general and the other officials of New York State, as well as the "friends of the fetus," objected to the chosen location and the fact that this official piece of legal business was to occur on the home turf of grassroots feminism. They won a sympathetic audience from the judges, who ordered a move to a more sober venue before any depositions were taken. However, neither the judges nor the lawyers on the other side were able to make the feminist lawyers play by traditional rules.

Kennedy and Schulder saw the lawsuit "as a very definite platform for exploring the extent of the legalized oppression of women." It was as important, they thought, to get public attention for the proceedings as to make cogent legal arguments. The judges found space for the depositions to occur in the federal courthouse itself. And so, on three days in January 1970, women giving depositions, observers, and the media crammed into a small room on the thirteenth floor of the federal courthouse in lower Manhattan—creating another kind of legal speak-out, this time in the veritable belly of what feminist legal thinkers were starting to conceptualize as a patriarchal legal beast. From Nancy Stearns's perspective, it was a lucky accident, "in a way, because it meant we were someplace where the press could easily come . . . so we had press covering all of our depositions." In addition, a smaller room made the audience seem larger, "so it turned out perfect for us."

The testimony included two sets of accounts by people who wanted abortions but were not able to get them legally. In the first group were women who carried pregnancies to term when they did not want to. The second group had abortions despite the fact that they were almost entirely illegal under New York law—by locating a safe abortionist through underground referrals, by risking everything with a shady practitioner, or by flying to Puerto Rico, where abortion was illegal but available to wealthy white women from the mainland, or to England or Japan, where the laws were more forgiving than in almost all U.S. jurisdictions. The testimony revealed the concrete harms suffered by women as a result of abortion restrictions. It also served to educate the federal courts about some of the ways in which law, as they saw it, discriminated unjustly against women.

A plaintiff whose name Schulder and Kennedy changed to Lucy Wilcox, in an effort to shield her identity, testified about bearing a child against her will. She gave her infant up for adoption via a home for unwed mothers on the fashionable Upper East Side of Manhattan. "For months after I left the home," she testified, "I'd wake up in the night crying and sort of rocking my pillow," with a sense of guilt about having birthed a child and then given it to adoptive parents she never met. When she testified about a later abortion that occurred outside New York State, an attorney for the "friends of the fetus" objected that her testimony was irrelevant. She responded: "To me it is most relevant." Kennedy then spoke to the media and the movement more than to the attorneys and judges in the room: "The relevance of the testimony regarding the ordeal of women, which somehow seems to escape the attorneys for the defendants and intervenors, is that a woman undergoes ordeals that people concerned about the fetus seem inclined to ignore." In response to the claim of a lawyer for New York that the testimony had nothing to do with the constitutionality of the state's laws, Kennedy continued: "If you're right, of course, we will not prevail. That does not for a moment stop us from building our case and stating our position and finding out how completely irrelevant these courts think women's experiences, ordeals, feelings, are, and we will be very much better informed about the nature and the proceedings of our government and our courts"—that is, we will learn how badly the game is rigged against women—"once this matter is ruled on."

When they finished the depositions, the legal team made its final arguments to the court. In their brief to the three-judge panel, written by Stearns, they argued that the federal courts had not yet "come to grips with the fact that approximately half of our citizenry is systematically being denied" the pledge in the Fourteenth Amendment that no person would be deprived by her government of "life, liberty, or property, without due process of law." Stearns went so far as to claim that New York's abortion laws had to fall because they violated the right to life—a more "compelling interest" for the state, she wrote, when it referred to pregnant people seeking abortions than when applied to their fetuses.

The feminist lawyers in the *Abramowicz* case made history by arguing that sex discrimination conflicted with the U.S. Constitution. Before the 1970s, there was little jurisprudence on constitutional sex discrimination, and none that treated unequal legal treatment on the basis of sex as a violation of the Fourteenth Amendment's promise of "equal protection of the laws." The idea generally was that women and men were different and so it was acceptable to treat them differently from each other. The U.S. Supreme Court did not rule until 1971, in a case for which a law professor and volunteer lawyer for the ACLU named Ruth Bader Ginsburg wrote the brief, that the "equal protection" clause forbade certain kinds of sex discrimination. Two years later, in the case *Frontiero v. Richardson*, Ginsburg, with the mass feminist movement behind her, persuaded the Supreme Court to go further. In a case about whether a husband who was economically dependent on his wife could claim the same benefits as a wife dependent on her husband, the court ruled that such flagrantly unequal treatment was unconstitutional and established a standard of "close judicial scrutiny" for laws that treated women and men differently. Although the standard was somewhat vague, by creating it the Supreme Court nonetheless acknowledged that women's claims for equality had succeeded at making sexist legal distinctions seem more problematic and less like common sense than they had ever seemed before.

In Nancy Stearns's original application to Judge Weinfeld, which predated Ginsburg's arguments in the Supreme Court, she had not argued that the laws violated equal protection on the basis of sex. Stearns argued that New York's abortion laws violated equal protection on the basis of race and income, since the state allowed legal abortions "almost exclusively to wealthy white women." But in her brief to the three-judge federal panel, Stearns made a claim for sex-based constitutional equality. This was bold: the last big sex-equality case the U.S. Supreme Court had considered was *Hoyt v. Florida* in 1961, in which a unanimous court had ruled that a system in which women only entered the pool from which people were chosen for jury service if they specifically requested to be included, while men were entered automatically, was constitutionally permissible. "Despite the enlightened emancipation of women from the restrictions and protections of bygone years," Justice John Marshall Harlan II argued, "woman is still regarded as the center of home and family," and so she should have the power to recuse herself from civic duties—even though this recusal produced lopsidedly male juries, and the criminal defendant who brought the case insisted that she had been denied a jury of her peers.

"At first glance," Stearns wrote, "it would appear that the concept of equal protection of the laws might not even apply since the laws relate only to women." But, she argued, equal protection was an essential lens through which to understand abortion law because of the ways in which women who were pregnant or raising young children faced "punishments, disabilities and limitations" not faced by men who fathered children. "If such a broad range of disabilities are permitted to attach to the status of pregnancy and motherhood," she concluded, "that status must be one of choice."

The *Abramowicz* litigation didn't wind up invalidating the nation's restrictive abortion laws, as reporter Linda Greenhouse thought it might, or becoming the vehicle in which the Supreme Court ruled on abortion rights. Thanks to the legislation first outlined by my mother, New York changed its abortion law before the federal judges had a chance to rule on the constitutional claims in the multipart case. But Stearns thinks that the litigation, born out of frustration with the clogged workings of representative government, "kind of helped the legislature along," that "maybe some of the legislators thought, well, we want to do it before the courts do," so that they had more control over the specifics of the final change.

Although the case did not go to the U.S. Supreme Court, the work of Stearns, Kennedy, Schulder, Lefcourt, and Garfinkle had a greater impact nationally than in New York. Consistent with Florynce Kennedy's emphasis on media and courtroom drama as tools for changing minds, she and Diane Schulder followed their participation in the case with a book called *Abortion Rap* that argued for a transformation in abortion law and policy, and more generally in women's status. The book offered an edited collection of documents from the case, including transcripts of the depositions collected in that small meeting room at the federal courthouse. Among its other legacies, *Abortion Rap* led to a discussion in a Boston taxi between Florynce Kennedy and her friend and sister on the public speaking circuit, Gloria Steinem. Their female cab driver chimed in with a feminist quip that became a movement standard: "Honey, if men could get pregnant, abortion would be a sacrament."

Nancy Stearns followed her participation in the case with a full-out legal push for abortion decriminalization and women's rights. She shared her groundbreaking brief and worked on strategy with activist lawyers and hundreds of woman-citizen plaintiffs in New Jersey, Connecticut, Rhode Island, Massachusetts, and Pennsylvania. These other cases followed the New York example with a few modifications. In several of them, the point about abortion being "every-woman's" problem was made by even bigger groups of plaintiffs: nearly six hundred in New Jersey, the post-*Abramowicz* case on which Stearns worked most closely, and around one thousand in both Connecticut and Pennsylvania. Stearns shared her original complaint in *Abramowicz* with Sarah Weddington, the Texas lawyer who argued *Roe v. Wade*, and Margie Pitts Hames, who argued the companion case from Georgia, *Doe v. Bolton*. Although neither of those lawyers used the women-as-class approach, they had the benefit of Stearns's thinking about the relationship between liberty and equality, constitutional rights and women's subordination. And they had the example of the groundbreaking work she and Kennedy, Schulder, Lefcourt, and Garfinkle did in New York.

The Connecticut litigation was particularly important. The case, *Abele v. Markle*, accomplished what Stearns and the others had aimed to do in *Abramowicz*: it struck down the state abortion statute on the strength of feminist argument and the willingness of those hundreds of women to add their names to the complaint. Stearns attributed this success to the lucky facts that the judges allowed a trial instead of asking that the feminists make their case only on paper, and that Stearns was working with the "truly extraordinary" Catherine Roraback, one of the attorneys in *Griswold v. Connecticut*. Stearns remembered Roraback, who had graduated Yale Law School when Ruth Bader was only fifteen, teaching her that their main job as feminist reproductive rights advocates was "to teach these male judges what abortion meant. And they had to start thinking about it in terms of their wives and their daughters and the women they socialized with at cocktail parties and all of this because they just didn't have a clue."

The attorneys who brought the Connecticut case had to bring it twice. The opinion Stearns and Roraback won in the first go-round was a slam-dunk victory for abortion law repeal. For the first time, a federal court seemed to them to have appreciated the meaning of unwanted pregnancy for women, and treated women as true agents in the world of constitutional law. "The decision to carry and bear a child has extraordinary ramifications for a woman," Judge Edmund Lombard wrote. "Pregnancy entails profound physical changes. Childbirth presents some danger to life and health. Bearing and raising a child demands difficult psychological and social adjustments. The working or student mother frequently must curtail or end her employment or educational opportunities. The mother with an unwanted child may find that it overtaxes her and her family's financial or emotional resources. The unmarried mother will suffer the stigma of having an illegitimate child. Thus, determining whether or not to bear a child is of fundamental importance to a woman." Justice Harry Blackmun echoed this paragraph in his *Roe v. Wade* opinion as the reason that constitutionally protected privacy was "broad enough to encompass a woman's decision whether or not to terminate her pregnancy."

After this feminist victory, the state legislature revised the abortion statute in an effort to skirt the court's decision. This led to an opinion by a different judge of the same court. Judge Jon Newman found that the state abortion law was still unconstitutional. But he also found that it was okay to limit women's constitutional rights at the point at which a fetus might theoretically be able to survive outside its mother's body. This approach hearkened back to the old common-law idea that abortion was acceptable before quickening, the time when a fetus would kick in the womb and was understood by early American religious and medical authorities to possess a life independent of its mother's, and problematic thereafter. It contradicted those "friends of the fetus" in the *Abramowicz* case who understood a gestating being that was in fact dependent on its parent's body as "parasitic" and yet independent enough to deserve constitutional recognition. This opinion became one example precedent from the lower federal courts on which Justice Blackmun and his brethren built in *Roe*, when they created a system in which women's constitutionally protected access to abortion was different in the first two trimesters of a pregnancy than it was in the final trimester.

Stearns built on the case she brought with Kennedy, Schulder, Lefcourt, and Garfinkle to make a feminist argument for abortion rights directly to the U.S. Supreme Court. Writing for a group called New Women Lawyers and two short-lived feminist groups that favored repeal, Stearns submitted a friend-of-the-court brief in *Roe v. Wade*. She repeated some of her best points and pithiest lines from her writing in the *Abramowicz* case to argue against restrictive abortion law as a lodestone of male supremacy. At a time when judges "didn't have a clue" about the arguments that animated the women's movement, Stearns urged the Supreme Court justices "not to shrink from redressing the constitutional wrongs perpetrated on women." As she had before, Stearns argued that abortion implicated the right to life—for adult women. Stearns again argued that state abortion statutes deprived women of equal protection of the laws; she asked the court to look at the manifold "forms of discrimination" created by the workings of the law.

Stearns ended her brief to the court by leaning into the idea that a forced pregnancy violated the Constitution because it imposed on women cruel and unusual punishment. She wrote of an undesired pregnancy as a twenty-five-pound pack a woman was forced to carry on her back for nine months, after which it would be tied to her wrist for the rest of her life. "Abortion laws," she summarized, "reinforce the legally legitimized indignities that women have already suffered under for too long and bear witness to the inferior position to which women are relegated. The total destruction of a woman's status in society results from compelling her to take sole responsibility for having the illegal abortion or bear the unwanted child, and suffer the physical hardship and mental anguish whichever she chooses. Only the woman is punished by society for an act in which she has participated equally." She demanded that men as a class stop treating the class of women cruelly. Much as constitutional law demanded that whites give up some of their brutally enforced privileges, she wrote, men, with their overwhelming majorities in all of society's political and legal decision-making bodies, "must now learn that they may not constitutionally impose the cruel penalties of unwanted pregnancy and motherhood on women."

The *Abramowicz* case was the first that gave form to the constitutional arguments for women's and abortion rights that emerged from the movement of the late 1960s. Stearns, Kennedy, Lefcourt, Schulder, and Garfinkle expressed the feminist demand for repeal of abortion restrictions in language federal judges could understand. They invented a vocabulary in which to describe the harms women experienced in a legal system that was not made by or for them—especially although not exclusively in the way it regulated their reproductive lives. They developed new modes of practice as activist feminist attorneys and advanced a critique of U.S. law that was the foundation for generations of thinking, writing, and teaching in women's, gender, and sexuality studies and in law school curricula.

The attorneys who later brought *Roe v. Wade* to the Supreme Court to defend the rights of "Jane Roe," a woman who sought an abortion and was unable to have one because of her state's restrictive statute, followed in the footsteps of Nancy Stearns and the whole *Abramowicz* team. In addition, as historian and journalist Cynthia Greenlee has argued, this case brought storytelling about women's lives into the courts—extending the impact of the 1969 abortion speak-out in lower Manhattan by bringing its spirit into an elite legal arena. They set the standard that activist litigators followed well into the twenty-first century, for example, in the friend-of-the-court brief that over one hundred women lawyers filed in the 2016 Supreme Court case *Whole Women's Health v. Hellerstedt*, in which they told about their own experiences with abortion.

Chapter Six

Game Changer

ASSEMBLYMAN FRANZ Leichter and Assemblywoman Constance Cook didn't leave it to the courts to finish the work they started. Neither did their network of supporters. As the attorneys for *Abramowicz v. Lefkowitz* and its companion cases were navigating constitutional law, the coalition Leichter and Cook served continued working to turn the dream of abortion law repeal into a legislative reality. Members of this coalition continued pushing until they won—not everything, but the greatest victory against nineteenth-century abortion laws anywhere in the United States.

Leichter and Cook did not get very far with their original repeal bill in 1969. But finally in April, 1970, the two legislators got to see their colleagues in the state assembly vote on a draft law that embodied what Leichter proudly termed the "Cook-Leichter approach," allowing women to choose abortion with no restrictions through twenty-four weeks of a pregnancy and making New York the first state in the nation to allow nonresidents to obtain abortions within its borders with no waiting period.

The roll call started: like a sailboat listing from side to side in stormy waters, the tally veered toward approving the law and then toward defeating it. Cook and Leichter needed a majority of the assembly members, 76 votes. When the result was announced, it was a tie: 74–74. Without two final votes, the bill would fail. Then Assemblyman George Michaels, a Jewish Democrat from a heavily Catholic district in central New York, rose to speak: "I realize, Mr. Speaker, that I am terminating my political career, but I cannot in good conscience sit here and allow my vote to be the one that defeats this bill—I ask that my vote be changed from 'no' to 'yes.'"

The people most closely involved experienced the final stage of the campaign to change New York's nineteenth-century abortion law as an infinity of petitions, letters, marches, presentations, lobbying visits, and off-the-record strategy meetings with leaders in both major political parties. In fact, only five years had passed since Percy Sutton's first reform bill and the passage of this one. It was only eleven years between the American Law Institute's model code and the new New York law.

Many advocates and activists outside New York were astounded at the victory. What finally made the impossible possible? It was the combined pressure of diverse groups that changed legislators' minds. The large body of advocates that had been forming since the middle 1960s finally brought enough force to bear on the Republican leadership of both legislative houses, and on Democrats who had not previously joined the pro-legalization column because they were afraid to face the wrath of conservative Catholic lobbyists and their own party hierarchy.

After the abortion speak-out and founding of NARAL in the early spring of 1969, the repeal movement started to move forward by yards rather than by inches. This happened in part because a bill that would only have reformed, but not repealed, existing law proved once again to be a spectacular failure in the legislature. In April, when Al Blumenthal, the bill's sponsor, thought the arithmetic was in his favor, the final vote on it ended up as 78–69. Despite what political insiders knew about quiet and not-so-quiet Catholic opposition, this decisive failure was a surprise. In part because of the increasing visibility of a movement for full repeal, the insiders thought that Blumenthal's bill had become a compromise position on which a majority could agree.

The New York Assembly voted down the Blumenthal bill after Assemblyman Martin Ginsberg, a Republican from Long Island, gave an impassioned speech against the bill's provision for abortion on the basis of likely fetal deformity, which he linked to Nazi-style eugenics. Ginsberg had lifelong effects from the polio he contracted as a child. "If we are prepared to say that a life should not come into this world malformed or abnormal," he declared, "then tomorrow we should be prepared to say that a life already in this world which becomes malformed or abnormal should not be permitted to live." Although Ginsberg's disability did not occur in utero, he damned the proposal in light of his own experience: "I don't know why God saw fit to let me live in this form and condition. Perhaps it was so I could be here on April 17 to speak on this specific bill." Ginsberg received a standing ovation, and fourteen of Blumenthal's "aye" votes melted away.

Constance Cook concluded while listening to the debate that the abortion-law reform approach would never succeed. Its advocates didn't seem to understand that "this was a political issue, not a moral issue," and that what would change its fortunes was not argument but political power. Moreover, the only way meaningful political power would be amassed against the restrictive abortion laws was if women mobilized against them—and "they were never going to get women aroused politically about a bill that required them to go to a committee of doctors, then to go to a committee of hospital administrators, and then to go to have consultations with psychiatrists, or social workers or priests. All these steps were in the Blumenthal bill by the time he had compromised the thing. No way would there be any political support from women, and there wasn't for that bill."

Specious in its specifics, Ginsberg's speech pointed to a dimension of the rhetoric favoring change in the abortion laws that adherents were reluctant to admit. Some advocates of changing the abortion laws did, indeed, suggest that certain children were better off not born and certain parents better off not parenting. These arguments were implicitly racist and reflected bias against poor and working-class people and disabled people. In 1969, neither the pro-reform nor pro-repeal factions was interested in engaging the arguments to which the success of Ginsberg's speech might have pointed them.

In a magazine article that took the form of a personal and political diary, journalist and Redstockings founder Ellen Willis chronicled her reaction to the defeat of the Blumenthal bill. "The abortion reform bill is unexpectedly killed," she wrote in an urgent present tense. "The bill was a farce, but that only makes the Assembly's action more shocking and disgusting. Key man in this spirited affirmation of the compulsory pregnancy system is Assemblyman Martin Ginsberg." She added: "My first reaction is simply that I want to kill him. A man who is more concerned about his own hypothetical death than about the real deaths of thousands of women is unsalvageable. [Anti-colonial theorist Frantz] Fanon says that an oppressed individual cannot feel liberated until he kills one of the oppressors. Women? Killing? The idea seems ludicrous. But the anger is there, and it's real, and it will be expressed. We have begun and we can't go back."

After the abortion law reform bill met ignominious defeat, the statewide advocacy network started a new, more intense season of pushing for repeal. Thanks to legislative rules, they would not have a new bill around which to rally until the start of 1970. But this did not deter them. Constance Cook, the Republican from upstate, and Manhattan Democrat Franz Leichter, were still the only sponsors of repeal legislation. And even they were only just becoming convinced, if Cusack is to be believed, that they had the wisp of a chance at success. On the day after the legislature rejected Blumenthal's bill, Cook and Leichter argued in a public statement that the repeal position was preferable, because it did not have the "moral and logical ambivalence" of a reform approach. The problem with reform was that it gave legislators the responsibility and power to figure out the appropriate grounds for abortion. This gave room to claims like Gins-berg's, that legislators were picking and choosing among more and less valuable potential lives. Cook and Leichter claimed that the climate in the legislature had changed within twenty-four hours of the reform defeat, with "numerous" colleagues coming out of the woodwork for repeal and a good chance of "many more" joining them soon.

Legislators and members of New Yorkers for Abortion Law Repeal met to outline strategy in Leichter's office in May 1969. In atten-dance were, among others, Cusack, then helping to found NARAL; Clergy Consultation Service coordinator Arlene Carmen; and Susan Brownmiller, the journalist who had covered the abortion speak-out in Greenwich Village. The group pressed Leichter to do everything in his power to convince Blumenthal it was time to give up on his bill. They wanted to leave people who opposed the nineteenth-century abortion laws with one choice: repeal or nothing. "There was some tension in the air," Cusack remembered. "I would say that Franz did not like" the advocates nudging him into a confrontation with Blumenthal, his senior colleague from the most liberal corner of the Democratic Party. However, Leichter and his staff agreed to move the repeal cause forward by lining up a cadre of additional Democratic sponsors for the Cook-Leichter bill.

As these advocates and officeholders worked within the legislature, repeal activists upped their game to change public opinion and get important interest groups on their side. Members of New Yorkers for Abortion Law Repeal worked closely with Betty Friedan, Law-rence Lader, and Ruth Proskauer Smith, all of whom were also busy creating NARAL as a national organization, to support the statewide repeal effort.

The campaign for repeal was in the streets as well as in the legislative suites. NARAL sponsored pro-repeal demonstrations on Mother's Day, May 11, 1969. The National Organization for Women dem-onstrated that day too, calling Mother's Day a "combination of All Saints Day and a Day of Atonement," a day of hypocrisy on which "sanctity is dished out in nauseating doses to 'Everywoman: Our Mother,'" despite the persistence of inequality on the basis of sex. These demonstrations capped off what NOW leaders dubbed Freedom for Women Week, which placed a spotlight on three central demands: an Equal Rights Amendment to the U.S. Constitution, a major expansion in available childcare, and the repeal of restrictive abortion laws, which they called "unconstitutional and a violation of women's civil rights."

Mass action for abortion law repeal wasn't confined to Mother's Day. At other times that spring, NARAL provoked "days of anger" protests in eleven cities, including New York, Philadelphia, Atlanta, Los Angeles, and Milwaukee. Its leaders called for demonstrations at hospitals that used the therapeutic abortion committee system, which privileged women who were wealthy, well connected, and white over everyone else. Lader remembered that almost two hundred people joined a "days of anger" protest at New York City's Lenox Hill Hospital, including nurses and medical school students in scrubs. Reverend Howard Moody from the Clergy Consultation Service "carried a placard" reading: "You don't have to be a woman to know this law is wrong." About a hundred radical feminists protested at New York's Criminal Court building during the trial of a doctor who performed abortions. Half of them demonstrated on the sidewalk outside, and half interrupted the proceedings inside to point out that they considered every criminal prosecution for providing an abortion an illegitimate use of government power.

One focus of the national and New York repeal campaigns was on recruiting professionals to the cause. Organizers for repeal shared a hunch that, much as groups like the American Medical Association (AMA) had been instrumental in spreading restrictive abortion laws across the United States in the nineteenth century, and some doctors and lawyers had helped start the push to reform those laws after World War II, so could professionals help the repeal campaign reach its goals. Leaders of the repeal movement did not complete this work before New York passed a version of my mother's bill in April 1970. But the wisdom of their approach was borne out a couple of years later, when the U.S. Supreme Court considered *Roe v. Wade*. In his opinion for the Supreme Court in that case, Justice Harry Blackmun referred repeatedly to the changes in policy by major medical, legal, and public health organizations.

Repealers worked both quietly and not so quietly to pull professional organizations to their side. In 1968, due, according to Ruth Cusack, to lobbying by New York abortion activist Ruth Proskauer Smith, the American Public Health Association became the first major health organization to go on the record for repeal. "Following that action," the *American Journal of Public Health* reported, "officers and members, as well as staff of the Association, participated vigorously in the nationwide effort to assure women the opportunity of deciding with their physicians whether or not to terminate an unwanted pregnancy." Repeal advocates worked to provoke a change in policy by Planned Parenthood. Although the medical committee of Planned Parenthood had led the conversation in the late 1950s about the need to reform abortion laws, Planned Parenthood was a relatively late convert to the repeal cause. Dr. Alan Guttmacher, then president of the Planned Parenthood Federation of America, argued in December 1968 that repeal was "obviously" the "eventual goal," but was out of reach for the foreseeable future. He began publicly to support repeal—and claim that passage of a reform bill in its stead would be a "catastrophe"—in late February 1969. He claimed this change as the consequence of decades of "medical practice and observation," although the introduction of a repeal bill in New York likely also inspired his change of heart. Only after New York's law changed in 1970 did the American Association of Planned Parenthood Physicians pledge itself to the cause of repeal—just in time to argue in a friend-of-the-court brief in *Roe v. Wade* that it was "desirable that provisions respecting abortion not be contained in State Criminal Codes."

New Yorkers for Abortion Law Repeal and NARAL worked together to move the AMA, the most conservative and prestigious of professional medical societies, toward repeal. The Education Committee of New Yorkers for Abortion Law Repeal mapped out a multipart plan of "demonstrating, leafleting, having pro-repeal physicians introduce a resolution to the convention, and inviting medical notables who are for repeal to hold a press conference" when the AMA came to New York City in mid-July, 1969, for its annual convention. Lucinda Cisler and James Clapp of New Yorkers for Abortion Law Repeal persuaded Bernard Nathanson, the New York doctor who admitted providing abortions, and psychiatrist Helen Edey to lend their names to a "Dear Colleague" letter asking other "eminent physicians in a variety of specialties" to sign a petition in favor of repeal. They pledged to circulate the petition at the conference and submit it to the AMA's policy-making body, the House of Delegates. By July 12, they had signatures from eighty-three AMA members, including prominent members of the New York County Medical Society. This should not be over-read as evidence of a feminist awakening in the medical community: "Most of us," one signatory wrote, referring to his doctor friends who also signed the petition, "are opposed to 'free choice' but are in favor of repeal so that *Medical Rx* [a doctor's ability to recommend abortion when he felt it was medically indicated] is not interfered with."

The campaign of pressure on the AMA, the most mainstream doctors' organization, was a watershed for the repeal movement. New Yorkers for Abortion Law Repeal, NARAL, and disparate feminists made the cause of repeal newly visible to a singularly powerful constituency. Lader remembered an explosion of energy when "women pickets surrounded" the midtown Manhattan convention center where the AMA was meeting, "with signs and leaflets demanding that doctors sign a petition for repeal. Dr. Lonny Myers of Illinois [a NARAL founder] invaded the hall to confront her colleagues, dressed in a white lab coat, her hands tied with red tape as a symbol of medical restrictions under present laws."

The AMA protest tied New York's legislative effort closely with the national network for repeal, and vice versa. The memberships and messages of the two were not entirely the same, but they overlapped in a Venn diagram of abortion-law-repeal organizing. New Yorkers for Abortion Law Repeal mapped out the campaign for the AMA protest and brought in the NARAL planning committee during its last stages. New York organizers created messages for the AMA action that were relevant to repeal efforts throughout the United States. Through the first year of NARAL's development, the new group borrowed the logo of New Yorkers for Abortion Law Repeal.

The next stage in getting New York to transform its abortion laws was to shore up the legislative coalition for repeal. Repeal forces needed to organize support downstate in the New York City area as well as upstate in the districts that Assemblywoman Constance Cook knew well. One priority was getting Democratic abortion-law reform champion Al Blumenthal to support repeal and agree not to re-introduce his reform bill in 1970. New Yorkers for Abortion Law Repeal communicated with him via Democratic Party insider networks: Barbara Gelobter, a Democratic district leader from Blumenthal's assembly district (a Black woman with Caribbean and Latin American roots married to an Ashkenazic Jew, both of them friends of my parents'), made the approach. She reported back that Blumenthal knew his constituents favored repeal, but he still raised objections to the Cook-Leichter bill. New Yorkers for Abortion Law Repeal circulated pro-repeal petitions in Blumenthal's district and created a coalition of groups to confront him on his position. This strategy worked: although Blumenthal once again introduced an abortion-law reform proposal for consideration in 1970, he did so half-heartedly while also supporting repeal.

At the same time that New Yorkers for Abortion Law Repeal were leaning on the liberal Democrats from Manhattan, their allies put the screws to a couple of Republicans from Long Island. Ruth Cusack, the tireless advocate, had spent much of 1969 sustaining a local repeal group in her Long Island county. The Suffolk Committee for Abortion Law Repeal was designed to support, and pressure, the powerful Speaker of the State Assembly, who lived in Suffolk County. Speaker Perry Duryea had pledged in a phone call in December 1968 to support a repeal bill "when the time came." Cusack kept up the activism because she "wanted people from throughout the state to know that Duryea had support"—and to make sure he didn't backtrack. Assemblywoman Cook recalled that Duryea flew to Puerto Rico to investigate a so-called "abortion mill" on the island and claimed afterward, at least to Cusack's group, that what he saw there increased his commitment to reforming the law. Cook also reported that members of the Suffolk group shared information with her whenever they met with the Speaker, so that she could press him further if need be. "That technique," of meeting repeatedly in his home district with a key legislator and telling the bill's lead sponsor what he said, "is not very nice, maybe," Cook opined, "but it's the only way I know of doing it."

The advocates were just as tenacious in dealing with Martin Ginsberg, the Republican who had polio as a child and spoke emotionally against abortion law reform, as they were with the Speaker. Ginsberg represented Nassau County, and so Cusack helped one of his constituents create the Nassau Committee for Abortion Law Repeal. Cusack attended the group's first meeting, at which she tried to persuade him that repeal, as opposed to the reforms he found objectionable, simply took government "out of the whole thing." Facing a pro-repeal audience and intrepid suburban white ladies who wanted him to change his position, Ginsberg claimed to have been in favor of repeal all along. He later tried to walk back this statement. The Nassau County women kept working on him, however, and eventually turned him into a real sponsor of the bill—an important switch both because of his notoriety and because he was among the few Republican legislators to join the repeal team.

＊　　＊　　＊

Even as it seemed like the repeal movement was poised for success, the coalition behind it hit an iceberg and broke apart. When Cook and Leichter were preparing for a final push on their bill, they added a stipulation that abortions must be performed by a physician—a minor shift, according to Cook, who believed that their original bill would also have required that the procedure be done by a doctor, although that was not spelled out in its text. To two leading members of New Yorkers for Abortion Law Repeal, Lucinda Cisler and James Clapp, this was a major shift. Cisler and Clapp responded by trying to get New Yorkers for Abortion Law Repeal to withdraw support from the Cook-Leichter bill. Things came to a head at a meeting just before Thanksgiving, at which most board members refused to follow Cisler's and Clapp's lead. NARAL, too, stuck with Cook and Leichter and against these two activists.

Cisler later explained why this change, which seemed innocuous to many of her colleagues, was in her view "one of the most insidious restrictions of all." By limiting abortion provision to credentialed physicians, Cisler argued, advocates were falling for a species of "fake repeal" that was actually a narrowing reform. It had the potential to "divide women from each other," making abortions expensive and difficult to access, and therefore separating the well-off (and white) from everyone else. "Looking not so far in the future," she wrote, "this restriction would also deny women themselves the right to use self-abortifacients when they are developed—and who is to say they will not be developed soon?" Aside from "self-abortifacients," Cisler may also have been thinking of initiatives from within the women's movement late in the 1960s and at the start of the 1970s, like the Jane project in Chicago. Jane members not only referred abortion seekers to competent physicians but, frustrated with the cost and the care patients received, learned to perform abortions themselves.

Cisler immediately became persona non grata with practical legislators like Assemblywoman Constance Cook. But Cisler's objections
seemed prescient from the perspective of the twenty-first century: a
doctors-only requirement did, as she warned, make it hard to create
what she termed a system of "efficient, inexpensive care on a mass
basis"—and this would matter greatly a few years later, when Congress passed the Hyde Amendment, which made federal health-care
funds off-limits for abortions. The fracturing Cisler anticipated in the
women's movement, between wealthier and poorer people, was latent
(or patent) all along, but stark differences in access based on the high
cost of abortion certainly didn't help. In the early 1970s, feminist
health-care activists developed a series of practices they called "self-
help" reproductive care. A California teacher named Lorraine Rothman invented a method of first-trimester abortion that one woman
could perform on another with the aid of a device they could make
inexpensively at home, no doctor or hospital required. The procedure
was called "menstrual exaction," and Rothman and self-help leader
Carol Downer traveled the country in the last two years before *Roe*
teaching women how to do it. In the twenty-first century, reproductive
rights activists in several states waged uphill battles to pass laws that
allowed physicians' assistants and nurses to perform abortions. They
also worked to enable pregnant people to self-manage their abortions
using medications they obtained through the mail.

The fracture in New York's repeal movement led to the creation
of a new advocacy organization to help carry Cook and Leichter's
legislation across the finish line. Cisler and Clapp remained in New
Yorkers for Abortion Law Repeal. That organization stood for full
repeal and opposed any legislation that departed from that standard.
People who were willing to modify the bill in order to pass it created
the Committee for the Cook-Leichter Bill to Repeal New York's
Abortion Laws, which elected officers and a board in January 1970.

The final attempt to pass the bill was a tag-team effort between
Cook and Leichter and a few colleagues and members of the

Committee for the Cook-Leichter Bill. Popular pressure made the repeal position more palatable than it had been just a year earlier. But the friends of repeal knew there was still a healthy likelihood that they would lose. The *New York Times* summarized the mood in the state capitol early in 1970: despite increased momentum behind replacing the nineteenth-century abortion law, repeal and reform proponents "sensed an indisposition on the part of other legislators to become embroiled in the issue" because they were afraid to earn the wrath of the Catholic leadership. From inside the legislative chambers and outside them, the game the repealers were playing became essentially arithmetic: counting votes.

The Committee for the Cook-Leichter Bill organized quickly to mobilize support. Its leaders distinguished support for the repeal legislation with the doctors-only compromise from Cisler's and Clapp's more uncompromising position and from Blumenthal's continued, if half-hearted, endorsement of a much more compromised bill. The committee gathered its forces at an early-February open meeting in Manhattan. Seventy-five people showed up to the Ethical Culture Society building for a pro-repeal pep talk by Franz Leichter, who said that the most important strategy they could employ was a mass of "visits, calls, and letters" from constituents to their legislators. The Committee for the Cook-Leichter Bill gathered endorsements from as many community groups as possible, eventually winning support from over fifty of them, including the Episcopal Diocese of New York, American Jewish Congress, Liberal Party (a third party active in New York with roots in the labor movement), New York State Council of Churches (mainline Protestants), National Organization for Women, American Women's Medical Association, New York branch of the National Council of Jewish Women, and liberal Democratic groups like the (Greenwich) Village Independent Democrats and Americans for Democratic Action.

One change in the legislative sausage-making this time was that the repeal bill started in the state senate and not in the assembly, where Cook and Leichter served. Both legislators believed that this occurred because the senate leadership, possibly after a huddle with the lieutenant governor, who, unlike Governor Rockefeller, opposed any change in the abortion laws, decided that this was a way to stop the momentum behind repeal. Cook believed that they meant to alienate her from the issue by leaving her name off the bill; once a new bill was written and introduced in the senate, it would go by the names of new lead sponsors. (Advocates would continue to refer to their pro-repeal position as the "Cook-Leichter approach.") It was a political truism, although not one the assemblywoman particularly respected, that no politician cared about an initiative for which they could not take ownership. But Cook never knew for sure if her assessments were correct. Although the decision makers were members of her own party, they did not consult with her. For his part, Franz Leichter suggested that it was better for the liberal Democrats to have the bill start in the senate, to remove the air of failure that surrounded the issue in the assembly after repeated defeats of bills for abortion-law reform.

The Committee for the Cook-Leichter Bill became the communications center of the repeal movement. It pointed its pressure at the state senate. Committee leaders wrote to every senator, arguing that repeal meant a separation of government from decision-making about intimate matters, a matter of liberty rather than personal morality. They worked hard, and successfully, to generate sympathetic press coverage of the repeal campaign. Then the Republican senate leader had his assistant counsel negotiate with Cook, who accepted a series of modifications to her original bill—not just the doctor-only provision but also a return of abortion to the penal code from which my mother's outline had plucked it, and "some kind of a time limitation" beyond which abortion would again be criminalized. In early March, however, Senator DeWitt Clinton Dominick III, at the behest of New York's Republican legislative leadership, introduced a bill that had none of those provisions: for reasons neither Cook nor Leichter could quite fathom, his draft law was a simple repeal on the Beatrice Kornbluh model.

It is hard to understand what happened next as anything but a product of the huge upsurge in feminist and other pro-repeal energy from outside the councils of political power. Certainly, nothing from the past made it predictable. The Committee for the Cook-Leichter Bill sent another mailing to every senator asking that they vote for repeal. The committee had planned an advertising campaign focused on upstate districts. But as the legislative effort quickly entered its final phase, Cook-Leichter committee members took the faster approach of inundating legislators across the state with telephone pleas to vote for repeal. Several members of the committee, including Cusack and Reverend Moody of the Clergy Consultation Service, made repeated lobbying trips to the state capitol.

The Republican Senate leader set debate for March 17, St. Patrick's Day. "Probably somebody on his staff thought that would be a clever way to get rid of it," Cook commented. "But, it didn't work." In response to an uproar from senators, who didn't even want to talk about abortion on the Irish-Catholic holiday, the vote was rescheduled. On March 18, 1970, then, Cook, Leichter, other long-term advocates of changing the law, and a mass of spectators watched the senate debate abortion law repeal for five hours. Television cameras struggled to capture the proceedings through a haze of cigarette smoke. Senator Dominick kicked off debate by relating a conversation he had with his wife, who said that if she became pregnant for a sixth time, she would have an abortion. "And you know," he added, "I would have helped her." At five o'clock, Senator Waldaba H. Stewart, a Black Democrat from Brooklyn, cast the deciding vote in favor of the motion. The final tally was 31–26 in repeal. Constance Cook was among the few people not surprised by the outcome. She credited it to a factor her anti-abortion Republican colleagues hadn't anticipated: "The women finally getting to their legislators. See," she said, "that's what it took."

Then it was on to the assembly. The Committee for the Cook-Leichter Bill continued to coordinate lobbying in person, on the phone, in letters, and in telegrams. New York State Catholic Women for Abortion Law Repeal, working with the committee, had already sent telegrams to most of the senators and the governor. The group followed up with letters to every member of the assembly, signed by seventy-five women. Then the powerful Codes Committee demanded two amendments as the price of reporting out the bill for debate and a vote: First, that an abortion could be performed only with the consent of the pregnant person (a reflection of concerns about population control and what some Black nationalists termed "Black genocide" by means of overly available contraception and abortion), and second, that after the twenty-fourth week of a pregnancy, abortion would be legal only to save the life of the pregnant person. Cook accepted both changes. "I believed in the outright repeal," she recalled. "So I backed down reluctantly." But she did back down. So did Assemblyman Leichter, who had favored some kind of time limit at the very start of his involvement in the repeal effort—a position from which my mother and others had initially dissuaded him. The twenty-four-week limit was a concession to assembly members for whom the six-month point was a reasonable approximation of the old standard of quickening from custom and common law. As Cook put it, despite her reservations: "It was historic, and it was traditional."

Lucinda Cisler, continuing to organize for full repeal, offered withering criticism of this particular species of compromise. A time limit at twenty-four weeks, or at any point, she wrote, violated the very principles of independent personhood, dignity, and civil rights that motivated the modern women's movement. It "essentially says two things to women: (a) at a certain stage, your body suddenly belongs to the state and it can force you to have a child, whatever your own reasons for wanting an abortion late in pregnancy; (b) because late abortion entails more risk to you than early abortion, the state must 'protect' you even if your considered decision is that you want to run that risk and your doctor is willing to help you." While Assemblywoman Cook was willing, in the end, to bend to the power of "historic" ideas about when life began, Cisler considered these ideas nonsense on sticks: "To listen to judges and legislators play with the ghostly arithmetic of months and weeks is to hear the music by which angels used to dance on the head of a pin." She predicted, accurately, that it would be very hard to remove such a time limit, once included, from the law; it was not until 2019 that New York widened abortion access past the point it reached with the legislation Cook and Leichter had compromised to pass. In the fifty years after *Roe*, the Supreme Court, which followed the New York law in allowing states to ban abortion in the third trimester, never reversed course and protected abortion access more fully than it had in the 1970s. "This is not repeal," Cisler warned.

Outside the state capitol, people at the grassroots took action against the abortion laws and may have had the biggest impact of all. "It became obvious" early in 1970, Diane Schulder and Florynce Kennedy wrote, "that the abortion issue was one that could mobilize large numbers of women." A coalition called People Against Abortion Laws, whose members hailed from many different corners of feminism and other kinds of anti-establishment protest, convened a mass march in New York City on March 28. The protest had three geographical foci: The first was St. Patrick's Cathedral, where organizers held a relatively small warm-up rally in the morning. St. Patrick's was the seat of the archbishop of New York, the single most important opponent of abortion law repeal—later, the most important opponent of scientifically based AIDS/HIV policy, famously protested by ACT UP New York. The second was Bellevue Hospital. Bellevue and other hospitals that served poor, Black, Puerto Rican, and immigrant New Yorkers were objects of protest by the militant Black Panthers and Puerto Rican Young Lords, and politicized doctors' organizations such as the Medical Committee for Human Rights. They charged Bellevue and the other city-funded hospitals with providing subpar, culturally insensitive health care *and* with being cogs in a restrictive abortion machinery that killed Black and Puerto Rican patients by driving them to unsafe practitioners because they could not access safe, legal abortions. The third focus was Union Square, a historic home of popular protest, including of mass actions for women's labor rights and woman suffrage.

This day of action demonstrated the depth and breadth of the repeal cause. It was, Schulder and Kennedy observed, "the first time in many decades that New York had seen masses of women in the streets on women's issues." Kennedy herself spoke at St. Patrick's. A sympathizer with the repeal cause handed out wire coat hangers covered with red lacquer, a then-new movement icon that represented the ways women harmed themselves in trying to terminate their pregnancies when legal abortion was unavailable. In the main march, a crowd of at least 1,500 streamed through the middle of town, from First Avenue on the East Side to Herald Square on the West, chanting, "Out of the house! Out of the stores! Up from under, women unite!" To a small number of hecklers, they answered: "Male chauvinists better start quakin'; today's pig is tomorrow's bacon!" Symbolizing the way that abortion law repeal united activists who had plenty of reasons to be disunited, the speakers to the crowd of over two thousand at Union Square ranged from NOW's Betty Friedan to Lucinda Cisler, who said that she opposed the bill Cook and Leichter were sponsoring (more than ever, thanks to the legislators' latest compromises), to Florence Rice, the Harlem Consumer Education Council leader who had told Kennedy and Schulder about her abortions when they were gathering depositions for the *Abramowicz* case.

The histrionic closing scenes of the legislative drama came on the heels of the mass march in New York City. On March 30, Assemblywoman Cook brought the amended repeal law to the floor. She and her colleagues debated it for eight hours. "I submit to you," she said, "we are not considering here today abortion on demand—we have that already. The only question is how abortions are to be had. Right now, if you have $25 you get an abortion in the back alley under the most abominable conditions, but if you have $2,500 then you can go elsewhere and get a proper abortion." She insisted that the point of the law she and Leichter endorsed was to "put the illegal abortionist out of business." Then her colleagues voted. The tally was 73–71, a slight majority for Leichter and Cook. But the measure still failed, since legislative rules stipulated that only a 76-member vote, representing a majority of the total number in the assembly, counted. Despite the fact that he had been cultivated for over two years by his dogged, pro-repeal Long Island neighbor Ruth Cusack, Republican Speaker Perry Duryea would not count the votes of assembly members who were not present for the balloting but had recorded their preferences with the clerk. Two of these would have been on the pro-repeal side.

With the fate of the bill uncertain, someone approached Cook with an offer. If she supported a further amendment, which would reduce access to legal abortion by making the time limit twenty weeks, then she would pick up one vote. This would be enough for victory, assuming that the assemblymen who left early eventually returned. Cook remembered taking it up with NARAL's Lawrence Lader. He was "sitting at the back of the chamber, and I said, 'Larry, this is it. They say we'll have it if we go down to twenty weeks.' I said, 'I really don't think we should,'" because of concern for people who did not realize they were pregnant before they hit that twenty-week point. Lader agreed, even if that meant the bill would fall. Pro-repeal forces had "reached the limit of compromise."

Then there was another flurry—or maybe a nor'easter?—of lobbying. The New York Catholic Conference mobilized to defeat the bill, meeting with political leaders, protesting, and organizing a pray-in on the lawn of at least one legislator. Three of Cook's and Leichter's yes votes switched and their near-victory slipped away. However, they noticed that they were also picking up a few votes from suburban districts on Long Island and Westchester. In these precincts, wealthy, white repeal partisans, some organized by Cusack, were making themselves known to their representatives. A few Black urban legislators, too, joined the yes column. Leichter remembered "a very progressive Democratic legislator from Erie County who had promised his local priest" to oppose the bill. He reneged on that pledge under pressure from senior Black Democrats, including Percy Sutton.

On April 9, 1970, the New York Assembly voted again on the "Cook-Leichter approach," the compromise bill with amendments demanded by other legislators. It took a bit of fancy parliamentary footwork to even schedule that vote. The Speaker, proving himself again a fair-weather friend to the repeal coalition, refused to let legislators vote on whether to reconsider the bill until every single one of them was present; twelve members of the assembly, who would have preferred not to go on the record about abortion, were ordered brought to the floor of the chamber "by whatever force necessary." The Catholic Conference and State Medical Society turned up the heat on their opposition to the bill. Some of its supporters described their chances of success as "a toss-up."

If the vote was in the affirmative, it was a near certainty that the years of effort by reformist legislators, population-control advocates, hardy demonstrators, hearing-interrupters, and champions of the speak-out would end in historic legal change. Despite the compromises, the New York law would become the most progressive state law on abortion in the country. What made it a true stand-out was its lack of a residency requirement. This meant that women from all over the world could come to New York—if they could afford to travel and manage the necessary logistics of their lives—and access legal abortions through the first six months of their pregnancies. Although the *Abramowicz* federal court case would be upstaged and preempted by the new legislation, its attorneys could take the win, too: They and their clients had chipped away at old stigmas and stereotypes. They fashioned new paradigms for thinking about reproductive rights and a new strategy for achieving them.

Constance Cook later insisted that she knew she had the vote sewn up. She and the other leaders who wanted the bill to pass, including the Democratic minority leader of the assembly, "worked up the list." They counted seventy-four supporters—plus, if his vote was decisive, a commitment from the Speaker, who seemed to be trying hard not to be forced to make good on that commitment. Cook also had a secret pledge from George Michaels, the liberal Democrat and father of a Reform Jewish rabbi, who represented a largely Republican upstate district near Cook's own. Unfortunately for Michaels, almost all the Democrats in his district were Catholic, and the state party leadership, which was loath to alienate the church, was more powerful there than it was in New York City. "As we came closer down the line, on that last abortion vote, he came to me several times," Cook remembered, to ask about her latest tally. About a week before the final vote, "he said, 'Connie, I will not be the vote that kills your bill.' He said, 'If it's one vote away, then you have my vote.' Now, he was not going to vote yes unless he had to." But Cook felt she could count on him if she needed him. "I never put anybody on the pan if I didn't have to," she insisted. But she knew there was a good chance that she would have to.

On the day after the vote, it was the lead story in the *New York Times*. The article about New York's 76–73 victory for abortion decriminalization edged out an account of a "bitter" President Nixon responding to the defeat of his two nominees to the Supreme Court, and a threat by the governor of Florida to fire on federal marshals if they tried to enforce a desegregation order in the public schools. Constance Cook had gotten the math right. The votes she spent over a year cultivating came through to bring the tally to a tie. Then Assemblyman Michaels, "his hands trembling and tears welling in his eyes, stopped the roll-call only seconds before the clerk was to announce that the reform bill had been defeated for lack of a single vote." He knew that what he was about to do would spell a challenge in the next Democratic primary, and that he'd lose that challenge. But he asked that his vote be changed. "In the confusion that followed—as secretaries applauded the move with tears streaming down their cheeks—few people saw Mr. Michaels slump in his chair holding his head in his hands, or heard Assemblyman Perry Duryea ask that his name be called so that he, as Speaker, could provide the final vote for passage."

Every stitch of effort from the past five years paid off. This imperfect and consequential legislative victory relied on all corners of the movement to decriminalize abortion. The final tipping point came from what Franz Leichter called "really a great act of political courage" by Assemblyman Michaels. But the coalition in favor of the bill earned every one of the votes that made the count close enough to pull that one legislator in from the sidelines. The mass march through Manhattan made a difference, and so did the Redstockings' speak-out and the radical feminist action to stop legislative hearings that didn't include women who wanted to repeal the laws. New Yorkers for Abortion Law Repeal and NARAL mattered, and so did the actions they organized or inspired at the hospitals, in the courts, and in professional associations. Letter writing and lobbying by members of the NOW abortion committee helped make it happen, even though by the spring of 1970 New York NOW was no longer a meeting place for every passionate partisan of women's civil rights. Nancy Stearns and Flo Kennedy, Diane Schulder, Anne Garfinkle, and Carol Lefcourt helped pass that law. So did my mother. And Ruth Cusack, with her indefatigable nudging of individual legislators. And Ellen Willis, Shulamith Firestone, Ti-Grace Atkinson, and Betty Friedan. Likewise Percy Sutton, Barbara Gelobter, and other Democratic leaders; and Reverend Howard Moody, Arlene Carmen, Rabbi Israel Margolies, and everyone affiliated with the Clergy Consultation Service. Lucinda Cisler and James Clapp helped, even though they objected powerfully to compromises the politicians made to get the bill past the post. And so did New York governor Nelson Rockefeller, who had himself been forced off the sidelines by rising movements for abortion law reform and women's rights. Since 1968, he had sent stronger and stronger signals of his willingness to sign any proposed reform of the abortion laws the legislature could pass.

Governor Rockefeller would soon have the opportunity to turn the bill into a law. Part of the reason the *New York Times* led with the vote in the state assembly was that George Michaels's switch made the success of the bill nearly a shoo-in. Since the New York Senate and Assembly bills were different from each other, the assembly version had to return to the other legislative chamber for approval. And so, the very next day, after just two hours this time of "quiet but emotional debate," the senate voted it up by a comfortable margin. The senate majority leader, whose apparent miscalculation had opened the door for the bill's passage, "openly wept" during the vote after reading from a lachrymose text called "The Diary of an Unborn Child." Another Republican, Senator Thomas Laverne from Rochester, insisted that he was a good Catholic who represented the majority of Catholics in his district—Catholics who disagreed with the church and thought that the government should stop regulating access to abortion. "I don't think," he told his colleagues, "I have the right to force my morality on anyone else." Then it was on to the governor. On the morning of April 11, Rockefeller, speaking in New York City, credited the grassroots troops of the women's movement, as well as the "wives of the Senate and the Assembly," and the Republican Party, for getting the proposal through the legislative process. Then he flew back to the governor's mansion in Albany and signed the bill. It would take effect July 1.

Chapter Seven

Palante

A FEW months after New York passed its new abortion law, Dr. Helen Rodríguez-Trías became the chair of the Department of Pediatrics at Lincoln Hospital in the South Bronx. She supported the abortion law, but she also saw its limitations up close from her vantage point as a doctor to Latino, Black, and working-class white New Yorkers. What she saw made her into a different kind of doctor than she had been before. The contrast between her patients' needs for health care and the more limited demands of the movement to decriminalize abortion turned her into a new kind of leader in the movement for reproductive rights.

In 1970, Helen Rodríguez-Trías went from being an extraordinary doctor in San Juan, Puerto Rico, to a department head at the most politicized hospital in New York City and an activist to whom the women's movement was "a personal matter of survival." In other words, she had become the person she would be for the rest of her life, a leader who could cofound the movement against sterilization abuse and rethink the reproductive rights movement so that it was about fighting against racism, imperialism, and inequality in health care as much as it was about fighting for access to birth control and abortion.

The transformation in Rodríguez-Trías's life started at Lincoln Hospital. Lincoln was perhaps the worst hospital in New York City's overburdened, underresourced municipal health-care system.

The hospital had a physical plant that was antiquated and in some ways as much of a threat to patients' health as the worst apartment buildings in the neighborhood that surrounded it. In the late 1960s, as part of a national movement for health-care civil rights and community control, Lincoln became a focus of protest by professional and nonprofessional health-care workers, neighborhood residents, the Black Panther Party, and the Puerto Rican Young Lords. The Young Lords occupied Lincoln Hospital in 1970 and developed a politics of reproductive health care that included the right to access abortion but did not stop there. Members of the Young Lords insisted that all people have decent care for all their health needs, and they decried an economic system in which poverty and racism (in their view) coerced people into sterilization and kept them from having the children they wanted to have.

Her experiences at Lincoln Hospital reconnected Rodríguez-Trías with her radical roots as a Puerto Rican *independentista* and left-wing critic of economic inequality. She joined what she had learned in her medical training with feminism, and with what she had long known about the depredations of imperialism and capitalism. Thanks to the Young Lords, Lincoln's doctors and other employees, and the nascent women's health movement, Rodríguez-Trías became a unique figure in both the women's movement and in public health, an advocate for reproductive justice two decades before that term was invented.

Lincoln Hospital began as the Home for Worthy, Aged, Indigent Colored People, a nursing home for former domestic servants, runaways, and freed people that opened its doors in Manhattan in 1842. Its aims were to offer "protection and a peaceful home for the respectable, worn-out colored servants of both sexes of our city," and to give them the "consolation of religion." Its white founders also sought to relieve the city's almshouses of young Black inmates, who would be encouraged "in habits of industry and propriety" and sent back into the labor market after a stay. The residents were people like

"Blind Sopha," abducted from Africa and enslaved at about seventeen, whose "life of accumulated suffering" ended at the home, according to a book that summarized the lives of its residents as a way to raise the private funds needed to pay its costs. The home prospered for a time. It moved to its own building, on First Avenue and 60th Street, in 1860. In 1882, its philanthropic leaders changed its name to the Colored Home and Hospital in recognition of its increasing role in providing medical care to Black residents of the city. In the 1890s, they moved it from Manhattan to a large lot on what was then the edge of New York City, at 141st Street and Southern Boulevard in the South Bronx.

In the late 1960s, Lincoln Hospital was still in that building on Southern Boulevard. It was part of New York's mammoth municipal health-care system. Lincoln's location was an inconvenient one for many Black New Yorkers who lived in Manhattan. However, Puerto Rican migration to New York City transformed the South Bronx and neighborhoods in Manhattan and Brooklyn after World War II, thanks to economic policies in Puerto Rico and from the U.S. government that led one-third of the island's population to move to the mainland between 1947 and 1970. Lincoln became the neighborhood hospital of tens of thousands of Boricuas (Puerto Ricans), while still serving Black patients who were not Puerto Rican, older immigrants from Eastern and Southern Europe, and other new migrants. Under an agreement with the New York City Health Department (and later the Health and Hospitals Corporation), Lincoln and other public hospitals were staffed by the city's major medical schools under public-private affiliation contracts, which were lucrative for the schools and which were supposed to produce high-quality health care for the patients. The heads of the public hospital departments were generally senior faculty at the medical schools. Hospital "house staff," who worked under these department heads, were doctors who had recently completed their educations and were in the final stages of their training.

Lincoln Hospital was an object of complaint and protest well before Rodríguez-Trías arrived. Community members and organizations like the Black Panther Party had complained for decades about the building, and about understaffing and gaps in the services offered to patients. They got little but empty promises from the mayor and city council. Although city officials had acknowledged that they needed to replace the building, and had approved a budget for a new building in the early 1960s, little had changed by the start of the 1970s.

Many of the people who lived near Lincoln Hospital and were its patients called their major neighborhood health-care institution "the butcher shop of the South Bronx." They likened the gap between butchery and real medicine to the gap between patients' experiences at Lincoln and the experiences they *would* have if the city cared about public hospital patients—people who didn't have a lot of political or economic power. Activists who referred to Lincoln as a butcher shop also suggested that the hospital was designed to make money for its administrators, and perhaps also to let them use Black and brown bodies for research purposes: A cartoon by Young Lords leader Denise Oliver, which appeared in the group's newspaper, *Palante* (named for a contraction in Caribbean Spanish made from "para adalante," meaning something like "straight ahead"), in July 1970, showed two pigs in white coats carving pieces out of a prostrate Puerto Rican patient and counting their money.

This was different from the way my mother and other abortion-rights activists referred to abortion providers in the years before the New York decriminalization law as "butchers." As a white woman who had first-class health insurance and used private doctors and hospitals, my mother expected her experiences of medical care to be mostly positive. She took it for granted that, in the main, doctors and other medical staff would demonstrate concern for her well-being, that the place where they saw her provided a sterile and comfortable environment, and that she would be attended by professionals with relatively reasonable workloads. Understanding health care this way was a privilege she didn't know she had. When my mother reminded me that the providers of illegal abortions were "butchers!" she marked the distance between her expectations of ordinary medical care and beliefs about abortion in the years when it was almost always a crime.

Lincoln Hospital was managed by Albert Einstein College of Medicine in the North Bronx, in an affiliation agreement with the city of New York under which senior faculty members ran hospital departments and supervised junior doctors and medical students. Einstein College of Medicine, part of Yeshiva University and a creature of mid-twentieth-century Jewish philanthropy, was close to the border between New York City and Westchester County, which contained some of the leafiest and most exclusive suburbs in the United States.

In addition to their work at Lincoln Hospital, the faculty at Einstein College of Medicine also supervised house staff at the Jacobi Medical Center, a larger and newer hospital than Lincoln, which was also closer than Lincoln to the College of Medicine. The geographic distance between the two resonantly named institutions, Lincoln and Einstein, was part of the problem with the condition of Lincoln Hospital. Patients and nonpatient activists believed that Lincoln was left out in the city hospital system generally and in the Einstein College of Medicine system in particular. But the embeddedness of Lincoln Hospital in the South Bronx also meant that Puerto Rican and Black neighbors felt ownership over the facility, more so than many of the senior physicians who worked there but spent relatively little time in the neighborhood.

At the end of the 1960s and beginning of the 1970s, a new grassroots health care politics arrived on the scene from several directions at once. One was a movement among radical doctors and other professionals. The lead organization was the Medical Committee for Human Rights, formed in New York City in 1963 to support the civil rights movement in the South. By the end of the 1960s, the group was active in the North as well. It was one of the original parties to the *Abramowicz* case, which tried to repeal abortion law through the federal courts. Some of the Medical Committee's individual members, such as Dr. Fitzhugh Mullan, who became a central figure in the drama at Lincoln Hospital, were among the doctor plaintiffs in that case.

Grassroots demands to change the health-care system also came from radicals in Black and brown communities. Initially, the most visible group was the Black Panther Party for Self-Defense, headquartered in California but powerful enough in New York City that twenty-one local members, including rapper Tupac Shakur's mother, Afeni Shakur, were arrested by New York City police on trumped-up charges in 1969 and remained in jail through the following year. Alongside their military-style training and posturing, Panthers served their communities by preparing free breakfasts for children, opening medical clinics, and testing for sickle cell anemia, which affected Black Americans disproportionately.

Starting a bit later, and inspired by the Panthers, was the Puerto Rican Young Lords Organization. Like the Panthers, the Young Lords were young socialist revolutionaries and anti-imperialists. The center of their early organizing was less *Puerto Rico Libre*—a Puerto Rican island free from U.S. military and economic control—than it was improving the lives of Puerto Ricans on the U.S. mainland.

The Young Lords started as a street gang in Chicago. Cha Cha Jiménez cofounded the gang with five other young Puerto Ricans and one young Mexican American when he was eleven years old. From 1959 to 1968, the Young Lords provided young Latinos in Chicago with a sense of pride and a measure of safety from assaults by violent white gangs and by the police. Jiménez, who described himself as having had a taste for nonviolent crime that was "like an addiction," was in jail for selling drugs in April 1968 when Reverend Dr. Martin Luther King, Jr., was assassinated. Thrown into solitary confinement for sixty days by guards who were afraid of a prison riot, Jiménez read King's *Where Do We Go from Here* and *The Autobiography of*

Malcom X. When he was released, Jiménez followed the example of the Black Panthers and started to remake the Young Lords as a political organization. The Young Lords participated in an opposition movement to "urban renewal" policies that drove Black and Latino city residents from their homes. By late 1969, they had also developed Black Panther–like community programs to provide free clothing, food, and health care and had been radicalized by the killing of one of their members by Chicago police.

The work of the Young Lords in Chicago attracted the attention of a group of college students in New York. The group, which included Miguel "Micky" Melendez, a student at the State University of New York at Old Westbury, and the "Black red diaper baby" Denise Oliver, had been meeting to figure out whether they wanted to organize on campuses or among Puerto Ricans in the cities. When they read a profile of Jiménez in the Black Panther Party newspaper, they decided to work in the cities. They called themselves the Sociedad Albizu Campos, named for the Puerto Rican nationalist who had recently died after decades of incarceration in a U.S. federal prison and possible radiation poisoning when he was an unwilling participant in a government medical experiment. (Albizu Campos was also the nationalist leader whose release from prison in 1947 had electrified Helen Rodríguez-Trías when she was a university student.) Members of the Sociedad Albizu Campus drove to Chicago and asked Jiménez to tell them more about the Young Lords and to grant his blessing for them to use the name for their project in New York. Jiménez told them about another germinating New York Young Lords chapter on Manhattan's Lower East Side. The Sociedad Albizu Campos combined with that group and others in East Harlem to create the New York Young Lords. Juan González, who had been expelled from Columbia University for participating in the 1968 student strike that shut the campus for a week, and Iris Morales, recently a student at the City College of New York and already a community organizer, were among those who joined within a few months of its founding.

The first major action by the New York Young Lords was a protest to get the city to clean up garbage on the streets in Puerto Rican neighborhoods. As Micky Melendez remembered, "No one in El Barrio [the heavily Puerto Rican neighborhood also known as East Harlem] seemed to know that just a few weeks before, we had announced the establishment of a branch of the young Lords in New York." So he and the other leaders decided to take on one of the neighborhood's most visible problems: dirty, smelly trash. "Marx, Lenin, Mao, Che, Albizu, Uncle Ho [Chi Minh] [African independence leader Amílcar Lopes] Cabral—none of them ever spoke of garbage," Melendez reflected. "But they all did, nevertheless, speak about 'the legitimate needs and aspirations of the people,'" one of which, in this instance, was for effective sanitation services.

The same desire to be relevant to their communities and speak to people's "legitimate needs" drove the Young Lords to focus on health care and ultimately to pursue a major campaign at Lincoln Hospital. With Afeni Shakur and the other Black Panther leaders busy fighting their arrests, the Young Lords became the leading radical organization in New York City naming, claiming, and ultimately seizing health-care rights.

The Young Lords protests at Lincoln Hospital were part of a wave of in-the-streets actions for what organizers in the late 1960s called community control, and which ended up laying the groundwork for a new politics of health. Participants in these actions were people who sympathized with the Black Panthers and Young Lords and were members of Black, Puerto Rican, and other neighborhood groups that were a little less militant than the Panthers and the Lords. The demand for community control was similar to what feminists like Ellen Willis and Betty Friedan demanded when they said that women were the "true experts" on abortion, the ones who should get to make decisions about policies that had a profound impact on their lives. Black and Puerto Rican New Yorkers, simultaneously with activists in other cities, declared that they should get to say what kinds of public services would be available to their families and in their neighborhoods, that they should direct the institutions that mattered in their lives.

The great flash-point struggle over community control came in a single school district in Brooklyn, the Ocean Hill–Brownsville district, starting in 1968. It became an inescapable topic of political discussion, and not just in New York. After decades of failing to integrate the schools, the city administration greenlit an experiment that gave Black and Latino parents in Ocean Hill–Brownsville control over hiring and firing in the neighborhood schools. The parent leadership forced nineteen unionized teachers out of the district. The United Federation of Teachers union responded with three successive citywide strikes. Charges of antisemitism toward the would-be community controllers and racism toward white (largely Eastern European Jewish) teachers abounded in public debate over the strikes. A resolution of sorts to the conflict came with the creation in 1969 of a new system of community school boards. This protracted struggle over schools publicized community control as a concept, a controversy, and a cri de coeur. From fighting for community control of public schools, it was a short leap to fighting for it in public hospitals that could have an even more immediate impact on people's lives.

After years of complaints from the staff of Lincoln Hospitals and members of its surrounding community, and inaction from the city administration, politics became heated while conflict in the Ocean Hill–Brownsville district was still smoldering. Early in 1969, a group of community mental health workers demanded the ouster of two psychiatrists at Lincoln. They called for reforms that would make the hospital more responsive to its patients. The administration fired four of the employees.

This set off a wave of activism that barely paused through the end of the following year. On March 3, 1969, over one hundred members of the hospital's mental health staff, all nonprofessionals, staged an occupation. They held the offices of their division of the hospital and kept its top administrators out. For three days, these mostly Black and

Puerto Rican workers ran the mental health clinic in conjunction with white professional allies. They demanded that the hospital's top brass find new money to sustain all the community-based mental health storefronts they had opened with the help of federal antipoverty dollars, operating on the theory that poverty itself was at least partly responsible for what was understood as mental illness. The clinics had lost their federal funding and were now threatened with closure. The protesters also demanded that nonprofessional or paraprofessional positions come with more opportunities for advancement. The Black Panthers helped them maintain their sit-in, providing security for the activists, making sure they had food, and organizing rallies with large crowds from the neighborhood. The action ended only when the top officials at Albert Einstein College of Medicine, with the political leadership of New York City acquiescing in the background, said that they would try to yank the professional licenses of psychologists, nurses, and psychiatrists who were working in the nonprofessionally led clinic. Twenty-three activists were arrested.

The last major factor that shaped politics at Lincoln Hospital, and ultimately shaped the perspective of Dr. Helen Rodríguez-Trías, was a wave of organizing by hospital employees. All the city's hospitals, public and private, employed Black people, Puerto Ricans, and new immigrants to do the large amount of nonprofessional labor they required. They underpaid these workers to the point that many needed welfare aid to pay their families' bills. In response, hospital workers organized a trade union to represent their interests: Local 1199, eventually part of the Service Employees International Union, started organizing "nurse's aides, orderlies, porters, cooks, elevator operators, and laundresses," a workforce the majority of which was women of color, in the city's private hospitals. After two strikes, in 1959 and 1962, the hospital employees won better wages, overtime, and the eight-hour day.

The union was slower to reach the employees of public hospitals than those at private hospitals because of a state law forbidding unionization among public-sector workers. After that law changed in 1967, an 1199 organizer arrived at Lincoln. The nonprofessional employees wanted union representation, but they also wanted the union to fight the war in Vietnam. Some insisted that the union endorse their perspective that, as Lincoln employee Cleo Silvers put it, "social and economic conditions were determinants" of patients' health.

In fall 1969, hospital workers in concert with the Black Panthers and Young Lords started to organize outside the union confines. They called themselves the Health Revolutionary Unity Movement, after militant Black workers in the auto industry who called themselves the Dodge Revolutionary Union Movement. They offered a class- and race-based analysis of health-care inequality. And they demanded simultaneous improvements in working conditions and in the care patients received. Although distinct from the union and the Panthers and the Lords, the Health Revolutionary Unity Movement was not entirely separate from them; its members pushed their trade union to the left, and they helped keep the Panthers and Lords focused on health care. By the middle of 1970, the head of the movement city-wide was Cleo Silvers from the Lincoln mental health services staff.

The Young Lords did not start out thinking that their mission was to change Lincoln Hospital or the circumstances of Puerto Ricans in the South Bronx. Their first goal was to serve El Barrio in Harlem and improve *its* terrible public health-care institution, Metropolitan Hospital. The Lords started to get involved when a supporter of theirs, a "brother off the block" they called Mingo El Loco, died when an ambulance from Metropolitan Hospital failed to pick him up in the hour after he was stabbed. They complained bitterly about the "butcher health care" that was routine in Puerto Rican communities. As an alternative to what they called "health oppression," they proposed a focus on prevention and neighborhood-based care via "mass health programs," like testing for lead poisoning and lead paint abatement in the old buildings that abounded in El Barrio. They attacked high salaries for M.D.s and "health empires," like New York Medical School, with its control over Metropolitan, and the Albert Einstein College of Medicine complex, which included both Lincoln and the Jacobi Medical Center. The affiliation arrangements between private medical schools and public hospitals ended up, they claimed, helping the former more than the latter. "The priorities for the medical schools are training and research. The needs of the people are for mass, quality free health care. The two are often antagonistic in our society."

A ten-point health program the Lords published in January 1970 demanded community control at Metropolitan Hospital. Major decisions, they insisted, should be in the hands of a community-staff governing board. Like the agenda of the Health Revolutionary Unity Movement, their agenda covered both employees and patients. They insisted that the hospital stop charging fees, provide "door-to-door preventive health services," and privilege local people in hiring.

The Young Lords didn't just analyze the health-care system. Like the Black Panther Party, they took action rather than waiting for authorities to care for their communities. Having concluded, for example, that locally based preventive care could make Puerto Rican New Yorkers healthier than an underresourced, research-oriented hospital could, they set out to provide preventive health services—combined with political education and recruitment to their revolutionary cause. In El Barrio, they started with a campaign against childhood lead poisoning after a two-year-old boy named Gregory Franklin died of it at Metropolitan Hospital. They organized a sit-in at the city deputy health commissioner's office and demanded more testing for excessive levels of lead in children's blood. Twenty-four hours later, the Lords and a flock of volunteers went from door to door with testing kits provided by the city government. This practice grew into a routinized system in which Young Lords, nonprofessional health workers from the Health Revolutionary Unity Movement, and medical professionals fanned out in teams on the weekends to screen for lead levels, as well as for tuberculosis and other medical conditions. They also let people know about services for which they qualified, including care at Metropolitan.

The Young Lords expanded their reach beyond El Barrio by opening an office in the South Bronx in April 1970. They sponsored the same kinds of door-to-door preventive health-care visits that had become routine in East Harlem. They began to focus even more on testing for tuberculosis than on testing for lead poisoning. Over three months in East Harlem and one in the South Bronx, they administered eight hundred TB tests. They used tuberculosis as a symbol of the need for a non-capitalist, non-racist medical system. It was, Young Lords Minister of Health Carl Pastor argued, "a disease of oppression, just like lead poisoning, anemia, malnutrition. It comes from being so oppressed by the man that we cannot get jobs that pay enough, houses that shelter us right, or hospitals to care for us: it comes from not being able as a nation, as Borinquenos [Puerto Ricans], to control all these things; it comes from being poor, oppressed, and powerless."

The Young Lords used flamboyant, militant action in their health-care work. To test for TB, they demanded in June 1970 that the New York Tuberculosis Association let them use its truck to survey Black and Puerto Rican neighborhoods. The goal was to serve people the association wasn't reaching in its middle-of-the-weekday rounds. When the association refused, the Young Lords stole the truck, raised the Puerto Rican flag over it, and named it the Ramón Betances Health Truck, after the Puerto Rican doctor who led the Grito de Lares, the 1868 rebellion against Spanish colonial rule on the island. The action ended with the city administration agreeing to pay for the Young Lords to continue operating their Health Truck every day of the week, for twelve hours a day.

The wave of health-care activism in New York City's public hospitals crested in July 1970, when the Young Lords occupied a portion of Lincoln Hospital. This takeover was different from the work they did at Metropolitan Hospital and from the protests by mental health and other nonprofessional employees. The Lincoln takeover had more broad-based support inside the hospital and in the neighborhood than the earlier protests, and it had bigger, more encompassing demands.

The context for the takeover was fear that the already understaffed hospital would soon face cuts that would make its services for the working-class people of the South Bronx even worse. In response to the threat, the Young Lords and lower-paid hospital employees created a new organization called the Think Lincoln Committee. They insisted that if cuts were needed, Einstein College of Medicine should make them at the better-resourced Jacobi facility and not at Lincoln, which already had the second-busiest emergency department in the United States—a department that would only get busier if, as anticipated, Einstein's administration closed the hospital's testing unit on the weekends, and people who required medical tests had to wait for the emergency room staff to do them. The group reached out to patients and employees to join their movement to transform the "butcher shop" into a "hospital to serve the people."

Without asking anyone for permission, the Think Lincoln Committee established a complaint table in the emergency room. Volunteers provided a kind of casework service or lay advocacy, helping patients get what they needed and voice their concerns to hospital higher-ups. As reported in the Young Lords newspaper, the complaints included "only one doctor available to deal with 70-80 patients, unsanitary health conditions," and hours-long waits in the emergency room. Based on what they heard at the table, and what they feared administrators at Einstein College of Medicine might do, leaders of the Think Lincoln Committee issued five demands: more-caring medical treatment for all patients, the provision of food for those waiting in the emergency room, a new hospital building, no cuts, and community control in the form of "a community-worker board which has control over the policies and practices of the hospital."

In addition to the Think Lincoln Committee, another group in the hospital that helped enable the Young Lords takeover was the Lincoln Collective. The Lincoln Collective was largely the brainchild of Dr. Fitzhugh Mullan, the member of the Medical Committee for Human Rights who had also been an individual plaintiff in the *Abramowicz* case. Mullan, who was a progressive medical student before he became a leading progressive physician, started his residency at Jacobi hospital in the North Bronx. He remembered that his "honeymoon with municipal medicine, the happy system of socialized health care I expected to find when I came to New York," ended shortly after he started working at the hospital. "Care at Jacobi was woefully impersonal."

Mullan and some of his colleagues started to develop the same critique of the public hospital–medical school affiliation system that the Young Lords and radical health-care workers developed. They criticized the Einstein medical school in particular for its two-hospital health empire in the Bronx. Why, they wondered, was there no sustained community involvement in decision-making around health care? Why was a medical school devoted to research and teaching allowed to control a hospital whose ostensible purpose was serving patients? Mullan organized successfully with community members to fight an increase in fees for Jacobi's patients. Then, he started imagining something more ambitious: going beyond protest to experiment with the kind of medicine he and other idealistic young doctors really wanted to practice.

The Lincoln Collective was a self-selected group of medical residents, recently minted M.D.s, who wanted to transform conventional medicine from the ground up. Mullan remembered that it was easy for them to imagine Lincoln Hospital as the place to start building something new. "We all knew Lincoln Hospital," he wrote, "a small, ancient, dilapidated city hospital in the South Bronx, serving one of New York's most oppressed neighborhoods. It was a poor-sister affiliate of the Einstein College of Medicine," and all the residents based at Jacobi had regular rotations as well at Lincoln Hospital. The Lincoln pediatrics department became the experiment's headquarters—because Mullan's specialty was pediatrics, and because the chair of the department, a Belgian Jewish immigrant to the United States named Dr. Arnold Einhorn, gave the project a green light he later regretted. Dr. Einhorn appears to have misunderstood the commitment to community control of the doctors who would soon be working under his supervision; he was accustomed to being accountable only to the pediatrics chair at Einstein medical school, and to running his department with what Mullan described as "an authoritarian hand." Dr. Einhorn was in no way ready for what was about to happen in his department or his hospital after the new, politically minded recruits arrived at the start of July 1970.

The Young Lords takeover started a little after five in the morning of July 14. One hundred and fifty people forced their way into Lincoln Hospital and assumed its administration for "the people." Although the success of their operation depended in part on support from doctors in the Lincoln Collective and the lower-paid staff and community members of the Think Lincoln Committee, the Lords kept their plan for occupying the hospital secret from those allies. To avoid any tip-offs about their plans to the police, the planners even kept their intentions secret from rank-and-file members of their own organization. Young Lord Carlos "Carlito" Rivera remembered that he and almost all the others who had gathered the night before the takeover "thought we were going to a party." Instead, they found out that they would be part of a large-scale illegal action to occupy a city-owned medical complex.

Each person received a specific assignment. After a mostly sleepless night, they stuffed themselves into what Rivera called a "giant-ass rented U-Haul truck" and pulled up to the hospital's loading dock. Within ten minutes of arrival they had barricaded themselves in and secured the doors. Cleo Silvers, who had left the staff of the Lincoln mental health service and become a Young Lord, had the job of asking top administrators to leave the building—a request that was backed up by the baseball bats and nunchuks several Lords brought for the occupation. The Lords unfurled a Puerto Rican flag on the roof and banners from upper-floor windows that read, "Welcome to the People's Hospital" or "Bienvenidos al Hospital del Pueblo." When the commotion woke him up in a side room of the hospital, Dr. Marty Stein, a Lincoln Collective member and third-year resident, turned to his friend Fitzhugh Mullan and said: "Wake up! The revolution is here."

During the occupation, the Young Lords reiterated their analysis of what was wrong with Lincoln Hospital and with the U.S. health-care system more generally. Gloria Cruz, the Lords' health lieutenant, described the hospital as a "butcher shop that kills patients and frustrates workers from serving these patients," a facility so bad that even an unequal, capitalist health-care system had condemned it decades earlier. They demanded promises from Einstein College of Medicine and the city of New York that there would be no cuts in Lincoln's emergency room or testing services and that there would be "immediate funds" for the promised new building; a "door to door preventive care program emphasizing nutrition, drug addiction, child and senior citizen care"; an official complaint table; a hike in the minimum wage for hospital employees; childcare for the children of patients, workers, and hospital visitors; and "total self-determination of all health services through a community-worker board."

With the building securely in their control, the Young Lords started implementing their own agenda. They turned the auditorium into a space for childcare—one of their most important demands, according to leader Iris Morales. With the help of hospital staff affiliated with the Health Revolutionary Unity Movement, the staff-heavy Think Lincoln Committee, and the doctors' Lincoln Collective, they established a mini-clinic providing preventative screening for anemia, lead poisoning, and tuberculosis. They opened a classroom for anyone who wanted to participate in health and political education, presumably of a revolutionary Marxist variety. Although some professionals and other hospital employees were scared of the (non-lethally) armed occupiers, radical doctors like Mullan were energized and hopeful: Thanks to the Young Lords, he wrote, Lincoln Hospital was no longer a forgotten backwater in the city's health-care system. "The press was listening; the city was listening; and the Lords had risen up and were telling the stories of the women and children waiting endlessly in the clinic, the old folks dying for lack of a Cardiac Care Unit, the humiliation of the Emergency Room, the flies, the pain, the degradation."

The occupation ended with more of a whimper than a bang. The city administration negotiated actively with the Young Lords but refused to make a public pledge to start work on the new hospital. Mayor John V. Lindsay's top advisers tried to get the activists out on the combined strength of a private promise that the city would soon break ground on a new building, and a threat that if they did not leave, the mayor's office would let the police in to bust heads and force them out. The two sides were close to an agreement when the Young Lords identified an undercover police officer trying to enter Lincoln Hospital. Negotiations ended immediately. Terrified of what a mostly white police force would do to them if allowed, the Young Lords slipped quietly out of the hospital in a stream of patients and staff leaving through the one exit not covered by the Police Department. "We walked out in between the police cars," Cleo Silvers remembered, many in doctors' coats and with stethoscopes around their necks, escorted by their radical allies from the Lincoln Collective and Think Lincoln Committee.

Protesters gathered at Lincoln in the name of community control and improved public services. They did not rally under the banner of reproductive rights. However, reproductive health care came to stand at the center of conflicts between the hospital's patients and activists, and the managers at Albert Einstein College of Medicine and in the city administration.

The most notorious source of controversy was a tragedy at Lincoln that happened only a few days after the occupation. Mrs. Carmen Rodríguez (no relation to Helen Rodríguez-Trías), a patient in a Lincoln drug treatment program, was the first to die in New York State from an abortion performed after the decriminalization law took effect. Carmen Rodríguez came to Lincoln for a therapeutic abortion, approved before the state implemented its new law because her doctors believed that continuing the pregnancy to term threatened her life. Nonetheless, coming on the heels of both the Young Lords takeover and the fight to repeal abortion laws, radical health-care activists interpreted her death as a sign that the kinds of reproductive rights that mattered to wealthy white women didn't offer much to the working-class people who used New York City's public hospitals.

Rodríguez did not die because abortion was dangerous in itself. This claim had long served as a rationale for state laws that criminalized abortion, but by the late 1960s that thinking was long out of date. She died, most likely, because she had rheumatic heart disease, which made pregnancy a major health risk for her, and because the hospital was overtaxed and under-resourced. The physician who performed Rodríguez's abortion did not have her chart and was not aware of her condition. This was particularly hard for activists and community members to accept, since she had been treated for heart disease at Lincoln Hospital, and it was a doctor at Lincoln who advised her to end her pregnancy. Moreover, she was a victim of the annual schedule of a teaching hospital, in which a new crop of medical residents arrived each July. Patients who were treated in the first weeks after their arrival sometimes saw the least experienced doctors on the staff. The absence of her chart may have been a mix-up related to the recent arrival of new residents, or related to chaos in the hospital following the occupation. The restrictive state abortion law prior to July 1970 may also have been a culprit here: tight controls had limited the number of abortions and training doctors received in performing them, and the infrequency of therapeutic abortion kept the city's municipal hospitals from developing standard protocols for the procedure.

Whatever the mix of reasons, Carmen Rodríguez's doctor made a big mistake. He chose the saline-infusion method, which was contra-indicated for someone with heart disease. When Rodríguez showed signs of distress, he diagnosed her as having an asthma attack, admin-istered asthma medicine, and continued the saline procedure. She died on July 19.

The Young Lords called Rodríguez's death a "murder." Within months, they would have a more nuanced view of abortion, but in the immediate aftermath of this tragedy, they condemned both the specific circumstances that led to her death and the decriminaliza-tion of abortion itself as signs of a planned "genocide." The Lords' Gloria Cruz argued that what had happened to Rodríguez pointed to the terrors of a whole system of population control that aimed to eliminate Puerto Ricans from the face of the earth. She also took Rodríguez's treatment at Lincoln Hospital as a signal case of poor people's health care under capitalism. She said it pointed to the weak-nesses of an affiliation system that paired medical schools like Einstein with the thousands of people who depended on a municipal hospital like Lincoln. "This death was no accident," she concluded bitterly. "Carmen died because amerikka is killing our people."

The death of Carmen Rodríguez had a huge impact on the conflict at Lincoln Hospital and on the Young Lords. It laid the groundwork for a new approach to reproductive rights and health care that Helen Rodríguez-Trías would later make her own. Coming on the heels of both the statewide campaign for abortion decriminalization and the hospital occupation, Rodríguez's death "just did it," Young Lords member and former hospital employee Gloria González remembered. "The abortion clinic had a reputation of giving totally bad care, malpractice, sterilizing sisters all over the place without letting them know." The death of this abortion patient seemed proof positive of the critique developed by low-paid hospital employees, Black Panthers, progressive doctors, and Young Lords of a separate and unequal system of health-care delivery. It "got people very furious," González wrote, "and the hospital workers and patients started moving."

The Young Lords, with the employees and community members from Think Lincoln, persuaded the top managers of the hospital to convene a kind of people's inquest at which patients and community members tried to hold to account doctors they believed did not care about their lives. "The meeting," wrote doctor-activist Fitzhugh Mullan, "was unique in the annals of American medicine." The groups that provoked this grassroots inquest did not get everything they wanted from Lincoln, Einstein, or the newly organized bureaucracy that managed them, the Health and Hospitals Corporation (HHC) of New York City. However, the hospital's director of obstetrics and gynecology was "fired by the people," in the words of the Young Lords' Pablo (Yoruba) Guzmán, for his role in Rodríguez's death. After a face-saving delay, he was replaced by his superiors at the hospital, too.

The death of Carmen Rodríguez made the Young Lords more sophisticated in their approach to sex, gender, and reproductive rights. Unlike the Black Panther Party, the Lords moved away from their initial position opposing abortion as a form of racial or imperial genocide. They came instead to favor "abortions under community control" and the freedom of all people to choose whether or not to raise children. They arrived at this new understanding at the end of an internal process that had already begun before Rodríguez's death. It was an earnest confrontation with the meaning of women's liberation for Puerto Ricans and the Young Lords, over one-third of whose members were female. Unlike many members of the overwhelmingly white Students for a Democratic Society, which is usually taken as the embodiment of the New Left of the 1960s, the new Puerto Rican left embodied by the Young Lords really wrestled with the problem of sexism.

The women of the Young Lords had been meeting since early in 1970 in a consciousness-raising group they called the women's caucus. They shared perspectives on male dominance in the party and society, and on women's liberation. Caucus member Olguie Robles remembered that they discussed their social conditioning as women, as well as "forced sterilization of Puerto Rican women and women of color in hospitals." They came to understand themselves as "third-class" citizens because they were poor, female, and Puerto Rican. In May 1970, they demanded changes: The Young Lords must remove a reference to "revolutionary *machismo*" from their Thirteen-Point Platform because, as founding caucus member Denise Oliver put it, "*machismo* was never gonna be revolutionary." And men must change alongside the Young Lords women—including by establishing a men's caucus that would help them deconstruct old modes of masculinity and build new ones.

All this internal work, and analyses of Rodríguez's death, produced an expansive and subtle approach to the politics of reproduction. By September 1970, the Young Lords Health Ministry was no longer decrying all abortions as genocidal. Health Ministry members zeroed in on inequality in reproductive health care, including the long waiting list at Lincoln Hospital, which forced patients to have later-term abortions, and the hospital's terrible physical plant, both of which made a relatively simple and now legal procedure unsafe for people in their community.

The party's Central Committee issued a formal paper on women, with a substantial section on birth control, abortion, and the threat of sterilization abuse. Its members, including, thanks to women's caucus demands, the recently elevated Denise Oliver, acknowledged that reproductive issues were part of a "complex situation." They raised the issue of genocide via coerced sterilization or coerced birth control. They also spoke about the lack of reproductive control that came from being deprived access to contraception and safe, affordable abortions. Carmen Rodríguez's death revealed that "butcher shops" like Lincoln nearly erased the positive impact of abortion decriminalization for Black, Latina, and poor white patients. "On the other hand," they argued, "abortions should be legal if they are community controlled, if they are safe, if our people are educated about the risks and if doctors do not sterilize our sisters while performing abortions." And if people were not coerced into choosing abortion or any other reproductive option by their poverty: "We say, change the system so that women can freely be allowed to have as many children as they want without suffering any consequences." As Denise Oliver put it the following year: "We have to have the kind of society where a woman can determine for herself whether or not she wants to have a child—not on the basis of whether that child will eat, because all children will be eating and will be well-clothed and well-educated, but just on the basis of how many children she feels like having at that time."

Dr. Helen Rodríguez-Trías applied to work at the Lincoln "butcher shop" in August 1970, with the controversy over Carmen Rodríguez's death aboil and the Young Lords in the midst of rethinking their gender and reproductive politics. An expert in neonatology credited with cutting infant mortality in half at the University of Puerto Rico medical center in just three years, Rodríguez-Trías directed her application to the Department of Pediatrics. By coincidence, that department headquartered the Lincoln Collective and the largest number of radically minded doctors at Lincoln.

The department head who received Rodríguez-Trías's application was Dr. Arnold Einhorn, who had initially approved the young doctors' experiment. But after the Young Lords seized the hospital and members of the Lincoln Collective seemed to be on their side, he soured on it and them. Einhorn was a distinguished physician and professor who had fled and then fought the Nazis in his youth. Having served at Lincoln Hospital for twelve years, he thought he knew the institution and its patients better than the upstart medical residents did. Einhorn interviewed Dr. Rodríguez-Trías but did not act on her application. She then applied directly to the Einstein College of Medicine, which had the ultimate power over staffing at Lincoln Hospital.

The demand for community control, as it was understood in the Ocean Hill–Brownsville school district and in battles over health-care equity across New York City, left Einhorn cold. He thought the complaint table in the emergency room was "an impertinence." He was alarmed by the Young Lords takeover and did not support the grassroots medical inquest that occurred after Rodríguez's death. On July 20, with conflict at Lincoln at a fever pitch, Einhorn complained that it was "impossible to operate" under the conditions prevailing in the hospital. As the conflicts continued, the residents of the Lincoln Collective and their supervisor grew even further apart from one another; they didn't respect him as much as they used to, and he barely spoke to them. After weeks and then months of this, the doctors working under Einhorn and community members demanded a change in the department's leadership. Finally, in November, the senior faculty in the pediatrics department at Einstein College of Medicine transferred Einhorn to another leadership position in the city's public hospital system and chose Rodríguez-Trías as the new director of pediatrics.

The doctors from the Lincoln Collective weighed in, uninvited, on the hire of their new department chair. They backed Rodríguez-Trías. Dr. Fitzhugh Mullan later insisted that her race and ethnicity were not at the heart of their assessment. They valued Rodríguez-Trías's expertise, her record in Puerto Rico, an understanding of health care that matched their own, and her personal warmth. "It was hard not to be drawn to her," he remembered. "We called her Helen from the outset because she felt like one of us."

Regardless of the reason that Lincoln's doctors preferred Rodríguez-Trías, Einhorn's replacement became major news as an example of precisely the kind of racial politics that many journalists and white readers believed had suffused the crisis in Ocean Hill–Brownsville, tagged as a high point of Black antisemitism. It did not help that a memorandum surfaced shortly after Einhorn's transfer in which Einstein College of Medicine dean Dr. Labe Scheinberg referred to the move as "political" and motivated by "ethnic" concerns. "Pediatrics Chief Out at Lincoln Hospital; Puerto Rican Named," summarized the *New York Times* on its front page. A profile of Einhorn the next day in the newspaper of record began: "Back in 1942, Arnold H. Einhorn, then a 17-year-old member of the French underground, was smuggled across the Pyrenees into Spain. Yesterday, as he prepared to leave his office at Lincoln Hospital, he said, 'I would do it twice again rather than go through what I have gone through here.'" The *Times* offered in an editorial that it was "nonsense" to suppose the quality of medical care a patient received could be linked to the ethnic origins or skin color of that patient's doctor, and indicated that Einhorn was removed "simply because he was not of Puerto Rican origin and would not knuckle under to his revolutionary subordinates." The Jewish Defense League, cofounded in 1968 by the right-wing Orthodox rabbi and later Israeli Knesset member Meir Kahane, plus the American Jewish Committee and other outside groups, got involved in the effort to save Einhorn's job and either demote or fire Rodríguez-Trías. The New York City Human Relations Commission started an investigation of the incident.

The powers at Lincoln Hospital, Einstein College of Medicine, and the New York City public health-care system started to backtrack. They never got Einhorn and the radical young doctors at Lincoln to work together again. However, after negotiating with Einhorn and not with Rodríguez-Trías, they arrived at a settlement that was far more favorable to him than his initial transfer: reinstatement in name only with the title of chair of the Department of Pediatrics, although Rodríguz-Trías as his deputy would be the one actually supervising the department's clinical work. This would be followed two weeks later by a transfer to Jacobi Hospital and, beginning the following summer, a year-long sabbatical in Paris at full pay ($47,000 in 1970 dollars, $337,000 in 2021 dollars).

The *Times* did not acknowledge her expertise, but Helen Rodríguez-Trías was a person with much to contribute to the Department of Pediatrics at Lincoln Hospital. The Lincoln experience also seems to have been a vital one for her. Lincoln Hospital exposed her to arguments about health-care inequity, community-centered care, and the need of Black and brown communities to mobilize on their own behalf. In the specifics of Carmen Rodríguez's death and the Young Lords' rethinking of reproductive politics, she received a crash course in the limits of feminism that focused only on abortion and not also on sterilization abuse, general health-care quality, racism, and a lopsided economic system. All these factors, combined with what she already knew as a Puerto Rican physician who had gained an early education in anti-colonialism and Marxism, led her to an expansive approach to reproductive rights.

For several years before she arrived at Lincoln Hospital, Rodríguez-Trías's anti-establishment bent had been somewhat submerged beneath the surface of her success as a medical professional. She had returned to San Juan from the U.S. mainland in the late 1950s, finished her undergraduate degree, and enrolled in medical school. She became an excellent student and outstanding young doctor, while also parenting four children (the fourth with her second husband). A 1964 *Look* magazine story on Puerto Rico quoted a senior colleague of hers, who called the thirty-five-year-old physician "a very brilliant girl" and "one of our hopes for the future."

Rodríguez-Trías described her medical training as informing her later approach to sexual and reproductive health mostly by negative example. She complained that her medical school in San Juan was "patterned after the most conservative schools in the United States." She described a range of reproductive health situations in which her medical colleagues failed their patients. "A woman with eleven children was denied sterilization by Catholic obstetricians," she remembered. "In another case, a mother of five died because of inadequate anesthesia at a poorly staffed, poorly equipped health center in a small town because the doctors there undertook to do a tubal ligation [sterilization surgery] so that they could practice their skills."

She moved seamlessly from discussing sterilization to discussing abortion: Rodríguez-Trías remembered the hypocritical enforcement of Puerto Rico's criminal abortion statute: "I could not stand the sanctimonious talk of my colleagues about abortion," she commented. "As an intern on the obstetrical service, just after I had my own fourth baby [Daniel], I saw woman after woman come in with bleeding or infection from incomplete abortions."

Rodríguez-Trías became a feminist activist with a distinctive approach to reproductive rights after she left Puerto Rico for the third time. Her first exposure to the women's movement occurred in 1970 at a conference at Barnard College about the New York abortion statute and ongoing decriminalization efforts elsewhere in the country. Although abortion, and not the wider health-care agenda outlined by the Young Lords, was the focus of the conference, Rodríguez-Trías remembered learning about racial and class differences in access to abortion care. She heard about these issues from Chicanas living in the Southwest, and from Black and white women from throughout the United States who highlighted "social inequities reflected in their treatment."

During the same period of her life in which her appointment as a hospital department head inspired citywide controversy, Rodríguez-Trías jumped into the women's movement with both feet when issues of sex-based subordination became personal. Toward the end of 1970, with conflict still roiling at Lincoln and the New York abortion decriminalization in its earliest months of implementation, her oldest daughter, Jo Ellen, came to New York to visit. Rodríguez-Trías was trying to figure out whether to send her son Daniel to San Juan for her ex-husband's impending wedding. "Mom, let me tell you what kind of a father he was," Jo Ellen began. She continued: "He would come into my room and fondle me and my sister until I was 14 and I refused to play dead." Rodríguez-Trías remembered later that she "first dared to speak publicly about the sexual abuse of my girls in a consciousness-raising group of fifteen women. When I finished, there was total silence. No one could deal with what I had said. Then my daughter Laura, sitting next to me, said, 'I want to talk about it, too. This is my mother; I am her daughter.'"

The incest revelation seems to have snapped the last cords connecting Rodríguez-Trías to her conservative medical training. In January 1971, she flew to San Juan to recruit new house staff for the Department of Pediatrics. She arranged to meet all three children from her first marriage and scheduled an appointment with her ex-husband. When she and her daughters arrived, Jo Ellen remembered, "Mom starts screaming at him, saying, 'I know what you did.'" She promised that "all Puerto Rico is going to know." Rodríguez-Trías then removed "her belt and starts whacking him across the face." Jo Ellen herself bit her stepfather to get him to release his grip on her mother. He jumped out of his office window to escape them. "I last saw him," Rodríguez-Trías recalled, "cowed and shaken, sitting on a grassy knoll ten feet from the window, a small crowd gathering. The man who had terrorized my children had become a nothing." Three days later, the women (but not their brother David, who had been nearby but not an active participant in the confrontation) were arrested at the airport on their way home and charged with attempted murder. Rodríguez-Trías's ex-husband eventually dropped the charges.

Back at Lincoln Hospital, Rodríguez-Trías and the doctors in her department worked to practice the kind of community-based care the Young Lords and their allies had demanded. Without naming it, they also started to participate in the women's health movement. She remembered that shortly after beginning her tenure at Lincoln, a "young woman doctor, training to become a pediatrician in the department of pediatrics I had just begun directing, gave me a copy of a book, by women and about women, printed on newspaper stock and cheaply bound. I was 41, working to heal from the traumatic last few years of a disastrous marriage. Recently arrived from Puerto Rico, I was also struggling to find my identity as a Puerto Rican professional and a single mother in New York City." When she read *Women and Their Bodies*, the groundbreaking feminist pamphlet that the Boston Women's Health Book Collective later expanded to create the bible of the women's health movement, *Our Bodies, Ourselves*, she "felt a surge of joy." As she and the politicized, committed physicians in training of the Lincoln Collective lurched forward in trying to create a new kind of hospital practice, "copies of the various editions of *Our Bodies, Ourselves* were dog eared and worn. Their contents were used for classes, discussions and teaching materials for community groups."

After Dr. Einhorn left Lincoln Hospital, Rodríguez-Trías and the physicians she supervised tried to prove that they could practice medicine in a way that their traditional colleagues couldn't or weren't willing to do. Fitzhugh Mullan described Einhorn's departure as a "paradoxical event," since the progressive doctors no longer had the luxury of merely criticizing a top-down medical regime. It was their responsibility to become partners with their chosen department head in delivering care—in a hospital that was still under-resourced and a building that was still condemned. Mullan found it difficult to meet the challenges that activists from the Health Revolutionary Unity Movement continued to pose to the way things worked at Lincoln Hospital; it was hard be a revolutionary while practicing medicine at Lincoln day-to-day. Rodríguez-Trías felt similarly about the demands that doctors in her department continued to make. She shared their political orientation and the goal of community-centered care, but she was a hospital administrator and supervisor with responsibility for delivering care in the here and now. While they did not always agree, the doctors who worked under her leadership continued to respect her and to appreciate her willingness to listen to all the groups that had a stake in Lincoln Hospital.

Thanks to the Young Lords, the organized doctors, the citywide health rights movement, the mobilization by lower-paid employees at the public hospitals, the engagement of community members who cared about those hospitals, and the work of leaders like Dr. Rodrí-guez-Trías, there was progress at Lincoln. In 1971, the pediatrics department became the administrative sponsor of a program called the Community Medical Corps, which institutionalized the neighbor-hood health screenings the Young Lords had initiated. With funds from New York City, the program hired eight community members to travel from door to door, testing people in the South Bronx for lead poisoning, tuberculosis, and other common diseases. The program continued to receive support from the city administration through 1973. The city broke ground for a new Lincoln Hospital building in August 1970—thanks, according to Young Lords member Juan González, to the occupation and the protests that followed the death of Carmen Rodríguez.

The new, seven-hundred-bed hospital rose slowly and behind schedule. When it finally opened in March 1976, it was still not a real match for the health needs of the neighborhood. But it was a genuine improvement.

Chapter Eight

To the Supreme Court

O N DECEMBER 13, 1971, the Supreme Court of the United
States heard oral arguments in the case *Roe v. Wade* and began
to consider whether state laws criminalizing abortion violated the Constitution. Justice Harry Blackmun quietly scribbled notes,
a near-constant habit, as the attorneys began their presentations. At
10:08 a.m., Sarah Weddington, four years out of the University of
Texas at Austin law school, stood to make her case against her state's
anti-abortion law. Blackmun judged her performance a C+. He also
noted the feminist advocate's "blond hair," and found her "rather
pretty, plump."

Weddington deserved a better grade. But it wasn't her arguments
or her looks that got Justice Blackmun to conclude, with a lopsided
majority of his brethren, that the laws at issue did indeed violate
the Constitution. Thirteen months after Weddington's star turn, the
Supreme Court invalidated the abortion laws of forty-six states and
recognized, incompletely but remarkably, what pregnancy and parenting mean to people who experience them. The historic rulings in this
case and its companion, *Doe v. Bolton*, were products of the work of
the same activist movements that had produced the historic change
in New York's law.

Roe has come to be regarded as a stroke-of-the-pen solution to
the problems generated by the old state abortion laws. However, the

Supreme Court's decision in that case was a product of the grassroots politics that preceded it, and grassroots politics in New York, which produced legislation decriminalizing abortion through twenty-four weeks and problematized the racial and class biases built into health care delivery, were especially significant. Decriminalization in 1970 had quickly made New York the abortion capital of the country, with a rapid expansion in abortion access for locals and for people throughout the United States who had the ability to travel to New York—an object lesson in both the need for abortion services and their relative safety. But activists didn't put away their marching shoes; a raft of immediate blocks to access, obvious inequities between people who could get to New York and those who could not, and the kind of unevenness in care that the Young Lords saw at Lincoln Hospital all helped create an even more passionate movement for abortion rights after New York changed its law than had existed before.

At the same time that it expanded abortion access, victory for decriminalization was, as David Garrow has written, "the single most important pre-1973 abortion-related event because it was New York's legalization that spurred the mobilization of anti-abortion activism." This counter-mobilization destabilized the New York law and came close to undoing it, and inspired forceful moves to block abortion law reforms in every state. An article in *Science News*, which Justice Blackmun kept in his files, argued that one tactic of the anti-abortion movement in New York, a court case that tried to overturn the New York law by claiming that fetuses had constitutional rights, proved "that a definitive ruling from the Supreme Court is necessary."

The change in New York's law shifted hospital and clinic practices. It transformed the Clergy Consultation Service and all other abortion referral networks. It led doctors and lawyers to rethink their stances on abortion and spurred their national organizations to take new policy positions—critically important for Justice Blackmun, who had been a lawyer for the Mayo Clinic, the premier Midwestern medical facility, and was highly attentive to doctors' perspectives.

My mother, Beatrice Kornbluh (then Cogan), in hat, a lawyer at a time when women made up just 4% of the profession, representing a female criminal defendant, 1950s.

Courtesy of the Kornbluh family.

Dr. Helen Rodríguez-Trías, a transformational leader of the reproductive rights movement, as chair of the pediatrics department at Lincoln Hospital in New York's South Bronx neighborhood, early 1970s.

Helen Rodríguez-Trías papers, Archives of the Puerto Rican Diaspora, Center for Puerto Rican Studies, Hunter College, City University of New York.

Karen Stamm, who had a legal abortion as a young woman and was pressured to agree to sterilization, in a photo by Rodríguez-Trías from 1977, when both were leaders of the Committee to End Sterilization Abuse (CESA).

Photo by Helen Rodríguez-Trías. Courtesy of Karen Stamm.

Loretta Ross, radicalized in the 1970s by her experience with a supposedly reliable IUD, became an organizer of women of color in the reproductive rights movement and a founder of the movement for reproductive justice.

Courtesy of Loretta Ross.

Percy Sutton, a reform-minded Democrat from Harlem, who as a member of the New York Assembly in 1965 introduced the chamber's first bill to liberalize the state's abortion laws.

Bettmann Archive, Getty Images.

Writer and activist Betty Friedan (right), who cofounded the National Organization for Women (NOW) as a civil rights organization to create sex equality, with the group's first chair, Kathryn Clarenbach.

Bettmann Archive, Getty Images.

Florynce Kennedy, who joined NOW at the first meeting of its New York chapter and then resigned because she found its members to be "boring and scared." She later became a public speaking partner to *Ms.* magazine founder Gloria Steinem.

Photo by Ray Bald. Courtesy of Gloria Steinem Foundation.

Reverend Howard Moody, who with Arlene Carmen, the administrator at Judson Memorial Church, headed the largest abortion referral service in the U.S., the Clergy Consultation Service on Abortion. After New York's law changed, the clergy service founded the nation's first free-standing abortion clinic.

Photo by Deborah Feingold, Corbis Premium Historical, Getty Images.

November 24, 1968

Honorable Franz Leichter

Dear Franz:
Enclosed is an abortion repeal law in the form which I understand
is followed in the House and Senate. You will note that there
are some sections referred to in other than the Penal Code.
Sec. 673 of the County Law, 1.(d) gives coroners or medical
examiners jurisdiction and authority to investigate the
deaths of persons ... which it appears to be (D) A death caused
by suspected criminal abortion. Section 6514(e) of the Education
Law provides for the revocation of certificates or annulments of
registrations if it is found "(e) That a physician, osteopath or
physiotherapist did undertake or engage in any manner or by any
ways or means whatsoever to perform any criminal abortion or to
procure the performance of the same by another or to violate Section
1142 of the penal law, or did give information as to where or by whom
such a criminal abortion might be performed or procured. "
619c.2(a),(b) and (c) of the Code of Criminal Procedure provide
for the conferring of immunity for offenses defined as
abortions (see the statute for exact language).

Ruth Cusick told me that you were concerned about outright
repeal of those Penal Code provisions referring to fetuses
of more than 24 weeks. She was on her way out of town, so our
talk was so hurried that I am not certain that I learned from
her just what problems you wished obviated. She said that
you had mentioned perhaps requiring certification by 2
physicians. But wouldn't such certification just result in
retaining 2 problems (1) Al Blumenthal's legislation is attacked
on the ground that since Al recognizes a distinction based on
the length of pregnancy, Al is thereby conceding the Catholic
viewpoint that abortion of any fetus is murder. We believe
that there are certain Catholics we will never persuade, but
that there are many to whom repeal of criminal penalties will
appeal whereas "reform" will not (2) Al has pointed out that
because hospitals do not wish to appear to be abortion "mills,"
hospital boards will not permit more than a self-imposed quota
number of abortions which are not illegal even under current
law. Thus, if the legislation you seem to have in mind would
be passed, the effect would be that doctors would be unwilling
to certify. The result is that many problems we wish remedied
will continue.

Please give us the opportunity to discuss with you again any
hesitancies you are having. We believe that only outright repeal
of the penal sections is the only course to follow.

                                        Sincerely,

800 West End Ave,
    apt 8B
NY 10025

                                        Mrs. David (Beatrice) Kornbluh

My mother's letter to the Democratic nominee for Assembly from her district, in which
she outlined what would soon become the first bill for a full repeal of all abortion
restrictions introduced into a legislative body in the United States and argued against
the nominee's effort to retreat from a full repeal to a twenty-four-week limit on access.

Beatrice K. Braun papers. Courtesy of the Kornbluh family.

Assemblyman Franz Leichter, Democrat from the Upper West Side of Manhattan, the object of my mother's lobbying and his party's lead sponsor of legislation to repeal all abortion restrictions.

Courtesy of Franz Leichter.

Assemblywoman Constance Cook, a Republican representing upstate New York and Vice President of the state chapter of NOW, who led the effort within the legislature to repeal or significantly reform the abortion laws.

Photo by Don Hogan Charles, the *New York Times*.

A meeting of the Governor's Commission to Review New York State's Abortion Law, with Governor Nelson Rockefeller, Dr. Alan Guttmacher of Planned Parenthood, and others. Note the gender composition of the group.

Bettmann Archive, Getty Images.

Thanks in part to the legislation my mother drafted, activists began to embrace full repeal of all abortion restrictions as their central demand—as in this 1969 protest in lower Manhattan.

Photo by Fred W. McDarrah. MUUS Collection, Getty Images.

The collaboration to defend Black activist H. Rap Brown, between radical lawyer William Kunstler and Florynce Kennedy, 1 of the 5 attorneys who worked on the landmark *Abramowicz* case, is one example of the ways in which other kinds of activist litigation set the stage for feminist legal work on abortion.

Photo by Fred W. McDarrah. MUUS Collection, Getty Images.

Nancy Stearns, lead attorney in the *Abramowicz* case, had a background in civil rights activism and was a staff lawyer at the progressive Center for Constitutional Rights at the time she conceptualized the litigation. Here, she is honored as Alumna of the Year by NYU Law School's Law Women Alumnae Association, 2019.

Photo by Brooke Slezak. Courtesy of NYU Law School Alumnae/i Association.

Regarding the mass abortion protest on March 28, 1970, Diane Schulder and Florynce Kennedy wrote that it marked "the first time in many decades that New York had seen masses of women in the streets on women's issues." Eleven days later, the New York State Assembly approved a modified repeal bill, assuring its victory.

Photo by Graphic House. Hulton Archive, Getty Images.

Assemblyman George Michaels switched from "no" to "yes," assuring the needed vote for New York's historic abortion bill three years before *Roe v. Wade*. "If I am going to have any peace in my family," he said, suspecting (correctly) that he would lose his seat because of his choice, "I cannot go back to them on Passover and say my vote defeated this bill."

Bettmann Archive, Getty Images.

The Young Lords Party, a militant Puerto Rican group inspired by the Black Panther Party, issued this platform before its members occupied part of Lincoln Hospital. Note the commitment to "revolutionary *machismo*" in Point #10, language members later changed under pressure from the Lords' women's caucus.

Richie Pérez Papers, Archives of the Puerto Rican Diaspora, Center for Puerto Rican Studies, Hunter College, City University of New York.

Gloria Cruz, Health Lieutenant of the Young Lords Party, and a man identified only as "Jack," speak to reporters about the takeover of Lincoln Hospital on July 14, 1970.

Bettmann Archive, Getty Images.

Denise Oliver, a "Black red diaper baby" who helped lead the women's caucus of the Young Lords and insisted that "*machismo* was never gonna be revolutionary."

Photo by Bev Grant, December, 1969.

Young Lords, including Denise Oliver, carry the Puerto Rican flag in a demonstration against the police killing of Black Panther Party leader Fred Hampton.

Photo by Bev Grant, December, 1969.

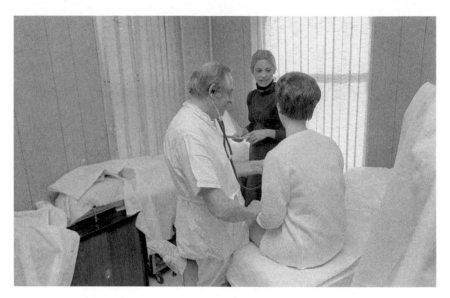

An abortion patient in January 1971, with a doctor and nurse or aide in "mod" clothing. The location was a private clinic that served some of the thousands who sought safe, legal abortions after New York State implemented its new law.

Bettmann Archive, Getty Images.

Demonstrators sit under a tree while participating in the Women's Strike for Equality, August 26, 1970. The strike had three main demands: free childcare, available twenty-four hours a day; sexual equality in employment and education; and free abortions "on demand."

Photo by Walter Leporati, Getty Images.

Supreme Court Justice Harry Blackmun, author of the majority opinion in
Roe v. Wade. Grassroots action that changed state laws, shifted the policies of
professional societies, and generated new research shaped Blackmun's thinking
and writing.

Bettmann Archive, Getty Images.

Helen Rodríguez-Trías with members of CESA, the first organization in U.S.
history dedicated to ending forced or coercive sterilization. Front row, from
left, Rodríguez-Trías, Netsy Firestein, RuthAnne Evanoff; second row, Roz
Everdell, Dale Stark, and Susan E. Davis.

Photo by Carol Marsh. Courtesy of Karen Stamm.

AGAINST STERILIZATION ABUSE

Regulations created during the last three years to control an epidemic of sterilization abuse affecting millions of Puerto Rican, Black, Mexican, Native American and poor white women are being challenged in Federal Court on Constitutional grounds by six New York City physicians and two unidentified patients.

The Plaintiffs are requesting permanent injunctions against the enforcement of certain provisions in New York City Health and Hospitals Corporation (NYCHHC), New York State, and Federal Department of Health, Education and Welfare (HEW), guidelines for elective female sterilization. They allege that the guidelines are "unlawful, unauthorized, and/or unconstitutional," and are "in violation of their First, Fifth, and Fourteenth Amendment rights of privacy, liberty, and property."

Regulations in Question

The HEW guidelines were drafted in 1974 after the Supreme Court case *Relf vs. Weinberger* exposed the forced sterilization of two young Black girls alleged to be "mentally retarded" by an Alabama social worker. These guidelines set minimum standards to be followed in any sterilization paid for with funds from the federal government, and contained a provision that a state or locality could amend them to increase protection, but could not go below those minimum standards.

New York State guidelines basically follow the HEW minimum standards. However, NYCHHC guidelines, which apply to all municipal hospitals, offer more protection than any regulations existing in the United States.

What is at Stake

The suit is attacking the prohibition by all three guidelines of the sterilization of persons under 21 years of age, and the "restrictive" definition of voluntary sterilization. It challenges the 72-hour wait between consent and sterilization by federal and state regulations, and the 30-day waiting period of the NYCHHC guidelines.

The suit focuses particularly on the NYCHHC guidelines. For instance, it sustains that the doctors' right to free speech is violated when he or she must discuss sterilization only in conjunction with alternative methods of birth control. It also contests the prohibition against obtaining consent at the time of hospitalization for childbirth or abortion or other medical treatment.

Puerto Rico—Case in Point

In 1973 the government of Puerto Rico printed a document titled "Opportunities of Employment, Education and Training" which correlated unemployment and overpopulation," and offered sterilization as a solution.

The sterilization program—until then run by private monies which were donated by rich U.S. industrialists, as well as funds from HEW—was turned over to the Puerto Rican government in 1974. Seventeen new clinics were opened, solely to sterilize.

...y has the highest rate of sterilizations ...three Puerto Rican women between ...ave been sterilized. Last year, the ...m performed more than 6,000

...ued by CESA to all individuals who ...potential victims should the guide-...to contact CESA as soon as possible. ...equests organizations and interested ...nicus briefs.

...ke our fight to the Supreme Court if ...rastia. "A unique opportunity has ... In the process of defending these ...be able to improve them and obtain ...n a federal level.

...now! It is no accident that Martin ...ntiffs, is on the Board of Directors of ...And whatever happens in court will ...ntire U.S. and Puerto Rico as well." ...acted by writing P.O. Box A-244, ...N.Y. 10003. V.W.

Rise in sterilization of PR women in NY

By Maritza Arrastía
CLARIDAD Staff

NEW YORK—An estimated 60 per cent of all sterilizations at Metropolitan Hospital in El Barrio, are being performed on Puerto Rican women, according to information recently received by CLARIDAD.

Preliminary studies underway by CLARIDAD's sources seem to indicate this is an alarming rise from figures in previous years and that the same trend is occurring in other city hospitals.

The alarmingly high rate is not proportionate to the population distribution in the area serviced by the hospital, which, as of the 1970 census was approximately 40 per cent Puerto Rican.

CLARIDAD's figures on Metropolitan Hospital come from a statistical breakdown of 200 sterilization requests there. Of these requests 133 were made by Puerto Rican women. One hundred and twenty five of these women were between the ages of 25 and 35.

Added to the figures for sterilization in Puerto Rico the numbers reach what the Puerto Rican Socialist Party has repeatedly called genocidal proportions.

Sterilization, which is an irreversible operation and involves complete impairment of a major bodily function, is the primary method of population control in effect in Puerto Rico.

While in 1939 seven per cent of the women in Puerto Rico were sterilized, at present 35 per cent of all women of child-bearing age have been surgically made sterile.

It was recently reported in CLARIDAD's Puerto Rico issue that the colonial government plans to reduce the Puerto Rican population by one million by 1985. This information is revealed in a report entitled Opportunities for Employment, Education and Training, prepared by members of the colonial cabinet.

As part of the recent escalation in government programmed "population control," 19 free sterilization clinics have been operating in Puerto Rico since last February, according to Dr. Antonio Silva—Puerto Rico's assistant secretary of health for family planning—as quoted in a New York Times interview published November 4th.

Silva said these centers are performing 1,000 sterilizations a month.

Thirty four years of contact with sterilization as the major means of population control, along with total lack of information as to its irreversibility, lack of contraception alternatives, and the socio-economic reality –unemployment, extreme poverty– which makes the prospect of child-bearing negative, have led to a cultural acceptance of sterilization as something normal.

This creates the psychological breeding ground that allows for the implementation of the genocidal sterilization program in New York City as well.

The same class that colonizes Puerto Rico controls the public health system here with its characteristic abuse of workers. And the continual back and forth flow of Puerto Ricans between here and the Island guarantees that the propaganda effects of the latest "population control offensive" will show up in statistics of the Puerto Rican population here.

Pressure stops

Sterilization of boricua women on the rise in New York

See page 3

you are holding the 1st issue of CLARIDAD diario

claridad

EL DIARIO DE LOS TRABAJADORES

December 1, 1974

New York, N.Y.

25¢

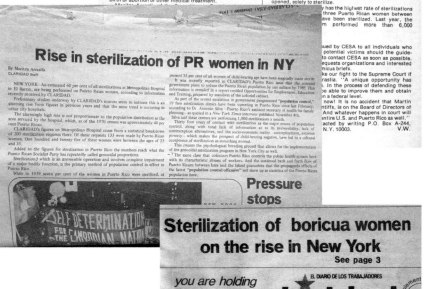

Campaigns against sterilization abuse are among the most forgotten activist efforts for reproductive rights: Above, an informational flyer from CESA, and, below, a front-page headline and article on the issue from the Puerto Rican Socialist Party newspaper, *Claridad*, by early CESA leader Maritza Arrastía.

Images courtesy of Carmen Vivian Rivera, from *Claridad Bilingue* and preserved as part of the Despierte Boricua! Recovering History Project.

Meredith Tax, a leader of the Committee for Abortion Rights and Against Sterilization Abuse (CARASA), who insisted that feminists should fight the Hyde Amendment's restrictions on abortion access by focusing on sterilization abuse and abortion rights at the same time.

Courtesy of Meredith Tax.

Meredith Tax and Ellen Ross flying the CARASA banner at a demonstration in 1978.

Photo by Michael Urquhart. Courtesy of Karen Stamm.

Sarah Schulman, Stephanie Roth, and Karen Zimmerman, all members of CARASA and of a just-created "Zap Action Brigade," insist that "A Woman's Life is a Human Life." Protest at congressional hearings on a Human Life Amendment to the U.S. Constitution, 1982. Mildred Jefferson, in white hat, president of the National Right to Life Committee from 1975–78, sits in front of the demonstrators.

Photo by Joan E. Biren (JEB). Joan E. Biren papers, SSC-MS-00587, Smith College Special Collections.

Graffiti by Wimmin for Womyn, the group Sarah Schulman, Stephanie Roth, Maxine Wolfe, and other lesbians founded after leaving CARASA. They continued to participate in the left-of-center Reproductive Rights National Network until it dissolved in 1984. Beginning later in the 1980s, Schulman and Wolfe were both active in ACT UP New York.

Photo by Maxine Wolfe. Courtesy of Lesbian Herstory Archives.

Most immediately germane to the Supreme Court, the legislative win in New York resolved Nancy Stearns's federal legal challenge in the *Abramowicz* case and the cases joined with it. This enabled litigation from Texas (and Georgia, in *Doe v. Bolton*) to take their place and become the contexts in which the court came to consider pregnancy, birth, and abortion in constitutional terms.

Perhaps befitting the rocky road it had followed to passage, the New York law faced a doubtful future even before the state implemented it on July 1, 1970. The "chaos" and challenges, wrote journalist Lawrence Lader, "began to build from the moment the law was passed." The only requirements of the state law were that abortion procedures be performed in the first twenty-four weeks of a pregnancy and that they be performed by licensed physicians. But there was a gap between the law as written and the law as it was to be practiced, which was filled in by local regulatory agencies and professionals with power to interpret it.

Underlying the controversy were two factors. First was the radicalness of the new law, a product of compromise that failed to satisfy some activists but a true departure from everything that had come before in the nearly century and a half of criminalizing abortions. Second was the fact that roughly 1.2 million courageous and/or desperate people were terminating their pregnancies in the United States each year by the time the New York law changed, although only thirty thousand to forty thousand of them had access to legal procedures. City and state officials, virtually all men who knew little about abortion and, if medically trained, virtually all with a learned antipathy to it, balked when faced with what the law might mean in reality.

The challenges to its implementation had little to do with the text of the law my mother played a role in passing. Abortion law reform advocate Dr. Robert Hall, plaintiff in the most important of the federal court cases from New York aside from *Abramowicz*, argued for a de facto residency requirement, lest the number of procedures overwhelm the capacity of qualified physicians to perform them—and so that a messy rollout of the New York law did not end up ruining the reputation of legal abortion altogether. With the legislation silent on where or how a legal abortion should occur, the state and city health departments accepted abortion on an outpatient basis in the first twelve weeks of a pregnancy. The state government insisted that it should happen in freestanding clinics only if these had hospital affiliations. The city said abortions could occur only on hospital premises. Both recommended in-patient, hospital procedures after twelve weeks. The state medical society circulated official guidance to doctors that classified abortion after twenty weeks as akin to infanticide. Its leaders warned that a procedure performed after twelve weeks was "fraught with tremendous danger," the legislature's intent be damned.

Advocates for wider abortion access couldn't ignore these immediate attempts to narrow the meaning of the law. Rulings of the city health department were binding on public hospitals under the management of the Health and Hospitals Corporation, hospitals like Lincoln in the South Bronx that served people on a sliding-scale-fee basis and were accessible only to residents of New York City. The guidance of the state agency had the power of law unless the assembly and senate passed specific legislation that made their intentions more clear. Insurance companies could use any of these guidelines to deny coverage to doctors or clinics that defied them. A doctor who did not follow the guidance of one or another level of government, or the recommendations of a medical society, could be accused of "malpractice"; if they were sued over a bad outcome, they could potentially lose their license, or a court could impose heavy fines on the clinic or hospital where they worked.

If these kinds of restrictions sound familiar, there is good reason. They are the same kinds of standards some state officials, who wanted to limit the number of abortions or the settings in which they were accessible, continued to create for decades after *Roe v. Wade*. The Supreme Court ruled twice, in 2016 and again in 2020, that for as long as *Roe* was good law, a requirement that all clinic staff have hospital affiliations, at least, was unconstitutional. The fact that these narrowing efforts appeared immediately after the New York law changed is evidence of how hotly contested abortion decriminalization truly was. In fact, all the tribulations of the New York law speak to this point—important reminders that the victories advocates achieved in this one state and then nationally were, among other things, victories over long-standing and hard-to-root-out ideas about sex, procreation, medicine, and women's roles.

Looking only at New York City, early estimates indicated that if all abortions had to be performed in hospitals, many of the people who wanted to terminate their pregnancies would not be able to do so legally. Combining public and private hospitals, there were seventy-nine obstetrics departments in the city. Lawyer Roy Lucas, the lead attorney in the doctors' case that had been combined with *Abramowicz* and an activist in the national repeal movement, estimated a potential need among only the city's own population for seventy-five thousand abortions per year. He thought it would take twenty-five doctors providing abortions more than full-time to meet that need, plus who knew how many hours to serve people from out of state or from other countries. Despite the city health department's guidance, the new idea that emerged in response to this situation was to create freestanding clinics off hospital grounds and outside the hospital system. For people in the first trimester of a pregnancy, these could perform a kind of procedure that was less invasive than the D&C my mother had back in 1964 and would therefore not require a general anesthetic or inpatient recovery.

Numbers alone did not persuade officials who may have been just as happy not to serve hundreds of thousands of people who wanted to end their pregnancies. The leadership of the National Association for the Repeal of Abortion Laws issued "A Radical Plan for Outpatient Clinics to Meet the Abortion Crisis" and agitated for both greater availability than the hospitals could ensure and lower prices.

Assemblyman Franz Leichter, the legislative cosponsor who had been needled by my mother to stay the course for repeal, went on the record to insist that the law had no hospital requirement. Women's liberationists protested hearings to consider the city guidelines, convened shortly after the new law went into effect, with signs claiming they had been "Raped by the Medical Bureaucracy."

When July 1 arrived, the city health department and heads of its public hospital network continued to insist that hospitals could meet the need. In response, the New York City Clergy Consultation Service disbanded. Arlene Carmen and Reverend Howard Moody at Judson Memorial Church replaced the service with an advocacy group for women who wanted to terminate their pregnancies in the city's hospitals, and for alternatives to hospital-based procedures. Carmen, Moody, and their colleagues pressured the city administration by documenting a three-week-long wait at municipal hospitals. They charged the Health and Hospitals Corporation with cruel treatment of abortion patients, for example the practice of having "a woman who was terminating her pregnancy . . . placed in a room with women delivering babies."

The Clergy Consultation Service headquarters at Judson Memorial Church continued to serve as the nerve center for a national referral network. That network changed dramatically as a result of the law change in New York. The clergy began referring virtually all abortion seekers on the East Coast and in the Midwest to New York for safe, legal, procedures. (The same was true of other abortion referral operations. Chicago's Jane service, for example, started sending all its patients with financial means to New York.)

From their redoubt in Greenwich Village, the Jewish church administrator Arlene Carmen and the Baptist minister Howard Moody made one more major contribution to ensure the success of the decriminalization project. They started their own abortion clinic. It was the nation's first freestanding clinic, founded months before Planned Parenthood had opened any, and soon the busiest in New York. Practically minded people, equally committed to meeting the immediate need and to forcing a change in public policy, Carmen, Moody, and other leaders of the clergy service had considered founding a clinic even before the law changed; one idea was to build it on a ship, sail into international waters where state laws did not apply, and operate under the flag of Japan, which had more liberal abortion laws than did any U.S. state. When the law changed, opening a clinic became part of the clergy service's advocacy for accessibility and affordability, which meant providing abortions outside the hospital context to prove this was possible. As Carmen put it: "There was no other organized group that was in a position, based on experience, to say without qualification that first trimester abortions" not only could be safely performed outside of a hospital setting but, under most circumstances, "ought not to be done in a hospital."

The clinic affiliated with the clergy service, known informally as Women's Services and officially as the Center for Reproductive and Sexual Health, became the standard-setter in New York in the early months of legal abortion and to some degree for years to come. Its founders were Barbara Pyle, a graduate student in philosophy at New York University, and Hale Harvey III, M.D., who had been studying for his Ph.D. at Tulane while Pyle worked on her master's degree. Both were interested in the ethics of abortion law and practice. When the law changed in New York, Pyle wrote to Harvey to suggest they start a clinic. Harvey, who had performed illegal abortions in New Orleans for patients referred by the clergy service, contacted his friends at Judson Memorial Church to find out if they would sponsor the venture. For them, "it seemed too good to be true." And so Barbara Pyle set to work with $30,000 of Harvey's money, to locate space and acquire two months' worth of clinic supplies. They were ready to open on July 1.

Women's Services was a success. It had the support of those Carmen called "celebrities," like NOW cofounder Betty Friedan. Soon, it was serving more patients than all of New York City's municipal hospitals combined, thanks to referrals from the far-flung chapters of the clergy service as well as to a new referral service managed by Planned Parenthood. It had a lower complication rate than places like Lincoln Hospital, which, in addition to all the problems cataloged by the Young Lords and other health reformers, did not have the benefit of a medical director who was an experienced provider of abortions—unlike Harvey, who was one of the few who had been willing to break the law in order to perform them.

The clinic offered professional medical procedures, performed by doctors, but was in other ways imbued with the anti-professional spirit of activist efforts like Chicago's Jane and the still-rising women's health movement. Each patient had a counselor dressed in regular clothing, who met with her for an hour and a half to help her understand the process and accompany her during the procedure. While the doctor was operating, the patient's legs would be supported by metal stirrups covered with flowered oven mitts. The patient's body was covered by a sheet, so that she could see the doctor but not the instruments he was using or any blood. The clinic was designed to be a kind of anti-hospital, suggesting through its layout and staffing that, in Arlene Carmen's words, "abortion was not a sickness, pregnancy was not a sickness, that a woman going through that experience doesn't need to be treated like a patient, in the same way that you treat a woman with a very serious illness, that the kind of things that were important were colors, concern, warmth, intimacy." The clergy service set the price, initially at $200 per procedure, the lowest going rate of which its leaders were aware. Within a year, they dropped the price to $125. With the endorsement of the clinic's board, one of every four patients was to pay only $25. Since Women's Services was among the first clinics licensed in New York, and became the busiest and most well known, its rates drove down the price of abortion at every clinic and perhaps even in the hospitals that were helping to meet the need.

The Women's Services clinic had one not-so-small problem. Dr. Harvey neglected to inform his colleagues in the Clergy Consultation Service that Louisiana authorities had yanked his medical license because he was caught performing abortions in violation of state law. He had never been licensed in New York, and so the clinic's medical director was in fact not licensed in any state. The city health department, with which the revamped clergy service had been fighting toe-to-toe over the availability of abortion in freestanding clinics, eventually discovered the lapse. Despite this bad blow to its reputation, leaders of the clergy service and the Judson Memorial Church board continued to support the project. The *New York Times* reported that Harvey "left the clinic and callers were told that he was on an indefinite vacation." Dr. Bernard Nathanson, chair of NARAL's medical committee, succeeded him as the clinic's medical director.

The contested win for legal abortion in New York inspired feminists to put their shoulders to the wheel even more for decriminalization. As advocates and authorities battled over the particulars of implementation, a coalition of women's movement groups with headquarters in New York City organized the national Women's Strike for Equality. The event was scheduled for August 26, 1970, days after the fiftieth anniversary of ratification of the woman suffrage amendment to the U.S. Constitution. The idea for a nationwide action on that day was Betty Friedan's: she issued the call for a twenty-four-hour-long women's "general strike" as she stepped down from the presidency of the National Organization for Women. Friedan reminded feminists of how far they had come since their battle to get the federal government to treat the sex discrimination named in the Civil Rights Act of 1964 seriously, and from NOW members' first demand for abortion law repeal. After a sideswipe at those in the movement who would oppose men, heterosexuality, or parenting, Friedan elegiacally asked women to desist from demeaning or underpaid work for one day and then, "when it begins to get dark, instead of cooking dinner or making love," to "converge the visible power of women at city hall" and recommit to feminist revolution.

Although relatively few actually withdrew their labor for the day, approximately ten thousand people marched in New York City, about fifty thousand total nationwide. Their motives and discontents were diverse. Officially, however, the strike had a platform of only three planks, expressed on a flyer for the largest rally in Manhattan as "FREE 24-hour child care centers—community controlled [as in the demands at Lincoln Hospital] / FREE abortion on demand / EQUAL Opportunities in Jobs and Education." Some strike activists paired the demand for free abortions, which by itself did the demand for repealing legal restrictions one better, with a protest over "forced sterilization"—perhaps an import into the movement from the Young Lords. A remarkably wide range of supporters was able to get behind these demands. The march was endorsed by former New York NOW member Florynce Kennedy; by *Ms.* magazine founder Gloria Steinem and Redstockings cofounder Shulamith Firestone; by Pauli Murray, the legal theorist who laid the groundwork for the women's civil rights movement, and Beulah Sanders, the public assistance client who led the New York City branch of the National Welfare Rights Organization; by Representative Patsy Mink from Hawaii and lawyer Bella Abzug, then making her first run for a seat in Congress; and by "comedienne" Joan Rivers.

At least in New York, the recent abortion law and its troubled implementation was a talking point in favor of the idea that women's revolution had only just begun. One fact sheet that organizers circulated to pump up interest in the strike underlined a gap between "myth and reality" on abortion in New York. Because of the city's requirement that people who received their health care through the public system could access abortions only at hospital-based clinics, the organizers argued, abortions were barely safer or easier to obtain than they had been before the law changed. Egregious waiting lists for care at the public hospitals, which couldn't handle the number of patients who needed their services, forced delays that made abortions more expensive and dangerous than they had to be. The solution to these

troubles? "Public Clinics For: SAFE, FREE, EARLY ABORTIONS"
and "Community-Controlled [Health Care] For: NO FORCED
STERILIZATIONS."

Although hard to quantify, the mass marching, in combination with
pressure from the advocates at Judson Memorial Church, in NARAL,
and in local women's groups, must have made a difference. In September, the city health department officially permitted abortions in
licensed clinics like the one the clergy service had been operating semi-
legally since July—although the city administration recommended
against abortions in doctors' offices like the many that had occurred
safely and illegally for years. The head of the Health and Hospitals
Corporation echoed the organizers of the Women's Strike for Equality
when he decried the hospitals' inadequate response to the influx of
patients. By December 1970, Arlene Carmen and Reverend Howard
Moody observed, "the situation began to look much better." The
combined efforts of city bureaucrats, doctors, and clinic and hospital staffs (including those working at the clergy service's own clinic)
proved that they could provide relatively inexpensive, safe abortions at
scale "with counseling and humane treatment." For Lawrence Lader
at NARAL, the rise of freestanding clinics meant that, by the middle
of 1971, "we had emerged from the crisis." The system was meeting
people's needs and the doomsaying about a potential drop in quality
or rise in terrible complications was disproved. A report in the *New
York Times Magazine* largely concurred: although care was unequal, even
hospital to hospital within the public system, within nine months of
implementation, the hospitals and clinics together had evolved to meet
the needs of local people and those who streamed in from elsewhere
seeking safe, legal abortions.

The data alone revealed a wealth of good news about the status
and future of legal abortion. New York City had the most reliable
statistics, as well as the largest number of abortions by far of any
place in the state. In the first year of the new law, there were slightly

more than 139,000 reported abortions in the city. Over 63 percent of the patients were from out of state. They arrived from every one of the fifty states, and over 3 percent of the nonresidents arrived from other countries—a testament to the need and an oblique way to measure the scale of the problem of unregulated, illegal medical care that prevailed before legal abortion in New York became an option. The numbers charted the increasing importance over time of clinics like Women's Services. In the first six months after July 1, clinics provided abortions for 12 percent of the nonresidents who sought them and for less than 1 percent of the residents. In the six months that followed, as the overall numbers kept climbing, the clinics were serving 51 percent of the nonresidents and 10 percent of the residents.

The law worked! It saved bodies and lives. New York City's practitioners were quickly able to match the safety record of those in Scandinavian countries and England, which had substantially more experience with legal abortions than the United States did. Soon, they even matched the record of Eastern Bloc countries like Hungary and Czechoslovakia, which performed the largest number of legal abortions in the world. New York City experienced what Dr. Alan Guttmacher called an "abrupt improvement" in maternal mortality in the first eight months of 1971. Deaths due to abortion dropped from 1.8 per 10,000 in the year before the law changed to 0.6 per 10,000 in the year after. Guttmacher was especially impressed with the drop in mortality for women who had live births; he hypothesized that it was due in part to the availability of abortions for younger teenagers and older women, for both of whom childbirth was more risky than it was for people in the middle age range. Women's Services, the clinic activist clergy built, was found in an independent evaluation to have a complication rate slightly higher than that in Czechoslovakia and roughly half that in Hungary.

The effects of the new law were far-reaching. The rate of infant mortality in New York City fell from 24.4 per 1,000 live births in 1969 to 20.7 in 1971, likely because people in the first or second trimester of risky pregnancies were able to terminate those pregnancies. The number admitted to city hospitals with "incomplete" abortions (i.e., with infections and other complications from unsafe or incompetently performed procedures) dropped by half in 1970 alone. At a time when childbearing outside marriage was profoundly stigmatized and could wreck educational or vocational aspirations, out-of-wedlock births declined in 1971 after fifteen years of increase.

Although still subject to unequal medical treatment, low-income people, Puerto Ricans and other Latinas, Black women, and poor whites, for whom legal abortion was a near impossibility when it required proof of psychological distress and approval by a hospital committee, were finally being served. In the first nine months of the new law, almost a third of pregnancy terminations in New York City were reimbursable under the Medicaid insurance program, used by people with low incomes. Of city residents, 35 percent had their abortions at public hospitals and 17 percent in the wards of nonprofit hospitals that were generally set aside for poor people. Data from the Centers for Disease Control revealed that only 7 percent of the patients for therapeutic legal abortions in New York City between 1951 and 1962 were nonwhite women. In the first year after the law changed, one-fifth of abortion patients in the city were not white. By the following year, nearly a quarter identified themselves as Black or Latina. Looking only at city residents, statistics from the end of 1971 found that over 43 percent of abortion patients were Black and an additional 10 percent were Puerto Rican. For advocates, the one major point of concern in these numbers was the overrepresentation of whites among the patients coming to New York from elsewhere: of these, only 10.4 percent were Black and 0.5 percent Puerto Rican. "One could assume," the leaders of the Clergy Consultation Service offered, "that the non-resident picture would more closely approximate that of the resident if travel expenses to New York were not a factor."

✳　✳　✳

As abortion providers and activist observers like Lawrence Lader started to breathe sighs of relief, abortion law in New York was unsettled all over again. From the pro-legal abortion corner, there was a renewed push for a full repeal of the kind my mother, NOW, and the original legislative sponsors of the 1970 law had favored before they bent to what they saw as the inevitability of political compromise. Lucinda Cisler, who continued to head New Yorkers for Abortion Law Repeal after more moderate advocates split off from that statewide coalition, led a push for new legislation in 1971 that would undo the compromises legislators had accepted in the prior year. The model state abortion law for Cisler's group was nothing more than a blank page. The leading sponsors of the bill for full repeal were Manhattan-based Democratic reformers who were by this time old hands in the fight for abortion rights, Assemblyman Franz Leichter and Senator Fred Ohrenstein. Republican assemblywoman Constance Cook supported the effort, too, as did an ad hoc coalition of groups including the New York Civil Liberties Union and the Women's Health and Abortion Project, which had grown out of the women's liberation movement. The advocates generated thousands of letters for full repeal. But the initiative never made it out of the assembly's powerful Rules Committee for a full vote in either house of the legislature.

More unsettling to the emerging world of safe, legal, and relatively equal abortion practice was a raft of challenges from abortion opponents. The Catholic hierarchy and some in the laity were shocked into action by the success of the new law, not only the fact of its passage but the magnitude of the shift it created in practice. Catholic lobbyists had been caught somewhat by surprise in 1970 when the repeal bill passed the state senate. Although they tried, they failed to prevent the dramatic victory that followed in the state assembly. Once the new law was implemented, abortion opponents across the country recognized the magnitude of their defeat. Even as conservative Catholics and a gradually rising number of Evangelical Protestants,

Mormons, and Orthodox Jews worked to oppose liberalization measures in other states, the opponents focused on New York because its lack of a residence requirement made abortion potentially accessible to people from every state, no matter how restrictive that state's own law. With support from elsewhere, the head of the state Right to Life organization, Ed Golden, decided it was time to "roll up our sleeves and really become political."

This newly energized movement made its first shots across the bow of New York politics right away. In the 1970 primaries and general election, Golden and other anti-abortion activists targeted for defeat a handful of the legislators who had voted for the abortion law. Given how close the vote had been for passage, switching out just a few legislators could end what they saw as the nightmare of abortion on demand. The state's Conservative Party, which had since its founding in 1962 contested the dominance of a form of liberalism in the Republican Party, was buoyed by reactions to the new abortion policy. The Conservatives backed a bid by James Buckley, brother of William F. Buckley, the Catholic conservative who founded *National Review* magazine, for a seat in the U.S. Senate representing New York. Abortion opponents also organized the new single-issue Right to Life Party, which used an image of a fetus as its marker on electoral ballots. On the day after the November election, in which James Buckley defeated a liberal Democrat and a liberal Republican for the biggest win in the history of the Conservative Party, Governor Rockefeller was quoted in the *Daily News* saying that twenty-four weeks of abortion access was too many. He now favored a limit of three months or less.

The next phase in what anti-abortion activist Ed Golden did to "really become political" was to try moving legislation in the state capitol. Running parallel to the initiatives of Lucinda Cisler and other repeal activists, abortion opponents persuaded their legislative allies to introduce thirty different bills to restrict abortion access in 1971. These covered every kind of restriction, from a straight-up repeal of the prior year's decriminalization law, to reductions à la Rockefeller to something less than twenty-four weeks, to a requirement that all abortions be performed in hospitals, to one that made a husband's or male partner's consent a necessary prerequisite for having an abortion. Abortion opponents created what Lader called "an increasingly potent coalition" of Catholic hierarchy and its lobbyists, the growing network of Right to Life organizations across the state, and Republicans elected with backing from the Conservative Party—or, presumably, others who were worried about being challenged in a primary by abortion opponents, as Assemblyman George Michaels, who had provided the critical final vote for decriminalization, had been.

Before the first anniversary of decriminalization, the season of political polarization around abortion had begun. It was not yet tightly mapped on to the two major political parties, but it is otherwise familiar from the decades of debate that followed. In February 1971, the state senate's Health Committee held hearings on abortion. The majority produced a report calling for curbs on the new law, while the minority called for full repeal of all remaining restrictions on abortion and contraception access. Governor Rockefeller, who had walked back his thinking-out-loud proposal for a twelve-week cutoff but toyed with a sixteen- or eighteen-week one, was reported to be helping get all the abortion bills out of committee and to the floor of the legislature for debate, in exchange for votes he needed to pass the state budget.

In the crucible of the abortion fight, Republican conservatives learned quickly how to use their clout to pull their party to the right. Five intransigent senators who refused to approve the budget were unable to pass a reversal of the abortion law in the legislature in 1971. But they got the Rockefeller administration to re-create the discrimination by race and class in abortion provision that the new law had dramatically reduced: by executive action, the state social services agency, for the first time in history, stripped this medical procedure from coverage by Medicaid. Advocates for legal abortion litigated to challenge the policy and garnered a mess of divergent rulings from judges in state courts. Finally, a federal court ruled that the Rockefeller administration and hospitals that turned people away on the basis of this policy had violated the federal Medicaid law; they had discriminated between medical patients solely on the basis of their income and "behavioral choice" without a compelling governmental rationale and thus had also violated the U.S. Constitution. This was the first airing of a strategy that abortion opponents would employ to great effect in the federal Hyde Amendment, first passed in 1976.

Abortion opponents used all the arguments and tactics that became familiar in the hardscrabble battles that followed in the later twentieth and twenty-first centuries. They also used many of the same strategies with which they knew pro-legalization forces had won the day. After their losses in the legislature, anti-abortion activists' next move was to practice what the feminist lawyer Nancy Stearns called an "affirmative challenge," going on the offense in court to undo the law. Fordham University law professor Robert Byrn, who had served on the Governor's Commission to Review the New York State Abortion Law, chaired the Metropolitan Right to Life Committee in New York City and would soon draft a "friend of the court" brief for the National Right to Life Committee in *Roe v. Wade*, challenged decriminalization as a violation of the citizenship rights of embryos or fetuses between four and twenty-four weeks of gestation. He asserted that these were living beings, persons whose right to life the state legislature had trespassed. Stearns argued on the other side against Professor Byrn. She thought that his legal claims mirrored the ones she, Florynce Kennedy, Diane Schulder, Ann Garfinkle, and Carol Lefcourt had made a few years earlier, to the point "where we said women have constitutional rights to liberty, to life, to privacy, and to be free from cruel and unusual punishment and to the equal protection of the laws, they said a fetus has those rights. It's virtually the same argument word for word." Byrn was granted legal guardianship over the embryos and fetuses for purposes of the suit. However, the Court of Appeals, New

York State's highest court, rebuffed his argument. He appealed to the U.S. Supreme Court to hear his case and, in the meanwhile, impose an injunction that would suspend operation of the New York law. Less than two weeks before announcing its opinion in *Roe v. Wade*, the court refused to impose the injunction.

While Professor Byrn's court case was making its way through the courts, abortion foes tried again in the legislature. This time, with the new reality of abortion in New York gaining greater notoriety and abortion politics becoming sharply polarized, they had more support from the outside, more grassroots activists within the state, and more success. Backing anti-abortion legislation became part of the effort by national Republicans to create a winning electoral coalition by recruiting sexual and gender conservatives, especially those who were Catholic or Evangelical Protestants, to their side.

The single year that elapsed between the first and second legislative sessions after New York decriminalized abortion through the twenty-fourth week was a banner one for the anti-abortion movement. By spring 1972, the state's once negligibly small state right-to-life organization had grown to fifty chapters across the state and an estimated two hundred thousand members. The movement was starting to branch out from its Catholic base; Catholic conservatives still comprised a super-majority of the membership, but whereas in 1971 only 5 percent were not Catholic, by 1972 15 percent were Orthodox Jews or Evangelical Protestants. The bulk of grassroots activists devoted to the anti-abortion cause were middle-class white housewives, "church ladies" whose public participation broadcast the message that there was more than one women's movement. With backing from national allies, the New York Right to Life organization had $10,000 to spend in 1972 to support its communications with members, to organize letter-writing and phone-calling efforts, and to bring people to the state capitol to lobby in person.

The result of all this change was a majority vote in each chamber of the legislature to undo the 1970 abortion law. A bill sponsored by an upstate Republican senator named James Donovan would have restored New York's old law, which allowed abortion only in the case of a threat to a pregnant person's life. Governor Rockefeller, with what one can only imagine was alarm about the widening place of this issue in his party (and the threat his pro-decriminalization stance might pose to his presidential aspirations), offered to endorse a reduction in the period during which abortion was legally allowed to sixteen or eighteen weeks—a compromise Donovan refused. Right-to-life forces made a huge push in response, perhaps energized by Donovan's hard-line stance in much the way feminists had been energized by the push for full repeal of all abortion laws. Terence Cardinal Cooke, the head of the Catholic hierarchy in New York State and one of the most prominent U.S. Catholic leaders, issued a letter to be read from pulpits across the state on April 9. The following weekend saw "Human Life Sunday," a day of political action whose focus was a march and rally in New York City that ended in Central Park. The New York City actions were sponsored by the Catholic fraternal organization the Knights of Columbus and drew at least ten thousand nuns, priests, and lay activists. In the largest of several coordinated trips to the state capitol, hundreds protested the law in Albany, and a group of women stormed the floor of the legislature yelling, "Stop abortion!"

At the crest of the lobbying effort, the New York abortion debate officially went national. On the advice of Patrick Buchanan, the cultural-conservative-whisperer in the White House, President Richard Nixon weighed in on behalf of Senator Donovan's bill. It was a transparent bid for Catholic support on the day after Nixon renounced the recommendations of his own Commission on Population Growth, headed by Governor Rockefeller's older brother, John D. Rockefeller III, for liberalizing access to abortion and contraception. In a letter to Cardinal Cooke, the president opined that unencumbered abortion access and laws like the one under fire in New York were "impossible to reconcile with either our religious traditions or our Western heritage." He pledged "admiration, sympathy, and support" to Cooke and anti-abortion activists.

The Nixon letter probably made more of a difference in his own election tally that year than in the New York legislature. But it doesn't seem to have hurt: Donovan's bill passed by a vote of 79–68 in the assembly and 30–27 in the senate. In other words, it did better than the decriminalization bill had two years before. Jon Margolis, who reported on the push to undo the 1970 law as Albany bureau chief for the Long Island paper *Newsday*, argued that the votes might have gone the other way if legislators had not known that Governor Rockefeller was primed to veto. As it was, they could garner political benefits from voting against abortion without incurring the wrath of their constituents, because they knew that the law would not in fact change.

Veto the governor did, as he had promised to do. His veto message defended the state's new approach, decriminalization up to twenty-four weeks, as a way to prevent discrimination "against women of modest means" and those who were "frightened, unwed, confused" and couldn't leave the state or the country to find good doctors. Showing signs of strain, he inveighed against the pressure campaign the anti-abortion movement had mustered and suggested that its strong-arm tactics had led to a form of minority rule. With his action, the bill was dead, but the movement that promoted it was not defeated.

Advocates for abortion decriminalization around the country were watching what happened in New York. They were also experiencing their own versions of the dynamics at play in New York, most importantly the effects of an energetic movement to stop the trend toward looser abortion policies. By the eve of *Roe v. Wade*, thirteen states allowed abortions for reasons beyond preserving a mother's health and four, including New York, had liberalized well beyond that point. Hawaii and Alaska, for example, had passed legislation repealing restrictions up to the point of fetal viability, with ninety-day residence requirements and mandates in both states that all abortions be performed in hospitals. The Hawaii measure, inspired by the years-long campaign in New York and other states, became law just before New York acted in April 1970. It might have been as significant as the New York change if it had not included a residence requirement and if the state had been easier to reach for most residents of the United States. Alaska followed suit soon after passage of the New York law.

Beyond these three states, perhaps the most significant change had been California's. This was not because the state's legislation was so ambitious (it was a reform statute, not an expansive repeal on the order of New York, Hawaii, or Alaska), but because the California Supreme Court had intervened in a way that loosened abortion access very significantly, and because attitudes on the ground shifted rapidly after that court's ruling. Early in 1970, a doctor in San Diego commented that, although abortion patients still needed the approval of hospital committees, these had loosened their criteria to the point of accepting "abortion on request." The situation was similar in Washington, D.C., where the U.S. Supreme Court had interpreted the law in a way that allowed the Clergy Consultation Service doctor Milan Vuitch to stay out of jail and permitted individuals to access abortion under an easy-to-reach standard of dangers to their "health," including mental or psychological distress. The last sizable victory for liberalization before *Roe* came in Washington State, with a referendum on the November 1970, ballot that ended in a 56 to 44 percent victory for something like repeal—no restrictions up to four months of fetal gestation, with a ninety-day residency requirement and mandates that all married women seeking abortions gain the consent of their husbands unless the couple was living apart and that minors gain the consent of their legal guardians.

Judged from one angle, it looked like the arc of history was bending toward liberalization of state abortion restrictions or even full legalization up to about the two-thirds point of a pregnancy. However, the arc bent less and less as the months passed in 1970 and stopped bending altogether in 1971. Anti-abortion organizing in response to liberalization in general, and to New York's law in particular, stopped the national decriminalization movement cold. In 1971, there were twenty-five efforts to liberalize abortion law in state legislatures. Abortion opponents, using graphic images and countering stories about women victims of harsh laws with stories about fetal victims of liberal laws, defeated every one. In 1972, the decriminalization movement set its hopes on a statewide referendum in Michigan that would have repealed all restrictions on licensed physicians operating on women who were up to twenty weeks pregnant. After a wealth of advertising from abortion opponents, the outcome wasn't even close, with 61 percent opposing the measure and 39 percent approving it.

This situation was the background to the Supreme Court's decision in *Roe v. Wade*, which overturned state laws restricting abortion in the first trimester entirely and laid out narrow bounds within which states could regulate access to abortion in the second trimester. Writing for the majority with six of his colleagues, Justice Blackmun found that the "right of personal privacy" that the Supreme Court had previously extended to cover people's choices about contraception "includes the abortion decision, but that this right is not unqualified and must be considered against important state interests." The *Roe* majority also rejected the idea of fetal personhood, as it had been expressed by Professor Robert Byrn in New York. Without ruling on the question of when life began, Justice Blackmun argued that the word "person," in the Fourteenth Amendment to the Constitution, did not refer to fetuses.

Before reaching these conclusions, Justice Blackmun and his brethren had followed Sarah Weddington's oral argument with several months of deliberation before concluding that the abortion cases had to be reargued and decided in the next term, which started in October 1972. As decriminalization advocates and abortion opponents battled in state after state, the justices had come to believe that the issue was too volatile to be decided by the seven-person court, depleted by the resignations of both Hugo Black and John Marshall Harlan II, that first heard the case. *Roe* and *Doe v. Bolton* would be revisited when President Nixon's two appointees, Lewis Powell and William Rehnquist, were present and accounted for—even if, as the most liberal justices suspected, this meant that the majority that seemed to have coalesced in favor of overturning restrictive state abortion laws were to fall apart. What this meant in practice was that the Supreme Court deliberated over abortion policy all through the year during which New York's statute faced its greatest challenge and survived, the year when the arc toward decriminalization was suspended in midair.

Traces of the New York statute and the troubled history that followed its passage are everywhere in *Roe v. Wade*. Although it has often been characterized as an absolutist opinion, a clear statement in favor of abortion legalization, *Roe* was in fact a compromise among competing forces that reflected the state of the debate at the moment it was decided. Justice Blackmun and his colleagues rejected the feminist preference (my mother's, Lucinda Cisler's, Florynce Kennedy's) for full repeal, abortion as easy to obtain as appendectomy. In remarks he drafted to give as he issued the opinion, Blackmun stressed, "The Court does not today hold that the Constitution compels abortion on demand. It does not today pronounce that a pregnant woman has an absolute right to an abortion." Blackmun knew that the opinion would be controversial and would likely be misinterpreted; he had a notion to share a written version of his remarks with the media so that they did not go "all the way off the deep end." This would have been an unprecedented move, and Justice William Brennan dissuaded him from adding more fuel to the anticipated fire by making it.

The court's majority echoed New York's decriminalization law when it ruled that states were for the most part to refrain from regulating abortion during the first two trimesters, or roughly twenty-four weeks, of a pregnancy. However, the justices compromised in ways that echoed the tussle between health authorities and activists when the New York law was implemented. In the middle period of a pregnancy, the justices decided, a state could regulate abortion access "to the extent that the regulation reasonably relates to the preservation and protection of maternal health," for example by demanding that an abortion provider be a licensed medical doctor or that the procedure occur in a hospital. The Supreme Court majority also appears to have recognized the rising anti-abortion movement and the barriers opponents had raised to liberalized laws in New York and a few other locations. After fetal viability, the point at which a gestating being might survive outside its mother's womb, or roughly six months into a pregnancy, a state could regulate abortion, even going "so far as to proscribe abortion" without offending the Constitution, the justices ruled, "except when it is necessary to preserve the life or health of the mother."

The fact that *Roe v. Wade* was argued a second time meant that Justice Blackmun and his clerks had time to gather materials and think through the issues the case raised more thoroughly in the summer and fall of 1972 than they had earlier. One branch of Blackmun's research, and eventually of the argumentation in his opinion, was historical. His main source for these reflections, which leading scholars Melissa Murray and Kristin Luker find glimmeringly present throughout the *Roe* opinion, was the work of law professor Cyril Means, Jr. Means was the repeal activist in New York who developed his read on the legal history of abortion in that context. An essay he wrote for Governor Rockefeller's commission on abortion law, published in 1968, used New York history to argue for the "cessation of constitutionality" of restrictive abortion laws. Means pointed out that English and early American law were far more liberal in their approach to abortion than New York's twentieth-century legislation was before 1970. He also argued that restrictive laws were constitutional when first passed as a response to the dangers of nineteenth-century abortion methods, like poisons women ingested to force themselves to miscarry and surgeries performed without effective antiseptics. The laws became unconstitutional when abortion in the mid-twentieth century became much safer. When Justice Blackmun wrote the final draft of his *Roe v. Wade* opinion late in 1972, there was nothing else like Means's work in print. In addition, Means had expanded his New York study into a national one arguing that the "phoenix of abortional freedom" was ready to rise from its ashes. Both essays appeared on a short list of "legal literature" Justice Blackmun reviewed while drafting his opinions, and both undergirded the justice's review of history in *Roe v. Wade*—especially his meditation on pre-nineteenth-century law.

As he had been doing since Weddington's first turn at the Supreme Court lectern, Blackmun relied on the library of the Mayo Clinic, for which he had worked for nearly a decade. Many of the books and articles he reviewed had to do with medical attitudes and practices, and this material became a centerpiece of his opinion in *Roe*. As journalist Jeffrey Toobin once pointed out, Blackmun mentioned physicians forty-eight times in the opinion and used the word "woman" forty-four times.

One aspect of the research that particularly interested Justice Blackmun was a review of the policies of the American Medical Association vis-à-vis abortion. The group's most important policy statement was its most recent: After a concerted effort to change AMA policy, which included protests by members of New Yorkers for Abortion Law Repeal and NARAL at the doctors' 1969 meeting, advocates for abortion decriminalization scored a near triumph in 1970. "For the first time in its 123-year history," the AMA's governing body ruled that it was medically ethical for doctors to perform abortions for a wide range of reasons. This policy included a hospital requirement and a standard that any doctor seeking to perform an abortion call in two colleagues for consultation, and so it was more restrictive than the laws of Hawaii, New York, Washington State, and Alaska. But it was more liberal than the laws in forty-six U.S. states. It arrived only three years after the AMA broke from one hundred years of endorsing the tightest feasible abortion restrictions, to endorse a reform approach that found abortion acceptable in case of dangers to a mother's physical or mental health, the potential deformity of her fetus, rape, or incest.

The rapid change in AMA policy was in large measure a result of what happened in New York. Activists had originally lobbied the AMA, and disrupted its conference, in order to get the organization to support the repeal campaign in New York State. They did not succeed at that goal. However, their success at passing the New York statute pushed the AMA to change its policy. The AMA approved its new approach to abortion only days before the New York law came into effect, after the organization's board of trustees underlined that "several states," most notably doctor-rich New York, had liberalized their laws in ways that created trouble for doctors who wanted "to perform a legalized medical procedure without violating the policy of their professional association." More explicitly, a committee on abortion that reported its findings at the AMA's 1970 meeting received testimony on "the logistic and other problems which will occur in New York when that state's new abortion law becomes effective."

The AMA was the most important professional organization whose policies Justice Blackmun reviewed in considering how the Supreme Court should intervene in the roiling politics of abortion. But it was not the only such organization or the only one whose policies shifted in response to grassroots pressure, especially in New York. The American Public Health Association (APHA), for example, came out for repeal in 1968, thanks, if we can believe repeal advocate Ruth Cusack, to lobbying by her colleague Ruth Proskauer Smith. APHA issued its set of Standards for Abortion Services, which built on that position, in October 1970. These standards were cited at length in *Roe*. APHA members participated in the last phase of the campaign for decriminalization in New York, and an editorial in the *American Journal of Public Health* used data exclusively from New York City to ground its new standard that legal abortion services should be available on an equal basis no matter one's income.

The American Bar Association (ABA), which liberalized its stance toward abortion in 1972, was not a medical organization. However, it was the most prominent national voice of the profession in which Supreme Court justices participated. Justice Powell, one of the new Nixon appointees who advocates feared would vote against Weddington's side of the case, had been president of the ABA in the mid-1960s. Shortly before the Supreme Court decided *Roe*, the ABA endorsed a model Uniform Abortion Act "based largely upon the New York abortion act," with the recommended time period for "unlimited" procedures pushed back from twenty-four to twenty weeks because "a number of problems appeared in New York"—perhaps a reference to the anti-abortion movement's charge that later procedures resulted in something like infanticide.

These changes appear to have had a powerful impact on the Supreme Court majority that decided *Roe v. Wade*. To be sure, the justices' starting point in evaluating the challenge to the Texas abortion law in *Roe* was a series of their own precedents, including *Griswold v. Connecticut*, which found that states could not prevent married people from obtaining contraceptives and established the modern idea of sexual privacy protected by the Constitution; *United States v. Vuitch*, which interpreted a local law broadly to permit women to choose abortion for a wide range of reasons; and *Baird v. Eisenstadt* (1972), whose criminal defendant was a New York activist named Bill Baird, and which extended the birth control right to people who were unmarried. In preparing his opinion, Justice Blackmun reviewed decisions on state abortion laws in lower federal courts and state courts, from the successful challenge to restrictive law in the California Supreme Court, to anti-abortion law professor Robert Byrn's unsuccessful challenge to New York's 1970 law, to the two different opinions Nancy Stearns's colleagues received from federal judges in Connecticut, one that opened the way to abortion access with no restrictions and another months later that permitted the state to criminalize abortions after fetal viability. Justice Blackmun concluded from reading the cases that he was not stepping too far past the point already reached in the lower courts; "most" of the state and federal judges who heard challenges to state abortion laws, he wrote, "have agreed that the right of privacy . . . is broad enough to cover the abortion decision."

Blackmun and the six justices who joined him in invalidating most state abortion laws ruled in a way that was consistent with trends in public opinion as much as it was with lower court rulings and the rapidly changing positions of groups like the AMA and ABA. Although less dramatically, general public opinion was moving in the same direction as the positions of professionals. In November 1970, a Gallup poll recorded 40 percent in favor of abortion in the first trimester, a new high. In October 1971, a front-page story in the *New York Times* reported on a poll that found 50 percent of Americans favoring policies that left the decision to a woman and her physician. On Justice Blackmun's copy of an August 1972 report on a Gallup poll finding that "64 per cent of the public and even a majority of Roman Catholics" believed "that the decision to have an abortion should be left solely to the woman and her doctor," either he or his clerks emphasized the data with heavy underlining.

The Supreme Court majority surprised nearly everyone with its opinion in *Roe v. Wade*. It may even have surprised the attorney who argued for the woman known as "Jane Roe." Sarah Weddington won election to the Texas legislature in November 1972. Her first major initiative, three days before the court gave her a historic win, was to sponsor a bill that would have repealed her state's abortion restrictions. In other words, she still believed that the road to changing policy on this issue most likely ran through contested legislative battles at the state level.

Weddington misjudged. Seven Supreme Court justices, including five Republican appointees, three named by Richard Nixon, chose in *Roe v. Wade* to make abortion policy at the national rather than the state level. Their decision promised to reduce what by the early 1970s had become profound inequality from state to state, and by race and income, in access to medical care that would determine the course of one's life.

Advocates for liberal abortion laws had built a mass base that created opportunities for women to tell their stories. They engaged in effective grassroots and insider tactics to earn legislative support, and they shifted overall public opinion and the elite opinion that mattered most in Supreme Court councils. Diverse, dogged coalitions succeeded at overcoming ancient prejudices and conservative tactics to make the democratic system in a few states work for them. However, what happened in the immediate aftermath of the New York law, from barriers to its implementation to the near-successful effort to undo it, demonstrated the frailty of their victory.

It may appear in retrospect that the Supreme Court was in conflict with its times, but the justices were followers as much as they were leaders. Members of the majority in *Roe v. Wade* ruled consistently with what likely seemed to them a new public consensus and particularly a consensus among professionals most immersed in the issue, those the justices assumed knew best. Behind those changes in public and professional opinion was a loosely coordinated, sustained movement that built attitudinal shifts and new policies from the foundations up.

Carol Marsh remembered exactly what she was doing when Justice Harry Blackmun announced the Supreme Court's decision in *Roe v. Wade*. She was sitting in the lower Manhattan office of the Women's National Abortion Action Coalition, the mostly forgotten feminist group that worked in parallel to NARAL as a national network of activists committed to repealing restrictive abortion laws. It was Marsh's job to organize busloads of feminists to the state capitol. Hundreds were ready to travel to Albany to defend the New York abortion law, not yet three years old and potentially facing its third major legislative challenge. On January 22, 1973, when Justice Blackmun issued his opinion, she realized they didn't have to demonstrate to defend that hard-won legislation. The buses were canceled, the protest called off. The Supreme Court had, unexpectedly, transformed the legal landscape of abortion in the United States.

Chapter Nine

Fighting Population Control
in 1970s New York City

THE COMMITTEE to End Sterilization Abuse started in in a "big, many-windowed room" in the Loeb Student Center at New York University. CESA rose on foundations that had been built before and during the federal court battles over abortion that resulted in *Roe v. Wade*. These ranged from efforts by Black civil rights activists to shine light on the problem of "Mississippi appendectomies" (involuntary sterilizations), to opposition to the sterilization program in Puerto Rico by independentists on the island, to protests of sterilization in New York City by groups like the Young Lords at Lincoln Hospital. Maritza Arrastía, whose mother was Puerto Rican and whose father was a Protestant minister from Cuba who had soured on the revolution and moved his family stateside, remembered that the progressive National Lawyers Guild had sponsored a meeting about colonization and Puerto Rico. It was natural for her to be there, since she was an active member of the Puerto Rican Socialist Party and a writer and editor for the party newspaper, *Claridad*. Arrastía joined "a small working group that was about reproductive rights, women's reproductive rights. And that working group, that's where I met Helen Rodríguez-Trías." By coincidence, or maybe not, since she was a reproductive rights diehard and lawyer committed to social change, Nancy Stearns, the original architect of New York's

Abramowicz case, was there too, as was her friend and colleague at the Center for Constitutional Rights, Rhonda Copelon. "And we talked a lot about sterilization abuse during that meeting," Arrastía remembered, about which "Helen was very active," and decided to continue meeting to see what could be done about it. With the party's blessing, Arrastía became the key "cadre," the committed member, assigned to participate in this new effort.

Dr. Rodríguez-Trías became a leader of the group, which met several times in her apartment. This was not yet the place on West End Avenue next door to my family, but "one of those sort of prewar or war apartments" elsewhere in upper Manhattan, fittingly grand for a hospital department chair. She helped write this new chapter in the history of the reproductive rights movement in close contact with leaders of the Puerto Rican Socialist Party, such as Arrastía and Digna Sánchez, head of the party's Women's Commission, whom Rodríguez-Trías had met previously at a demonstration for Puerto Rican independence. The Puerto Rican Socialist Party was a lineal descendent of the Movimiento Pro Independencia (Movement for Independence) formed at the time of the Cuban Revolution. It was as radical as the Young Lords but maintained a stronger emphasis than the Lords did on the struggle against U.S. control in Puerto Rico. Party members were also more diverse in terms of age than the Young Lords. Via its Women's Commission, the Puerto Rican Socialist Party did similar internal work to overcome male dominance. Rodríguez-Trías was not a member of the Puerto Rican Socialist Party. She was "what we called a sympathizer," Sánchez said, "all but card-carrying"—that is, believing in the cause of Puerto Rican independence and working every day at Lincoln Hospital to make things better for low-income Latino, Black, and white patients.

Together, and with Arrastía and Rodríguez-Trías in the lead, the group that had met that night at NYU and a small number of additional recruits took major steps to expand the movement for reproductive rights beyond abortion. CESA was the first organization in

U.S. history whose mission was fighting involuntary or coercive sterilization. It was also more than that: a testing ground for ideas and strategies that continued to stand at the cutting edge of the movement for decades, a standing critique of feminists who believed in *Roe v. Wade* as an end point and not a bare beginning.

For Dr. Helen Rodríguez-Trías and the others who came together to form CESA, there was plenty of evidence that Justice Blackmun's opinion in *Roe v. Wade* didn't guarantee reproductive rights to all Americans. They were all aware of the mass sterilization program in Puerto Rico, which resulted by 1968 in 35 percent of women of childbearing age having been sterilized. Women consented to sterilization in a context in which abortion was illegal and difficult for all but the wealthiest to access, and other forms of contraception had negative reputations because of the years' worth of birth control experiments U.S. inventors and companies had conducted on Puerto Rican women. CESA's founders, like members of the Young Lords, also knew that Latinas and Black women in public hospitals on the U.S. mainland were pressured to consent to sterilization surgeries and were sometimes sterilized, as Fannie Lou Hamer had been, without their consent.

Among CESA's founders were Karen Stamm and Carol Marsh, white women who missed that first meeting at New York University but attended almost all the planning meetings that followed. After *Roe v. Wade*, Stamm and Marsh understood that the Supreme Court had fundamentally changed reproductive rights for American women—at least in theory. Both had had abortions before the New York law changed in 1970. Marsh could have died from hers. Stamm had to fight her doctor and her mother to avoid being sterilized against her will—a potential victim of the old "package deal," as Rodríguez-Trías called it, that women were pressured to accept when they had so-called therapeutic abortions under the old restrictive laws. Marsh and Stamm saw the difference legal abortion could make. However, they were socialist feminists, critics of a top-down society that shaped health care and mainstream feminism alike. They knew that the words of a Supreme Court opinion did little to reverse the gaping differences people experienced in the health-care system based on economic class and health insurance, race, ethnicity, language, age, and citizenship status, as well as gender. They knew that access to legal abortion was not the same thing as social or reproductive justice.

Even before they heard about the meetings Arrastía, Rodríguez-Trías, and the others were having, Marsh and Stamm were primed to join a reproductive rights group focused on sterilization abuse. They learned about the sterilization crisis in Puerto Rico and in mainland Black and brown communities as activists with the Women's National Abortion Action Coalition, which convened a Women's National Abortion Conference in 1971 and condemned "forced sterilization" while demanding the repeal of restrictive abortion laws. However, almost immediately after the Supreme Court ruled in *Roe v. Wade*, Marsh said, "it was the end of WONAAC." Although originally an offshoot of the Socialist Workers Party, the group's lifeline was "basically individual rich peoples' donations. And once their goal had been achieved, they didn't see any reason to keep funding the organization." Marsh and Stamm "kept asking them to stay on and work on sterilization abuse. And they said no."

After the Women's National Abortion Action Coalition folded, Karen Stamm traveled to China. She found out about the anti-sterilization meetings early in 1974 from a friend in a Marxist-Leninist study group. She and Marsh joined Arrastía, Rodríguez-Trías, Stearns, and the others as they decided to start a new organization and hashed out its mission. Marsh remembered that next, the group was ready for a name. At a meeting Stamm missed, she recalled, "there was something, I don't know if 'magical' is the right word, but something extraordinary when Maritza came up with the name of CESA"—which means "cease!" in Spanish—"and it was the perfect name. I mean, we didn't really have to struggle about it or come up with anything else. There it was laid out right in front of us."

The people who attended these early meetings were a mélange of activists, all still up to their ears in politics after the disappointments of the end of the 1960s and the victories, such as the *Roe* decision, of the early 1970s. In addition to members of the Puerto Rican Socialist Party, like Arrastía, there were the socialist feminists Marsh and Stamm and, a little later, Workers World Party member Susan E. Davis; the feminist reproductive rights attorneys Stearns and Copelon; a psychiatrist from Metropolitan Hospital in East Harlem named Ray Rakow and his wife, Cornelia Rakow, from the combustible politics of New York City health care; and Esta Armstrong, a veteran administrator in the city's public hospital bureaucracy, the Health and Hospitals Corporation. Armstrong was a politically minded official who had gotten interested in sterilization abuse while working earlier in the 1970s at the Urban League. In 1974, at the time of CESA's founding, she held a position of authority and a flexible portfolio as special assistant to the senior vice president for quality assurance of HHC.

Dr. Helen Rodríguez-Trías "was really the heart of CESA," as Marsh put it. Thanks to the takeover of Lincoln Hospital by the Young Lords and the community mobilization that elevated her to the chair of Lincoln's pediatrics department, Rodríguez-Trías was well known. She was connected simultaneously to Puerto Rican and independentist radicals, the majority-white women's liberation and women's health movements, to socialist feminists (also mostly white), and to organizing by doctors and other hospital employees, which was especially intense in her own department at Lincoln. CESA alums remember her as beautiful, although humble about her beauty, warm and welcoming, brilliant, and strategically savvy. She commanded respect with her expertise in medicine and public health, her vision and tactical smarts.

The small group that founded CESA came to understand that sterilization abuse was just as serious a problem in liberal New York

City as the independence movement had found it to be in Puerto Rico. They connected the Puerto Rican mass sterilization program with what was happening in cities with large Latino and Black populations, "because," Arrastía remembered, "it was going on in New York at the time that women would go in and they'd be railroaded into a C-section [cesarean birth]," or they would go in seeking an abortion, "and then during that also be railroaded into having a tubal ligation," a sterilization surgery. "And so a lot of the work there was making the connection that what had gone on in Puerto Rico and was still going on, to a certain degree, was going on in New York, that Puerto Rican women were being targeted for basically genocide." CESA members were aware of an incarcerated woman who was sterilized against her will at Kings County Hospital in Brooklyn. When they spoke publicly, as Rodríguez-Trías did in Harlem shortly after CESA started, "everybody in the audience said this happened to my mother and to me and to my neighbor." The issue, in Stamm's words, had "a huge domestic footprint."

CESA became ever more focused on the mainland United States, as opposed to fighting the sterilization program in Puerto Rico. This, and maybe the prominence of Dr. Rodríguez-Trías, as well as the presence in the group of women who were known for their dedication to improving the lives of Puerto Ricans, like Arrastía and other women from the Puerto Rican Socialist Party, made CESA a four-leaf clover among groups fighting for reproductive rights, interracial in membership and even more in the people who cared about its agenda. Rodríguez-Trías's particular genius, which became CESA's, was to ground the group's actions in what came later to be known as an "intersectional" approach—the idea that different subgroups of women had radically different experiences and political needs. As the women's health movement, in which Rodríguez-Trías also participated, had begun to argue, nearly all women were mistreated in mainstream medicine by doctors who didn't listen to them or governments that limited their options for abortion and birth control.

But white, wealthy, able-bodied and -minded women had a totally different experience of sterilization—not being able to get it, thanks to standards by which doctors multiplied age by number of children and did not perform the sterilization if they believed the number was too low—than poor, Black and brown, and disabled women did. "It was just great," Stamm remembered, "that we finally had some kind of a women's organization that managed, maybe because of the issue, to bridge the gap."

Although Puerto Rico was always on their minds, the CESA founders wound up spending most of their time in the first few years working to stop sterilization abuse in New York. The issue of sterilization abuse had leaped onto front pages only half a year after *Roe v. Wade*. The occasion for the headlines was the announcement in June 1973 that the Southern Poverty Law Center was representing a Black family with two daughters who had been sterilized by a clinic in Montgomery, Alabama. The clinic received its funding from the federal antipoverty agency, the Office of Economic Opportunity.

The Relf children, Minnie Lee and Mary Alice, were fourteen and twelve years old, respectively. They had participated in a birth control program, which involved receiving repeated shots of the then-experimental drug Depo-Provera. The head of the clinic said later (as paraphrased in the *New York Times*) that nurses "told Mrs. Relf and the girls—Mr. Relf was not home at the time—that the birth control shots, given every 90 days, were no longer authorized because some studies indicated they might cause adverse side effects. The nurses then suggested," the director added, "that sterilization would be an alternative, particularly since the clinic had never considered the girls disciplined enough to take daily birth control pills." Mrs. Relf, who reportedly could not read or write, signed consent forms for the sterilization of her two young daughters with an "X." She said later that she thought she was authorizing a different form of reversible birth control, not permanent sterilization.

As the Relfs' case made its way through the courts, the media revealed a disturbing backstory to their treatment. In 1970, Congress had added Title X to the Public Health Service Act, creating for the first time a dedicated national program to fund birth control for people who could not otherwise afford it. In the next year, the Nixon administration authorized local offices funded by the notoriously decentralized Office of Economic Opportunity to make sterilization available as a tool to fight poverty. It contracted with the American Public Health Association to produce draft guidelines for informed consent, which a young agency employee named Dr. Warren Hern shepherded through an internal review process. The administration finalized the guidance and printed twenty-five thousand copies of it to send to local agencies funded by the Office of Economic Opportunity. However, on the eve of the 1972 presidential election, which President Nixon saw as an opportunity to remake the Republican coalition by bringing Catholic voters into the fold, top administration officials decided not to call attention to the sterilization program by issuing the guidelines. All twenty-five thousand copies were remanded and left in a warehouse. When the Relf sisters and their parents started speaking publicly about their experiences, doctor-bureaucrat Warren Hern concluded that, as he had feared, the lacuna between the allowance of sterilization and the lack of standards for patient consent had created opportunities for abuse.

In an effort to save face after the guidelines were discovered, the federal Department of Health, Education, and Welfare assumed management of the Montgomery clinic. In February 1974, the agency issued sterilization guidelines that administrators argued would prevent any questionable surgeries in the future. But the guidelines allowed for the sterilization of children under eighteen without their parents' consent if a five-member committee recommended it, and of other people who were deemed "mentally incompetent" on recommendation of the committee and approval by a state court.

Relf v. Weinberger was heard by Judge Gerhard Gesell of the federal District Court for the District of Columbia. He was the same judge who had struck down D.C.'s restrictive abortion law in the case named for Clergy Consultation Service doctor Milan Vuitch. Gesell ruled in October 1973 that the Nixon administration's firing of special prosecutor Archibald Cox in the "Saturday night massacre"—President Nixon's Hail Mary pass to avert an honest accounting for the crimes of Watergate—was unlawful. Gesell ruled against the administration again in the *Relf* case, writing that "federally assisted family planning sterilizations are permissible only with the voluntary, knowing and uncoerced consent of individuals competent to give such consent." The administration's standards did not ensure such consent.

Judge Gesell wrote movingly that involuntary or coerced sterilization, whether of an adult or a child, like one of the Relf girls, violated "the basic human right to procreate." He decried the fact that "an indefinite number of poor people have been improperly coerced into accepting a sterilization operation under the threat that various federally supported welfare benefits would be withdrawn"—or even, in the case of some with public health insurance under the Medicaid program, that they would be denied medical care. This was one of the rare moments in American history when someone with a lot of mainstream power acknowledged the significance of the right *to have children*, alongside the right to end a pregnancy recognized in *Roe*. At the same time, even this liberal champion revealed that if it were Congress and not a federal agency authorizing it, he might view sterilization as an appropriate tool in population control. "The dividing line between family planning and eugenics is murky," Gesell wrote. He argued that it was appropriate in certain circumstances for government entities to make policies aimed at "limiting irresponsible reproduction, which each year places increasing numbers of unwanted or mentally defective children into tax-supported institutions."

Dr. Rodríguez-Trías brought the *Relf* case and the issue of sterilization abuse to the women's movement and started to see how fractured that movement was by race and class. She and others discussed what happened to the Relf sisters at a panel on sterilization abuse at an early meeting of the women's health movement attended by thousands. She remembered getting "a lot of flack from White women who had private doctors and wanted to be sterilized" but whose doctors wouldn't approve their surgeries. The reaction revealed to her that feminists disagreed about the very thing that seemed to unite them during the effort to repeal criminal abortion laws: reproductive rights. Much as the death of Carmen Rodríguez at Lincoln Hospital revealed unequal experiences of abortion and of health care in general, these responses to the sterilization issue were an object lesson in tensions among feminists. Rodríguez-Trías "began to understand that we were coming to different conclusions because we were living different realities."

After the frustration she experienced when talking about it with mostly white activists in the women's health movement, Rodríguez-Trías went to work on the issues raised by the Relf sisters' case with her comrades in New York. In November 1974, she and the activist health-care bureaucrat Esta Armstrong persuaded the leaders of the Health and Hospitals Corporation to appoint an Advisory Committee on Sterilization. The committee's mission, informed by the abuses on display in the *Relf* case—the sterilization of very young women, faux consent procedures that deprived patients or their guardians of the ability to make genuinely informed decisions, racist and elitist opinions on the part of professionals who were apparently empowered to act without review or repercussions—was to draft new sterilization guidelines for the city's public hospitals, including Lincoln in the Bronx and Metropolitan in El Barrio. Judge Gesell's ruling in the *Relf* case provided the rationale for the committee: if, as Gesell had said, the federal government's sterilization guidelines were not protective enough of people who might be coerced or misled into sterilization, then what kinds of regulations would do the job?

The sterilization guidelines committee was a product of Armstrong's and Rodríguez-Trías's knowledge of the health system. Armstrong herself cochaired the committee with the director of obstetrics and gynecology at Morrisania Hospital, another in the municipal hospital network. Technically, CESA was one of several groups represented on the committee. However, as Stamm put it, "we set up the organizations, or really Helen and Esta set it up, so that CESA was the outside organization, the inside organization was the ad hoc advisory committee" on sterilization. Maritza Arrastía remembered that CESA provided "movement support" for the work of the guidelines committee, organizing pickets and demonstrations and doing political education about its work in Puerto Rican and other communities that had a stake in the committee's work.

In addition to Rodríguez-Trías and Armstrong, other CESA members served on the committee. These included Karen Stamm and attorneys Nancy Stearns and Rhonda Copelon. The Puerto Rican Socialist Party was represented, and so was Health/PAC, the progressive group that had helped Stearns find plaintiffs for her woman-centered abortion litigation, *Abramowicz v. Lefkowitz*. Also on the committee were representatives of *Ms.* magazine and the National Black Feminist Organization and representatives of some of the neighborhood groups that were already participating in advisory bodies at the city's health centers and hospitals. These advisory bodies had become politicized thanks to the Young Lords takeover of Lincoln Hospital and other grassroots campaigns for community control of health care and education. Stamm remembered these groups as a critical base of support. Although their members did not attend CESA meetings, they were aligned with CESA's goals, and vice versa. Stamm credited Rodríguez-Trías and Armstrong, with their years of work inside the city's public health care system, with even knowing that these local advisory groups existed, and with the insight to know how important it was to include them in the work of making sterilization guidelines more rigorous.

Although CESA members still hoped to address the sterilization crisis in Puerto Rico, the Advisory Committee on Sterilization was a response specifically to what Stamm had called the "domestic footprint" of the issue. This was a first effort from the grassroots to create rules that could serve as a model for other cities and states around the country, even for the federal government. The goal from CESA members' perspective was to keep racist, ableist, or elitist doctors from pressuring women into ending their reproductive lives—and to make sure that doctors never (again) took it upon themselves to end that part of women's lives willy-nilly, without even the pretense of consent.

The committee worked quickly and had a draft report and set of guidelines in May 1975. In the report, Armstrong and the other authors described reproductive rights as rights people needed to exercise against the medical experts and social workers in their lives. This was a far cry from Justice Blackmun's *Roe* opinion, which aimed to get government out of the way so that doctors could act in their patients' best interests. The report pointed to evidence that doctors in the New York City system were ordering hysterectomies as sterilizations (as opposed to less risky and invasive tubal ligations) in order to give trainees experience in surgical techniques—a form of abuse that Rodríguez-Trías had seen as well in Puerto Rico. They cited data to prove that hospital personnel didn't understand or follow the existing federal guidelines, the ones Judge Gesell had rejected as too permissive. "These factors, combined with the fact that New York municipal hospitals serve primarily a poor, undereducated minority population, many of whom have cultural biases about sterilization"—by which they meant Puerto Rican women who had begun to choose sterilization during decades when they had few options for reliable birth control—"and lack specific information or are misinformed about the irreversibility of the procedure, create an atmosphere for concern."

Committee members treated doctors, hospital bureaucracies, and the federal government with great skepticism. They suspected that the doctors were biased and that public hospital patients would be unable to fend off pressure or make choices that were truly in their self-interest. An early version of the guidelines would have imposed a sixty-day-long waiting period after a woman's initial request before she could have a tubal ligation, with no exceptions. In the final proposal, this was reduced to thirty days, and the wait time could be waived under certain circumstances. The committee suggested refusing sterilization entirely to women under twenty-one or to those not legally competent to consent. It created high barriers to what was considered "consent," including mandatory counseling on post-sterilization regret and a requirement that patients affirm their desire for sterilization twice. The forms were to be written "in at least Spanish, French, Chinese, Yiddish and English."

Two of the guidelines spoke specifically to the treatment of the Relf sisters, and to the situation Karen Stamm had faced in the early 1960s, when she went for an abortion and hospital staff recommended sterilization. Even though abortion was mostly legal after *Roe*, Armstrong, Rodríguez-Trías, and the other CESA members heard stories of women being pressured into sterilization during abortion appointments. They also heard about Black, brown, and poor women in New York and elsewhere being pushed to agree to sterilization in the middle of labor or delivery. The proposed guidelines would treat as "presumed involuntary" any sterilization a woman consented to while in the hospital for an abortion or for childbirth. In response to the Relfs' situation, in which the same government employees who helped the family maintain their public assistance benefits implicitly threatened (or could be thought to have threatened) to withdraw this lifeline if the family refused sterilization, the guidelines insisted that every consent form and informational flyer include, in loud capitals: "IF YOU DECIDE YOU DO NOT WANT TO BE STERILIZED, YOU WILL NOT LOSE ANY BENEFITS OR MEDICAL SERVICES. YOU CAN CHANGE YOUR MIND AT ANY TIME PRIOR TO THE OPERATION."

The consent form was four pages long. In response to a concern that many women did not understand that "tying your tubes," the colloquial way many referred to tubal ligation, was not a reversible procedure, the form underlined that what the patient was considering "should not be performed if you think you might ever wish to have a child again. The chances of undoing this operation are limited." It had patients affirm specifically that they had been advised about all methods of birth control and of the availability of abortion. The largest portion of the form was an extensive, plainspoken, *Our Bodies Ourselves*–ish description of tubal ligation, in three surgical variants. These descriptions were followed by a blank in which the patient had to write in the name of the type of surgery she was to have and the doctor who explained it to her and was to perform it. Finally, the patient made her request. A month or more later (unless there were extenuating circumstances), she affirmed once again prior to surgery that she had "carefully considered all the information, advice and explanations given."

The Health and Hospitals Corporation draft sterilization guidelines lit a fire of opposition under doctors and some white feminists, as well as advocates for voluntary sterilization. In the New York City public hospital system, senior physicians in obstetrical and gynecological departments (who also served as professors at the city's major medical schools) said that the guidelines, if adopted, would narrow doctors' right to recommend and perform sterilization when they thought it was appropriate for their patients. Dr. Myron Gordon, the chief of service at Metropolitan Hospital and a professor at New York Medical College, complained to the committee cochair, Dr. Norman Herzig, about the "tone of distrust and dismissal of the physicians' role" in one of the committee's many drafts. Herzig responded to the complaints of his professional colleagues by withholding endorsement from his own committee's work. He protested the committee's language on post-sterilization "regret"—a concept supported by research at the time. In

Puerto Rico, for example, a research study found that 36 percent of sterilized women regretted their operations and 75 percent of them desired children and had not been aware that the surgery was irreversible at the time they had it. A study of sterilization patients on the mainland found the highest rates of regret among those who were sterilized at the same time that they were having abortions, perhaps a testament to the amount of pressure that was placed on women before and even after the abortion laws changed.

In hindsight, the willingness of CESA and the HHC committee to use the idea of regret may, as Karen Stamm suggested, have unintentionally provided the anti-abortion movement with an idea for how to frame its own arguments. After years of using the idea of abortion regret as a talking point, the anti-abortion movement won a major victory from the U.S. Supreme Court. Without the support of research data, Justice Anthony Kennedy used the idea of potential abortion regret as a basis for upholding the constitutionality of a federal law banning so-called partial-birth abortion in the 2007 case *Gonzalez v. Carhart*. "Respect for human life finds an ultimate expression in the bond of love the mother has for her child," he wrote. "While we find no reliable data to measure the phenomenon, it seems unexceptionable to conclude some women come to regret their choice to abort the infant life they once created and sustained."

After months of negotiation, the doctors who were alarmed about some of the advisory committee's recommendations simply stopped responding to revisions and refused to endorse the guidelines. The American College of Obstetricians and Gynecologists opposed the proposal—as the organization's California chapter opposed a law years later forbidding the state prison system from using public funds to perform sterilizations on women who were incarcerated. A group of doctors filed suit to block the HHC guidelines from becoming policy. They argued that the new rules would rob them of their First Amendment rights to speak and to practice their profession and would prevent individuals from exercising reproductive autonomy. CESA's "short answer" to their suit was, as Stamm put it, "Listen, you don't have a First Amendment right to commit fraud. So you don't tell people it's not permanent, you don't tell people it's a nothing, which is what people were being told. You don't tell them it's reversible; it's not really reversible. And you don't say stupid things to people, like, 'When you're a good girl again, I'll undo it'"—reportedly the words a doctor from Kings County Hospital used before he operated on the incarcerated woman whose story had inspired the CESA members to take action.

Some of the most ardent advocates of abortion rights opposed the guidelines. However, this did not mean that CESA was alone. The political coalition in favor of the guidelines had less mainstream power than the coalition that won New York's game-changing abortion law. But it was a broad and fierce coalition nonetheless. Coming from the perspective that women were not a unified group with shared experiences that could be improved with more "sisterhood" but a collection of people with diverse experiences and needs, CESA was "in sync with welfare rights, civil rights, consumer rights, women's health, feminist, Native American, Puerto Rican and anti-imperialist organizations, and almost everyone else except the professional medical and population organizations."

The Association for Voluntary Sterilization and Planned Parenthood worked together closely to oppose the guidelines. The Association for Voluntary Sterilization had started early in the twentieth century as a group committed to *involuntary* sterilizations and reinvented itself after World War II as a defender of families' right to access sterilization when they wanted to—in the face of hospital and government policies that kept (white, relatively well-off, nondisabled) people from having the sterilization procedures they chose. These two organizations argued that the waiting period and cumbersome consent procedure violated the rights of doctors and of women or couples who wanted the option of sterilization as reliable birth control.

On the other hand, the representative of *Ms.* magazine who served on the Health and Hospitals Corporation advisory committee remained an ardent backer of the guidelines. The National Black Feminist Organization, which was represented on the committee, never withdrew its support. The American Civil Liberties Union initially opposed the new rules and then, amid internal debate, supported them: It was difficult for white lawyers from the ACLU to see the through-line from supporting a woman's freedom to end a pregnancy, and to have a sterilization surgery if she so wished, to trying to keep her from being pressured to end her reproductive life. Well-off white people, including feminists in the ACLU Women's Rights and Reproductive Freedom Projects, had few experiences that led them to believe that doctors and policy makers had racist and class biases that might make them operate against a patient's will or manipulate her into giving consent for a procedure she did not really want. In the end, the heads of the New York Civil Liberties Union and ACLU Reproductive Freedom Project offered "strong support for the policies embodied by" the proposed guidelines. Quiet dissent from a few white feminists affiliated with the organization continued.

The Committee to End Sterilization Abuse defeated its powerful opponents and won unanimous approval for the guidelines from the board of the Health and Hospitals Corporation. This meant that all thirteen hospitals in New York City's public system—hospitals that saw many thousands of patients each year—were instructed to abide by the thirty-day waiting time for sterilization, to provide translators and translated forms to patients who didn't speak or read English, and to give each woman who requested sterilization a counseling session in which she heard about alternative means of birth control that were both reliable and reversible, and about legal abortion.

The victory was one result of the inside/outside strategy masterminded by Esta Armstrong and Helen Rodríguez-Trías. While battling "inside" the committee, they and the other CESA members mobilized a campaign of public education and protest. They spoke to virtually every community group that would have them and took interviews with every media outlet that expressed interest. As Stamm explained, the "outside" part of the strategy was not always far outside: "On the one hand," she remembered, "we were in the city's parks doing street theater and throwing darts at a target with the face of Antonio Silva, who headed the sterilization program in Puerto Rico" and was being considered for a permanent job at Lincoln Hospital. On the other hand, they made repeated presentations to get buy-in for the guidelines from each hospital's community board. "So almost to a one they approved our proposal." In an era of community control, members of those boards were able to counter the doctors' opposition by saying, for example, "We represent Bellevue Hospital and we want to see the guidelines passed."

After their triumph with the public hospital rules, Karen Stamm remembered, CESA members "were thinking what were we going to focus on." They considered a frontal challenge to national Medicaid regulations that reimbursed states at a higher rate if a patient had a sterilization surgery than if she had an abortion, or returning to CESA's roots in the Puerto Rico crisis by fighting State Department programs that pushed population control in low-income countries across the globe.

Before they had a chance to decide, Stamm said, "I got a phone call from the city council, which said, . . . 'We're taking the regulations that you guys have enacted, we're going to make a law out of them, and you are going to do the organizing.' I said we're not ready." The staff person on the other end of the line replied, "Yes, you will be." If it passed, then the law would apply to all hospitals, health clinics, and doctors' offices in New York City, and not just to the municipal hospitals covered by the guidelines Armstrong and Rodríguez-Trías had ushered to passage. It would cover male and female patients, whereas the HHC guidance applied only to women. Although the HHC guidelines were also a form of law, city council legislation had a higher profile and would be enforced by the city's health department.

The city council member who expressed interest was Carter Burden, a progressive patrician politician who was eager to make his mark. "Not everybody in CESA was thrilled about it," Stamm remembered, since organizing around the city council law kept the group from returning its attention to Puerto Rico and U.S. international policy. "But I thought this is a fabulous opportunity"—to pass the nation's first law to fight sterilization abuse. "I mean, it may never come again. So we put together a campaign." That campaign was a replay of the one CESA conducted to win new sterilization guidelines in the public hospital system—including the organizing that members did with hospital staff and community boards. The guidelines were opposed, once again, by doctors of obstetrics and gynecology, Planned Parenthood locally and nationally, the Association for Voluntary Sterilization, and the national leadership of NARAL and the National Organization for Women, as well as New York City's own health department. The result was a 38–0 victory for CESA and Councilman Burden, with three abstentions, a rout for their opponents.

How did the anti-sterilization-abuse David win against the Goliath of its more powerful allies? Stamm, who had by this time become CESA's sole paid staff person and chief organizer, remembered the huge effort that went into the win. You can almost hear an exhausted yawn behind the details: CESA members and allies spoke to "thousands of people," wrote "hundreds of letters," testified at two public hearings the city council convened on Burden's proposal, "lobbied councilmembers, personally, unannounced," and monitored "the enemy," a phrase that referred to Planned Parenthood and the Association for Voluntary Sterilization, including by infiltrating their closed-door meetings. By February 1977, CESA's tirelessness had won endorsements from progressive medical groups including the Medical Committee for Human Rights, liberal Protestant congregations such as those represented by the Brooklyn Council of Churches, the New York Civil Liberties Union, the Community Advisory Board of the private St. Luke's Hospital, and at least four city council members in addition to Burden. By the time the proposal came to a vote, it had support from the National Black Feminist Organization and, in a coup born of persistence and persuasion, the New York City chapter of the National Organization for Women, which departed from the stance of the group's national leaders and switched from a no on the public hospital guidelines to yes on Councilman Burden's draft law.

CESA won by regenerating and expanding the coalition that had pushed the HHC to change its sterilization guidelines. CESA members accepted quiet, unsolicited support from people who opposed both abortion and sterilization abuse (which are both, at least in theory, anathema to Catholic doctrine). While this didn't win Stamm and Rodríguez-Trías any friends at NARAL or NOW, it served their goal of passing the law—and suggested that it might someday be possible to create a new political coalition dedicated to ensuring that all people had what they needed to make genuine choices about when and whether to parent. One city council member declared publicly that he felt compelled to vote for the initiative because it was endorsed by the New York chapter of NOW and the anti-abortion movement at the same time.

Thanks to CESA's focus on an issue that was immediately germane to Black and Latino communities, and to poor people across New York, the group had ties to communities that treated most feminist organizations as irrelevant at best. One turning point for the campaign occurred when a Black woman called the CESA office with a story about the staff of a private hospital, Lenox Hill in Manhattan, pressuring her to consent to sterilization. She agreed to testify publicly about her experience. When a council member asked her why she felt she had been pressured, the woman replied, "'Because I'm poor, black, and on welfare,' and," Stamm remembered, "the room erupted. That told everybody what the strength of the issue was." CESA's endorsements and lobbying operation were diverse—in contrast to their opponents, who were virtually all white and socially prominent.

CESA members and allies showed up to lobby in "multi-racial groups of four (often including a NOW member)." The fact that they were new to the business of influencing politicians worked in their favor, as did the fact that many, including Stamm, whose salary came from a federal government training program, didn't have a lot of money. They "looked respectable but never 'well-heeled.' One of the legislative assistants said later that they owed their success to the fact that they represented no special interest, came from diverse backgrounds and let their inexperience convey the depth of their conviction. In contrast, the opposition were well-heeled professional lobbyists who often alienated the legislators they visited."

The creation of CESA, the first activist group in U.S. history dedicated to fighting sterilization abuse, and passage of the Burden bill, the first law to curb the abuse, were national news. Activists around the country followed New York's lead and created grassroots groups to fight sterilization abuse and public policies of population control. Some of these other groups were called CESA, but others took different names. They never coalesced into a formal national network or centralized organization with a single agenda. Instead, each local chapter, whether in New Haven, Connecticut, or in Boston, Western Massachusetts, Philadelphia, Baltimore, Chicago, or Northern or Southern California, worked on issues that were most relevant to its members. In Saint Louis, Missouri, for example, the CESA affiliate focused on fighting a program funded by the U.S. Agency for International Development, which trained foreign doctors in "advanced fertility management techniques" at Washington University hospital. The aim of the government program they protested was to enable the sterilization of up to one quarter of the world's women of reproductive age. A CESA affiliate in Western Massachusetts focused exclusively on fighting sterilizations of Puerto Ricans and other women from Latin America and the Caribbean in that area. Activists in Hartford, Connecticut, focused on the problem of sterilization of cognitively disabled people in institutions, fighting surgeries that were performed on people who could not meaningfully consent to them, and the sexual abuse that occurred in institutions, to which sterilization to avoid pregnancy was seen as a backward kind of solution. In Boston, the radical Black lesbians of the Combahee River Collective worked with white socialist feminists to form a local CESA chapter that demonstrated at Boston City Hospital against sterilization abuse and for abortion rights. Barbara Smith of the collective remembered the white women from CESA being the only feminists she had met up to that time who "actually understood that you could not really deal with sexism and the exploitation of women if you didn't look at capitalism and also at racism." She recalled Dr. Rodríguez-Trías "inspiring us and teaching us about—strategically—how we could indeed bring this issue to the fore."

As CESA's impact and the awareness of the *Relf* case grew nationally, scandals in Los Angeles and the federal government's Indian Health Service made clear that the problem of forced sterilization in communities of color went far beyond New York City. At L.A. County Hospital, a whistleblower found a 742 percent increase in elective hysterectomies and 470 percent increase in tubal ligations in the recent past. Chicanas organized the Committee to Stop Forced Sterilization separate from the abortion-centered activism of well-off white feminists and from the male-led Chicano movement. Ten women sued the hospital, claiming they were sterilized without having given genuine, informed consent—because the procedure was not explained fully to them, or because it was explained only in English and they spoke Spanish, or because, as one patient testified, she was denied medication for her labor pains until she consented to sterilization.

The women were Mexican American, not Puerto Rican, but their treatment echoed the stories CESA members had heard about the treatment of Spanish-speaking public hospital patients in New York City. Although four of the women were so uninformed about what doctors had done to them that they sought birth control after having been sterilized, the judge in their civil case ruled against them. He found that there was no "sinister, invidious social purpose" at work in what the whistleblower and one witness at the trial reported was a well-known policy within the hospital to push sterilizations on low-income Mexican American mothers. He held the individual doctors harmless because they operated under the "bona fide belief" that their patients either consented or "would have consented" had they been able (as, for example, with a woman who was under general anesthesia on the operating table when her husband consented on her behalf).

For anyone who wasn't convinced by CESA's public education campaign or the publicity about sterilization abuse in Los Angeles, Indigenous women, too, started reporting sterilization abuse in the middle 1970s. They charged that the very worst violations of women's reproductive autonomy came in the same years when mainstream feminists were celebrating abortion rights victories like New York's 1970 reform law and the Supreme Court decision in *Roe v. Wade*. Reports of involuntary or coercive sterilization originated with nonprofessional health-care workers called community health representatives, with Native American nurses, and with a Choctaw Cherokee physician named Dr. Constance Redbird Pinkerton-Uri. Pinkerton-Uri reported that a twenty-six-year-old patient on whom an Indian Health Service doctor had performed a full hysterectomy had come to her in 1972 seeking a "womb transplant" so that she could have children, now that she was ready to do so. Clearly, she had not been fully informed of, or had not understood fully, the surgery her doctor performed.

Senator James Abourzek responded to the grassroots and demanded a government assessment of sterilization in the Indian Health Service. In 1976, the Government Accounting Office published its report, which was damning and yet incomplete. Reviewing four of twelve regions the Indian Health Service covered, for the years 1973–76, the report concluded that doctors and hospitals serving Native women did not follow the government's own sterilization guidelines. These were the guidelines Judge Gerhard Gesell found wanting in the *Relf*

case, which CESA members considered so inadequate that they organized to create something more protective in New York. The report
did not consider the sterilizations within histories of which Native
activists were well aware—generations of land grabs by white settlers, and over a century of efforts to stamp out Native culture by
taking children from their communities and raising them in Indian
boarding schools. Pinkerton-Uri estimated, on the basis of data in
the government report, that 25 percent of all Indigenous women
of reproductive age had been sterilized. In 1978, women from over
thirty Nations formed Women of All Red Nations to battle against
sterilization abuse and for their "personal sovereignty."

Before the campaign against sterilization abuse went national, but
after CESA had won rigorous guidelines across New York by making it urgent for the city council to pass a law that included them,
Karen Stamm paused for a moment to consider CESA's success. The
victory in New York, she wrote, not only helped the organization
and its cause gain recognition from the powerful in city hall. It also
gave a bloody nose to their opposition and punctured the bubble that
surrounded elite thinking about race, class, population, and women's
bodies in post–World War II America. Perhaps most important, the
diverse, multiracial membership of the movement against sterilization
abuse gained "inner cohesion and love for each other." Together, they
formed a powerful, resourceful instrument of social change, connected to nearly everyone who had a stake in the issue, except a set
of leading doctors, professionals committed to lowering population
growth, and a subgroup of mainstream feminists. Their opposition,
she wrote, was "at a loss to comprehend what we are and how this
happened to them."

Chapter Ten

Toward Reproductive Freedom

L ATE IN the evening of July 13, 1977, lightning struck, the local power companies failed, and nine million New Yorkers were left in darkness. Dr. Helen Rodríguez-Trías and a group of activists were meeting at her apartment to plan their next moves. The Committee to End Sterilization Abuse had just won historic legislation in the city council, and yet their fight was far from over. The law was supposed to prevent hard-sell sterilization techniques, but low-income women with narrow options were still the ones most likely to be sterilized in New York hospitals. The evidence indicated that some doctors were still pressuring them into it. Even abortion rights, which seemed relatively secure after initial skirmishes over New York State's decriminalization and the Supreme Court's decision in *Roe*, were anything but. With the Hyde Amendment, a majority-Democratic Congress chose to forbid states from using federal Medicaid funds to cover abortions—meaning that women with low incomes, disproportionately Black and brown women, could face a major barrier to abortion access. A ruling from a New York judge prevented the amendment from going into effect, but only temporarily. The future of abortion access for poor women was not looking rosy.

After the blackout started, a few women navigated their way down the narrow stairwell in the darkness and walked east to Broadway to see what was going on. There was a promise of chaos in the summer air. Atina Grossmann, a graduate student leftist and feminist activist, concluded that it "was going to be a pretty dicey night." She and the others made their way back to Rodríguez-Trías's place. Karen Stamm was there, too. "Helen," Stamm remembered, "cool as a cucumber, invited us all to stay on the couches, floors, bathtubs, wherever we could fit."

Sheltered by Rodríguez-Trías's hospitality, many of the activists talked and snacked all night. From the bleakness of that night, the women in apartment 8A started to imagine a new politics of reproductive rights that encompassed both abortion access and the fight against sterilization abuse. They committed both to sustaining CESA and to building on its work—and to building on the contributions of Black, Puerto Rican, Mexican American, and Native American women across the country who were stretching the limits of a feminism that had come to focus narrowly on abortion. Although they didn't yet know it, they were starting to build a movement for "Reproductive Freedom," including the freedom to bear and to raise a child.

What these activists accomplished, with the help of hundreds of others around New York City and eventually the United States, deserves the attention of feminists, reproductive rights advocates, and everyone who wants to understand movements for social change. They critiqued established organizations and their understandings of both feminism and reproduction. They developed ideas and an agenda that still matter today. And they hit roadblocks that kept them from going forward. If we are ever going to revive a winning movement for reproductive rights, then we need to study the strengths of these predecessors, and their roadblocks, too—the differences over race, sexuality, and organizing strategy that tore their efforts apart as the need for them was becoming incredibly urgent.

The meeting at Rodríguez-Trías's was a follow-up to a mass gathering in response to the impending cuts in low-income women's access to abortion under the Hyde Amendment, which had occurred a few days earlier. Meredith Tax, a writer and intellectual in her midthirties who had worked in a range of feminist and left-wing groups without finding one that quite fit, was one of the scores of feminist activists who had come out for that mass gathering to figure out how to respond to this new threat. Tax had just arrived in New York City, too late to join the local CESA campaigns for heightened sterilization guidelines. But she was already attuned to the issue of sterilization abuse. "The Hyde Amendment came down," she remembered. "All of a sudden there was this panic, which spread through the telephone lines." Friends of hers who were part of women's liberation groups in lower Manhattan called and said, "Come down, there's going to be a big meeting."

They gathered at the Village Vanguard jazz club, "a huge meeting," Tax remembered. Unusually for a feminist gathering later in the 1970s, after the women's liberation movement had crested and started to recede, "I didn't see anybody I knew because there were so many people there." Tax recalled that feminists with diverse styles and politics showed up because they all cared about the Hyde Amendment. The audience included members of the New York City chapter of NOW, "downtown" feminist radicals, "uptown" academic feminists, and the Puerto Rican and white socialists of CESA. Women from NOW focused on Democratic Party politics and specific policies. By contrast, radical feminists in the mold of writer Ellen Willis saw the crux of the issue as "punishing women for having sex. And I got up," Tax recalled, "and I said I thought we had to find a way to frame the issue that would reach into other communities, and we should couple it with sterilization." Her suggestion dropped with the force of a lead balloon. However, it served as her introduction to the CESA members in the room, who came over excitedly when the meeting was over to ask, "Who are you?"

The diverse crowd at the Village Vanguard couldn't agree on how best to fight the Hyde Amendment. They organized two follow-up meetings, scheduled for the same night, which turned out to be the night the city's lights went out. The first meeting, uptown, was the one at Rodríguez-Trías's place. The second occurred downtown in the apartment of Rosalyn Baxandall, the woman whose story had been the lead-off for the abortion speak-out back in 1969. Writer Alix Kates Shulman, who remembered being "completely freaked out by the Hyde Amendment," was in attendance downtown, along with Tax and Willis.

Her spine stiffened by support from CESA members, Tax again pressed the point she had started to make at the jazz club. As she recalled, the most vocal people in the room wanted to frame a response to the Hyde Amendment, and to any other efforts to narrow abortion access, as endangering women's "sexual freedom. And I said I thought that was the wrong thing tactically or strategically, that we had been doing that for years and we were still all white and middle-class and . . . we were never going to be strong enough, have a strong enough movement as long as we were all white and middle-class. And so I was arguing with Ellen [Willis] about that and the lights went out."

Everyone made it home safely, and the two groups, from downtown and uptown, convened again. They were coming to understand that they had to create a new organization but had yet to settle on an agenda or name. Netsy Firestein, a CESA member who joined the group relatively late, remembered getting involved with this new organization after seeing a flyer posted in her neighborhood, which announced yet another planning meeting, this time at a church uptown. Tax remembered attending that gathering, too, and she remembered that it was just as big and lively as the meetings that preceded it: the radical feminists with whom she had been arguing when the lights went out were there, as were CESA members, "and a whole bunch of other people who I didn't know who were just from all over the place," diverse in terms of class but not, except for Latinas affiliated with CESA, in terms of race or ethnicity, and all eager to find new strategies for the reproductive rights and women's movements.

It was this post-blackout meeting that really birthed the new effort. The group agreed that it was time to create a new organization, and then engaged in a protracted debate about what it should advocate and what it should be called. CESA activists insisted that, in addition to abortion, the agenda and the name both had to include sterilization abuse. Eventually, the assembled chose to call their new entity the Committee for Abortion Rights and Against Sterilization Abuse, CARASA. Unlike the CESA acronym, which spells out a real and relevant Spanish word, CARASA only sounds like Spanish. The word has no particular meaning, but it captured the essence of these feminists' concerns.

Susan Davis, another CESA member, became active in the new group as it was forming. She remembered that it was especially important to include abortion rights *and* sterilization abuse because public policy joined the two issues. As the Hyde Amendment withdrew federal funding from abortions, federal Medicaid dollars continued to cover 90 percent of the costs of a sterilization. Fighting the Hyde Amendment meant, at the same time, fighting the covert or overt pressure women might face to get sterilized because they had low incomes and knew that they couldn't access abortion. CESA organizer Karen Stamm, who also became a founding member of CARASA, underlined this point, too. As they were when she was a young abortion patient, and hospital staff offered a consent form that not at all coincidentally had a consent form for sterilization on its flip side, access to legal and affordable abortions and resistance to coercive sterilizations were two sides of the same page.

In responding to the Hyde Amendment, advocates re-created the broad coalition that had changed the abortion laws in New York and the nation. But the bitterness and divisions that emerged in policy debates about sterilization never disappeared. Tax remembered that even members of NOW in New York City, the one feminist organization that had opposed sterilization guidelines initially and came to support them before the city council, were leery of joining CARASA. The impression she got from NOW members was that they thought the progenitors of this new effort were "crazy leftists"—and, to be sure, Tax and some of the other leaders were people of the political left who might have called themselves "democratic socialists" before they identified themselves as members of the Democratic Party. In Tax's view, the NOW feminists seemed to have had class biases that made them uncomfortable in the company of someone like her, an activist intellectual and single parent with a "crappy little apartment" and not enough chairs for everyone to sit down at the same time during a meeting.

Tensions were sharper between this new group and Planned Parenthood and the Association for Voluntary Sterilization than they were with NOW. Planned Parenthood and the Association for Voluntary Sterilization collaborated with CARASA to fight the federal Hyde Amendment. At the national level, they lost that fight, with Congress ultimately settling on a compromise that allowed Medicaid-funded abortions only in cases of rape, incest, or risk to the pregnant person's life. But a unified movement for abortion rights succeeded at making the Hyde Amendment effectively moot in New York State, mobilizing repeatedly to ensure that abortion coverage was included in the state portion of the program's budget. This was remarkable at a time when thirty-three states eliminated public funding for abortion either significantly or altogether in the wake of the Hyde Amendment.

Even while working together to keep state Medicaid funding in the budget, CARASA members battled Planned Parenthood and the Association for Voluntary Sterilization over their policies on sterilization abuse. Many CESA activists, including Karen Stamm, began at this point to wear two organizational hats, remaining committed to the important single-issue politics of CESA and participating in CARASA, and particularly in its committee on legislation, the center of the new group's work against sterilization abuse. CESA and CARASA, together, opposed an attempt by a state legislator who was close to Planned Parenthood and the Association for Voluntary Sterilization to pass a state law that would have preempted and essentially nullified the New York City sterilization guidelines CESA had worked hard to get passed.

The debate between CARASA and CESA, and Planned Parenthood and the Association for Voluntary Sterilization, was not merely a philosophical one. The latter two groups were preparing to loan hundreds of thousands of dollars (they had put up $300,000 of their own money, and banks had contributed $450,000) to freestanding abortion clinics to encourage them to add sterilization procedures to the services they provided. Their intention was to train medical staff at the clinics to perform the relatively simple, quick—too quick for the comfort of anti-sterilization-abuse activists—and inexpensive procedure called the mini-laparotomy, which would be affordable for the patient and her health insurance company. They wanted storefront laparotomy provision in New York City to become a model for the nation. The bill they backed in the state legislature contained a waiting period of seventy-two hours for sterilizations performed outside hospital settings, considerably shorter than the thirty-day-long waiting period that the city council had specified in its law. The longer waiting period would have made it far more difficult for the clinics to provide efficient and inexpensive sterilization procedures, and therefore to perform them en masse.

Members of the CARASA legislation committee and of CESA viewed this legislative attempt to clear the way for thousands of storefront sterilizations as a direct threat to progress against sterilization abuse that CESA had forged in New York City. Committee chair and attorney Anne Teicher wrote on behalf of CARASA, and Stamm on behalf of CESA to warn members of the state senate's Health Committee that the bill left "wide loopholes through which abuse will occur and would invalidate" the city council law. CARASA and CESA members mobilized to oppose the proposal, and thanks to their work, the legislation's sponsor withdrew it from consideration. As in New York City's public hospital system and city council, the anti-sterilization-abuse forces scored a victory, and their opponents suffered an embarrassing loss. After defeating the bill, Teicher and Stamm underlined the relationship between abortion and sterilization in a coauthored letter to the editor of a local newspaper. They argued that a "grossly abusive situation" would have emerged if the plan for storefront sterilizations had gone forward while the federal government was withdrawing Medicaid funds for abortion and continuing to pay 90 percent of the cost of sterilizations. (They did not yet know that New York would retain abortion coverage in its state Medicaid plan year after year.) The thirty-day waiting period, they insisted, was a necessary policy "made against a background of past and continuing abuse, characterized by the insistence of the medical establishment on usurping women's decision-making power over their own bodies."

NOW and NARAL did not go into business with the Association for Voluntary Sterilization. But "they were ready to kill us," in the words of progressive bureaucrat Esta Armstrong, for policies on sterilization abuse that supposedly infringed reproductive rights and started down a slippery slope to greater government control of people's options for contraception—at the very moment when the federal government was itself narrowing access to abortion.

These philosophical differences were concrete and long-lasting. Five years after *Roe v. Wade* an attendee at a "teach-in" about abortion rights and public funding "asked angrily how some of the speakers could justify abortion on demand, but not sterilization on demand." Dr. Helen Rodríguez-Trías responded that she balanced "the slight inconveniences of [a] 30-day waiting period versus the danger of many instances of abuse. . . . Frankly," she said, "I would choose to inconvenience the few."

These same divisions came to the fore when CARASA members and their allies in CESA had the opportunity to change policy at the national level. After CESA's repeated wins and the founding of CARASA, loosely affiliated partisans of the anti-sterilization-abuse movement met for a National Conference on Sterilization Abuse in September 1977. A delegation from the conference, including veterans of the New York policy fights, met with representatives of the Department of Health, Education, and Welfare (HEW, later

Health and Human Services) about the kinds of regulations needed at the federal level. A short time later, Stamm received a call from someone in the agency's Office of the General Counsel. "We have been watching" developments in New York City, the official said, first in the municipal hospital system and then citywide. The Carter administration wanted to make the city's sterilization standards "a federal project": HEW was ready to go public with a proposal to make a version of CESA's guidelines its own.

Stamm knew that if the agency followed through, this would be a huge development. Like all other federal agencies, the department issued regulations that specified how it would implement the laws passed by Congress and signed by the president. These regulations had the force of law. Millions of people in the United States would be covered by new HEW rules, including many from the groups that faced the greatest threat of coercive sterilization, because they participated in health-care programs that were part of HEW. These included people with low incomes who utilized the federal Medicaid program, disabled people covered by Medicare, and Indigenous Americans on and off reservations whose health care was financed by the Indian Health Service. Although it did not affect the health care of every person in the United States, HEW touched every hospital and every doctor who accepted payments under these programs. CESA and CARASA members had reason to believe that, if they could get HEW to issue new regulations on sterilization, they could change policy throughout the health care system.

The only catch was that administration officials needed to see support for the guidelines before adopting them. The department would convene ten hearings on the proposal, one in each city where it had regional headquarters, and one in Washington, D.C. If Stamm and her allies in CESA, CARASA, and related groups testified powerfully at every hearing, then there was a good chance that their proposals would be written into the agency's regulations.

On December 1, 1977, the administration issued proposed sterilization regulations that largely mirrored the New York City law. The regulations covered both men and women, and required a written consent form for the patient in their primary language, a thirty-day waiting period, and an additional form on which the doctor had to attest to having informed the patient about the permanence of sterilization and having made it clear that the patient's public benefits were not at risk, no matter what the patient decided about sterilization. In addition, the regulations barred the use of hysterectomy for the purpose of contraception, since sterilization by other methods was safer and less invasive. Building on the New York City law, the draft regulations included a new approval system for patients who expressed a desire for sterilization and who were incarcerated, or who were held in other institutions or cognitively impaired. The public had ninety days to comment on the regulations before they became final—and eleven hearings at which to air questions and concerns.

Stamm and other CARASA and CESA activists organized the necessary national campaign to support the proposed guidelines. Their allies, members of CESA from outside New York and comrades from affiliated groups, testified at each of the hearings. Meanwhile, CARASA members kept up their pressure on Joseph Califano, Jr., the secretary of Health, Education, and Welfare, for his role in implementing the Hyde Amendment. Democratic president Jimmy Carter had signed the budget bill to which the Hyde Amendment was an amendment, making it law. One of CARASA's biggest early actions was a protest of about two thousand people at New York University Law School during a lecture by Secretary Califano.

Dr. Helen Rodríguez-Trías spoke on behalf of CESA at the most significant of the hearings, in Washington, D.C. She supported the regulations but also critiqued them. Rodríguez-Trías placed the need for new guidelines and their limitations in political and economic context. She argued that, while they would go a long way toward eliminating the most overt forms of sterilization abuse, they couldn't reach "the coercive aspects" of a person's life, which made people choose sterilization because of their "social and economic conditions."

She urged the federal administration to make its rules even more like New York's than the proposed regulations already were, by including requirements that consent be given twice, that mandatory counseling be provided in the patient's primary language, and that the range of specific medical options for sterilization be described on the consent forms so that people could more clearly choose among them. Rodríguez-Trías ended with a plea that was right out of her experience at Lincoln Hospital—for "patient advocacy with local consumer control," because no one was going to care as much about sterilization abuse in a particular hospital, or work as hard to prevent it, as those on whom the abuse was practiced.

The national debate that accompanied the proposed regulations mirrored the ones in New York. It lit up conflicts among feminists, and among members of the coalition for legal abortion, in Times Square neon: Black people, Latinos, Native Americans, and whites who thought about reproductive issues through a lens of race, class, and opposition to colonization favored heightened sterilization rules. The feminists who did not place race, class, and empire, and their impacts on people's experiences of reproduction, at the center of their world views, worried more about denying people their reproductive right *to* access sterilization than about their reproductive right to make a different choice.

At the end of an intense internal debate, NOW's executive board opposed the new federal guidelines. The organization's national leadership stuck to this position despite receiving "indignant letters from women's health groups all over the country," and from their own members, opposing that position. NOW joined Planned Parenthood, the Association for Voluntary Sterilization, and NARAL, as well as individual doctors and the American College of Obstetricians and Gynecologists, on the anti-guidelines side. Karen Mulhauser from NARAL spoke at the Washington, D.C., hearings. She decried the guidelines as a form of income-based discrimination, since they established a different standard for accessing sterilization for patients who received their health insurance via the Medicaid program or

Indian Health Service (that is, from programs that were under the HEW umbrella) than for those with private insurance. In New York City, CESA had addressed a similar concern with legislation that made the sterilization guidelines apply to all patients, and not only those who utilized public hospitals. Mulhauser did not propose this kind of solution. The National Medical Association, a membership organization for Black doctors, was the only professional medical group that favored the regulations.

As in New York, the forces that joined to endorse the new federal guidelines proved stronger than those that opposed them. It took a full year, but the Carter administration officially published the regulations on November 8, 1978, with an effective date of March 8, 1979. They didn't include the extra provisions Dr. Rodríguez-Trías had proposed at the hearings. They did include a minimum age of twenty-one for all sterilizations, a thirty-day wait, a bar on the federal government reimbursing any hospital that performed a hysterectomy as a form of contraception, and limitations on the sterilizations that could be performed on people who were institutionalized. Emblazoned on the first page of the government's information booklet on sterilization was the assurance: "Your decision at any time not to be sterilized will not result in the withdrawal or withholding of any benefits provided by programs or projects receiving federal funds." The administration left unsettled, for the time, whether cognitively disabled people who were capable of consenting to sterilization would be able to have them if certain procedures were followed, or if the presumption in favor of coercion would be so strong that the federal government would never support their sterilizations.

CARASA and CESA member Susan Davis used the Yiddish word "*verklempt,*" meaning overwhelmed with emotion, when she remembered the victory she and her friends won with the new regulations. "It was the first time," she said, "when I realized the terrific importance of political action. And it made me feel it was a signpost that yes, this struggle is really important."

✳   ✳   ✳

These hard-fought campaigns, for abortion funding in the face of the Hyde Amendment and for robust sterilization guidelines, raised fundamental questions that the broad coalition in favor of abortion decriminalization had downplayed: Who had the right to have a child? Or to refrain from having a child? Under what circumstances? Could a citizen whose access to health care was subject to public debate truly have the kind of privacy the Supreme Court had endorsed in *Roe v. Wade*? What was the price of reproductive rights for all—and were mainstream activists willing to demand that the government pay that price in terms not only of public funding for abortion but also the full range of supports that would enable people to exercise all of their reproductive options?

To answer these questions, CARASA members engaged in a searching inquiry about what was required for true reproductive rights for all people. This meant lots of meetings, some of them contentious and prolonged, to plan the group's activist agenda and, at the same time, to figure out what exactly the group stood for. Netsy Firestein recalled two kinds of meetings, general meetings of "hundreds of people," which were "really different than CESA in Helen's living room," and a rich diet of committee meetings that focused on specific topics or projects. CARASA member Rayna Rapp remembered, "We just met all the time."

CARASA was unlike perhaps all prior reproductive rights organizations in covering both sides of the coin, or the page, from the very beginning. As Rapp understood it, the victories CARASA and CESA won for heightened sterilization guidelines were "so, so important," and at the same time obviously limited in a way that made it urgent that the activists in these groups expand what they were asking for. If they were really going to eliminate what Rodríguez-Trías had called "the coercive aspects" of people's lives, which prevented genuine freedom of reproductive choice, then the movement "wasn't just going to be about abortion. And it wasn't just going to be about steriliza-tion abuse. It was going to be about neighborhoods where you could raise children. It was going to be about nutrition" that would lead to healthy pregnancies. The goal became, in Rapp's words, creating "the conditions that made it safe for people to actually be able to choose to have children, not only to not have children."

After many meetings, members of CARASA came to call their encompassing feminist vision an agenda for reproductive freedom. They developed this language in response to what they saw as a cramped understanding of reproductive rights by NOW and Planned Parenthood. For Susan Davis, "the whole thing about the concept" of reproductive freedom was that the movement's goal was "not just abortion, but it's everything that is involved in women's lives that are important to the whole issue of reproduction." At once vast and con-crete, the concept encapsulated their shared socialist feminist ideals. Speaking in terms of freedom was, too, a hat tip to feminists like Ellen Willis, who had wanted to start fighting the Hyde Amendment by asserting women's inalienable rights to sexual freedom. Reproductive freedom was "like liberation, women's liberation," as Davis put it, and at the same time captured the members' sense that no true liberation could be achieved without fighting economic inequality and "racial inequality, and all of the other elements that are part of our lives, culture as well, the whole shebang."

CARASA member Rayna Rapp couldn't remember when the group started speaking the language of reproductive freedom. She did remember that taking on that goal meant an ever-widening mandate— and more meetings! Freedom in the realm of reproduction required universal access to good health care, secure housing, and a range of safe birth control options. It encompassed the rights of lesbians, who, if they had come from heterosexual marriages, were routinely denied custody of their children by biased family court judges. Those who had not been in straight marriages but wanted to raise children were prevented by policy and custom from adopting as a couple, and the partners of women with children were prevented from second-parent adoption. "And all of those things came up," Rapp recalled. "And each one I'm sure was a struggle and a meeting and an 'Oh no, do I have to sit through another meeting?' But yes, you do have to sit through another meeting until you understand that the shitty state of New York City playgrounds means that it's not safe to have children in a lot of those housing projects." Despite what could seem sometimes like an overwhelming commitment to CARASA, all the meetings and all the thinking-through led the members to agree that, "yeah, safe housing and safe playgrounds and safe streets for children," and health care and freedom from police violence, "that, too, is part of reproductive freedom. Because what does it mean to have a child, only to spend your life potentially losing that child?"

CARASA members didn't just formulate their new approach to reproductive politics in their meetings. They worked through a committee system that developed their understanding of particular issues, and they joined action-oriented coalitions with other organizations to move parts of their agenda forward. The childcare committee, for example, sponsored a conference in 1980 headlined "Child Care: What We Want and How to Get it." CARASA was one sponsor of a demonstration that demanded that New York governor Hugh Carey allocate more funds to childcare so that fifty centers slated to close could stay open. In 1983, CARASA joined the coalition that supported students and faculty at Medgar Evers College in the City University of New York system, who demanded that the college—and the whole university system—provide subsidized childcare so that the students, many of whom were working-class Black and white women raising young children, could finish their educations and so that faculty could do their jobs. They protested for weeks, and, with help from CARASA members, created their own temporary child care center that students could use.

Members of the CARASA Trade Union/Workplace Committee protested the policy of the company American Cyanamid, announced in 1978, compelling women who wanted to work in its paint factory to be sterilized so that they would not have children with birth defects caused by the toxic chemicals in the paint. CARASA joined a coalition with labor, women's, and environmental activists that grew into a Committee for the Reproductive Rights of Workers, which challenged the policy and worked to inform the public about it. (This activism gave rise to a federal court case that challenged the company's policy, first as a workplace hazard under the Occupational Safety and Health Act, and then as an instance of sex discrimination, forbidden by Title VII of the Civil Rights Act of 1964. The U.S. Court of Appeals ruled in favor of the company in the former case, and in the latter, the women workers who brought the suit settled with the company out of court.) In remarks she gave at a conference on sterilization at work that CARASA cosponsored, Rodríguez-Trías drew similarities between corporate policies like American Cyanamid's and coerced sterilizations of Black women and Latinas in U.S. hospitals.

The CARASA Research Committee produced a book, *Women Under Attack*, which the group published in 1979. It was a shared effort, which involved a long list of CARASA members as writers and consultants. The main author and editor of *Women Under Attack* was Rosalind Pollack Petchesky, a political science professor at New Jersey's Ramapo College and later a recipient of a MacArthur Foundation "genius" award, who worked closely on the project with Rapp, an anthropologist teaching at the New School for Social Research in Manhattan. Grossmann, a historian of Germany who was then in graduate school, was a junior member of the team and felt that the project offered a precious opportunity to integrate scholarship with activism.

The main project of the book was to define and explore the idea of reproductive freedom. Echoing Rodríguez-Trías's testimony in favor of sterilization regulations before the Department of Health, Education, and Welfare, the group wrote: "When we say women must have reproductive freedom, we mean the possibility of controlling for themselves, in a real and practical way—that is, free from economic, social, or legal coercion—whether, and under what conditions, they will have children." They emphasized the two sides of "reproduction control": restrictions on opportunities to have children and on the ability to refrain from having children.

CARASA offered a New York diner menu's worth of supports that would enable reproductive freedom. These included "among other things, the universal availability of good, safe, cheap birth control; and adequate counseling for all women and men about all currently existing methods. It must mean adequate abortion services and an end to involuntary sterilization. It must mean the availability to all people of good public childcare centers and schools; decent housing, adequate welfare, and wages high enough to support a family and quality medical, pre- and post-natal and maternal care."

Beyond the social or political, *Women Under Attack* outlined the psychological and cultural shifts that would also be necessary foundations for reproductive freedom. True reproductive freedom, the women of CARASA wrote, "must mean freedom of sexual choice, which implies an end to the cultural norms that define women in terms of having children and living with a man; an affirmation of people's right to raise children outside conventional families; and, in the long run, a transformation of childcare arrangements so that they are shared among women and men." They concluded by acknowledging the ambitious sweep of group's agenda: "Women have never had reproductive freedom in this sense."

Except for Dr. Helen Rodríguez-Trías and other Puerto Rican CESA alums who joined the group, CARASA's membership was virtually all white. That was a problem, which members acknowledged without knowing how to solve it. At the same time, CARASA members were not the totally clueless white feminists of popular lore. Their political approach encompassed issues that mattered to Black women and Latinas. First of all, the group worked on the problem of sterilization abuse. Beyond its efforts around state legislation and the federal

HEW guidelines, CARASA joined with community members in the Bronx to prevent a doctor named Antonio Silva, who had been a leader in the government family planning agency in Puerto Rico that was responsible for promoting sterilization as a primary means of birth control, from gaining a permanent position at Lincoln Hospital. Despite an article in the Puerto Rican Socialist Party's newspaper, *Claridad*, in which Silva indicated a preference for an inexpensive one-time sterilization procedure over providing ongoing access to reversible contraception, he had been appointed interim director of the Department of Obstetrics and Gynecology at Lincoln. (An article by Deb Kayman in CARASA's newspaper claimed that neighbors referred to the hospital as a "slaughterhouse," a dramatic heightening of the charge contained in its old nickname, "the butcher shop of the South Bronx.") The agitation paid off, and Silva's position was not made permanent.

CARASA also included welfare rights, an issue that mattered to many women who were not white, on its list of concerns and worked in coalition with at least one local activist welfare rights organization. Leaders like Meredith Tax understood that welfare, government financial aid that enabled parents to access income and raise their children in health and dignity, was a matter of reproductive freedom. However, in Tax's recollection CARASA did not work on the issue consistently or embrace it as a core concern, although members joined temporary coalitions that worked on welfare policy.

As imperfect as they surely were, these white feminists acknowledged the ways in which policies that prevented childbearing, and those that blocked access to contraception and abortion, affected "different groups of women differently." In other words, building on the understanding that Rodríguez-Trías had helped bring to CESA, their feminist theory was what later generations would call an "intersectional" one. Writing in the increasingly conservative late 1970s, they saw better-off white women facing pressure "to resume the 'woman's role' of full-time motherhood and housework. At the same time," they wrote, "low-income women—particularly those on welfare and those who are black, Hispanic, and Native American—are the targets of systematic, heavily funded programs of 'population control' as well as programs that aim to remove their children from them and into 'foster care' or state institutions." In addition, the authors of *Women Under Attack* acknowledged an "almost categorical" lack of reproductive freedom for women who were cognitively or physically disabled, and those in prison and other institutions.

Along with the major change CARASA helped produce in sterilization guidelines, the idea of reproductive freedom and the book that dug into its meaning were among the group's greatest contributions. CARASA distributed hundreds of copies of *Women Under Attack* to its allies in the women's health movement, the independent clinics that sprang up around the country to provide abortions after decriminalization, labor unions that were interested in a progressive take on reproductive rights, and the kinds of liberal church groups that had supported the Clergy Consultation Service in its heyday and after *Roe v. Wade* formed the backbone of its successor organization, the Religious Coalition for Abortion Rights. Rayna Rapp had free mailing privileges and friends in the mail room at the unconventional university at which she taught. From being "second in command" on the writing and editing, she became the book's mailer in chief.

CARASA published a second edition of the book in 1988. This time, the lead editor was Susan Davis, who considered it "one of the great offshoots of CARASA because it centralized our politics." She was joined on the writing and editing team by, among others, Kristin Booth Glen (then a judge on the New York County Supreme Court), Karen Stamm, and legislative committee chair Anne Teicher. This time, *Women Under Attack* took up the setbacks in the 1980s for the broad agenda they termed reproductive freedom. Davis and her collaborators met the politics of the era with a brief discussion of AIDS/HIV and an extensive catalog of cuts in social welfare programs and challenges to abortion access. They mentioned the meeting points between disability rights and reproductive freedom, and they explored lesbians' reproductive challenges—via an extended discussion of alternative reproductive technologies that lesbians (and others) might use, and a photo of a lesbian couple pushing a baby carriage while they walked in the 1987 National Lesbian and Gay March on Washington.

The second edition of *Women Under Attack* circulated widely. (I own a copy that I bought in 1991, when I was a young staff member at a Washington, D.C., think tank.) However, by the time it appeared, CARASA itself had basically ceased to exist. Despite the increased focus on lesbians' rights in this later version of the book, sexuality and lesbianism were at the center of conflicts that tore CARASA apart. The first explosion around these issues occurred early on, when Meredith Tax, as cochair of CARASA, invited an important radical feminist to educate the group on the earlier movement for abortion rights in New York. "And what did I know?" Tax asked. As she told the tale, the speaker "talked about two seconds on abortion rights" and then, unbidden, ranted about "how the problem was that gay people had infiltrated the women's movement and they were working for the CIA to break it up. And everybody starts screaming and yelling at her, and I said . . . 'Stop. Go.' Everybody is so mad at me for having her, and I had no idea." In the wake of this incident, a group of CARASA members formed a Lesbian Caucus whose mission was to explore relationships between lesbian rights and reproductive rights.

Then there was what Karen Stamm called "the great disruption." This was a more serious and sustained conflict in the organization, primarily between three lesbians who were very active in CARASA and a majority-straight membership. The three were Maxine Wolfe, Sarah Schulman, and Stephanie Roth. Wolfe was later a leader, and Schulman a member, of the paradigmatic (and paradigm-changing) AIDS activist group ACT UP, and both Schulman and Wolfe were founders in the early 1990s of Lesbian Avengers. Roth served as the sole staff person to CARASA and was also active in New York

Women Against Rape. Schulman joined the organization already out of the closet, but Roth came out while serving as CARASA's staff person, and Wolfe was a bisexual mother of two. The three, with other CARASA members, formed a Lesbian Action Committee (deliberately separate from the earlier Lesbian Caucus) that brought a new, politicized lesbian perspective into the group.

One of the most important moments in "the great disruption" was not overtly about sexuality. However, members' reactions were likely linked to already mounting anxiety about their staffperson (Roth) and a leader of their effort to organize nationally (Wolfe) coming out and bringing lesbian politics to the fore. Schulman, Roth, and members Libby Smith, Maureen Angelos, and Karen Zimmerman traveled to Washington, D.C., to protest congressional hearings on the Human Life Amendment. The amendment embodied the great goal of the anti-abortion movement, to rewrite the Constitution to cancel *Roe v. Wade* and make all abortions, as well as forms of contraception such as the IUD, illegal. As Schulman told the story in 1983: "No witnesses advocating abortion rights were allowed to speak. As one man testified that 'the fetus is an astronaut in a uterine spaceship,' we stood up in the chamber and shouted, 'A Woman's Life is a Human Life.'" She added later that they raised signs that advertised what they saw as the full reproductive rights agenda, including Lesbian Rights. Since the hearings were being covered live on television, the protest wound up on the evening broadcasts of all three national networks. "A Woman's Life is a Human Life" became a key slogan of the movement for reproductive freedom, printed on innumerable CARASA buttons, signs, and stickers and posted on walls throughout New York City. The CARASA members were arrested, charged with contempt of Congress, and convicted. They escaped a six-month sentence in federal prison in part because Schulman and Roth were open about both their politics and their sexuality. The judge, who appears to have been sympathetic to their feminism and was mother to an activist lesbian daughter, sentenced them to $100 fines.

This risky and effective action was reminiscent of earlier feminist protests that helped decriminalize abortion. However, Schulman found that some CARASA members were uncomfortable with the tactics she and the other protesters used—tactics of "direct action," immediate and often illegal moves that provoked a direct confrontation with people in positions of power—and others were simply unhappy that they had not cleared the tactics in a CARASA meeting before leaving New York. One member accused those who favored direct action, including the members of the CARASA Lesbian Action Committee, of "substitutionalism," a term from the old Marxist left that implied that one had taken on a role in the struggle that should more appropriately have been taken by someone from the working class. However, the activist lesbians and some other CARASA members saw themselves as people who were under attack and therefore the right ones to respond to a rising anti-feminist and anti-lesbian and -gay conservatism; in other words, they were not working to foment a working-class uprising, as an old Marxist politics might have asked them to, but carrying out the uprising themselves, for themselves.

Discomfort over tactics by some members seems to have been layered atop and intermixed with homophobia and the discomfort of some CARASA activists over the way Schulman, Wolfe, and Roth placed lesbianism at the center of their politics. The arguments of members of the Lesbian Action Committee seem to have confused and angered other CARASA members, who believed that they had been making progress toward incorporating lesbian rights into their platform for reproductive freedom. However, as Roth argued in CARASA's newspaper, *CARASA News*, the women on the committee didn't think of lesbianism as "simply another separate issue to add to our long list, but also as a way of understanding and analyzing all of the issues we address." Alison Colbert wrote an open letter to CARASA members in which she suggested that lesbians in the group "may not live with abortion as a gut/personal issue," and that straight members in her view did not treat lesbianism as a "gut" matter, at the core of their concerns.

After they were arrested in the capitol but before their trial, Schulman and Roth invited Andrea Dworkin, who was best known at that time for a book called *Woman Hating* (1974), to address a fundraiser for their legal defense. Unbeknownst to them, Dworkin's new book project on pornography had convinced her that progressives willfully ignored the misogyny that some porn made graphically visible. Dworkin thanked Schulman and Roth for inviting her and then offered her critique, "delivered in her humorless affect in a sweaty hot room," as Schulman remembered, to an audience of CARASA members and many of their male partners. Audience members started talking to drown out the rest of Dworkin's remarks. They threw things at the stage, and a group of them walked out.

A low point of the battle within CARASA, for Wolfe, was the time when other members referred to her behind her back as an "unconscious lesbian separatist." This, she thought, was little more than a cover for the others' discomfort with the work she, Schulman, and Roth were doing to weave lesbian liberation into CARASA's philosophy—to think of lesbianism, which challenged male-centered families and traditional social structures, as not merely one issue area among others but as a basis for a new radical politics of reproduction. Wolfe considered the "separatist" tag evidence of disrespect for her years in mixed-gender organizations and groups dedicated to child care and abortion rights. She retorted decades later: "I was the person who came up with the [slogan] 'a woman's life is a human life', okay?" But she believed homophobia, intertwined with fear of the three activists' confrontational style, erased her other work in the eyes of her CARASA colleagues. "As soon as we coalesced and formed a lesbian group," she insisted, "it was as if nothing else that I had ever done in CARASA existed."

Although, as Stamm insisted, no one was forced to leave the organization, Schulman had an experience of being pushed out of CARASA after the direct-action protest at the U.S. Congress and the Dworkin debacle. "We, who had spent years working for a broad vision of freedom, with a wide range of people, were accused of being lesbian separatists, as though that was an accusation of shame." It was, she wrote, "one of the most painful experiences of my political life."

For her part, Stamm remembered a wave of conflict that lasted a full year before driving most members away, "demoralized" and "disheartened." In her view, it ate away at CARASA, which, with its penchant for long meetings and deep deliberation, lacked mechanisms for keeping internal challenges from becoming all-consuming. The divisions were so bitter and effective at tearing CARASA asunder, she remembered, that "depending on the speaker's point of view, they will tell you that these were either police spies or misguided people or lesbian activists," perhaps on a deliberate mission to bring CARASA to its knees. Davis, who, like Stamm, blamed Schulman, Wolfe, and Roth for the organization's dissolution, called the conflict "devastating."

Stamm underlined the good work CARASA did on lesbian rights issues before and after the "great disruption," and the number of bisexual and lesbian members of CARASA who did *not* feel obliged to leave. She pointed out, for example, an insightful piece in *CARASA News* by member Janet Price, which analyzed the links between "Lesbian Rights and Reproductive Rights" and observed that, in Price's view, CARASA had become "far more committed to the gay rights issue than we would have dreamed possible in the early days," when the group formed in response to the Hyde Amendment. "Today," Price wrote in 1982, "gay and lesbian issues are usually covered in any CARASA material or speech." In its early years, she noted, CARASA "tended to emphasize the economic guarantees in our outreach efforts and therefore gave short shrift to gay and lesbian rights whereas internally, we talked more about control over own bodies and therefore more about gay rights . . . It was scary enough to talk about abortion to the unconvinced let alone the love that dares not speak its name." The rise in the 1980s of right-wing politics that sought to undercut lesbian, gay, and reproductive rights, while cutting social programs and weakening workers' power, made it easier to understand the necessary connections between CARASA's founding emphasis on abortion rights and economic inequality, and lesbian rights.

Meredith Tax, who had left the organization by the time these troubles emerged in 1982–83, understood that there was homophobia at work in the conflicts. However, she saw them primarily in terms of her own struggle against radical feminism, which was in the founding DNA of CARASA. Having misunderstood the lesbian feminist politics Schulman, Wolfe, and Roth were bringing to CARASA, Tax interpreted the main source of the conflict as a resistance by the majority of members, including those who identified as lesbian or bisexual, to making lesbian liberation central to their mission or worldview because it was centrally about sex. "We were trying to avoid, at least I was, the whole thing about this being about sexual freedom. We wanted to emphasize reproduction rather than sexuality," she said, because she "was trying to get away from" the radical feminist politics of many of her friends—a kind of politics that she thought had little traction with the majority of women in the United States and which she believed didn't address many of the most important obstacles to women's well-being. "And I wasn't gay so I didn't think about it as much as I should have."

Although it was the most explosive issue, the place of lesbianism in CARASA's agenda was not its only weak point. The most obvious additional challenge was the group's nearly all-white membership. To a certain degree, the narrowness of its membership base was emblematic of 1960s-era feminism in general. But it stood out as a problem in CARASA because the group emphasized the importance of racial and other differences among women while it was not racially diverse. Many active members were similar in other ways, too; as Schulman observed, one subgroup was made up of members of Marxist parties or political factions, a second of feminists loosely affiliated with the women's liberation movement, and a third of socialist feminists, many of whom were academics or professionals with advanced degrees. Members of this last group tended to migrate to the research committee, which produced *Women Under Attack*. The similarities among members may have been among the things that made CARASA a "really, really, really quite wonderful place to be" for Grossmann as a young activist intellectual. It was not as natural a fit for people who did not share her background or academic training—especially if they did not fit into either of the other major subgroups of members, either.

Individual CARASA members and committees tried to build bridges with Black women activists. Firestein, for example, working through the CARASA labor committee, attended meetings of the Coalition of Labor Union Women that were "like ninety-eight percent African American," hoping to create alliances against sterilization abuse and for abortion rights and reproductive freedom. She found that the Black trade union women just weren't interested—in part because they thought the issues would be controversial among their members, and in part because "it might have been like these sort of young white women going into this largely group of African American women who were probably a little older" and didn't see the young whites as obvious or dependable allies. Tax approached Black feminist activist and sociologist Barbara Omolade, who was active in the women's caucus of New York's Black United Front, about working with CARASA. Omolade gave the idea an unqualified no. "She said those are not our main issues. Our main issues are subsistence. How are we going to survive? We all have kids. We're working all of the time. We're dealing with these guys who are really sexist and trying to bring better politics in there. That's all we can do."

Before CARASA folded, it went national to fight the rising conservative politics of the early 1980s. Tax, Wolfe, and others in the group worked to build the Reproductive Rights National Network (R2N2), which linked together groups from all over the country. R2N2 formed the basis for an activist, multi-issue, militant, and grassroots movement for reproductive freedom. It stood for abortion access plus the many changes in society and public policy that would truly allow people to parent when they opted to do so.

In some ways the creation of this network was the ultimate achievement of reproductive rights activism, perhaps of the women's movement itself, in the late twentieth century. Except that it also wasn't, since it was bedeviled by the same conflicts that had bedeviled CARASA—over sexuality, race, economic class, and political strategy. A movement that could capture the strengths of R2N2 while incorporating the lessons organizers have learned in the years since it folded would really be one to watch.

The people who participated in R2N2 understood earlier than almost any other progressives that they faced a multipronged challenge from a powerful national conservative movement, which was exemplified by Ronald Reagan's presidency but had deep organizational roots and deeper pockets. As committed as many were to saving the lives of embryos and fetuses, conservatives also used abortion as an issue to galvanize constituents behind an agenda that went far beyond abortion. This agenda included simultaneous efforts to reduce levels of unionization, roll back laws that that enhanced Black civil rights, reduce funding for antipoverty policies, weaken environmental regulations, and limit the scope of feminism and the movements for lesbian and gay rights. It was the beginning of a new strategy to achieve a rollback of the social, economic, and cultural trends of the 1960s and 1970s. In response, activists all over the country joined R2N2.

The Reproductive Rights National Network was less a membership organization than a coalition of organizations working together and parallel to one another. Some were groups that formed independently of CARASA in New York—born out of participation in the anti-sterilization movement, or independent activism ignited by the threat the Hyde Amendment posed to abortion access. Others were specifically inspired by what they saw CARASA achieving and theorizing: there were CARASA chapters in Buffalo, Los Angeles, and the state of New Jersey, for example, and lots of groups elsewhere that did not share the CARASA name but affiliated with CARASA under the R2N2 banner because they had a similar understanding of the way to move forward. A single issue of the R2N2 newsletter listed member organizations including CESA, Women's Liberation of Rochester, the Federation of Feminist Women's Health Centers, the Abortion Rights Coalition of Cincinnati, the International Socialist Organization, St. Louis Women's Rights Action Group, and the Sojourner Truth Organization (this last, a Marxist group that was not necessarily a home for Black women like its namesake but did take race seriously as the centerpiece of its social analysis).

As Karen Stamm put it: "Since NOW wasn't going to be helpful on a national level," as was demonstrated by its role in the fight over sterilization guidelines, CARASA members decided that they would have to build the national infrastructure to fight conservatives themselves. By the start of 1982, Sarah Schulman was ready to announce "a national network of radical reproductive rights organizations" encompassing at least the seventy different groups that participated in a national conference of R2N2.

The Reproductive Rights National Network was "pretty white," in the memory of national steering committee member Marlene Gerber Fried. But it was more diverse than CARASA and more so than other national groups working on reproductive rights. Wolfe and Schulman both remembered that there were more out-of-the-closet lesbians and more women of color involved in the groups that helped form the network, and in the network's leadership, than there were in CARASA. By the time of R2N2's end, Wolfe estimated, the national board was "basically all lesbians, and half lesbians of color." Most of these women were from the working class, "and so, we were trying to put all of those politics really in"—not merely pay lip service to the full range of needs that would allow people to make free choices about having and raising children.

After leaving CARASA, Wolfe, Schulman, and Roth, with other lesbians from CARASA, formed a new organization called Wimmin for Womyn. Wimmin for Womyn, the name a playful riff on the ways some feminists in the 1970s were trying to expunge the male roots of the English language, affiliated on its own with R2N2 so that its members could continue participating in the movement. They committed themselves to "fighting for women's liberation with warmth and a sense of humor."

The Reproductive Rights National Network was short-lived. By the time of its 1984 conference, the network's future was in doubt, and by March 1985, it lacked an office and staff, and had almost no money and no steering committee. Although many of the organizations that participated were still active, the network among them barely existed.

R2N2's demise was the result of relatively long-term trends, chief among them pressure from the outside exerted by a multifront conservative campaign that caused even people who thought of themselves as socialists to back away from struggles for abortion rights and gay and lesbian liberation. Money dried up. Volunteer people power was in short supply as activists burned out or prioritized other movements or issues. Wolfe argued, moreover, there were never as many people involved as there might have been because their coalitional style of organizing involved only the heads of groups and not actual masses of people. (She, Schulman, and others would work to make ACT UP a different kind of organization.)

Characteristics of the network itself gnawed away at its strength and cohesion. Worst was a gap between rhetoric and reality, between a laundry list of objectives and the narrow program on which many groups in the network actually took action. It was here, betwixt word and deed, that racism, homophobia, and class biases appeared—for example, in the resistance of local groups to plastering walls in their areas with stickers that advertised Lesbian Liberation, part of what was sometimes a default position of devoting resources only or primarily to the effort to defend abortion rights even while arguing for a broader vision of reproductive freedom.

Conflict over race led most directly to the end of the Reproductive Rights National Network. An exasperated-seeming Women of Color Task Force issued a statement in November 1984, withdrawing from the network and explaining why. "We came here to work on reproductive rights issues. We came here because we thought there would be other women of color, that we would be able to find a place for our experience and perspectives as women of color organizing in Third World communities on Third World issues. We came here finding that we can't work on these issues, that we can't be who we are, and instead we spend all of our time working on educating white women." Much as members of the Lesbian Action Committee of CARASA objected to making "lesbian issues" merely one item among many on a list of concerns, the women of color who resigned from R2N2 found it "oppressive" to treat racism as separate from "everything we do." They expressed a continued commitment to working politically with white women, but for the moment advised white members of the network to deal with their racism on their own.

The white women in R2N2 hesitated but had little appetite for or capacity to sustain R2N2 after that point. Stephanie Roth, R2N2 staff member Margie Fine, and former steering committee member Marlene Gerber Fried seemed a little shell-shocked as they wrote to the people on their mailing list about the iffy "future of both R2N2 and national multi-racial reproductive rights organizing." Eleven white women who had attended the conference met and "affirmed [their] commitment to confront racism within ourselves, our movement, and beyond." But they alone couldn't create, or re-create, a transformative national movement.

CESA, too, dissolved at around the same time as R2N2. It had diminished as an active organization even earlier than R2N2 did, although Karen Stamm would sometimes break out a piece of stationery to represent the CESA perspective in a coalition or in response to a particular threat of sterilization abuse. There were no dramatic confrontations between or among members, no flash-point foot-in-mouth lectures. CESA had always been a different kind of animal from CARASA and R2N2, smaller, more focused on the immediate problem it was trying to solve.

Stamm suggested that CESA's organizational problem was tied to its success in forging new policies. The publication of new sterilization guidelines by the Carter administration appeared to complete a process that had begun with the government's abuse of the Relf sisters, had then spurred the creation of CESA and activism for new policies in New York City, and then made its way back to the federal Department of Health, Education, and Welfare. In 1982, the Reagan administration indicated a desire to lift or rewrite the guidelines. CARASA opposed the move, as did the Center for Constitutional Rights and leadership of the New York City Health and Hospitals Corporation, which, under Esta Armstrong's watchful eye, continued to embrace its own sterilization guidelines. Reagan's secretary of Health and Human Services backed down. "There seemed to be no particular need for [CESA] anymore," Stamm concluded, "which was too bad."

The operative word here, of course, is "seemed." If anyone had had the time or energy, if they had not needed to finish their educations, raise their children, or get on with their careers—or if there had been a new generation of anti-sterilization-abuse activists ready to take their places—there would have been plenty for CESA members to take on. The years-long effort to create new sterilization rules in the United States had, for example, led CESA away from its original focus on the population control movement around the world. The organization had pointed out, but hardly made a dent in, the conditions of people's lives that pushed them toward sterilization as much as aggressive health-care providers did.

One of the most important aspects of the CESA-inspired guidelines in New York City and nationally was a requirement they included for collecting data on sterilizations. In the early 1980s, these data indicated that wide disparities remained between the rates of women's sterilization based on race and ethnicity, with whites still having the fewest and Latinas the most. The overall trend in numbers of sterilizations, from the middle 1970s to the early 1980s, was steadily upward, perhaps in part because the Medicaid program continued to cover the bulk of the cost for sterilizations. However, Stamm took heart from another trend the data revealed: the virtual disappearance of hospital sterilizations performed on girls like the Relf sisters or very young women, those who were most likely to be pressured by professionals who were racist or biased against welfare recipients and least likely to know for sure whether they wanted ever to bear children.

Even though CESA was no longer in the streets or bureaucratic suites, the sterilization guidelines for which its members fought continued to make a difference. Wendy Chavkin, a doctor and public health expert who was mentored by both Helen Rodríguez-Trías and Esta Armstrong, saw this up close from the New York City health department. Chavkin directed the department's reproductive health unit from 1984 to 1988. She was responsible for monitoring compliance with the guidelines in all the city's private hospitals, while Armstrong monitored compliance in the public ones. Chavkin periodically found "technical noncompliance" but saw nothing she would have called "actual abuse."

In 1991, the city's public hospital system itself organized a symposium about the guidelines. Stamm remembered that the audience was almost all people on the "front lines, so nurses, physician assistants, counselors, social workers, all of the people who would be involved in counseling, in-patient care," although not a large group of M.D.s. "And everybody, speaker after speaker," said that the sterilization guidance was "part of the landscape. We don't have to fight about it anymore. It's here to stay. It's part of how we practice."

On abortion rights, the direct action of CARASA members and more conventional tactics of other advocates defeated the anti-abortion initiative for a Human Life Amendment to the Constitution. But the

Hyde Amendment remained, making access to abortion a privilege of economic class by denying federal Medicaid funds for this one medical procedure. Most galling to the people who favored abortion rights, the amendment wasn't part of a regular piece of congressional legislation. It was a rider added repeatedly to budget bills, at the discretion of congressional majorities, whether the House and Senate were in Democratic or Republican hands. This continued for decades, with only a slight liberalization in its terms in the early 1990s.

In an often forgotten but vastly important case, *Harris v. McRae*, which arguably set the nation on the road that led ultimately to overturning *Roe v. Wade*, the U.S. Supreme Court found the Hyde Amendment to be constitutional. When Representative Henry Hyde first tacked his amendment on to a budget bill in 1976, and Congress passed the bill, feminist lawyers had challenged it immediately. The lead attorney on the case was Rhonda Copelon, a close friend of attorney Nancy Stearns's. Copelon was a staff member of the Center for Constitutional Rights, a founding member of CESA, and an active member of CARASA. Like the legal cases that had worked to decriminalize abortion through the courts, *Harris v. McRae* was as much a piece of movement strategy as legal strategy. As with those earlier cases, and the movement for abortion decriminalization itself, the coalition backing *McRae* was a wide one. Copelon and Stearns were CESA and CARASA people, but Planned Parenthood of New York City was among their plaintiffs in the case, too. So was a women's group within the Methodist Church, reminiscent of the role liberal Protestants played in the Clergy Consultation Service at the height of the push for decriminalization.

With this wide coalition behind them, Copelon and her legal team, which included Stearns, persuaded federal judge John Francis Dooling, Jr., to block implementation of the Hyde Amendment. Dooling's order applied not only to his own jurisdiction but to the whole country. However, after the Supreme Court ruled that individual states could deny public funds for "elective" abortions (those not specifically recommended by a doctor), Dooling lifted the block he had placed in the way of implementation of the Hyde Amendment. The Department of Health, Education, and Welfare started denying federal Medicaid funds for abortions in August 1977.

Judge Dooling then considered the Hyde Amendment on its merits. Copelon, Stearns, and their colleagues who worked on the case posed the constitutional question of whether people whose health insurance was through Medicaid could actually exercise the rights the Supreme Court announced in *Roe v. Wade* if their health insurance didn't cover abortions. These feminist legal activists spent fourteen months thickening the record with data and, following the pattern established in the *Abramowicz* case, the stories of individual women—lest the judge think that the questions presented were abstract matters of constitutional theory. Judge Dooling considered at length the religious issues involved—whether it was a violation of the First Amendment to the Constitution for laws like the Hyde Amendment to respect mainstream Catholic doctrine while ignoring mainstream Reform and Conservative interpretations of Jewish law and the beliefs of several mainline Protestant denominations. CARASA legislation committee chair Anne Teicher submitted a "friend of the court" brief on behalf of CARASA, CESA, and the Comisión Feminil Mexicana Nacional, which supported the Copelon-Stearns side of the case. Stamm, by then a law student, was part of the team that checked citations on the brief.

Dooling spent an additional thirteen months deliberating and writing. In January 1980, he published a 642-page-long opinion that found the Hyde Amendment unconstitutional and ordered the federal government again to stop enforcing it. He echoed Justice Harry Blackmun from *Roe v. Wade* in finding that a woman's decision to abort, made in consultation with her doctor, was an exercise of fundamental rights. These included the right to liberty anchored by the Constitution's Fifth and Fourteenth Amendments and were "doubly protected when the liberty is exercised in conformity with religious belief and teaching protected by the First Amendment." The government violated these rights just as much, he suggested, by denying medical coverage for abortion to one class of people who were differentiated by income from the rest of the population as it had by criminalizing abortion in the pre-*Roe* days.

The Carter administration appealed Judge Dooling's ruling to the Supreme Court. When she argued before the Court, Rhonda Copelon spoke for the whole community of feminists in CESA and CARASA. They believed that reproductive rights required, at the very least, the financial means to exercise them. To little avail. In handwritten notes from the justices' meeting to consider the case, Justice Blackmun chronicled this watershed ending to the settlement in abortion policy that he had tried to achieve in *Roe v. Wade*. When Justice Lewis Powell made it clear that he would be the fifth vote for upholding the Hyde Amendment as constitutional, Blackmun scribbled a note that appears to read, "& so ends the ballgame."

In the court's opinion in *Harris v. McRae*, Justice Potter Stewart wrote for a bare majority that the Hyde Amendment placed "no governmental obstacle in the path of a woman who chooses to terminate her pregnancy," but simply expressed a governmental preference for her not to make that choice by failing to fund it. Even though the Reagan administration, with its openly expressed desire to curb anti-poverty programs, had not yet started, the Supreme Court majority appears to have been inspired by a similar sentiment. Justice Stewart wrote that a woman's constitutionally guaranteed right to choose abortion carried with it no "constitutional entitlement to the financial resources to avail herself of the full range of protected choices." The justices who voted in the minority dissented sharply from Stewart's reasoning and conclusions. Justice John Paul Stevens, a Republican, went so far as to read his dissent from the bench after Stewart finished reading his.

The Supreme Court in *Harris v. McRae* accepted a class-based bar to exercising reproductive liberty, rejected Protestant and Jewish claims that restrictive abortion policy violated their faiths, and initiated decades of federal court cases that narrowed the reach of *Roe v. Wade*. And so ended the ballgame.

Epilogue

What Then? What Now?

THIS STORY didn't end in the early 1980s. There have been two major trends in reproductive rights since then. One is a steady erosion in the politics of abortion, from the high point when my mother's draft repeal law seemed to have a chance at becoming a model for the nation, through the compromises woven into the New York law and *Roe v. Wade*, to the way the Hyde Amendment and *Harris v. McRae* ratified differences in abortion access by race, class, and geography, to the carve-outs, limitations, and restrictions that built on that precedent to create a crazy quilt that has left us barely able to remember the way activists like Florynce Kennedy, members of Redstockings, and Betty Friedan understood the right to terminate a pregnancy as a bedrock of women's citizenship.

The quilt got crazier. The law began to normalize even more inequality after the late Justice Ruth Bader Ginsburg, a veteran of the women's civil rights movement of the 1970s, was succeeded on the bench by a conservative Catholic, Justice Amy Coney Barrett. Leaping ahead of high court precedents, in 2021 the Texas legislature passed Senate Bill 8, which denied abortions after the sixth week of a pregnancy, earlier than most women realize they are pregnant, and blocked routine legal avenues for challenging it. The U.S. Supreme Court and other appellate courts declined to prevent Texas from implementing the law, effectively stopping a majority of constitutionally protected abortions in the state. Mississippi's legislature passed a more conventional but still highly restrictive law that forbade abortions at fifteen weeks, prior to the long-standing standard of fetal viability. In a brief filed after Coney Barrett's ascent, the state asked the Supreme Court to overturn *Roe v. Wade* and rule that no constitutional rights covered a person's decision to end a pregnancy. It seemed clear from the tenor of the colloquy in the Mississippi case, *Dobbs v. Jackson Women's Health Clinic*, that a majority of justices agreed with the state's arguments and would either accept the fifteen-week ban or overturn *Roe v. Wade*. And then, on May 2, 2022, the journal *Politico* reported on a draft opinion and vote in the Mississippi case that was even more extreme than the state's brief, overruling *Roe*, denying that there was ever a constitutional foundation for the right to access abortion, and opening the door on possible total or near-total state legislative bans on abortion in twenty-three states. The draft opinion included withering remarks about Supreme Court precedents protecting LGBTQ rights, and seemed to invite cases that would give the majority of justices opportunities to overrule them, too. As the world learned in late June 2022, the draft was no more radical than the final majority opinion in this case.

The second trend was more encouraging. Often far from the limelight, ideas like those of the Young Lords, the Puerto Rican Socialist Party, and the groups CESA, CARASA, and the Reproductive Rights National Network moved ever closer to the political center. More and more, the women's movement (whose members learned increasingly to think of themselves as a movement against all forms of gender-based oppression) and reproductive rights advocates placed race, class, gender identity, and sexuality at the center of their analyses and programs. They encapsulated the new approach in the phrase "reproductive justice," using a framework learned from Black women activists and thinkers, who built on generations of experience and reflection in their communities to reimagine the movement. Reproductive justice expanded CARASA's understanding by shifting from the reproductive freedom of all parents to make unencumbered choices about their bodies to the *justice* of answering with long-due reparation centuries of oppression that had denied people the family lives they wanted. The idea was most closely associated with SisterSong: Women of Color Reproductive Justice Collective, founded in the late 1990s by Black women, Latinas, Native Americans, and Asian Americans. SisterSong defined reproductive justice as a matter of "human rights, not choice." Unlike a movement dedicated to abortion rights, one committed to reproductive justice, the group wrote, cares about "contraception, comprehensive sex education, STI [sexually transmitted infection] prevention and care, alternative birth options, adequate prenatal and pregnancy care, domestic violence assistance, adequate wages to support our families, safe homes, and so much more."

Although CESA, CARASA, and the Reproductive Rights National Network didn't survive the 1980s, the National Organization for Women, Planned Parenthood, and NARAL (since 2003, NARAL Pro-Choice America) remained in the field for decades more. Chastened by persistent critiques from the members of CESA and CARASA, as well as women of color feminists who asked them to encompass the needs of all people, they started to change. NOW did not fully embrace reproductive freedom or reproductive justice as the movement's goal, but its leaders made strides in that direction. They increased NOW's dedication to lesbian and, later, queer rights, and increasingly accommodated the voices of people of color. In August 2020, Christian Nunes began her tenure as NOW's second-ever Black president—following Aileen Clarke Hernandez, the friend of legal theorist Pauli Murray whose parents taught her never to back down from a fight and who headed NOW for a year after Betty Friedan stepped down from the post.

Spokespeople for Planned Parenthood and NARAL stopped arguing for abortion and birth control as aids to population control—distancing the organizations from population control organizations and fielding other arguments by the end of the 1970s, in part because

of the rise to leadership of women of color in the feminist movement. In the twenty-first century, they addressed the last vestiges
of population control arguments, like the suggestion that abortion
could help lower welfare costs or save the environment. In November 2021, NARAL welcomed Mini Timmaraju, a veteran political
organizer, as its first nonwhite president. She described herself on
Twitter as "mom, anti-racist, feminist, indian/south asian american,
immigrant, president @NARAL." Within Planned Parenthood, leaders of the New York City chapter did not discuss their predecessors'
role in opposing sterilization guidelines. But they took the symboli-
cally important step of removing the name of founder Margaret
Sanger from a lower Manhattan health clinic. Alexis McGill Johnson,
the national organization's second Black president, did not address
the controversy over sterilization. However, she condemned Sanger's
backing of birth control experiments in Puerto Rico that didn't fully
inform participants of the risks they faced. "We will no longer make
excuses or apologize for Margaret Sanger's actions," McGill Johnson
wrote. "But we can't simply call her racist, scrub her from our history, and move on. We must examine how we have perpetuated her
harms over the last century—as an organization, an institution, and
as individuals." The Association for Voluntary Sterilization changed
its named to the Association for Voluntary Surgical Contraception
and, in 2001, to EngenderHealth.

The happiest development in the post-CARASA years was the emergence of organizations by and for women of color. The National Black
Women's Health Project (later, Black Women's Health Imperative),
headed by a Florida abortion clinic cofounder named Byllye Avery, was
in the lead. Avery and Dr. Helen Rodríguez-Trías had served together
on the mostly white board of the National Women's Health Network, the advocacy arm of the women's health movement. With other
women of color, they pushed for the network to sponsor a national
conference on Black women's health. That 1983 conference, a first,

drew nearly two thousand people to Spelman College in Atlanta—to talk and work with one another, and practice a version of feminist consciousness-raising they called self-help. Emerging from that meeting, Black women demanded their own organization. In 1984, coincidentally as the Reproductive Rights National Network was falling apart, they created the National Black Women's Health Project.

Byllye Avery's genius, the genius of the National Black Women's Health Project, was to address everything that determined women's health and not to separate reproductive health care from all other kinds. This was in contrast to the narrowest understanding of reproductive rights as access to birth control and abortion. It was even in tension with the broader mandate of reproductive freedom. The National Black Women's Health Project embodied a commitment to Black women's health and well-being, whether or not it related immediately to reproduction. As Avery put it: "Whether you die from illegal abortion or die from diabetes, you're dead." The National Black Women's Health Project was about keeping Black women alive in the face of their health challenges, reproductive or otherwise. Doing this, Avery came to understand, meant giving Black women opportunities to talk about their experiences, since health is tied to every other aspect of life. By 1988, the project was overseeing ninety-six self-help discussion and action groups in twenty-two U.S. states, plus groups in Kenya, Barbados, and Belize.

Other groups by and for women of color followed. The next of the national efforts was the National Latina Health Organization, founded in 1986. It was supported by Byllye Avery and inspired by the efforts of Helen Rodríguez-Trías, CESA, and the Mexican American women who had battled sterilization abuse in Los Angeles. Luz Martinez, leader of the National Latina Health Organization, described ongoing efforts to get majority-white women's organizations to shift their understandings: Despite feeling tokenized when she was the only woman of color in the room, Martinez tried all the time to "make sure that it was more inclusive and that their agenda opened up. It is not just about abortion. What about the abuses? What about the access? What about the cultural access? What about the language? What about that we don't even get information? We're invisible. They do their organizing and don't even know or think, care to think, about our issues."

Women of color increasingly demanded their rightful places in leadership, whether forming new organizations or transforming older, historically white groups. The next key person in this history was Loretta Ross, who joined the National Organization for Women in 1985 as director of Women of Color Programs. Ross had a double role while at NOW. On the one hand, she mobilized women of color who supported NOW's reproductive rights agenda, for example, by organizing delegations of women of color to national marches for abortion rights of which NOW was a chief sponsor. At the same time, she built and strengthened networks of women of color who could create their own agendas. Ross led mini-conferences around the country, on a Native American reservation in South Dakota, among Black people in Atlanta, and in Latino communities in Hartford, "all trying to find pockets of women of color that we could pull together to talk about reproductive health issues." In the summer of 1987, she convened the first national meeting on reproductive rights for women of color at Howard University. She remembered: "Just like the white girls had their little girls' network, those of us who did that work in the '80s, we formed our own little girls' network," a group of people who continued to support one another for decades.

One high point in this period was Ross's collaboration with Donna Brazile, later an important Democratic Party strategist, and others to publish a 1989 pamphlet titled *We Remember: African American Women Are for Reproductive Freedom.* (They did not yet have the language of reproductive justice.) The sixteen signatories included Avery, Brazile, and Faye Wattleton, the first Black head of the Planned Parenthood Federation of America. They defined reproductive freedom in terms of eleven rights. The second was the right to have a child; the third, the "right to good, affordable health care"; and the eighth, present but fairly far down the list, the "right to safe, legal, affordable abortion services." *We Remember* was a response to the Supreme Court's opinion in *Webster v. Reproductive Services*, which built on the court's prior decision to uphold the Hyde Amendment. The majority in *Webster* found constitutional a Missouri law that forbade abortions in all public hospitals, even if the patient paid out-of-pocket. Five justices agreed that "nothing in the Constitution requires States to enter or remain in the abortion business," or entitled citizens to access constitutionally protected health-care options in taxpayer-supported health facilities. This would have the effect of deepening inequalities of access to abortion by driving up the price and the difficulty patients faced in locating a hospital or clinic to provide their care.

These events in the 1980s set the stage for even bigger changes in the reproductive rights movement. In 1992, the Supreme Court affirmed the central holding of *Roe* in *Planned Parenthood of Southeast Pennsylvania v. Casey*. However, a fractured court also said that the right to abort was not "fundamental," and it granted states latitude to regulate abortion access as long as the regulations didn't impose an "undue burden" on the person seeking to terminate their pregnancy. In response, the National Black Women's Health Project joined with groups of Indigenous, Latina, and Asian American health activists in a short-lived coalition effort to put a specifically women-of-color stamp on the politics of reproductive rights. In 1994, Ross and eleven other Black women named reproductive justice as the movement's framing goal. In 1997, women of color gathered to create SisterSong as a national organization. This time, the organization lasted. In 2003, the idea of reproductive justice "became more sharply defined and crystallized," Ross said, "at the first SisterSong national conference because I organized the plenary panel asking the question 'What is reproductive justice?' and could it be used to organize a new movement of women of color. And the six hundred people who came to our conference said, 'Hell yes,' so it took off from there." It helped that Ross herself, who coordinated the participation of women of color in the one-million-strong March for Women's Lives in 2004, became the national leader of SisterSong in 2005.

The women of color feminists who had their heyday in the late twentieth and twenty-first centuries were more successful at reframing the reproductive rights movement than CESA and CARASA had been. The call for reproductive justice, which encompassed so much more than abortion rights, proved more enduring and influential than CARASA's bid for reproductive freedom. The leaders of the 1990s and 2000s also had greater success than the earlier groups had at reimagining the movement as a global one. CESA, for example, at its start emphasized the sterilization program in Puerto Rico and fought the worldwide elite consensus around population control. Its members succeeded at changing policies on the U.S. mainland but made little headway against the global problems of which those policies were a part. But in the 1990s, Loretta Ross and other leaders, including Dr. Helen Rodríguez-Trías in a post-CESA phase of her career, participated in international policymaking. When SisterSong discussed reproductive justice as a matter of human rights, its members spoke a language people around the world could understand.

The movement's international work occurred in the context of two separate series of meetings sponsored by the United Nations, one for and about women and the other on population. The first global women's conference occurred in Mexico City in 1975. At the urging of the conference, the U.N. as a whole chose to focus for the next ten years on eliminating gender discrimination, allowing women's full participation in economic development, and inviting women to contribute fully to the making of a peaceful world. Ross missed the gathering in Mexico but attended the next global women's conference in Copenhagen in 1980, and organized a delegation of women of color from the United States to attend the meeting after that, in

Nairobi in 1985. She helped bring a similar delegation to the fourth World Conference on Women in Beijing in 1995.

These women's conferences were in some tension with the series of meetings on population. U.N.-backed gatherings on population occurred in 1954, 1964, and 1974. They provided few opportunities for people who felt that their communities had been victims of population control to share the stage with those who believed in population control—that is, thought that the most effective way to promote economic development in poor countries, or poor parts of rich countries, was to institute policies that would entice residents to have fewer children. The meeting in 1984 allowed more critique of population control ideology than ever before, and the International Conference on Population and Development in Cairo ten years later was a serious departure from the pattern. As one sign of change, the U.S. government asked Dr. Helen Rodríguez-Trías to serve in the years before the Cairo conference as an adviser to the team drafting the nation's position papers for it.

It was in preparing for the Cairo meeting that Loretta Ross and her eleven Black women colleagues named reproductive justice as the movement's goal. They called themselves Women of African Descent for Reproductive Justice and drafted a statement that outlined their understanding of the necessary agenda. Although on their way to an international meeting, they directed their demands to the U.S. Congress: "Reproductive freedom is a life and death issue for many Black women and deserves as much recognition as any other freedom," they wrote. This freedom (or justice) included support for "the full range of reproductive services," including accessible abortions, prenatal care, birth control, cancer screening and treatment, and care for people with HIV/AIDS. After only a few weeks of sharing it, over eight hundred Black women, including novelist Alice Walker and activist intellectual Angela Davis, endorsed the statement. Women of African Descent for Reproductive Justice printed it, under the title "Black Women for

Health Care Reform," in full-page ads in the *Washington Post* and the political insider's journal, *Roll Call*.

Rodríguez-Trías attended the Cairo population meeting as part of the official U.S. delegation. In addition to representing the United States, she also represented the American Public Health Association as its immediate past president. Loretta Ross attended the Cairo meeting with a women of color delegation, not as an official U.S. representative but as what she called "the loyal opposition." She joined delegates from the rest of the world in arguing that economic development came first, as both more important than and a precondition to reducing population. "And of course, the U.S. was saying, Reduce the population and then you develop," Ross remembered. "Halve your babies and then those babies you have can finally figure out how to go to school. Well, not if there's no schools. And those babies aren't going to build those schools. So it was just the wrong approach." In part because the U.S. population control establishment was relatively isolated in its views, the Cairo meeting that Rodríguez-Trías and Ross attended proved to be historic—a population conference that refuted the population control ideology that had led to the Puerto Rican sterilization program and many abuses in poor communities and communities of color on the U.S. mainland.

What happened in and around the Cairo meeting, thanks to Loretta Ross's delegation and others like it, represented great progress since the early 1960s. The conference produced a program for the next twenty years called the Cairo Consensus, which 184 governments endorsed. The Consensus didn't encapsulate reproductive freedom quite as CARASA understood it, or reproductive justice as Ross understood it; Rodríguez-Trías and Ross both argued that the program failed to acknowledge that the global economic system favored certain countries, and communities in them, over others. But the Cairo signatories retreated from the old article of faith that lowering population numbers (i.e., getting people to have fewer children by any means necessary) was an end in itself. They were squishy on abortion, emphasizing the negative threat to people's health posed by illegal abortion but not a positive need for safe, accessible abortion care. However, their program affirmed the primary importance of basic health care, including a range of options for reproductive health, and called for improvements in all people's standard of living and in women's rights.

The Cairo meeting changed the reproductive rights movement in the United States. After the Women of African Descent for Reproductive Justice returned home from Cairo with new connections to women of color in the United States and in the rest of the world, the coalition dissolved. There was, Loretta Ross remembered, "no money to continue the work." So she and others "formed another huge delegation, coalition, to go to Beijing." Then, "Beijing was over, and there's no money to do the domestic work." She and other women of color finally had enough of "that yo-yo." With the help of Reena Marcelo, a Filipina program officer at the Ford Foundation, they built Sister-Song in 1997, from an idea formulated by the Puerto Rican health activist Luz Rodríguez in partnership with Marcelo. Marcelo granted the sixteen reproductive rights and health groups that were in on the ground floor of the collective all the money she had to distribute that year, $4 million in three-year grants. They used the support to build their individual organizations, which allowed them to create a more sustainable national network than had ever existed before.

By 2022, SisterSong was the most well-known national group of women of color advocating reproductive health, rights, and justice. Reproductive justice was still not a completely mainstream concept. In the movement, however, reproductive justice was ever present—as a demand, an analysis, a critique, and a hope for the future.

There has been so much bad news about public policy, especially about abortion access, in the twenty-first century. What can we possibly learn from a history of reproductive politics thirty or sixty years ago? Here are a few thoughts, offered in a spirit of love toward our predecessors and ourselves, in honor of the memory of my mother and our amazing next-door neighbor:

First, there's no substitute for organizing. Organizing means gathering together people who want social change, deciding on a mission and tactics, and applying pressure to people in power to do what you want them to do. Without organizing, the past teaches, there would have been no victories for abortion rights or against sterilization abuse, no progress toward reproductive freedom or reproductive justice.

For reasons I don't fully understand, the fact that reproductive rights—both abortion decriminalization and regulation to prevent sterilization abuse—were achieved through relentless, local grassroots organizing has been nearly erased from conventional memory. As far from my mother's vision, or that of the abortion repeal militant Lucinda Cisler, as it was, Justice Harry Blackmun's opinion in *Roe v. Wade* did as much to recognize women's humanity as the Supreme Court had ever done before. This seems to have blotted from vision the very movement that led Blackmun and his brethren to rule as they did.

Maybe a thin silver lining around events in the early 2020s is that they made it possible to remember what really happened in the past. The Supreme Court was never a savior. *Roe v. Wade* was a compromise decision, built on the earlier compromises written into the landmark New York law of 1970 and the work of a few other states. Only seven years after *Roe*, the court basically crumpled up and threw away its defense of women's dignity and autonomy, and allowed the Hyde Amendment to turn abortion access into a privilege of class, race, and geography. The court never had much to say about the broad agenda for reproductive freedom or reproductive justice.

The Supreme Court didn't give us our rights, and it won't save us now. When a majority of justices ruled in 1973 to make abortion legal under most circumstances in the first two trimesters of a pregnancy, they responded to a massive, diverse grassroots movement that organized like hell to change the law. Insofar as they recognized women's humanity, they responded to feminists who organized like hell to demand recognition.

The same happened in New York, on the road to the major legislative change that transformed abortion access not only in that one state but across the country and across the world: Legislators and the governor alone didn't change the law. The people most responsible for its change were individuals who continued seeking abortions in spite of the law and who forced doctors and other professionals to confront its impact, plus ministers and rabbis who broke the old law by referring people for safe abortions, members of the National Organization for Women like my mother who drafted bills and supported them tirelessly, and more daring activists who disrupted legislative hearings and gathered in church basements to speak out about their abortions.

The fight against sterilization abuse proves this even more. After a national furor over what happened to the Relf sisters in Alabama, it was up to the Committee to End Sterilization Abuse to spur the creation of new policy. Without the work of Rodríguez-Trías, Maritza Arrastía, Esta Armstrong, Karen Stamm, and others, who applied pressure from inside the New York City bureaucracy while mobilizing people who knew the most about how sterilization abuse happened on the ground, there would have been no new policy in the city's public hospital system and no city council law. Without the organizing that created CARASA and the Reproductive Rights National Network, and without their efforts to support changed policy, there would have been no rigorous new sterilization guidelines from the Department of Health, Education, and Welfare.

Second, to build something new, start with the tools that are ready-to-hand. After *Roe v. Wade*, we sometimes forgot that it was only a fluke of history that made sexual self-determination a matter of constitutional law. The campaign against unjust abortion laws was mostly a campaign in the states, pointed, like the New York effort, at getting state legislatures that criminalized abortion in the nineteenth century to undo what they had done. As in New York, before becoming statewide, the movement to change abortion laws germinated in a handful of neighborhoods, like Harlem and the Upper West Side in New York City, whose political representatives were part of a fight to pull the Democratic Party to the liberal left. The movement entered the courts only when it seemed like its legislative campaign had reached a stalemate. The federal case *Abramowicz v. Lefkowitz* was an extension of the movement, brought by activist attorneys and with scores of plaintiffs, which used collective, in-your-face strategies as much as they used constitutional argument. Nobody in the movement thought that courtroom law alone would get the job done.

Beyond legislatures and courts, activists used an even wider array of tools. To control sterilization abuse, CESA members worked on hospital policy before they ever changed the law. They built from a victory in the public health-care system to one in the chambers of the city council. With CARASA and allies around the country, they won a change in the regulations that governed a critical federal agency. We don't usually think about hospitals, city governments, or agency rules as the guarantors of reproductive rights. But they can be, and, as was clear in the immediate aftermath of the decriminalization law in New York in 1970, when ambivalence about abortion generated restrictive policies by hospitals and local governments, they can also be tools for limiting reproductive rights.

Third, choose your allies with care. The great learning from the three victories against sterilization abuse is that the right coalition can defeat even the most powerful-seeming opponents. Elite physicians, some of them national leaders in their fields, opposed the heightened guidelines that CESA members drafted. So did Planned Parenthood, NARAL, the Association for Voluntary Sterilization, and, except for the New York City chapter, NOW. But they were no match for the combined force of what Stamm called a "people's organization" of Puerto Rican radicals, left-of-center feminists, health-care workers, critics of conventional medicine, and, when the movement went national, Native Americans, Mexican Americans, Black nationalists, civil rights activists, "and almost everyone else except the professional medical and population organizations."

The coalition that won legal abortion was similarly broad. But it was different, and it raises different questions. What did it mean for the movement for abortion rights to win in statehouses and the federal courts with the aid of people and organizations committed to population control, including the Association for Voluntary Sterilization, founded on a commitment to sterilizing disabled people against their will, and a Planned Parenthood that had not yet confronted its founder's ties to eugenics?

The problematic allies, and problematic things some abortion advocates said and believed, worked to alienate communities that were at the center of both the harms from illegal, unsafe, and too-expensive abortion care and the struggle against sterilization abuse. When middle-class white feminists like my mother didn't call out these allies or statements, they built a barrier in the way of creating the powerful, progressive, interracial political movement that CARASA and the Reproductive Rights National Network struggled to fashion, a movement that might have had the ability to sustain the gains of the 1970s in the decades that followed. Who knows how much more might have been accomplished to counter the wave of anti-feminist and economically unequal policy if the movement for abortion decriminalization had not argued for abortion as a way to avoid giving birth to disabled children, or as a means to lower the welfare rolls? What if advocates of decriminalization had made a stronger bid for liberal Catholic support, agreeing to disagree about the substantive morality of abortion but arguing more strongly for public policy that simply removed government from the role as abortion gatekeeper—and uniting on behalf of people's right to bear and raise the children they want, at the very least by fighting coercive or involuntary sterilization?

With a different coalition and a different program, maybe the movement would have won more, or lost less. If the forces favoring abortion decriminalization had sought different allies and lost the support of powerful people with ties to population control, they might have had to wait longer to produce victories like the New York law and to create the pressure that encouraged the Supreme Court to endorse their campaign. Who knows? Maybe those victories would never have come, and the pushback would have been just as strong. As a professional historian, I'm not supposed to indulge hypotheticals, but the most tantalizing remains: What if the fight had from the beginning joined the right to bear and raise children, in health and dignity for all people, with the right to end a pregnancy when someone decides that is the appropriate or necessary next step for them? This demand, rather than a demand for abortion rights alone, would speak to the many ways in which economic inequality and inadequate health care for all people shape our most intimate and life-changing decisions. Rather than, as in the 1960s abortion decriminalization movement, giving a platform to wealthy whites who thought it was good public policy to help other women limit the size of their families, a movement dedicated to the right to parent would privilege Black, brown, Indigenous, disabled, queer, and working-class people, and the agenda required to undo the barriers that have long stood in the way of their reproductive autonomy.

It's hard to separate the coalition that won legal abortion from that coalition's political program. If the architects of the campaign to decriminalize abortion had not included population controllers, if the feminists who demanded the repeal of the laws had not been so overwhelmingly white and well-off, then perhaps the movement's mandate and the whole of its history would have traveled a different road. Maybe it would not have taken until the late 1970s for the movement to demand reproductive freedom, or the middle 1990s to name reproductive justice. Maybe the white socialist feminists in CARASA and people of color throughout the movement would not have spent so much of their precious time schooling others on what it really takes for most people to experience reproductive choices and good health.

I would have liked to see what a better-resourced version of Karen Stamm's "people's organization" could have accomplished, standing on a platform that ran the gamut from opposing sterilization abuse to battling police violence to enabling people to terminate pregnancies without fear of legal repercussions. I long to see it still. In a head-to-head battle with activists who call themselves pro-life because they advocate for fetal life without working to preserve the lives of children like Tamir Rice, the twelve-year-old shot by police in Cleveland, Ohio, or those who seek to ensure that everyone has basic health care, my money would be on the people's movement.

Some of the lessons this history hopes to teach refer to particular moments in it and not to the whole. For example, the risk-taking contributions of the Clergy Consultation Service on Abortion and the work of its lineal descendant, the Religious Coalition for Reproductive Choice and the group Catholics for Choice, founded in 1973, should remind everyone in the United States that conservative Catholics and Evangelical Protestants hardly have a monopoly on faith-based views of reproductive health care. The mainline Protestants and Reform and Conservative Jews who led the clergy service were acting out of deeply held beliefs and the teachings of their sacral traditions.

A country and federal judiciary that offer constitutional protection for diverse religious faiths ought to notice the ways in which proscriptive reproductive policy keeps a huge portion of the population from exercising its beliefs. The legal teams that brought the *Abramowicz* case and *Harris v. McRae* (with Nancy Stearns on both teams) raised this argument in the federal courts. In *Roe*, Justice Blackmun acknowledged the "divergence of thinking" on the morality of abortion, noting specifically the thinking of wide swaths of Jews and Protestants. Judge Dooling of the Eastern District of New York found the argument compelling. In *Harris v. McRae*, a majority of the U.S. Supreme Court did not. This does not mean the argument is wrong.

For people today who identify with one faith tradition or another, including of course dissident Catholics and Evangelical Protestants who can find themselves within a movement for reproductive justice, one implication is clear: You need to be heard on these issues and demand action on them by your clergy, early, often, and at volume. For non-Orthodox Jews and mainline Protestants, for whom endorsing reproductive justice should be a no-brainer, this history indicates that it is time to take risks in support of our beliefs. The kinds of social action in which our communities typically engage—racial-equity reading groups and canned-food drives for the local food shelf—are not going to move the needle on these issues. Concerted political action from the grassroots up just might.

Rank-and-file members of faith communities are not the only ones who need to assume more risk. The history of the Young Lords takeover of Lincoln Hospital shows the difference it can make when communities join together in campaigns to make local public services do the jobs for which they are designed—demanding, for example, that health-care institutions support our and our neighbors' health by providing free, neighborhood-based preventive screening and treatment, and insisting that local people have opportunities for employment that sustain them economically and allow them to serve as bridges between neighborhood and hospital. The Young Lords and Puerto Rican Socialist Party were outlier political organizations, products of a particular moment in the history of the Puerto Rican left. But they still have much to teach in their remarkable efforts to practice race-conscious and empire-conscious protest, and in the ways they grappled with sex, reproduction, and women's place in their organizations.

The Young Lords takeover is also a reminder of the difference it can make when professionals join the ranks of activists. The doctors of the Lincoln Collective kept providing medical care during the takeover so that the Lords could negotiate for more resources and better care for hospital patients. These doctors were part of a forgotten national movement of progressive M.D.s who wanted to upend conventional medical practice and support activists who were doing the most to transform society.

In addition to the young doctors at Lincoln Hospital, medical professionals must remember their predecessors who continued to provide abortions in the face of rigid state laws, legal harassment, and even arrest. Dr. Henekh "Henry" Morgentaler in Montreal and Dr. Milan Vuitch in Washington, D.C., each of whom performed hundreds of abortions for patients referred to them by the Clergy Consultation Service, spent years fending off criminal charges. Morgentaler served eighteen months in jail. Both became subjects of landmark court cases that liberalized abortion law, Vuitch in the United States and Morgentaler in Canada. Who today is ready to take those risks and pay that price for a real chance of changing policy?

For models, academics and writers could do worse than look to CARASA members Meredith Tax, Atina Grossmann, Sarah Schulman, and Rayna Rapp, who interrupted the workaday business of their careers with an infinity of meetings in service of reproductive freedom. Lawyers can, and should, look to activist litigators like Nancy Stearns and Rhonda Copelon of the Center for Constitutional Rights, and the endlessly innovative Florynce Kennedy. These attorneys didn't simply make smart arguments. They built cases that were themselves occasions for organizing, activism, and public education. Clergy can of course look to the Clergy Consultation Service for examples of effective faith-based action. Not only did ministers Howard Moody and Finley Schaef of New York start the project, but their colleagues Rabbi Max Ticktin and Reverend Robert Hare, of Chicago and Cleveland, respectively, faced aggressive legal prosecution for their roles in helping people find safe ways to end their pregnancies—as every clergy member in the network knew they might. Ticktin and Hare both remained under indictment at the time the Supreme Court decided *Roe v. Wade*.

Most important, this history offers a wealth of object lessons on why not to give up. The legal status of abortion rights is dire.

Reproductive justice seems far-off and almost more than we're allowed to want. Remember: At the start of the 1960s, major wins for abortion rights and against sterilization abuse seemed just as far off. They happened in less than two decades.

Two images on the way out: September 2018, in a cool venue deep in the borough of Brooklyn. Even though the candidate on stage was conceding defeat, the crowd was ebullient. Cynthia Nixon's hard-fought gubernatorial campaign capped a wave of change in New York's Democratic Party unlike anything since the 1960s. After more than a year of ads, speeches, and debates, she was as well known for political activism as for acting. She is also my oldest friend. I ditched a weekend of regional Planned Parenthood board meetings to honor Nixon's bid for office, and to remember my mother. The day of Nixon's concession would have been Beatrice Kornbluh Braun's ninetieth birthday.

"We have already won," Nixon announced to the crowd. "We have fundamentally changed the political landscape in this state." The crowd erupted in cheers, because everyone knew she was right. Before her campaign was halfway through, Governor Andrew Cuomo, a Democrat but not a progressive reformer, switched his position on the legalization of recreational marijuana—a matter of racial justice, Nixon had argued, given that young Black and Latino men were overwhelmingly the ones who suffered legal consequences for marijuana use. He promised to use the pardon power to restore voting rights to felons and paid greater attention to conditions in public housing. Even more important, under pressure from Nixon and other progressives, the governor ceased backing a legislative caucus that had prevented passage of liberal Democratic initiatives by allying against them with Republicans. The movement Nixon symbolized defeated members of that anti-liberal caucus at the polls, changing the political balance in state government.

The impact of Nixon and the dissidents within the state's Democratic Party didn't stop with primary season. When a new legislature sat in 2019, one of its first achievements was passage of the Reproductive Health Act, which the governor signed on January 22, the forty-sixth anniversary of Justice Blackmun's opinion in *Roe v. Wade*. It was the first time since 1970 that New York State had expanded access to abortion. The Reproductive Health Act wasn't the no-barriers law respecting sex-based civil rights that Betty Friedan, my mother, Florynce Kennedy, and Lucinda Cisler all wanted in the late 1960s. It wasn't the expansive menu of reproductive freedoms Dr. Helen Rodríguez-Trías, Karen Stamm, and their friends pushed in CARASA. Feminists still haven't gotten that, even in New York. But the Reproductive Health Act secured in one state the right to end a pregnancy past the twenty-four-week point that had been established in 1970 if the pregnant person and their physician agreed that their health (including mental health) or life was at risk from continuing that pregnancy, or if their fetus was not viable. This was a gain for abortion rights that activists won by creating a strong coalition that pushed the Democratic Party to honor its rhetoric and ideals. They built power from the local grassroots that reshaped their political party from the bottom up, scoring victories for criminal justice reform before provoking a new state abortion law. They proved that change was still possible.

Second, Vermont 2022: By a vote of 107–41, the state's House of Representatives approved Proposition 5, an amendment to the state constitution called the Reproductive Liberty Amendment, the first such amendment in U.S. history. It promised all citizens of the state "personal reproductive autonomy." That meant, at a minimum, freedom from mandatory or coercive sterilization, legal abortions, and access to a full range of reproductive health care for same-sex couples and transgender or nonbinary people. Having followed the procedure for passing a constitutional amendment and passed each house of the legislature twice, during successive sessions, the proposal will go directly to voters as a ballot measure in the November election. It is expected to win.

The amendment isn't the absolute ideal. It ensures reproductive liberty, not justice—meaning, it promises to keep the government from interfering in people's decisions but does not promise all the supports (childcare, decent wages, universal health care) that would allow truly free choices about parenting. Still, its legislative success showed what was possible when the movement for safe and legal abortion acknowledged at least some of the concerns that lived on the other side of the page—when advocates did not sever the right to refrain from parenting from at least some of the needs implied in the right to parent.

At a conference in the 1990s on the health of women of color, Dr. Helen Rodríguez-Trías remembered her "formative experiences as an advocate" in the movements for abortion rights and against sterilization abuse. "Women activists in the women's movement, who were primarily concerned with removing all legal obstacles to abortion, opposed the notion of guidelines, regulations or legislation that in any way might restrict access to sterilizations. As we thrashed out the differences, we . . . began to listen to each other and to understand that our personal experiences were different because our race, class or ethnicity exposed us to different institution[s] and practices. A basis for working together was solidly laid"—and manifest in CESA and CARASA. Rodríguez-Trías concluded on a note of optimism, celebrating the progress of advocates for reproductive rights in "identifying and understanding our commonalities." But she knew there was more work to do to make common cause in the face of our differences. She implored her audience "to consolidate our ranks and focus our strength that we may create a universal equitable system fully consonant with our best values of compassion and fairness."

Abbreviations

ACLU: American Civil Liberties Union records, Seeley G. Mudd Manuscript Library, Princeton University, Princeton, NJ.

ACT UP: ACT UP Oral History Project Videotapes, a Program of MIX—the New York Lesbian and Gay Experimental Film Festival, Manuscripts and Archives Division, New York Public Library, New York, NY; transcripts held at the New York Public Library and at https://actuporalhistory.org/.

AG: Alan F. Guttmacher papers (H MS c155), Center for the History of Medicine, Francis A. Countway Library of Medicine, Harvard University, Boston, MA.

Blackmun: Harry A. Blackmun papers (MSS84430), Library of Congress, Washington, DC.

Braun: Beatrice Kornbluh Braun papers, in possession of the author.

CSE: Catherine Shipe East papers (MC 477), Schlesinger Library on the History of Women in America, Radcliffe Institute for Advanced Study, Harvard University, Cambridge, MA.

DJG: David J. Garrow papers, privately held, Pittsburgh, PA.

FPOHP 1: Family Planning Oral History Project Interviews (OH-1), Schlesinger Library on the History of Women in America, Radcliffe Institute for Advanced Study, Harvard University, Cambridge, MA.

FPOHP 2: Records of the Family Planning Oral History Project (MC 223), Schlesinger Library on the History of Women in America, Radcliffe Institute for Advanced Study, Harvard University, Cambridge, MA.

Friedan: Papers of Betty Friedan (MC 575), Schlesinger Library on the History of Women in America, Radcliffe Institute for Advanced Study, Harvard University, Cambridge, MA.

HRT: Helen Rodríguez-Trías papers, Archives of the Puerto Rican Diaspora, Center for Puerto Rican Studies/Centro de Estudios Puertorriqueños Archives, Hunter College, City University of New York, New York, NY.

Kennedy: Papers of Florynce Kennedy (MC 555), Schlesinger Library on the History of Women in America, Radcliffe Institute for Advanced Study, Harvard University, Cambridge, MA.

Lader: Lawrence Lader papers (H MS c304), Center for the History of Medicine, Francis A. Countway Library of Medicine, Harvard University, Boston, MA.

MLC: Papers of Maren Lockwood Carden (MC 504), Schlesinger Library on the History of Women in America, Radcliffe Institute for Advanced Study, Harvard University, Cambridge, MA.

MSC: Papers of Mary Steichen Calderone (MC 179), Schlesinger Library on the History of Women in America, Radcliffe Institute for Advanced Study, Harvard University, Cambridge, MA.

NAR-ACW: Nelson A. Rockefeller Personal Papers, Ann C. Whitman—Politics, Series P, Miscellaneous Materials, Abortion, Rockefeller Archive Center, Sleepy Hollow, Mount Pleasant, NY.

NARAL-State: National Abortion Rights Action League State Affiliates Newsletter Collection (Pr-5), Schlesinger Library on the History of Women in America, Radcliffe Institute for Advanced Study, Harvard University, Cambridge, MA.

NOW: Records of the National Organization for Women (MC 496), Schlesinger Library on the History of Women in America, Radcliffe Institute for Advanced Study, Harvard University, Cambridge, MA.

NOW-NYC: National Organization for Women, New York City Chapter records (TAM.106), Tamiment Library and Robert F. Wagner Labor Archive, Elmer Holmes Bobst Library, New York University, New York, NY.

NYS-CC: Collection of the New York State Constitutional Convention, 1967, New York State Archives, Albany, NY.

NYS-GC: Governor's Committee Appointed to Review New York State's Abortion Law, Reports and Public Hearing Transcript (Series 10996), New York State Archives, Albany, NY.

NYS-KB: Senator Karen Burstein Women's Issues Files (Series L0101), New York State Archives, Albany, NY.

NYS-MO: Subject and Bill Files of Senator Manfred Ohrenstein (Series B1952), New York State Archives, Albany, NY.

NYS-SCH: Senate Committee on Health, Abortion Legislation File (Series L0236), New York State Archives, Albany, NY.

NYS-TC: Temporary Commission on Revision of the Penal Law and Criminal Code Administrative and Working Files (Series 13828), New York State Archives, Albany, NY.

RPS: Papers of Ruth Proskauer Smith (77-M164–77-M183), Schlesinger Library on the History of Women in America, Radcliffe Institute for Advanced Study, Harvard University, Cambridge, MA.

Seaman: Papers of Barbara Seaman (82-M33–84-M82), Schlesinger Library on the History of Women in America, Radcliffe Institute for Advanced Study, Harvard University, Cambridge, MA.

Stamm-NYU: Karen Stamm papers (TAM 212), Tamiment Library and Robert F. Wagner Labor Archive, Elmer Holmes Bobst Library, New York University, New York, NY.

Stamm-Private: Karen Stamm papers, privately held (now Karen Stamm Collection of Committee for Abortion Rights and Against Sterilization Abuse [CARASA] records [SSC-MS-00811], Sophia Smith Collection of Women's History, Special Collections, Neilson Library, Smith College, Northampton, MA).

Teicher: Anne Teicher papers, privately held, New York, NY (now part of Sophia Smith Collection of Women's History, Special Collections, Neilson Library, Smith College, Northampton, MA).

Voices: Voices of Feminism Oral History Project, Sophia Smith Collection of Women's History, Special Collections, Neilson Library, Smith College, Northampton, MA.

Endnotes

PROLOGUE

xiv **I determined to** Telephone contact list, Professional Women's Caucus, New York City, n.d. [1972?], Braun.

xv **She represented APHA** Helen Rodríguez-Trías, M.D., F.A.A.P., "Foreword" to *Reproductive Rights and Wrongs: The Global Politics of Population Control*, by Betsy Hartmann (Chicago: Haymarket Books, 2016; originally 1987), xxii.

xv **"poverty, violence, joblessness"** Dr. Helen Rodríguez-Trías, draft foreword to *Wings of Gauze: Women of Color and the Experience of Health and Illness*, ed. Barbara Bair and Susan E. Cayliff (Detroit: Wayne State University Press, 1993), unnumbered typescript, HRT, Box 2, Folder 5.

xv **Rodríguez-Trías and the** Karenna Gore Schiff, *Lighting the Way: Nine Women Who Changed Modern America* (New York: Miramax Books, 2005), 341–89, is the only published work to explore Rodríguez-Trías's life and career in some depth.

xvi **The most influential** Thomas M. Shapiro, *Population Control Politics: Women, Sterilization, and Reproductive Choice* (Philadelphia: Temple University Press, 1985), 139–40, 154–55.

xvi **Also important were** Collection description, Association for Voluntary Sterilization Records, Social Welfare History Archives, University of Minnesota, https://archives.lib.umn.edu/repositories/11/resources/2395, accessed January 19, 2021.

xvii **And I reviewed** Beatrice Kornbluh Braun, interview with Felicia Kornbluh, July 5, 2016, transcript in possession of the author.

xviii **With the narcissism** Marguerite Rewalt, Chairman, Legal Committee, NOW , "Report . . . .To All Members of the Legal Committee, National Organization for Women . . . as at September 12, 1968," Braun.

xviii **"perhaps only a"** Senator Franz Leichter (D-NYS retired), remarks, Memorial Service for Beatrice Kornbluh Braun, Marlene Myerson Jewish Community Center, April 16, 2017.

xix **But a J.D.** Kornbluh Braun, with Kornbluh.

xx **"D&C"** Beatrice Kornbluh, New York, New York, to Meryl and Andy Steigman, Washington, D.C., August 30, 1966, Braun; and Daria Steigman, interview with Felicia Kornbluh, April 30, 2020, transcript in possession of the author.

xx   **legal abortion** Even at the height of the "illegal abortion era," and even in a highly restrictive state such as New York, doctors performed thousands of abortions each year to preserve women's health (sometimes interpreted broadly to include psychological health). Edwin M. Gold, Carl L. Erhardt, Harold Jacobziner, and Frieda G. Nelson, "Therapeutic Abortion in New York City: A 20-Year Review," *American Journal of Public Health*, vol. 55, no. 7 (July 1965): 964–72.

xx   **Luckily, though, I** Daniel Curet-Rodríguez, interview with Felicia Kornbluh, September 22, 2019, transcript in possession of the author; and Felicia Kornbluh, notes from an interview with Jo Ellen Brainin-Rodríguez, August 19, 2019, in author's possession. There is no transcript of the latter interview because the equipment failed to record.

xx   **Thanks to her** HRT.

xxi **School administrators must** "Biography: Helen Rodriguez-Trias," *Changing the Face of Medicine*, National Library of Medicine, U.S. National Institutes of Health, https://cfmedicine.nlm.nih.gov/physicians/biography_273.html, accessed January 19, 2021.

xxi **"The year of"** Helen Rodríguez-Trías, Jo Ellen Brainin-Rodríguez, and Laura Brainin-Rodríguez, "A Mother's Story," typescript chapter for *The Conversation Begins: Mothers and Daughters Talk About Living Feminism*, ed. Christina Looper Baker and Christina Baker Kline, December 13, 1995, HRT, Box 2, Folder 7.

xxi **She dropped out** Joyce Wilcox, "The Face of Women's Health: Helen Rodriguez-Trias," *American Journal of Public Health*, vol. 92, no. 4 (April 2002): 567.

xxii **"as suited two"** Rodríguez-Trías, Brainin-Rodríguez, and Brainin-Rodríguez, "A Mother's Story."

xxii **They asked Representative** Gore Schiff, *Lighting the Way*, 349–50.

xxii **At the time** Rodríguez-Trías, Brainin-Rodríguez, and Brainin-Rodríguez, "A Mother's Story."

xxii **With her husband** Rodríguez-Trías, Brainin-Rodríguez, and Brainin-Rodríguez, "A Mother's Story."

xxii **"revelation," she recalled** Rodríguez-Trías, Brainin-Rodríguez, and Brainin-Rodríguez, "A Mother's Story."

xxiii **In 1977, as** Wilcox, "Face of Women's Health," 568.

xxiii **With the endorsement** Carmen Vivian Rivera, interview with Felicia Kornbluh, May 1, 2020, transcript in possession of the author.

xxiii **She and González** Wolfgang Saxon, "Helen Rodriguez-Trias, Family Health Care Advocate," *New York Times*, January 4, 2002: C11.

xxiv **"better patient care"** President William J. Clinton, "Remarks on Presenting the Presidential Citizens Medal," January 8, 2001, American Presidency Project, University of California, Santa Barbara, https://www.presidency.ucsb.edu/documents/remarks-presenting-the-presidential-citizens-medal, accessed March 3, 2022.

xxiv **She shared the** Clinton, "Remarks on Presenting the Presidential Citizens Medal."

xxiv **"a complex and"** Jo Ellen Brainin-Rodríguez, draft eulogy, Memorial Service, Helen Rodríguez-Trías, St. Matthew–St. Timothy Episcopal Church, New York, HRT, Box 1, Folder 11.

xxiv **"There was proximity"** Mike Nichols and Elaine May, "Back to Bach," on the album *Improvisations to Music* and discussed in Mitchell Cohen, *Lost in a Fool's Parade*, http://emscee.com/foolsparadise/?p=2612, accessed January 15, 2021.

xxv **But it was** Alexandra Minna Stern, *Eugenic Nation: Faults and Frontiers of Better Breeding in Modern America* (Berkeley: University of California Press, 2016), 93 (for a complex quantitative scale of "delinquent, retarded, diseased, and otherwise unfit individuals"), 176–77 (on the rebirth of eugenic thinking and policies in the postwar period).

INTRODUCTION: BOTH SIDES

1 **It was 1963** Karen Stamm, interview with Felicia Kornbluh, October 25, 2019, transcript in possession of the author.

1 **of New York** Cyril Means, Jr., "The Law of New York Concerning Abortion and the Status of the Foetus, 1664–1968: A Case of Cessation of Constitutionality," *New York Law Forum*, vol. 14, no. 3 (1968): 411–515. New York passed the relevant law in 1828 as part of a general revision of the state legal code but did not implement it until 1830.

1 **Authorities rarely prosecuted** James Mohr, *Abortion in America: The Origins and Evolution of National Policy* (New York: Oxford University Press, 1978), 1–6.

1 **Starting in 1830** Means, "Law of New York," 437–38, 450, 454.

1 **By the 1960s** Leslie Reagan, *When Abortion Was a Crime: Women, Medicine, and Law in the United States, 1880–1973* (Berkeley: University of California Press, 1997), 200–201.

2 **It helped that** Stamm, with Kornbluh.

2 **"Otherwise, who knows"** Karen Stamm, private communication with the author, February 24, 2022.

2 **"was going to"** Stamm, with Kornbluh.

2 **Many doctors who** Lawrence Lader, *Abortion* (Indianapolis, IN: Bobbs-Merrill, 1966), 30–31; Dr. Helen Rodríguez-Trías, "Two Lectures," the Reid Lectureship, Barnard College, November 10–11, 1976 (Barnard College Women's Center, 1977), Stamm-Private, unnamed accordion folder, file titled "Helen Rodriguez-Trias," 21; and Susan Brownmiller, "Everywoman's Abortions: The Oppressor Is Man," *Village Voice*, March 27, 1969.

2 **"There was no"** Stamm, with Kornbluh.

3 **only a trained** Linda Gordon, *Woman's Body, Woman's Right* (New York: Penguin Press, 1990; originally 1974), 172 and footnote same page, 281, 289.

4 **Ross aborted that** Loretta Ross, interview by Joyce Follet, transcript of video recording, November 3–5 and December 21–3, 2004 and February 4, 2005, Voices, 70–71.

4 **Loretta Ross would** Loretta Ross, interview with Felicia Kornbluh, October 11, 2019, transcript in possession of the author; and Loretta Ross and Rickie Solinger, *Reproductive Justice: An Introduction* (Berkeley: University of California Press, 2017).

4 **The student medical** Morton Mintz, *At Any Cost: Corporate Greed, Women, and the Dalkon Shield* (New York: Pantheon Press, 1985); and Harriet Washington, *Medical Apartheid:*

The Dark History of Medical Experimentation on African Americans from Colonial Times to the Present (New York: Anchor Books, 2008; originally 2006), 201–2.

4 **"And of course"** Ross, with Follet, 76–78.

5 **"To be told"** Ross, with Kornbluh.

5 **"didn't get any"** Ross, with Kornbluh.

5 **"And so I"** Ross, with Follet, 79–80.

5 **From there, she** Ross with Follet, biographical introduction, no page.

5 **The group coined** "The Herstory of Reproductive Justice," SisterSong Women of Color Reproductive Justice Collective, https://www.sistersong.net/reproductive-justice, accessed April 21, 2021.

7 **Second was a** Mary Ziegler, *After Roe: The Lost History of the Abortion Debate* (Cambridge, MA: Harvard University Press, 2015), 152–53.

7 **After all, the** Daniel K. Williams, *Defenders of the Unborn: The Pro-Life Movement Before Roe v. Wade* (New York: Oxford University Press, 2016), 57 (on the middle-1960s era of Vatican II); Jack Rosenthal, "Survey Finds Majority, in Shift, Now Favors Liberalized Laws," *New York Times*, August 25, 1972: 1; and Blackmun, Box 152, Folder 5 (a majority of Catholics favored abortion law reform).

8 **"into concepts of"** Nell Irvin Painter, *The History of White People* (New York: W.W. Norton, 2010), Kindle edition, location 87.

8 **White privilege shapes** Peggy McIntosh, "White Privilege: Unpacking the Invisible Knapsack," *Peace and Freedom Magazine*, July–August 1989: 10–12; Robin DiAngelo, *White Fragility: Why It's So Hard for White People to Talk About Racism* (Boston: Beacon Press, 2018); Janet Halley, Prabha Kotiswaran, Rachel Rebouche, and Hila Shamir, *Governance Feminism: An Introduction* (Minneapolis: University of Minnesota Press, 2018); Karen Brodkin, *How Jews Became White Folks—and What That Says About Race in America* (New Brunswick, NJ: Rutgers University Press, 1998); and Ruth Frankenberg, *White Women, Race Matters: The Social Construction of Whiteness* (Minneapolis: University of Minnesota Press, 1993). Thanks to Matthew Horton for citations and for discussing these issues with me.

8 **"invisible knapsack"** McIntosh, "White Privilege."

8 **"second-sight" and "double-consciousness"** W.E.B. DuBois, *The Souls of Black Folk: Essays and Sketches* (Project Gutenberg, 2008, e-book #408; originally 1903), "Of Our Spiritual Strivings," no page.

8 **"one main piece"** McIntosh, "White Privilege."

8 **"vision as does"** Dr. Helen Rodríguez-Trías, draft foreword of *Wings of Gauze: Women of Color and the Experience of Health and Illness*, ed. Barbara Bair and Susan E. Cayliff (Detroit: Wayne State University Press, 1993), unnumbered typescript, HRT, Box 2, Folder 5.

10 **Harlem's assemblyman Percy** Dr. Cynthia Greenlee, "Percy Sutton's 1966 Abortion Rights Bill: Groundbreaking, but Often Unremembered," *Rewire*, February 24, 2015, https://rewirenewsgroup.com/article/2015/02/24/percy-suttons-1966-abortion-rights-bill-groundbreaking-often-unremembered/, accessed May 21, 2021.

10 **Labor leader and** State of New York: In Convention, May 23, 1967—Introduced by Mrs. ROBINSON—read once and ordered printed and when printed,

referred to the Committee on Bill of Rights and Suffrage, A PROPOSITION TO REPEAL SECTION ELEVEN OF ARTICLE ONE OF THE CONSTITUTION, RELATING TO EQUAL PROTECTION OF LAWS AND PROHIBITING DISCRIMINATION IN CIVIL RIGHTS . . . [and] TO AMEND THE CONSTITUTION, IN RELATION TO THE RIGHT TO TERMINATE A PREGNANCY UNDER MEDICAL SUPERVISION, attached to letter from Jean Faust, President, NOW–New York, New York City, New York, to Andrew R. Tyler, Chairman, Committee on Rights and Suffrage, Constitutional Convention, Albany, New York, August 9, 1967, NYS-CC.

10   **Activist attorney Florynce** Diane Schulder and Florynce Kennedy, *Abortion Rap* (New York: McGraw Hill, 1971).

11   **My mother's draft** Florynce Kennedy quoted in Grace Lichtenstein, "Abortion Laws Opposed at Rally," *New York Times*, March 29, 1970: 35.

11   **The role my** Senator Franz Leichter (D-NYS retired), remarks, Memorial Service for Beatrice Kornbluh Braun, Marlene Myerson Jewish Community Center, April 16, 2017; and Leichter, interview with Felicia Kornbluh, July 14, 2017, transcript in possession of the author.

11   **By eliminating criminal** Alan F. Guttmacher, "The Genesis of Liberalized Abortion in New York: A Personal Insight," *Case Western Reserve Law Review*, vol. 23, no. 4 (1972): 764.

11   **After implementation of** Arlene Carmen, interview with Ellen Chesler, FPOHP I, January 1976.

11   **Maternal mortality dropped** David Harris, M.D., M.P.H., et al., "Legal Abortion 1970–1971: The New York City Experience," *American Journal of Public Health*, vol. 63, no. 5 (May 1973): 409–18.

12   **"we all looked"** Stanley Katz, interview with Felicia Kornbluh, November 9, 2020, transcript in possession of the author, and private communication.

12   **If nothing else** Keisha N. Blain, *Until I Am Free: Fannie Lou Hamer's Enduring Message to America* (Boston: Beacon Press, 2021), xv, 34.

12   **"In the North"** DeNeen L. Brown, "Civil Rights Crusader Fannie Lou Hamer Defied Men—and Presidents—Who Tried to Silence Her," *Washington Post*, October 6, 2017, https://www.washingtonpost.com/news/retropolis/wp/2017/10/06/civil-rights-crusader-fannie-lou-hamer-defied-men-and-presidents-who-tried-to-silence-her/, accessed February 5, 2020.

12   **"too many side"** Daniel Immerwahr, *How to Hide an Empire: A History of the Greater United States* (New York: Picador, 2019), 249.

13   **In 1960, the** Elaine Tyler May, *Americans and the Pill: A History of Promise, Peril, and Liberation* (New York: Basic Books, 2011), 28–34 (noting that her own father, Dr. Edward Tyler, slowed down the FDA approval process by voicing reservations based on the Puerto Rico trials).

13   **"Close the Institutions"** "1970—Present: Close the Institutions, Parallels in Time, a History of Developmental Disabilities," State of Minnesota, Governor's Council on Developmental Disabilities," https://mn.gov/mnddc/parallels/five/5f/1.html, accessed March 4, 2022.

13 **"socially inadequate"** Kim Nielsen, *A Disability History of the United States* (Boston: Beacon Press, 2012), 113.

13 **Because of these** Nielsen, *Disability History*, 100.

13 **Affirming the legality** Paul A. Lombardo, *Three Generations, No Imbeciles: Eugenics, the Supreme Court, and Buck v. Bell* (Baltimore: Johns Hopkins University Press, 2008); and Adam Cohen, *Imbeciles: The Supreme Court, American Eugenics, and the Sterilization of Carrie Buck* (New York: Penguin, 2016).

13 **"It is better"** *Buck v. Bell* [274 U.S. 208] (1927).

13 **The targets of** Alexandra Minna Stern, *Eugenic Nation: Faults and Frontiers of Better Breeding in Modern America* (Berkeley: University of California Press, 2016), 175–78; and Joanna Schoen, *Choice and Coercion: Birth Control, Sterilization, and Abortion in Public Health and Welfare* (Chapel Hill: University of North Carolina Press, 2005), 61–62.

14 **Disabled people continued** Mag Segrest, *Administrations of Lunacy: Racism and the Haunting of American Psychiatry at the Milledgeville Asylum* (New York: New Press, 2020), 301–2, offers one example of eugenic practices (racist and ableist) in an institution for disabled people at their height in the 1950s and continuing until the 1970s.

14 **As Thomas Shapiro** Thomas Shapiro, interview with Felicia Kornbluh, June 4, 2020, transcript in possession of the author.

14 **"The prevailing idea"** Thomas M. Shapiro, *Population Control Politics: Women, Sterilization, and Reproductive Choice* (Philadelphia: Temple University Press, 1985), 67.

15 **The environmental argument** Population Connection (formerly Zero Population Growth), "Our Mission and Goals," https://populationconnection.org/about-us/, accessed March 20, 2022.

15 **For her, transforming** Ruth Cusack, interview with David Garrow, June 25, 1993, Part I, cassette recording DJG, transcript in possession of the author.

16 **"the unwanted child"** Ruth Cusack, Miller Place, New York, to Honorable Albert H. Blumenthal, Member of Assembly, New York, New York, November 13, 1967, DJG, Box 5.3, Folder 15.

16 **After World War II** Stern, *Eugenic Nation*, 4; and Betsy Hartmann, *Reproductive Rights and Wrongs: The Global Politics of Population Control* (Chicago: Haymarket Books, 2016; originally 1987), 57 (on the greater involvement of the International Planned Parenthood Federation in these efforts starting in the 1960s), 97 (on IPPF's founding and explicit ties to eugenics), 233–35 (on IPPF in Puerto Rico and Colombia from the late 1940s to the 1980s).

16 **Within the United** Mary Steichen Calderone, M.D., ed., *Abortion in the United States: A Conference Sponsored by the Planned Parenthood Federation of America, Inc. at Arden House and the New York Academy of Medicine* (New York: Paul B. Hoeber, Medical Book Department of Harper and Brothers, 1958).

16 **The Sterilization League** "Historical Note," Inventory of the Papers of the Association for Voluntary Sterilization, Archives and Special Collections, University of Minnesota Libraries, https://archives.lib.umn.edu/repositories/11/resources/2395, accessed December 17, 2021.

16 **"somewhat single-handedly"** Hugh Moore, Easton, Penn., to Ruth Proskauer Smith, New York, New York, November 2, 1964, RPS, Box 1, Folder 5. At the time she headed it, the group was called the Human Betterment Association for Voluntary Sterilization. Its publications made direct links between population programs abroad and the supposed need for them in impoverished U.S. communities, and argued that high numbers of welfare recipients proved the need for more sterilization. See "$25,000 Gift Speeds Voluntary Sterilization Program in Appalachia," press release, and Memorandum, Proskauer Smith [to Board of Directors], Re: Hartman Plan—Florida Project, October 26, 1964, ibid.

17 **The New York** Alan Guttmacher, M.D., "Sterilization: Facts and Arguments," *The Nation*, April 6, 1964, AG, Box 11, Folder 36; and Guttmacher, "Too Many People Too Fast," *Hadassah Magazine*, November 1964, ibid., Box 11, Folder 38.

17 **He served at** Extract of Board of Directors Meeting, Human Betterment Association for Voluntary Sterilization, November 19, 1964, with Guttmacher on letterhead as chair of Medical Committee, RPS, Box 1, Folder 5.

17 **He titled it** Lawrence Lader, *Breeding Ourselves to Death* (New York: Ballantine Books, 1971).

17 **"the function of"** Lawrence Lader, *Abortion II: Making the Revolution* (Boston: Beacon Press, 1973), 218, 220.

17 **Nelson Rockefeller, the** Matthew Connelly, *Fatal Misconception: The Struggle to Control World Population* (Cambridge, MA: Harvard University Press, 2010), 61, 135, 155–59.

17 **"concluded that no"** Report of the Commission on Population Growth and the American Future, March 1972, https://www.populationsecurity.org/rockefeller/001_population_growth_and_the_american_future.htm#Chapter%201, accessed February 5, 2020.

17 **"influenced particularly by"** Constance Cook, interview with Ellen Chesler, FPOHP 1, 44.

18 **It was also** Hartmann, *Reproductive Rights and Wrongs*, 233–34.

18 **"foreign in a"** Bartholomew H. Sparrow, *The Insular Cases and the Emergence of American Empire* (Lawrence: University of Kansas Press, 2006); and Christina Duffy Burnett and Burke Marshall, eds., *Foreign in a Domestic Sense: Puerto Rico, American Expansion, and the Constitution* (Durham, NC: Duke University Press, 2001).

18 **Staff of the** Laura Briggs, *Reproducing Empire: Race, Sex, Science and U.S. Imperialism in Puerto Rico* (Berkeley: University of California Press, 2002), chapter 3.

19 **He advocated the** Schoen, *Choice and Coercion*, 205; and Shapiro, *Population Control Politics*, 52.

19 **"health reasons"** Iris López, "Sterilization in Puerto Rico: Coercion or Personal Choice?," *Genetic Determinism and Children*, ed. Ethel Tobach and Betty Rosoff (New York: Gordian Press, 1980), 68.

19 **Others, like the** Frances Hand Ferguson, interview with James Reed, FPOHP 1, 23–25.

19 **Two-thirds of** López, "Sterilization in Puerto Rico," 71.

19 **But sterilization was** Briggs, *Reproducing Empire*, has done the most careful historical work on this issue and has shaped my understanding.

20 **At the same** Iris López, *Matters of Choice: Puerto Rican Women's Struggle for Reproductive Freedom* (New Brunswick, NJ: Rutgers University Press, 2008); López, interview with Felicia Kornbluh, September 18, 2020, transcript in possession of the author; and Rickie Solinger, *Beggars and Choosers: How the Politics of Choice Shapes Adoption, Abortion, and Welfare in the United States* (New York: Hill and Wang, 2001).

21 **The second concern** Linda Gordon, *Woman's Body, Woman's Right: Birth Control in America* (New York: Penguin Press, 1990; originally 1974), 132–38.

21 **The American Medical** Rebecca Kluchin, *Fit to Be Tied: Sterilization and Reproductive Rights in America, 1950–1980* (New Brunswick, NJ: Rutgers University Press, 2011), 22–23.

21 **People who wanted** Kluchin, *Fit to Be Tied*, 114–47.

22 **By contrast, Justice** *Roe v. Wade* [410 U.S. 113] (1973).

22 **"on the pan"** Constance Cook, interview with Ellen Chesler, FPOHP I, 31.

23 **"recreative" versus "procreative"** Alice Rossi, "Sociological Argument in Support of Effect of Denial of Right to a Woman to Control Her Own Reproductive Life," [1967], Friedan, Identifier 127-1552.

24 **They stumped for** [Karen Stamm], "Lessons of the Campaign for the Guidelines," n.d., Stamm-NYU, Box 2, Folder 4.

24 **Mexican American and** Maya Manian, "Coerced Sterilization of Mexican-American Women: The Story of *Madrigal v. Quilligan*," *Reproductive Rights and Justice Stories*, ed. Melissa Murray, Katherine Shaw, and Reva B. Siegel (St. Paul, MN: West Academic/Foundation Press, 2019), 97–116; and Brianna Theobald, *Reproduction on the Reservation: Pregnancy, Childbirth, and Colonialism in the Long Twentieth Century* (Chapel Hill: University of North Carolina Press, 2019), 1–4, 155–64.

25 **"possibility of controlling"** Rosiland Pollack Petchesky, Rayna Rapp, et al., *Women Under Attack: Abortion, Sterilization, and Reproductive Freedom* (New York City: Committee for Abortion Rights and Against Sterilization Abuse, 1979), 9.

ONE: REFORMERS AND REFORM

27 **"I was in"** Carol Rosenberg Marsh, interview with Felicia Kornbluh, August 6, 2020, transcript in possession of the author.

27 **"and he said"** Marsh with Kornbluh.

28 **"And the resident"** Marsh with Kornbluh.

28 **Carol Marsh's experience** David Garrow, *Liberty and Sexuality: The Right to Privacy and the Making of* Roe v. Wade (Berkeley: University of California Press, 1998; originally 1994), 304–5.

29 **Enforcement was haphazard** Leslie Reagan, *When Abortion Was a Crime: Women, Medicine, and Law in the United States, 1867–1973* (Berkeley: University of California Press, 1997), 160–215.

29 **In 1958, Steichen Calderone** Mary Steichen Calderone, ed., *Abortion in the United States*, with an introduction by M.F. Ashley Montagu (New York: Hoeber-Harper, 1958), and MSC, Identifiers 12–24.

30 **In 1959, the** Reagan, *When Abortion Was a Crime*, 220–22.

30 **Americans for Democratic Action** Joseph P. Lash, *Eleanor Roosevelt: A Friend's Memoir* (Garden City, NY: Doubleday, 1964), 317–18.

31 **When I got** Beatrice Kornbluh Braun, interview with Felicia Kornbluh, July 5, 2016, transcript in possession of the author.

32 **In New York, my** Senator Franz Leichter (D-NYS retired), interview with Felicia Kornbluh, July 14, 2017, transcript in possession of the author; and David Kornbluh, interview with Felicia Kornbluh, August 17, 2017, transcript in possession of the author.

32 **One of Harlem's** Douglas Martin, "Percy E. Sutton, Political Trailblazer, Dies at 89," *New York Times*, December 27, 2009, https://www.nytimes.com/2009/12/28/nyregion/28sutton.html, accessed May 24, 2021.

32 **Ohrenstein, a Jewish** Eleanor Roosevelt, "My Day," May 26, 1960, Eleanor Roosevelt Papers, digital edition, George Washington University, https://www2.gwu.edu/~erpapers/myday/displaydoc.cfm?_y=1960&_f=md004755, accessed May 26, 2021.

33 **He may have** Manfred Ohrenstein, with Jack Kliger, "Stories Survive," Museum of Jewish Heritage, a Living Memorial to the Holocaust, April 21, 2021, https://www.youtube.com/watch?v=T9sYkaARopQ, accessed May 26, 2021.

33 **The Upper West** Walter H. Waggoner, "Albert H. Blumenthal Dies at 55," *New York Times*, July 10, 1984: B6.

33 **Friedan was a** Betty Friedan, *The Feminine Mystique* (New York: W.W. Norton, 2013; originally 1963).

33 **At her birth** Daniel Horowitz, *Betty Friedan and the Making of "The Feminine Mystique": The American Left, the Cold War, and Modern Feminism* (Amherst: University of Massachusetts Press, 1998), 17–19.

33 **Bettye Goldstein dropped** Horowitz, *Betty Friedan*, 87.

33 **In *The Feminine*** Friedan, *Feminine Mystique*, 6–7.

34 **She opposed U.S.** Horowitz, *Betty Friedan*, 76–82

34 **She finally supported** Horowitz, *Betty Friedan*, 81–82.

34 **"the largest communist-led"** Daniel Horowitz, "Rethinking Betty Friedan and *The Feminine Mystique*: Labor Union Radicalism and Feminism in Cold War America," *American Quarterly*, vol. 48, no. 1 (March 1996): 1–42. On the United Electrical Workers, Horowitz is quoting labor historian Ronald Schatz.

34 **It was also** Dorothy Cobble, *The Other Women's Movement: Workplace Justice and Social Rights in Modern America* (Princeton, NJ: Princeton University Press, 2003), 52, 57.

34 **In 1952, Friedan** Horowitz, "Rethinking Betty Friedan," 1, 15.

34 **Friedan didn't acknowledge** Horowitz, *Betty Friedan*, 205.

35 **The commission, a** Cobble, *Other Women's Movement*, 159.

35 **Title VII also** National Archives and Records Administration of the United States, transcript of Civil Rights Act of 1964, from *Our Documents: 100 Milestone Documents from the National Archives*, https://www.ourdocuments.gov/doc.php?flash=false&doc=97&page=transcript, accessed May 12, 2021.

35 **In the first** Sonia Pressman Fuentes, *Eat First—You Don't Know What They'll Give You: The Adventures of an Immigrant Family and Their Feminist Daughter* (Xlibris, 1999), ebook edition, location 1782.

35 **"I arrive at"** "Aileen Clarke Hernandez (1926–2017), 'A Pioneer for Women and Civil Rights,'" Veteran Feminists of America, https://www.veteranfeminist-sofamerica.org/vfa-pioneer-histories-project-aileen-hernandez/interview-aileen-hernandez/, accessed June 11, 2021.

36 **Before President Johnson** "Aileen Clarke Hernandez—Biography," based on interviews conducted April 12, 2007, and November 8, 2013, The History Makers, https://www.thehistorymakers.org/biography/aileen-clarke-hernandez, accessed June 11, 2021; and "Aileen Clarke Hernandez," Veteran Feminists of America.

36 **"sex maniac"** Pressman Fuentes, *Eat First*, title of chapter 23.

36 **"I had been"** Pressman Fuentes, *Eat First*, location 1717.

36 **"with tears in"** Pressman Fuentes, *Eat First*, location 1836. Friedan told the same story somewhat differently: "Sonia Pressman shut her office door and said, 'I'm not a feminist. . . . Who appointed me to worry about women? . . . You have to start a national organization to fight for women, like the civil rights movement fights for blacks.' And there were tears in her eyes." Friedan, *"It Changed My Life": Writings on the Women's Movement* (Cambridge, MA: Harvard University Press, 1998; originally 1976), 100.

37 **In 1965, Justice** I avoid using a gender-specific pronoun here because Murray's private writing reveals a gender identity that was closer to what people in the twenty-first century would call a "trans" or "nonbinary" one than to a female one. Murray's gender is addressed at length in the documentary *My Name Is Pauli Murray*, directed by Julie Cohen and Betsy West, distributed by Amazon (2021).

37 **"at the risk"** Letter from Pauli Murray, First Year Law Student, Howard University, to Attorney Dobbins, President, Sigma Delta Tau Legal Fraternity, Washington, D.C., November 7, 1941, Friedan, Identifier 143-1798. Murray shared the letter with Friedan as "my first reaction to 'Jane Crow,'" in support of comments in an interview with Friedan for the latter's second book (never completed). Memo from Pauli Murray to Betty Friedan, Re: P. Murray Interview, June 9, 1966, ibid. Murray asked Friedan to return the letter after reviewing it, which Friedan apparently never did.

37 **Murray and Eastwood's** Headnote, "Document 10, Pauli Murray and Mary Eastwood, 'Jane Crow and the Law: Sex Discrimination and Title VII,' *George Washington Law Review*, vol. 34, no. 2 (December 1965): 232–56," published as part of the Women and Social Movements collection, section on "Why and How Was Feminist Legal Strategy Transformed, 1960–1973?" (Alexander Street Press), https://documents.alexanderstreet.com/d/1000687209, accessed June 8, 2021.

37 **"The addition of"** Murray and Eastwood, "Jane Crow," 235.

38 **They countered the** Murray and Eastwood, "Jane Crow," 239–41.

38 **It didn't take** Betty Friedan, "Report of the President," National Organization for Women, Second National Conference, Washington, D.C., November 18, 1967, typescript with her handwritten edits, Friedan, Identifier 127-1553; and Friedan, "The First Year: President's Report to NOW, 1967," *"It Changed My Life,"* 124.

38 **"that night a group . . . 'an NAACP for women'"** Cobble, *Other Women's Movement*, 185.

39 **"The purpose of"** National Organization for Women, "Statement of Purpose," adopted at the Organizing Conference, Washington, D.C., October 29, 1966, NOW, Identifier 23-1. (Also published as "The National Organization for Women [NOW] Statement of Purpose," Friedan, *It Changed My Life*, 109–15.)

39 **"There is no"** NOW, "Statement of Purpose."

39 **"lawyers, doctors, and"** Lawrence Lader, *Abortion II: Making the Revolution* (Boston: Beacon Press, 1973), 26.

39 **"America's first notably"** Garrow, *Liberty and Sexuality*, 297.

40 **Originally from Baltimore** "Biographical Note," Finding Aid, Guttmacher.

40 **ASA's founding executive** Garrow, *Liberty and Sexuality*, 297.

40 **Members of the** Rosemary Nossiff, *Before Roe: Abortion Policy in the States* (Philadelphia: Temple University Press, 2001), 79.

40 **Spokespeople Guttmacher and** Garrow, *Liberty and Sexuality*, 298; and *Griswold v. Connecticut* [381 U.S. 49] (1965).

40 **A legislative campaign** Nossiff, *Before* Roe, 79.

40 **In New York** Reagan, *When Abortion Was a Crime*, 213–14.

40 **A report in** Edwin M. Gold, Carl L. Erhardt, Harold Jacobziner, and Frieda G. Nelson, "Therapeutic Abortion in New York City: A 20-Year Review," *American Journal of Public Health*, vol. 55, no. 7 (July 1965): 964–65.

41 **"This background," he**: Quoted in Dr. Cynthia Greenlee, "Percy Sutton's 1966 Abortion Rights Bill: Groundbreaking, but Often Unremembered," Rewire News Group, February 24, 2015, https://rewirenewsgroup.com/article/2015/02/24/percy-suttons-1966-abortion-rights-bill-groundbreaking-often-unremembered/, accessed May 21, 2021.

41 **This included, in** Reagan, *When Abortion Was a Crime*, 160–92.

41 **"consistent downward trend"** Gold et al., "Therapeutic Abortion in New York City," 965.

41 **At Manhattan's Mount** Alan F. Guttmacher, "The Genesis of Liberalized Abortion in New York: A Personal Insight," *Case Western Reserve Law Review*, vol. 23, no. 4: 759–60.

41 **"outmoded" . . . "letter of the law"** Alan F. Guttmacher, "Therapeutic Abortion: The Doctor's Dilemma," *Journal of the Mount Sinai Hospital–New York*, vol. 21, no. 1 (May–June 1954): 118–19.

42 **While the systems** Guttmacher, "Doctor's Dilemma," 118.

42 **The committee structure** Reagan, *When Abortion Was a Crime*, 178–79.

42 **"No case is" . . . "a material reduction"** Guttmacher, "Doctor's Dilemma," 118–19.

43 **Of women who** Lader, *Abortion II*, 13, 22.

43 **Sutton started with** James C. Mohr, *Abortion in America: The Origins and Evolution of National Policy* (New York: Oxford University Press, 1978), 177–82.

43 **"For a price"** Percy Sutton, "Is Abortion Ever Right?," *Amsterdam News*, January 29, 1966: 1.

44 **"right to be born"** Sutton, "Is Abortion Ever Right?," *Amsterdam News*, February 5, 1966: 1.

44 **"Is abortion ever"** . . . **"vegetable"** Sutton, "Is Abortion Ever Right?," *Amsterdam News*, February 19, 1966: 1.

44 **"opposed to abortions"** Sutton, "Is Abortion Ever Right?," *Amsterdam News*, February 26, 1966: 1.

44 **"Humiliation, agony and"** Sutton, "Is Abortion Ever Right?," *Amsterdam News*, March 5, 1966: 36.

45 **But they represented** Nossiff, *Before* Roe, 79, noting that hearings on the Sutton bill were covered on the front page of the *New York Times*.

45 **While his abortion** Martin, "Percy E. Sutton."

45 **It drew, similarly** Lader, *Abortion II*, 62.

45 **Blumenthal added an** Nossiff, *Before* Roe, 80.

46 **"with all their"** Lader, *Abortion II*, 59.

46 **"The opposition concentrated"** Lader, *Abortion II*, 59.

46 **Paterson's involvement helped** Garrow, *Liberty and Sexuality*, 311.

46 **But the compromise** Lader, *Abortion II*, 60.

47 **The people who** Lader, *Abortion II*, 58–60.

47 **The vote was** Nossiff, *Before* Roe, 79.

47 **In the midst** Nossiff, *Before* Roe, 80.

Two: Change the Law NOW

48 **As the delegates** Lawrence Lader, *Abortion II: Making the Revolution* (Boston: Beacon Press, 1973), 36.

48 **"the right to"** State of New York: In Convention, May 23, 1967—Introduced by Mrs. ROBINSON—read once and ordered printed and when printed, referred to the Committee on Bill of Rights and Suffrage, A PROPOSITION TO REPEAL SECTION ELEVEN OF ARTICLE ONE OF THE CONSTITUTION, RELATING TO EQUAL PROTECTION OF LAWS AND PROHIBITING DISCRIMINATION IN CIVIL RIGHTS . . . [and] TO AMEND THE CON-STITUTION, IN RELATION TO THE RIGHT TO TERMINATE A PREG-NANCY UNDER MEDICAL SUPERVISION, attached to letter from Jean Faust, President, NOW–New York, New York City, New York, to Andrew R. Tyler, Chairman, Committee on Rights and Suffrage, Constitutional Convention, Albany, New York, August 9, 1967, Collection of the NYS Constitutional Convention 1967, Box 4, Folder 33, New York State Archives, Albany, NY.

48 **The Democratic Party's** Sam Roberts, "Democratic Infighting, Old-Time Party Bosses, and Gridlock That Lasted Weeks, in 1965," *New York Times*, June 22, 2009, https://www.nytimes.com/2009/06/23/nyregion/23gridlock.html, accessed February 25, 2022.

48 **in the midst** Greenlee, "Percy Sutton's 1966 [*sic*] Abortion Rights Bill"; and Mark Uhlig, "Ohrenstein: A Career That Began with Reform," *New York Times*, September 17, 1987, https://www.nytimes.com/1987/09/17/nyregion/ohrenstein-a-career-that-began-with-reform.html, accessed May 26, 2021.

49 **New York's Constitution** Richard I. Nunez, "New York State Constitutional Reform—Past Political Battles in Constitutional Language," *William & Mary Law Review*, vol. 10, no. 2 (December 1968): 366–77, https://scholarship.law.wm.edu/wmlr/vol10/iss2/ 5, accessed May 3, 2021.

49 **The person who** Dorothy Sue Cobble, *The Other Women's Movement: Workplace Justice and Social Rights in Modern America* (Princeton, NJ: Princeton University Press, 2004), 44, 185.

49 **To boot, she** "Biographical/Historical Information," Ann Petry Papers, New York Public Library, http://archives.nypl.org/scm/24832, accessed June 18, 2021.

50 **However, once NOW** Stephanie Gilmore, *Groundswell: Grassroots Feminist Activism in Postwar America* (New York and London: Routledge Press, 2012), 29.

50 **the National Organization** Gilmore, *Groundswell*, generally.

51 **"Abortion reform is"** Betty Friedan, "Abortion: A Woman's Civil Right" (1969), in *"It Changed My Life": Writings on the Women's Movement* (Cambridge, MA: Harvard University Press, 1998; originally 1976), 157.

52 **Indeed, activists and** Patricia Hill Collins, *Black Feminist Thought: Knowledge, Consciousness, and the Politics of Empowerment* (New York and London: Routledge Press, 1990); and Denise Riley, *"Am I That Name?" Feminism and the Category of 'Women' in History* (Minneapolis: University of Minnesota Press, 2003; originally 1988).

52 **Abortion law reform** David Garrow, interview with Felicia Kornbluh, January 14, 2021, transcript in possession of the author.

53 **One Philadelphia-area** Carol Joffe, *Doctors of Conscience: The Struggle to Provide Abortion Before and After Roe v. Wade* (Boston: Beacon Press, 1995), 110–11.

53 **on a forbiddingly** Florynce Kennedy, *Color Me Flo: My Hard Life and Good Times* (Englewood Cliffs, NJ: Prentice-Hall, 1976), 62.

53 **Nationally, nearly 114** "Minutes of Meeting of NOW Members from New York, New Jersey and Connecticut, Monday, February 6, 1967 at 5 East 75th St.," Friedan, Identifier 131-1631.

53 **pioneering women's historian** Gerda Lerner, *Fireweed: A Political Autobiography* (Philadelphia: Temple University Press, 2003).

53 **Atkinson, an art** Breanne Fahs, "Ti-Grace Atkinson and the Legacy of Radical Feminism," *Feminist Studies*, vol. 37, no. 3 (Fall 2011): 568.

53 **Kennedy who was** Sherie Randolph, *Florynce "Flo" Kennedy: The Life of a Black Feminist Radical* (Chapel Hill: University of North Carolina Press, 2016), 99, 101, 111–12.

54 **"She felt this"** "Minutes, February 6, 1967."

54 **"not as part"** "Minutes, February 6, 1967."

54 **"went bonkers"** Kennedy, *Color Me Flo*, 62.

54 **Atkinson remembered, "[Kennedy]"** Fahs, "Ti-Grace Atkinson," 569–70.

54 **The overwhelmingly white** Randolph, *Florynce "Flo" Kennedy*, 113.

55 **They started discussing** Hendrik Hartog, *Man and Wife in America: A History* (Cambridge, MA: Harvard University Press, 2000), Kindle edition, location 1010.

55 **But several members** Randolph, *Florynce "Flo" Kennedy*, 84.

55 **"to recommend that"** "Minutes, February 6, 1967."

55 **"All the work"** Jean Faust, interview with [Jacqui Cabellos], Veteran Feminists of
America, published as "Jean Faust—First President of the First Chapter of NOW,
New York City NOW," n.d. [after 2009], https://www.veteranfeministsofamerica.
org/legacy/Jean_Faust_Bio.htm, accessed May 25, 2021.

56 **"I don't know"** Faust, with [Cabellos].

56 **Representatives to the** Benediction by Cardinal Spellman, *Proceedings of the Constitutional
Convention of the State of New York*, vol. 2, part 1, p. 3, digitized version of Albany, New
York, April 4–September 26, 1967, proceedings from the collections of the New
York State Library, https://nysl.ptfs.com/data/Library1/103918.pdf, accessed
May 25, 2021.

56 **The overwhelmingly male** Henrik Dulea, Ph.D., "We the People," in *Making a Modern
Constitution: The Prospects for Constitutional Reform in New York*, ed. Rose Mary Bailly and
Scott N. Fein (Albany: New York State Bar Association, Continuing Legal Education
Division, 2016), 39–40, https://nysba.org/NYSBA/Publications/Books/Con-
stitutionalConvention/Making%20a%20Modern%20Constitution%20(4106E).
pdf, accessed May 25, 2021; and *Proceedings of the Constitutional Convention*, vol. 4.

56 **Parochial-school funding** Andrew Hacker, "The 'Blaine Amendment'—Yes or
No?," *New York Times Magazine*, October 1, 1967: 234–35+.

56 **Dollie Lowther Robinson's** *Proceedings of the Constitutional Convention*, vol. 4.

57 **"right to terminate"** Lowther Robinson proposal, attached to letter from Jean Faust
to Andrew R. Tyler, August 9, 1967.

57 **Jean Faust wrote** Faust to Tyler, August 9, 1967.

57 **"mailings on NOW"** Faust with [Cabellos].

57 **"make abortion the"** Letter from Gloria Nelson (Mrs. Charles Nelson), Massapequa,
NY, to Honorable Henry L. Ughetta, Chairman, Judiciary Committee, Constitutional
Convention, Albany, NY, July 28, 1967, NYS-CC, Box 4, Folder 30.

57 **"women the respect"** Letter from (Mrs.) A. Weissenfels, Massapequa, NY, to Hon.
Andrew Tyler, Chairman, Committee on Bill of Rights and Suffrage, Constitutional
Convention, Albany, NY, June 22, 1967, ibid.

58 **Population control was** Betsy Hartmann, *Reproductive Rights and Wrongs: The Global
Politics of Population Control* (Chicago: Haymarket Books, 2016; originally 1987);
and Hartmann, interview with Felicia Kornbluh, October 3, 2019, transcript in
possession of the author.

59 **The first was** U.S. Centers for Disease Control and Prevention, "Rubella in the
U.S.," https://www.cdc.gov/rubella/about/in-the-us.html, and "Pregnancy and
Rubella," https://www.cdc.gov/rubella/pregnancy.html (both accessed February
27, 2022); and Leslie Reagan, *Dangerous Pregnancies: Mothers, Disabilities, and Abortion in
Modern America* (Berkeley: University of California Press, 2012).

59 **The second was** Katherine A. Donavan et al., "Thalidomide Promotes Degradation
of SALL4, a Transcription Factor Implicated in Duane Radial Ray Syndrome,"
eLife Sciences, 2018, https://elifesciences.org/articles/38430, accessed February
27, 2022.

59 **A woman named** Reagan, *When Abortion Was a Crime*, 203; and Karina Bland, "54 Years After
Abortion, No Regrets for 'Romper Room' Host, But Still Sadness," *azcentral*, April 15,

2016, https://www.azcentral.com/story/news/local/karinabland/2016/04/15/sherri-chessen-miss-sherri-romper-room-abortion-reproductive-rights-donald-trump/82957074/, accessed April 27, 2022.

59 **"take into consideration"** Letter from (Mrs.) Lillith Lehner, Carle Place, NY, to Hon. Raymond Rice, Manhasset, NY, June 17, 1967, NYS-CC, Box 4, Folder 30.

60 **"the fact that"** Letter from Sylvia Burgman, Bethpage, LI, to Honorable Paul Widlitz, Albany, n.d., ibid.

60 **"No person," it** State of New York, In Convention, Proposed Constitution of the State of New York, Article I, Section 3, a. and b., September 2, 1967, digitized version of materials held at the New York State Library, Albany, NY, https://nysl.ptfs.com/data/Library1/Library1/pdf/454143.pdf, accessed May 26, 2021 (emphasis mine.)

61 **This was language** Proposed Constitution, Article I, Section 1.

61 **"right of the"** Proposed Constitution, Article I, Section 4, b.

61 **By a two-to-one** Peter Galie and Christopher Bobst, "Constitutional Revision in the Empire State: A Brief History and Look Ahead," in Bailly and Fein, *Making a Modern Constitution*, 88.

61 **Legislators and advocates** Garrow, *Liberty and Sexuality*, 327–32.

61 **Proposals to liberalize** [Dr. Alice Rossi?], National Organization for Women, "The Right of a Woman to Determine Her Own Reproductive Process," Document II in materials prepared for NOW Membership Conference, Washington, D.C., November 18–19, 1967, with Rossi, "Sociological Argument in Support of Effect of Denial of Right to a Woman to Control Her Own Reproductive Life," Friedan, Identifier 127-1552.

62 **Advocates who followed** Garrow, *Liberty and Sexuality*, 332.

62 **But compared with** Garrow, *Liberty and Sexuality*, 332.

62 **"chapter push"** Faust, with [Cabellos].

62 **In 1964, she** Randolph, *Florence "Flo" Kennedy*, 84.

63 **"My theme was"** [Jacqui Cabellos], "Alice Rossi, Feminist Icon," Veteran Feminists of America, https://www.veteranfeministsofamerica.org/legacy/ALICE%20ROSSI.htm, accessed June 2, 2021.

63 **She found that** Garrow, *Liberty and Sexuality*, 302–3.

63 **"be replaced with"** [Dr. Alice Rossi?], "The Right of a Woman to Determine Her Own Reproductive Process."

64 **She participated in** Rossi, "Sociological Argument."

64 **"The right to"** Rossi, "Sociological Argument."

64 **"from the penal"** Rossi, "Sociological Argument."

64 **Atkinson issued a** "Minutes, February 6, 1967."

64 **"rests on the"** E.J. Farians, "A Statement on Abortion and Birth Control from the Catholic Viewpoint"; and Ti-Grace Atkinson, "Refutation," n.d. [marked by hand, "1967 Conf"], post-conference mailing, National Organization for Women, January 1968, NOW, Box 23, Folder 3.

65 **"the right of"** Betty Friedan, Report of the President, National Organization for Women (NOW), Second National Conference, Washington, D.C., November 18,

1967, typescript, Friedan, Identifier 127-1553. (The text is virtually identical to that published as "'The First Year': The President's Report to NOW, 1967," in "*It Changed My Life*," 123–31.)

65 **In 1972, for** Leandra Ruth Zarnow, *Battling Bella: The Protest Politics of Bella Abzug* (Cambridge, MA: Harvard University Press, 2019), 137.

65 **The Women's National** Women's National Abortion Action Coalition, "Petition for Abortion Rights Act of 1972," n.d. [1972], assorted Women's National Abortion Action Coalition papers, Firestone Library, Princeton University.

65 **They reintroduced the** Planned Parenthood, "In Historic Vote, House Passes Women's Health Protection Act, a Critical Step Toward Protecting Access to Abortion Across the Country," September 24, 2021, https://www.plannedparenthood.org/about-us/newsroom/press-releases/in-historic-vote-house-passes-womens-health-protection-act-a-critical-step-toward-protecting-access-to-abortion-across-the-country, accessed February 25, 2022.

66 **"all-conference discussion"** Schedule, 1967 National Conference of National Organization for Women, circulated as part of a mailing to members in advance of the meeting, NOW, Box 23, Folder 2.

66 **"NOW endorses the"** Minutes, National Conference of National Organization for Women, November 18 and 19, 1967, NOW, Box 23, Folder 2.

Three: Want an Abortion? Ask Your Minister—or Your Rabbi

68 **The journalist at** Lawrence Lader, *Abortion* (New York: Bobbs-Merrill, 1966).

68 **"The fairly well-off"** Lawrence Lader, interview with [Ellen Messer and Kathryn E. May], in Messer and May, *Back Rooms: An Oral History of the Illegal Abortion Era* (New York: Touchstone/Simon and Schuster, 1988), 201.

69 **The four men** New York State first criminalized advising a woman on how to procure an abortion in 1845. James C. Mohr, *Abortion in America: The Origins and Evolution of National Policy* (New York: Oxford University Press, 1978), 124.

69 **"It seemed to"** Arlene Carmen and Howard Moody, *Abortion Counseling and Social Change: From Illegal Act to Medical Practice* (Valley Forge, NY: Judson Press, 1973), 19.

69 **Working alongside other** Laura Kaplan, *The Story of Jane: The Legendary Underground Feminist Abortion Service* (Chicago: University of Chicago Press, 1995).

71 **Lader approached Reverend** Lader, *Abortion II: Making the Revolution* (Boston: Beacon Press, 1973), 24–26.

71 **Moreover, Lader understood** Arlene Carmen, interview with Ellen Chesler, FPOHP I, January 1976, 6.

72 **Early in the** Christine Stansell, *American Moderns: Bohemian New York and the Creation of a New Century* (Princeton, NJ: Princeton University Press, 2010; originally 2000).

72 **After World War II** Diane di Prima, *Memoirs of a Beatnik* (New York: Penguin, 1998; originally 1969).

72 **"carefully planned nuclear"** Howard Moody, "The Beatitude of the Beat Generation," February 16, 1958, in "Excerpts from Howard Moody's Book, a Voice in the

Village: A Journey of a Pastor and a People," http://classic.judson.org/avoicein-thevillage, accessed June 30, 2021.

72 **In 1963, a** Ed Koch was later a fairly conservative New York City mayor, who resisted calls for major police reform in response to violence against Black and Latino residents and failed to respond adequately to the AIDS crisis.

72 **dealt a blow** My father served as the reform Democratic district leader in our uptown neighborhood a few years later—although he didn't have to beat a leading machine candidate to earn the role.

72 **With the Village** R.W. Apple, Jr., "Koch Won't Run on Ryan's Ticket," *New York Times*, August 17, 1965: 22; and editors, "Ed Koch—American Politician," *Encyclopedia Britannica*, https://www.britannica.com/biography/Ed-Koch, accessed June 28, 2021.

73 **"heavily involved in"** Carmen, with Chesler, 3–4.

73 **He was one** Carmen, with Chesler, 6, 44; and Clarence Taylor, *Knocking at Our Own Door: Milton Galamison and the Struggle to Integrate New York City Schools* (New York: Columbia University Press, 1998).

73 **Other clergy who** Joshua Wolff, "Ministers of a Higher Law: The Story of the Clergy Consultation Service on Abortion" (senior thesis, Amherst College, 1988), 118, available on the Judson Memorial Church website, http://classic.judson.org/MinistersofaHigherLaw, accessed June 29, 2021; and Carmen and Moody, *Abortion Counseling and Social Change*, 21.

73 **Reverend Finley Schaef** Wolff, "Ministers of a Higher Law," 4–5, 7; and Adelle Banks, "News Profile—Finley Schaef: Memories of the Abortion Underground Before *Roe v. Wade*," Religion News Service, January 1, 1998, https://religionnews.com/1998/01/01/news-profile-finley-schaef-memories-of-the-abortion-underground-before-roe/, accessed June 29, 2021.

73 **Later in the** George Dugan, "Parishioners Conduct Service at Church in 'Village,'" *New York Times*, January 5, 1970: 42.

74 **Rabbi Israel Margolies** "Rabbi Israel Raphael Margolies Dies at 72," *New York Times*, February 1, 1988: B4.

74 **Five years before** Marian Faux, Roe v. Wade: *The Untold Story of the Landmark Supreme Court Decision That Made Abortion Legal* (New York: Macmillan, 1988), 48.

74 **"The truly civilized"** N.A., "Rabbi Attacks Abortion Laws," *New York Times*, November 18, 1962: 76; and Mary Ziegler, "The Disability Politics of Abortion Rights," *Utah Law Review*, vol. 3, no. 4 (2017), 594.

74 **A pollster found** Williams, *Defenders of the Unborn*, 42–43.

74 **Following the model** Reverend Dr. Martin Luther King, Jr., *Letter from Birmingham City Jail* (pamphlet, American Friends Service Committee [Quakers], May 1963), Firestone Library Stacks, Princeton University.

75 **"a threshold for"** Quoted in Wolff, "Ministers of a Higher Law," 120.

75 **"a faith-based"** N.A., "Overview," Judson Memorial Church, http://classic.judson.org/Historical-Overview, accessed July 1, 2021.

75 **"this church to"** ... **"was meant to do"** Carmen, with Chesler, 7, 40–41.

75 **By the time** Kristin Luker, *Abortion and the Politics of Motherhood* (Berkeley: University of California Press, 1984), 123.

75 **These denominations built** Daniel K. Williams, *Defenders of the Unborn: The Pro-Life Movement Before Roe v. Wade* (New York: Oxford University Press, 2016), 41.

76 **In May 1967** David Garrow, *Liberty and Sexuality: The Right to Privacy and the Making of Roe v. Wade* (Berkeley: University of California Press, 1998; originally 1994), 333.

76 **Reverend Moody and** Robert Wuthnow and John H. Evans, ed., *The Quiet Hand of God: Faith-Based Activism and the Public Role of Mainline Protestantism* (Berkeley: University of California Press, 2002).

76 **Few were deeply** Williams, *Defenders of the Unborn*, 57.

77 **"Abortion on request"** Dr. Robert F. Drinan, S.J., "The Right of the Foetus to Be Born," *Dublin Review*, Winter 1967–68: 371, DJG, Box 5.3, Folder 17.

77 **According to most** Exodus 21:22, in Robert Alter, *The Hebrew Bible: A Translation with Commentary* (New York: W.W. Norton, 2018), 425.

77 **"The woman is"** Rachel Biale, *Women and Jewish Law: The Essential Texts, Their History, and Their Relevance for Today* (New York: Schocken Books/Random House, 1995; originally 1984), 220. Thanks to Kim Scheppele for this citation.

77 **"strong preponderance of"** Responsa RRR 188–193, originally published in Central Conference of American Rabbis Yearbook, vol. 58 (1958), under the heading "Abortion," https://www.ccarnet.org/ccar-responsa/rrr-188-193/, accessed July 12, 2021.

78 **"permit abortions under"** Reform (UAHC) Resolution: 49th General Assembly, November 1967, Montreal, Quebec, under the heading "Abortion Reform," https://urj.org/what-we-believe/resolutions/abortion-reform, accessed July 12, 2021. The organization later changed its name to the Union for Reform Judaism.

78 **One of Willis's** Joyce Antler, *Jewish Radical Feminism: Voices from the Women's Liberation Movement* (New York: NYU Press, 2018), 76–77, 80–88, 90–98, 100–05; and Alix Kates Shulman, interview with Felicia Kornbluh, August 11, 2020, transcript in possession of the author. See also the memoir by Shulamith Firestone's sister, who also rejected her family's Orthodoxy but became a rabbi affiliated with the "Jewish Renewal" movement: Rabbi Tirzah Firestone, *With Roots in Heaven: One Woman's Passionate Journey Into the Heart of Her Faith* (New York: Dutton, 1998).

79 **She was active** Karen Stamm, interview with Felicia Kornbluh, October 25, 2019; Atina Grossmann, interview with Felicia Kornbluh, July 9, 2020; and Carol (Rosenberg) Marsh, interview with Felicia Kornbluh, August 6, 2020.

79 **The late Justice** Neil S. Siegel and Reva B. Siegel, " 'Struck' by Stereotype: Ruth Bader Ginsburg on Pregnancy Discrimination as Sex Discrimination," *Duke Law Journal*, vol. 59 (2010): 779–98.

79 **Ephraim London, a** Wolff, "Ministers of a Higher Law," 44; and Doris Dirks and Patricia Relf, *To Offer Compassion: A History of the Clergy Consultation Service on Abortion* (Madison: University of Wisconsin Press, 2017), Kindle edition, location 818.

79 **"tall and willowy"** Carmen, with Chesler, 9.

80 **"I never counseled"** Carmen, with Chesler, 9–10.

80   **In May 1967** Edward B. Fiske, "Clergymen Offer Abortion Advice," *New York Times*, May 22, 1967: 1, 36. (The *Times* story referred to the group as the "Clergymen's Consultation Service on Abortion.")

80   **Their founding statement** "Clergy Statement on Abortion Law Reform and Consultation Service on Abortion (1967)," from Howard Moody, *A Voice in the Village: A Journey of a Pastor and a People* (Xlibris, 2009), reprinted in Linda Greenhouse and Reva B. Siegel, *Before* Roe v. Wade: *Voices That Shaped the Abortion Debate Before the Supreme Court's Ruling* (New York: Kaplan, 2010), 29–31.

80   **"procedural covenant" that** Carmen and Moody, *Abortion Counseling and Social Change*, 25–27.

81   **"There was no"** Carmen, with Chesler, 34–35.

81   **It was a** Rickie Solinger, *The Abortionist: A Woman Against the Law* (Berkeley: University of California Press, 2019; originally 1994).

81   **Moody, the other** Carmen, with Chesler, 5.

81   **At the start** Clergy Consultation Service on Abortion, Message for Code-a-Phone Tape, n.d., FPOHP-1, Box 1, Folder 7.

82   **She insisted that** Carmen, with Chesler, 13.

82   **"we were of"** Carmen and Moody, *Abortion Counseling and Social Change*, 40.

82   **"Any gas station"** Carmen, with Chesler, 13–14.

82   **"Often," she recalled** Carmen, with Chesler, 14-16.

83   **Some were outside** Lader, *Abortion II*, 45-46; and Dirks and Relf, *To Offer Compassion*, Kindle edition, location 1141.

83   **When my New** Isabel M. Cordova, *Pushing in Silence: Modernizing Puerto Rico and the Medicalization of Childbirth* (Austin: University of Texas Press, 2017), 37, 113, 119.

83   **"Over the years"** Carmen, with Chesler, 14.

83   **Farther afield, the** Kate Gleeson, "Persuading Parliament: Abortion Law Reform in the UK," *Australasian Parliamentary Review*, vol. 22, no. 2 (Spring 2007): 23–42.

83   **Despite their professional** Lawrence Lader, "First Exclusive Survey of Non-Hospital Abortions," reprinted from *Look*, January 21, 1969, Lader, Box 9, Folder 10.

83   **Although some doctors** Carmen and Moody, *Abortion Counseling and Social Change*, 40–43.

84   **One of the** Warren Hern, M.D., interview with Felicia Kornbluh, December 9, 2019, transcript in possession of the author.

84   **"The image I"** Carole Joffe, *Doctors of Conscience: The Struggle to Provide Abortion Before and After* Roe v. Wade (Boston: Beacon Press, 1995), 99.

84   **A 1969 reform** Linda Long, "Abortion in Canada," *The Canadian Encyclopedia*, February 2006, revised 2020, https://www.thecanadianencyclopedia.ca/en/article/abortion, accessed July 15, 2021.

84   **He served eighteen** Joffe, *Doctors of Conscience*, 105; and *R v. Morgentaler* (*Dr. Henry Morgentaler, Dr. Leslie Frank, and Dr. Robert Scott v. Her Majesty the Queen and the Attorney General of Canada*), 1 S. C. R. 30, 1988 SCC 19556, https://scc-csc.lexum.com/scc-csc/scc-csc/en/item/288/index.do, accessed July 15, 2021.

84   **"a brusque and"** Garrow, *Liberty and Sexuality*, 318.

84   **"Women cry for"** Linda Greenhouse, "Dr. Milan Vuitch, 78, Fighter for Abortion Rights," *New York Times*, April 11, 1993: 30.

84 The clergy service Lader, *Abortion II*, 1.

84 Dr. Vuitch gained Lader, *Abortion II*, 15.

84 The U.S. Supreme *United States v. Vuitch* [402 U.S. 62] (1971).

85 His conviction was Garrow, *Liberty and Sexuality*, 509, 561.

85 Margaret Sanger Bureau Carmen, with Chesler, 27.

85 At first, abortions Carmen and Moody, *Abortion Counseling and Social Change*, 62–63; and "U.S. Inflation Calculator," 1967–2022, https://www.usinflationcalculator.com, accessed February 27, 2022.

85 "it wasn't easy" Carmen, with Chesler, 15–16.

86 Few Black clergymen Doris Dirks and Patricia Relf, *To Offer Compassion: A History of the Clergy Consultation Service on Abortion* (Madison: University of Wisconsin Press, 2017), Kindle edition, location 290.

86 "never" Black clergy Carmen, with Chesler, 45.

86 "It didn't take" Carmen, with Chesler, 20.

86 Data the Judson Carmen, with Chesler, Appendix 2.

87 "located Clergy Consultation" Byllye Y. Avery, interview by Loretta Ross, transcript of video recording, July 21–22, 2005, Voices of Feminism Oral History Project, 15.

87 Arlene Carmen estimated Carmen, with Chesler, 21.

87 "Ignorant of the" Carmen and Moody, *Abortion Counseling and Social Change*, 47.

88 Thanks to the Wolff, "Ministers of a Higher Law," 93–97.

88 "starting in about" Wolff, "Ministers of a Higher Law," 97–98; and Dirks and Relf, *To Offer Compassion*, locations 1212-38.

89 "would call the" Rev. Robert Hare, interview [with Ellen Messer and Kathryn E. May], in Messer and May, *Back Rooms: An Oral History of the Illegal Abortion Era* (New York: Touchstone/Simon and Schuster, 1988), 213 (editors' headnote), 214–15.

89 By the time Howard Moody, "Dear Colleague," *National Clergy Consultation Service on Abortion Newsletter*, vol. 1, no. 1 (February 1970): 1, FPOHP, Box 1, Folder 7.

89 By November 1970 Howard Moody, "Dear Colleague," *National Clergy Consultation Service on Abortion Newsletter*, vol. 1, no. 2 (November 1970): 1, ibid.

89 By July of N.A., Up-to-Date List of Public Clergy Services, *National Clergy Consultation Service on Abortion Newsletter*, vol. 2, no. 1 (July 1971): 4, ibid.

89 In May 1972 Up-to-Date List of Public Clergy Services, *National Clergy Consultation Service on Abortion Newsletter*, vol. 3, no. 1 (May 1972): 4, ibid.

90 "feel free to" Carmen and Moody, *Abortion Counseling and Social Change*, 36.

90 "they knew that" Carmen, with Chesler, 34–35.

90 Religious leaders were Dirks and Relf, *To Offer Compassion*, location 1901.

91 Rabbi Max Ticktin Dirks and Relf, *To Offer Compassion*, locations 2025–2135; and "Charge Rabbi with Abortion Conspiracy," *National Catholic Reporter*, vol. 6, no. 12 (January 12, 1970), Catholic News Archive, https://thecatholicnewsarchive.org/?a=d&d=ncr19700121-01.2.11&e=-------en-20--1--txt-txIN--------, accessed July 29, 2021.

91 "We hammed it" Rev. Robert Hare, interview [with Messer and May], in Messer and May, *Back Rooms*, 219, 223.

91 After months of Lader, *Abortion II*, 96.

92 **"prominent individuals, including"** Edith Evans Asbury, "Four Seized Here in Abortion Raid," *New York Times*, May 25, 1969: 34.

92 **Roberts called sixty** Lader, interview with [Messer and May], in Messer and May, *Back Rooms*, 203; and Dirks and Relf, *To Offer Compassion*, location 2240.

92 **On the advice** Carmen and Moody, *Abortion Counseling and Social Change*, 56–57.

93 **"right to the"** Letter from Rev. Jesse Lyons, Riverside Church, New York City, to Burton Roberts, Esquire, District Attorney, Bronx County, September 17, 1969, DJG, Box 5.4, Folder 2.

93 **The two different** Dirks and Relf, *To Offer Compassion*, location 2252.

Four: Repeal Gets a Hearing

95 **"Enclosed is an"** Mrs. David (Beatrice) Kornbluh, New York, NY, to Franz Leichter, New York, NY, February 24, 1968, DJG, Box 5.3, Folder 18.

95 **The law my** Ruth Cusack, interview with David Garrow, June 25, 1993, Miller Place, NY, cassette tape in DJG, transcript in possession of the author.

95 **It may have** David J. Garrow, communication with the author, March 5, 2022; and Leslie J. Reagan, communication with the author, March 6, 2022.

95 **As of September** Alan Guttmacher Institute, "An Overview of Abortion Laws," September 1, 2021, https://www.guttmacher.org/state-policy/explore/overview-abortion-laws#, accessed October 4, 2021.

96 **Feminist organizing for** Reva Siegel, "*Roe*'s Roots: The Women's Rights Claims That Engendered Roe," Yale Law School Legal Scholarship Repository—Faculty Scholarship Series, Paper 1128, January 2010, originally *Boston University Law Review* (2010), http://digitalcommons.law.yale.edu/fss papers.

97 **"middle-class, middle-age"** Cusack, with Garrow, Part I.

97 **"There is no"** Florynce Kennedy quoted in Grace Lichtenstein, "Abortion Laws Opposed at Rally," *New York Times*, March 29, 1970: 35.

97 **over a year** Florynce Kennedy, "Memorandum to the Officialdom of NOW: National and New York," submitting her resignation, November 18, 1968, Friedan, Identifier 125-1536b.

97 **A "chain of"** Lucinda Cisler, "Abortion Law Repeal (Sort Of): A Warning to Women," *Women's Liberation! Feminist Writings That Inspired a Revolution and Still Can*, ed. Alix Kates Shulman and Honor Moore (New York: Library of America, 2021; essay originally published 1970), 137.

98 **"All women are"** Cisler, "Abortion Law Repeal (Sort Of)."

98 **Men as a** Alice Echols, *Daring to Be Bad: Radical Feminism in America, 1967–1975* (Minneapolis: University of Minnesota Press, 1989), 3–6.

99 **"nobody is doing"** Cusack, with Garrow, Part I.

99 **"in a welfare"** Garret Hardin, "The Tragedy of the Commons," *Science—New Series*, vol. 162, no. 3859: 1246.

99 **In a book** Garrett Hardin, *Exploring New Ethics for Survival: The Voyage of the Spaceship Beagle* (New York: Viking Press, 1968), 180–81 (on abortion as a key method of birth control), 187 (against the portion of the Universal Declaration of Human

Rights that grants each family "choice and decision with regard to the size of the family"), and 189 ("The community, which guarantees the survival of children, must have the power to decide how many children shall be born").

99 **Thomas Malthus made** Donald Gunn MacRae, "Thomas Malthus," *Encyclopedia Britannica*, https://www.britannica.com/biography/Thomas-Malthus, accessed October 14, 2021.

99 **She contacted him** Cusack, with Garrow, Part I; and Cusack to Pat [Maginnis], March 7, 1968, DJG, Box 5.3, Folder 17. (The letter indicates that Cusack and Maginnis were both part of the same Unitarian Fellowship, so Cusack's memory of meeting Maginnis through Hardin, in her oral history interview with David Garrow, may have been mistaken.)

99 **When interviewed thirty** Cusack, with Garrow, Part I.

99 **founder of NARAL** "History," Inventory, Papers of the National Abortion Rights Action League, 1968–1976, Schlesinger Library, Radcliffe Institute, Harvard University.

99 **"white nationalist"** Southern Poverty Law Center, "Garrett Hardin," https://www.splcenter.org/fighting-hate/extremist-files/individual/garrett-hardin, accessed September 27, 2021.

100 **"the right of"** Ruth P. Cusack (Mrs. John H. Cusack), Lafayette, CA, to Assemblyman John T. Knox, Sacramento, CA, May 16, 1965, DJG, Box 5.3, Folder 11.

101 **"Criminal abortions will"** Ruth Cusack, Social Responsibility Committee of the Unitarian Fellowship of the Three Village, East Setauket, NY, to Fellow Unitarians, December 1967, with attached petition, DJG, Box 5.3, Folder 15.

101 **"was just sort"** Cusack, with Garrow, Part I.

101 **"Almost any personal"** Cusack to Honorable Albert H. Blumenthal, Member of Assembly, New York, NY, November 13, 1967, DJG, Box 5.3, Folder 15.

101 **"obvious benefits to"** Cusack to Perry Duryea, Member of Assembly, Montauk, NY, November 21, 1967, DJG, Box 5.3, Folder 15.

101 **She communicated with** Cusack to Honorable Anthony J. Travia, Speaker of the Assembly, Brooklyn, NY, January 22, 1968, DJG, Box 5.3, Folder 17; and Cusack to New York State Legislators, January 25, 1968, DJG, Box 5.3, Folder 17.

101 **"to review the"** *Report*, State of New York, Governor's Commission Appointed to Review New York State's Abortion Law, March 1968, NYS-GC, Box 1, Folder 2.

102 **Rockefeller appointed Dr.** Alan F. Guttmacher, M.D., "Therapeutic Abortion: The Doctor's Dilemma," *Journal of the Mount Sinai Hospital–New York*, vol. 21, no. 1 (May–June 1954): 111.

102 **Cyril Means, Jr.** Cyril Means, Jr., "The Law of New York Concerning Abortion and the Status of the Foetus," March 1968," NYS-GC, Box 1, Folder 1.

102 **a law professor** Robert M., Byrn, "The Future in America," *America*, December 9, 1967: 710–13 (this article appeared in a special issue on abortion of a leading Catholic magazine/journal); and Daniel K. Williams, *Defenders of the Unborn: The Pro-Life Movement Before* Roe v. Wade (New York: Oxford University Press, 2016), 93.

102 **and religious leaders** Report of the Governor's Commission; and Ari L. Goldman, "Louis Finkelstein, 96, Leader of Conservative Jews," *New York Times*, November 30, 1991: 9.

102 **The only women** New York City Hearing of the Governor's Commission, Transcript, NYS-GC, Box 1, Folder 3.

102 **"also known as"** For Mrs. Mark (Margaret) Hughes Fisher, For Mrs. Charles Hayden, aka, Phyllis McGinley, Transcript, NYS-GC, Box 1, Folder 3; and "Phyllis McGinley," Poetry Foundation, https://www.poetryfoundation.org/poets/phyllis-mcginley, accessed October 14, 2021.

102 **"those women who"** Testimony of Miss [*sic*] Betty Friedin [*sic*], before the Governor's Commission, NYS-GC, Box 1, Folder 6.

102 **"the inextricable relationship"** Ti-Grace Atkinson, "Resignation from NOW," October 18, 1968, *Amazon Odyssey: The First Collection of Writings by the Political Pioneer of the Women's Movement* (New York: Links Books, 1974), 1–3.

103 **"I think this"** Testimony of Miss T. Grace Atkinson, before the Governor's Commission, NYS-GC, Box 1, Folder 6.

103 **"Frankly," Cusack offered** Cusack to Pat [Maginnis], March 7, 1968, DJG, Box 5.3, Folder 17.

103 **Soon afterward, Cusack** Cusack, with Garrow, Part I.

104 **"since that is"** Ruth Cusack to Honorable Constance E. Cook, Member of the Assembly, Ithaca, NY, July 19, 1968, DJG, Box 5.3, Folder 18.

104 **"told everybody to"** Cusack, Memorandum for Lawrence Lader, December 19, 1971, DJG, Box 5.5, Folder 3.

104 **"old-fashioned liberal"** Constance Cook, interview with Ellen Chesler, FPOHP-1, January 1976, 17–19.

104 **Receiving none, Cusack** Cusack, with Garrow, Part I.

105 **"a majority is"** Assemblyman Albert Blumenthal, Chairman, Committee on Health, New York State Assembly, New York, NY, to Mrs. John H. Cusack, Miller Place, NY, February 19, 1968, DJG, Box 5.3, Folder 17.

105 **He did not** Cusack, with Garrow, Part I.

105 **A member of** Cusack, Memorandum for Lawrence Lader.

105 **At the same** Senator Franz Leichter (D-NYS, retired), interview with Felicia Kornbluh, July 14, 2017, transcript in possession of the author.

105 **"And I just"** Franz Leichter, with Felicia Kornbluh.

105 **He was a** Harriet Friedenreich, "Käthe Leichter," Jewish Women's Archive, https://jwa.org/encyclopedia/article/leichter-kaethe, accessed October 5, 2021; and *Käthe Leichter: A Woman like That*, directed by Helene Maimann (2016, Austria), film.

106 **She continued to** Sarah Helm, *Ravensbruck: Life and Death in Hitler's Concentration Camp for Women* (New York: Anchor Books, 2015), 81–87, 139–43, 151–52; and Käthe Leichter, "To My Brothers in the Concentration Camp," Voices of Ravensbruck, a project by Pat Binder, https://universes.art/en/voices-from-ravensbrueck/hope/leichter-an-meine-brueder/info, accessed October 5, 2021.

106 **The Austrian government** Gerda Lerner, *Why History Matters: Life and Thought* (New

York: Oxford University Press, 1997), 50–55 (essay on receiving the Käthe Leichter award from the Austrian government).

106   **"that we would"** Franz Leichter, with Felicia Kornbluh.

107   **Ruth Cusack wrote** Cusack to Franz L[e]ichter, New York, New York, October 11, 1968, DJG, Box 5.3, Folder 18.

107   **"because hospitals do"** Mrs. David (Beatrice) Kornbluh, New York City, NY, to Honorable Franz Leichter, November 24, 1968, DJG, Box 5.3, Folder 18.

107   **"would never have"** Cusack, with Garrow, Part I.

107   **"reiterated her desire"** Cusack, Memorandum for Lawrence Lader.

108   **Cook pre-filed the** New York(ers) for Abortion Law Repeal "Help Repeal Abortion Laws Now," [December 1968-January 1969], Abe Books, https://www.abebooks.com/Help-Repeal-Abortion-Laws-Now-New/30716053280/bd, accessed October 13, 2021.

108   **Carmen, Reverend Moody** Cusack to Arlene Carmen, New York, NY, August 31, 1968, DJG, Box 5.3, Folder 18.

109   **By calling themselves** Echols, *Daring to Be Bad*, 140.

109   **"struggle to break"** Shulamith Firestone, *The Dialectic of Sex* (London: Women's Press, 1988; originally 1970), 23.

109   **"*All men* have"** [Firestone and Ellen Willis], "Redstockings—Manifesto and Principles," *Women's Liberation!*, 110–11.

109   **The members of** Kennedy, "Memorandum to the Officialdom of NOW"; and Atkinson, "Resignation from NOW."

109   **Two of Cusack's** Cusack, Memorandum for Lawrence Lader.

110   **"truly expert in"** Robert Hall, M.D., New York, New York, to Jean Faust, Vice President, New York NOW , New York, New York, DJG, Box 5.3, Folder 18.

110   **The group included** Cusack, with Garrow, Part I.

110   **New Yorkers for** Emery, *New Yorkers for Abortion Law Repeal Newsletter*, February 3, 1969.

110   **"SUPPORT CONSTANCE COOK'S"** N.A. [Ellen Willis], Women's Liberation Movement Flyer, "WHO ARE THE EXPERTS?," n.d. [February 14, 1969], NYS-SCH, Box A555, Folder 3; and Nona Willis Aronowitz, fn #1, "Talk of the Town—Hearing," *The Essential Ellen Willis*, ed. Nona Willis Aronowitz (Minneapolis: University of Minnesota Press, 2014), Kindle edition, location 1145 (confirming that Ellen Willis authored the flyer).

111   **"They argue that"** Ellen Willis, "Hearing," *New Yorker*, February 22, 1969, https://www.newyorker.com/magazine/1969/02/22/hearing, accessed October 8, 2021.

111   **"About thirty women"** Willis, "Hearing."

112   **"We're tired of"** Willis, "Hearing."

112   **"why don't we"** Florynce Kennedy, quoted in Gloria Steinem, "City Politic," *New York Magazine*, vol. 2, no. 10 (March 10, 1969): 8.

112   **"I would bet"** Brian Barrett and Lewis Grossberger, "Women Invade Abortion Hearing," *Newsday*, February 14, 1969, NYS-SHC, Box A555, Folder 3.

112   **The first steps** Lawrence Lader, edited oral history transcript in *Back Rooms: An Oral History of the Illegal Abortion Era* (New York: Touchstone/Simon and Schuster, 1988), ed. Ellen Messer and Kathryn E. May, 203–4.

113 **Its individual sponsors** Program, First National Conference on Abortion Laws, "Modification or Repeal?," November 14–16, 1969, Drake Hotel, Chicago, IL, Friedan, Identifier 103-1182; and *Griswold v. Connecticut* [381 U.S. 479] (1965).

113 **Helping to lead** Program, First National Conference on Abortion Laws.

114 **"women move out"** Betty Friedan, "Abortion: A Woman's Civil Right," Keynote Speech, First National Conference for Repeal of Abortion Laws, Chicago, IL, February 14, 1969, Friedan, Identifier 103-1182.

114 **"no expert on"** Friedan, "Abortion: A Woman's Civil Right."

114 **Half the committee's** "History," Inventory, Papers of the National Abortion Rights Action League.

114 **"pivotal state"** Lader, *Abortion II*, 91–92.

115 **"Abortion: Tell It"** Susan Brownmiller, *In Our Time: A Memoir of Revolution* (New York: Dell, 1999), Kindle edition, location 1123.

115 **"And she said"** Alix Kates Shulman, interview with Felicia Kornbluh, transcript in possession of the author, August 11, 2020.

115 **"consciousness-raising about"** Shulman, with Felicia Kornbluh.

115 **"The Personal Is"** Carol Hanisch, "The Personal Is Political," *Women's Liberation!*, 82–85.

116 **"But that's the way"** Shulman, with Felicia Kornbluh.

116 **Activist and writer** Susan Brownmiller, interview with Felicia Kornbluh, August 10, 2020; and Alice Echols, *Daring to Be Bad*, 187.

116 **"I went to"** Brownmiller, "Redstocking Rap—Everywoman's Abortions: 'The Oppressor Is Man,'" *Village Voice*, March 27, 1969, no page, https://womenwhatisto-bedone.files.wordpress.com/2013/09/1968-03-27-village-voice-full.pdf, accessed October 12, 2021.

116 **"If you don't"** Nona Willis Aronowitz, "The First Time Women Shouted Their Abortions," *New York Times*, March 23, 2019, https://www.nytimes.com/2019/03/23/opinion/sunday/abortion-speakout-anniversary.html, accessed November 5, 2020.

117 **"I was just"** Gloria Steinem, interview with Evelyn White, transcript of video recording, September 30, 2007, Voices.

117 **"that if these"** Steinem, with White. (The article was "After Black Power, Women's Liberation," *New York Magazine*, April 4, 1969, https://nymag.com/news/politics/46802/, accessed October 13, 2021.)

117 **The New York** "Women Tell the Truth About Their Abortions," *Ms.* preview issue, Spring 1972, cover, https://msmagazine.com/about/, accessed October 13, 2021.

FIVE: INTO THE COURTS!

119 **"dignitary harm"** Reva B. Siegel, "*Roe*'s Roots: The Women's Rights Claims That Engendered *Roe*," *Boston University Law Review*, vol. 90 (2010): 1883.

120 **"sex-class"** Alice Echols, *Daring to Be Bad: Radical Feminism in America, 1967–1975* (Minneapolis: University of Minnesota Press, 1989), 6.

120 **Leading the charge** Headnote to Plaintiff's Brief, *Abramowicz v. Lefkowitz*, in *Before Roe v. Wade: Voices That Shaped the Abortion Debate Before the Supreme Court's Ruling*, ed. Linda Greenhouse and Reva Siegel (Creative Commons, 2012; originally 2010), 140–41.

120 **"boring and scared"** Florynce Kennedy, *Color Me Flo: My Hard Life and Good Times* (Englewood Cliffs, NJ: Prentice-Hall, 1976), 62.

121 **This large group** [Nancy Stearns], Complaint for Declaratory and Injunctive Relief, *Abramowicz v. Lefkowitz*, [October 1969], Kennedy, Box 10, Folder 12; Florynce Kennedy, Affidavit, *Abramowicz, et al., versus Lefkowitz, et al., United States District Court for the Southern District of New York*, October 22, 1969, ibid., with attached List of Additional Plaintiffs.

121 **At a time** Linda K. Kerber, *No Constitutional Right to be Ladies: Women and the Obligations of Citizenship* (New York: Hill and Wang, 1999).

121 **This is because** Stearns, with Kornbluh, Part I; and Schulder and Kennedy, *Abortion Rap*, 92.

122 **"The very phrase"** Linda Greenhouse, "Constitutional Question: Is There a Right to Abortion?," *New York Times Magazine*, January 25, 1970: 30–31, 88+.

122 **This was especially** *People v. Belous* [71 Cal. 2d 954] (1969).

123 **"wholly unexpected"** David Garrow, *Liberty and Sexuality: The Right to Privacy and the Making of Roe v. Wade* (Berkeley: University of California Press, 1998; originally 1994), 382.

123 **Gesell vacated the** *United States v. Vuitch* [305 F. Supp. 1032] (D.C. Circuit, 1969).

123 **"all others similarly"** Diane Schulder and Florynce Kennedy, *Abortion Rap* (New York: McGraw-Hill, 1971), xiii; *Abramowicz, et al., v. Lefkowitz, et al.*, Memorandum of Law in Support of Plaintiffs' Motion to Convene a Three-Judge Court and for a Preliminary and Permanent Injunction, U.S. District Court for the Southern District of New York, Kennedy, Box 10, Folder 10.

124 **"female citizens of"** "Complaint for Declaratory and Injunctive Relief," *Abramowicz, et al., v. Lefkowitz, et al.*, United States District Court, Southern District of New York, Kennedy, Box 10, Folder 12; and Nancy Stearns, interview with Felicia Kornbluh, Part I, October 30, 2020, transcript in possession of the author.

124 **The last defendant** Edith Evans Asbury, "Four Seized Here in Abortion Raid," *New York Times*, May 25, 1969: 34.

124 **"a very tacky"** Kennedy, *Color Me Flo*, 23–24.

124 **"They want an"** Kennedy, *Color Me Flo*, 39.

124 **Her worst suspicions** Kennedy, *Color Me Flo*, 47–52.

125 **"Jim Crow advertising"** Randolph, *Florynce "Flo" Kennedy*, 103.

125 **Kennedy got Northern** Randolph, *Florynce "Flo" Kennedy*, 140–43.

125 **Kennedy and Ti-Grace** Randolph, *Florynce "Flo" Kennedy*, 144–48.

125 **Stearns was still** Howard Ball, *Murder in Mississippi: United States v. Price and the Struggle for Civil Rights* (Lawrence: University Press of Kansas, 2004).

126 **"needed a skill"** Stearns, with Kornbluh, Part I.

126 **He urged Stearns** Nancy Stearns, interview with Felicia Kornbluh, Part II, November 11, 2021, transcript in possession of the author.

126 **She also stayed** Stearns, with Kornbluh, Part II.

126 **When she finished** Stearns, with Kornbluh, Part I.

126 **"a women's group"** Stearns, with Kornbluh, Part I.

126 **She started conceptualizing** The Health/PAC Digital Archive: Three Decades of Health and Social Justice, http://www.healthpacbulletin.org/credits-2/, accessed October 30, 2021.

127 **"What I did"** Stearns, with Kornbluh, Part I.

128 **"So we were"** Stearns, with Kornbluh, Part I.

128 **Stearns recruited help** Diane Schulder [Abrams], "Brains vs. Beauty: How the 1968 Miss America Pageant Led to the First 'Women and the Law' Course in America," New York University Law School, n.d. [2013], https://www.law.nyu.edu/sites/default/files/upload_documents/Brains%20v%20Beauty.pdf, accessed October 30, 2021; Schulder, "Does the Law Oppress Women?" *Sisterhood Is Powerful*, ed. Robin Morgan (New York: Vintage Press, 1970), 153–75; Board of Trustees, Maryland Institute College of Art—Ann M. Garfinkle, https://www.mica.edu/mica-dna/leadership/board-of-trustees/ann-m-garfinkle-esq/, accessed October 30, 2021; Nick Ravo, "C.H. Lefcourt, 47, Lawyer and Fighter for Women Is Dead," *New York Times*, August 25, 1991: 42; and Garfinkle, Lefcourt, and Schulder, *Women's Servitude Under Law*, pamphlet (Detroit, MI: Radical Education Project, 1971).

128 **Schulder introduced her** Stearns, with Kornbluh, Part II.

129 **"deep concern for"** *Abramowicz, et al., v. Lefkowitz, et al.,* "Memorandum of Law in Support of Plaintiffs' Motion to Convene a Three-Judge Court and for a Preliminary and Permanent Injunction," Kennedy, Box 10, Folder 10.

129 **"the New Left"** Fitzhugh Mullan, quoted in John Dittmer, *The Good Doctors: The Medical Committee for Human Rights and the Struggle for Social Justice in Health Care* (Jackson: University Press of Mississippi; originally Bloomsbury, 2009), 205.

129 **The first stop** Jennifer Nelson, *Women of Color and the Reproductive Rights Movement* (New York: NYU Press, 2003), 41.

130 **"invidious discrimination"** "Memorandum of Law," 1. (Schulder and Kennedy, *Abortion Rap*, xv, footnote, says that Stearns prepared the complaint, the injunction application, and the brief in the case.)

130 **"Every woman"** "Memorandum of Law," 6.

130 **"cruel and unusual punishment"** "Memorandum of Law," 6–7.

130 **"personal privacy"** "Memorandum of Law," 7–8.

130 **Probably all the** Garrow, *Liberty and Sexuality*, 381; and Randolph, *Florynce "Flo" Kennedy*, 168.

131 **"the luxury" of** Stearns, with Kornbluh, Part I.

131 **But** *Hall v. Lefkowitz* Garrow, *Liberty and Sexuality*, 379.

131 **Lucas's paper on** Roy Lucas, "Federal Constitutional Limitations on the Enforcement and Administration of State Abortion Statutes," *North Carolina Law Review*, vol. 46, no. 4 (June 1968): 730–78.

131 **Lucas's team, including** *Hall v. Lefkowitz* [305 F. Supp. 1030] (S.D.N.Y., 1969), Justia.com, https://law.justia.com/cases/federal/district-courts/FSupp/305/1030/2244909/, accessed October 31, 2021.

132 **"place a heavy"** Thomas J. Ford, Memorandum of Law in Support of Motion to Intervene, *Hall, et al., v. Lefkowitz, et al.,* n.d. (December 1969), Kennedy, Box 10, Folder 12; and Schulder and Kennedy, *Abortion Rap*, 94.

132 **"the unborn infant"** Charles E. Lapp, Jr., and Edward J. Walsh, Jr., Attorneys for Intervenor-Defendant, Memorandum of Law in Support of Motion by "Baby" Poe to Intervene, *Hall, et al., v. Lefkowitz, et al.,* n.d. [November–December 1969], Kennedy, Box 10, Folder 13.

132 **"its own life"** William H. Beckert, Affidavit, *John and Mary Doe, et al., v. Lefkowitz, et al.,* December 9, 1969, Kennedy, Box 10, Folder 13.

132 **"friends of the"** Schulder and Kennedy, *Abortion Rap,* 94. (They say that Atkinson heard the term "friends of the fetus," to refer to abortion opponents, at an international conference on abortion.)

132 **"really didn't want"** Stearns, with Kornbluh, Part I.

133 **They decided that** Schulder and Kennedy, *Abortion Rap,* 95.

133 **"people who wanted"** Schulder and Kennedy, *Abortion Rap,* 97.

134 **They would have** Schulder and Kennedy, *Abortion Rap,* 98–99.

134 **"And it was"** Stearns, with Kornbluh, Part I.

134 **"as a very"** Randolph, *Florynce "Flo" Kennedy,* 173.

134 **The judges found** Schulder and Kennedy, *Abortion Rap,* 102–3.

135 **"so it turned"** Stearns, with Kornbluh, Part I.

135 **"For months after"** Schulder and Kennedy, *Abortion Rap,* 23.

136 **"once this matter"** Schulder and Kennedy, *Abortion Rap,* 30.

136 **"come to grips"** [Nancy Stearns], Plaintiffs' Brief, *Abramowicz, et al., v. Louis Lefkowitz, et al.,* United States District Court for the Southern District of New York, in Schulder and Kennedy, *Abortion Rap,* 208

136 **"compelling interest"** [Stearns], Plaintiffs' Brief, 209.

136 **The U.S. Supreme** *Reed v. Reed* [404 U.S. 71] (1971).

137 **In a case** *Frontiero v. Richardson* [411 U.S. 677] (1973).

137 **"almost exclusively to"** "Memorandum of Law," 24.

137 **"Despite the enlightened"** *Hoyt v. Florida* [368 U.S. 62-63] (1961).

138 **"At first glance"** Plaintiffs' Brief, *Abramowicz v. Lefkowitz* (March 9, 1970), excerpt in Greenhouse and Siegel, *Before* Roe v. Wade, 144. (Greenhouse and Siegel list the authors of the brief as Stearns, Catherine Roraback, Kathryn Emmett, Marjorie Gelb, Barbara Milstein, and Marilyn Seichter.)

138 **"punishments, disabilities and"** Plaintiffs' Brief, *Before* Roe v. Wade, 144–45.

138 **"kind of helped"** Stearns, with Kornbluh, Part I.

138 **The book offered** Schulder and Kennedy, *Abortion Rap.*

139 **"Honey, if men"** Gloria Steinem, *Outrageous Acts and Everyday Rebellions* (New York: Holt, Rinehart, and Winston, 1983), 8.

139 **In several of** Siegel, "*Roe's* Roots," 1887; Nancy Stearns, "*Roe v. Wade:* Our Struggle Continues," *Berkeley Women's Law Journal* (1988): 4; and Stearns, email to the author, November 11, 2021.

139 **Stearns shared her** Stearns, email to the author.

139 **"truly extraordinary"** Stearns, with Kornbluh, Part I.

139 **"to teach these"** Stearns, with Kornbluh, Part II.

140 **"The decision to"** Judge Edmund Lumbard, quoted in Stearns, "*Roe v. Wade:* Our Struggle Continues," 5.

140 **"broad enough to"** *Roe v. Wade* [410 U.S. 153] (1973).

140 **This approach hearkened** James C. Mohr, *Abortion in America: The Origins and Evolution of National Policy* (New York: Oxford University Press, 1978), 3–5.

141 **This became one** Siegel, *"Roe's* Roots," 1894.

141 **"not to shrink"** [Nancy Stearns], "Amicus Curiae Brief in Support of Jane Roe—New Women Lawyers; Women's Health and Abortion Project, Inc.; and National Abortion Action Coalition," in Greenhouse and Siegel, *Before* Roe v. Wade, 329.

141 **Stearns again argued** [Stearns], "Amicus Curiae Brief," 333.

141 **She wrote of** [Stearns], "Amicus Curiae Brief," 335

142 **"must now learn"** [Stearns], "Amicus Curiae Brief," 337–38.

142 **In addition, as** Cynthia Greenlee, "How Abortion Storytelling Was Born," *Rewire News Group*, January 22, 2016, https://rewirenewsgroup.com/article/2016/01/22/abortion-storytelling-born/, accessed April 29, 2022; and *Whole Women's Health v. Hellerstedt* [579 U.S. _] (2016).

SIX: GAME CHANGER

144 **"Cook-Leichter approach"** Franz Leichter, interview with Felicia Kornbluh, July 14, 2017, transcript in possession of the author.

145 **"I realize, Mr."** Bill Kovach, "Abortion Reform Is Voted by the Assembly, 76 to 73; Final Approval Expected," *New York Times*, April 10, 1970: 1.

145 **This happened in** Ruth Cusack, interview with David Garrow, June 25, 1993, part I, DJG, transcript in possession of the author.

145 **In part because** John Kifner, "Abortion Reform Dies in Assembly," *New York Times*, April 4, 1968: 1.

146 **"If we are"** Martin Ginsberg, as quoted in Rosemary Nossiff, *Before* Roe: *Abortion Policy in the States* (Philadelphia: Temple University Press, 2001), 94–95.

146 **Ginsberg received a** Sydney H. Schanberg, "Assembly Blocks Abortion Reform in Sudden Switch," *New York Times*, April 18, 1969: 1.

146 **"this was a"** Constance Cook, interview with Ellen Chesler, FPOHP I, January 1976, 41–42.

146 **Some advocates of** Leslie Reagan, *Dangerous Pregnancies: Mothers, Disabilities, and Abortion in Modern America* (Berkeley: University of California Press, 2010).

147 **In 1969, neither** Anne Finger, *Past Due: A Story of Disability, Pregnancy and Birth* (Seattle: Seal Press, 1990), provides an excellent primer on these arguments the reform and repeal movements failed to address.

147 **"The abortion reform"** Ellen Willis, "Up from Radicalism: A Feminist Journal," *US Magazine*, 1969, in *The Essential Ellen Willis*, ed. Nona Willis Aronowitz (Minneapolis: University of Minnesota Press, 2014), Kindle edition, location 578.

147 **And even they** Ruth Cusack, Memorandum for Lawrence Lader, December 19, 1971, DJG, Box 5.5, Folder 3.

148 **"many more"** Statement by Assemblywoman Constance E. Cook and Assemblyman Franz S. Leichter, April 18, 1969, For Immediate Release, DJG, Box 5.4, Folder 1.

148 **In attendance were** Cusack, Memorandum for Lawrence Lader; Minutes, Planning Committee, National Association for Repeal of Abortion Laws [June 3, 1969], DJG, Box 5.4, Folder 1.

148 **"I would say"** Cusack, Memorandum for Lawrence Lader.

148 **Members of New** Planning Committee minutes, National Association for Repeal of Abortion Laws, June 3, 1969, New York City, DJG, Box 5.4, Folder 1.

148 **NARAL sponsored pro-repeal** Lawrence Lader, *Abortion II: Making the Revolution* (Boston: Beacon Press, 1973), 95.

148 **"combination of All"** Memo from Dolores Alexander, [Executive Secretary], NOW National Headquarters, To All NOW Officers, Board Members, Chapter Presidents and Convenors, Task Force Chairman [*sic*], n.d. [April 1969], on Freedom for Women Week, Friedan, Identifier 121-1473.

149 **"unconstitutional and a"** Memo from Dolores Alexander to NOW Officers.

149 **"You don't have"** Lader, *Abortion II*, 95–96.

149 **About a hundred** Lader, *Abortion II*, 82.

149 **Organizers for repeal** Leslie Reagan, *When Abortion Was a Crime: Women, Medicine, and Law in the United States, 1867–1973* (Berkeley: University of California Press, 1997), 10.

150 **In 1968, due** Cusack, with Garrow, Part I.

150 **"Following that action"** Reprint of editorial, "Standards for Changing Practice in Abortion," *American Journal of Public Health*, vol. 61, February 1971, 215–17, Blackmun, Box 152, Folder 5.

150 **Although the medical** Mary Steichen Calderone, ed., *Abortion in the United States: A Conference Sponsored by the Planned Parenthood Federation of America, Inc., at Arden House and the New York Academy of Medicine* (New York: Paul B. Hoeber, the Medical Book Department of Harper and Brothers, 1958); and Reagan, *When Abortion Was a Crime*, 219.

150 **"obviously" the "eventual goal"** Alan F. Guttmacher, M.D., President, [Planned Parenthood Federation of America], to Mrs. Charles Nelson, Massapequa, NY, December 23, 1968, DJG, Box 5.3, Folder 18.

150 **"medical practice and"** Guttmacher quoted in Garrow, *Liberty and Sexuality*, 368.

150 **"desirable that provisions"** Planned Parenthood Federation of America, Inc., and American Association of Planned Parenthood Physicians, Amicus Curiae Brief in Support of Jane Roe, *Before Roe v. Wade: Voices That Shaped the Abortion Debate Before the Supreme Court's Ruling*, ed. Linda Greenhouse and Reva Siegel (Creative Commons, 2012), 337–38.

151 **"demonstrating, leafleting, having"** *New Yorkers for Abortion Law Repeal Newsletter*, June 13, 1969, RPS, Carton 1, Folder 6.

151 **"eminent physicians in"** Bernard Nathanson, M.D., Obstetrics and Gynecology, and Helen Edey, M.D., Psychiatry, to Dear Colleague, July 3, 1969, RPS, Carton 1, Folder 6; and Memorandum from James Clapp and Lucinda Cisler, to the NARAL Planning Committee, on the Medical Petition for Abortion-Law Repeal, July 14, 1969, ibid.

151 **"Most of us"** Quoted in Memorandum from Clapp and Cisler to NARAL Planning Committee.

151 **"Dr. Lonny Myers"** Lader, *Abortion II*, 82.

152 **New York organizers** Memorandum from Clapp and Cisler to NARAL Planning Committee; and James Clapp, "Abortion Facts," July 1969, RPS, Carton 1, Folder 6.

152 **Through the first** New Yorkers for Abortion Law Repeal, NARAL, press release, "Doctors Urge AMA to Back Repeal" (on stationery with NYALR at the top and NARAL at the bottom, with same logo); memorandum from Carol Greitzer and Ruth Smith to Arleen Emery et al., December 5, 1969 (on NARAL stationery with borrowed logo of New Yorkers for Abortion Law Repeal), RPS, Carton 1, Folder 6; and letter from James Clapp to NYALR Board Members, August 22, 1969, ibid.

152 **One priority was** Minutes, Meeting of the Board of Directors, New Yorkers for Abortion Law Repeal, August 13, 1969, RPS, Carton 1, Folder 6.

152 **Barbara Gelobter, a** "Barbara Elcantara Engaged to Ludwig Gelobter, Student," *New York Times*, August 18, 1959: 26.

152 **She reported back** Minutes, Board of NYALR, August 13, 1969.

152 **This strategy worked** *New Yorkers for Abortion Law Repeal Newsletter*, vol. 2, no. 1 (September 1969): 2 (with text of petition), no box or folder but designation "New York—New Yorkers for Abortion Law Repeal," NARAL State; and Nossiff, *Before Roe*, 95.

153 **"wanted people from"** Cusack, with Garrow, Part I. Cusack's purposes are confirmed by Nossiff, *Before Roe*, 104, fn. #74; Cusack, Memorandum for Lawrence Lader; and Ruth (Mrs. John) Cusack, Miller Place, NY, to Hon. Perry Duryea, Jr., Montauk, NY, January 5, 1970, DJG, Box 5.4, Folder 3.

153 **"That technique,"** Cook, with Chesler, 58.

153 **"out of the"** Cusack, with Garrow, Part I.

153 **Facing a pro-repeal** Annabelle Kerins, "OK Abortions: Ginsberg," *Newsday*, August 15, 1969, 7, DJG, Box 5.4, Folder 1, with accompanying photo.

153 **The Nassau County** Cusack, Memorandum for Lawrence Lader.

154 **When Cook and** Cook, Ellen Chesler, FPOHP I, 58.

154 **NARAL, too, stuck** Memo from Ivan Shapiro, New York City, to James Clapp et al., November 21, 1969, RPS, Box 1, Folder 6; and [Ruth Proskauer Smith], "Chronicle of the Activities of the Committee for the Cook-Leichter Bill (For Repeal of N.Y. State's Abortion Law)," n.d., ibid.

154 **"one of the"** Lucinda Cisler, "Abortion Law Repeal (Sort Of)," *Women's Liberation! Feminist Writings That Inspired a Revolution and Still Can*, ed. Alix Kates Shulman and Honor Moore (New York: New American Library, 2020), 140.

154 **"fake repeal"** Cisler, "Abortion Law Repeal (Sort Of)," 143.

154 **"this restriction would"** Cisler, "Abortion Law Repeal (Sort Of)," 141.

154 **Jane members not** Laura Kaplan, *The Story of Jane: The Legendary Underground Abortion Service* (Chicago: University of Chicago Press, 1995).

155 **Cisler immediately became** Cook, with Chesler, 45.

155 **"efficient, inexpensive care"** Cisler, "Abortion Law Repeal (Sort Of)," 141.

155 **The procedure was** Jessica Bruder, "The Abortion Underground: Inside the Covert Network of Activists Preparing for a Post-*Roe* Future," *The Atlantic*, vol. 22, no.

4 (May, 2022): 22-32; and Sadie Bograd, "The Feminist Self-Help Movement Helped Women Seek Reproductive Care," *Teen Vogue*, January 21, 2022, https://www.teenvogue.com/story/feminist-self-help-movement-abortion, accessed May 1, 2022.

155 **They also worked** Tracy A. Weitz et al., "Safety of Aspiration Abortion Performed by Nurse Practitioners, Certified Nurse Midwives, and Physician Assistants Under a California Legal Waiver," *American Journal of Public Health*, March 2013, https://ajph.aphapublications.org/doi/full/10.2105/AJPH.2012.301159, accessed November 11, 2021; and Carrie N. Baker, "Self-Managed Abortion Is Medically Very Safe. But Is It Legally Safe?," *Ms. Magazine*, April 1, 2020, https://msmagazine.com/2020/04/01/self-managed-abortion-is-medically-very-safe-but-is-it-legally-safe/, accessed November 10, 2021.

155 **The fracture in** [Smith], "Chronicle of the Activities"; Memo from Ivan Shapiro; Memorandum from Carol Greitzer and Ruth Smith, To Arleen Emery, Ruth Frey, Kit Kulak, Ivan Shapiro [and, written by hand, Betty Friedan, Lucy Komisar], Re: Letter to the Editor of *Village Voice*, December 5, 1969, RPS, Box 1, Folder 6 (on the stationery of the National Association for Repeal of Abortion Laws); and Pamphlet, Committee for the Cook-Leichter Bill, n.d., DJG, Box 5.4, Folder 3.

156 **"sensed an indisposition"** William E. Farrell, "Opponents of the Abortion Law Gain Strength in Legislature," *New York Times*, January 26, 1970: 19.

156 **"visits, calls, and letters"** [Ruth Proskauer Smith], "Chronicle of the Activities of the Committee for the Cook-Leichter Bill (For Repeal of N.Y. State's Abortion Law)," RPS, Carton 1, Folder 6.

156 **The Committee for** [Smith], "Chronicle of the Activities"; and Pamphlet, Committee for the Cook-Leichter Bill, RPS, Carton 1, Folder 6.

157 **Although the decision** Cook, with Chesler, 58–61.

157 **For his part** Leichter, with Kornbluh.

157 **"some kind of"** Cook, with Chesler, 61.

157 **In early March** Leichter, with Kornbluh; and Cook, with Chesler, 62–63.

158 **But as the** [Smith], "Chronicle of the Activities."

158 **Several members of** Ruth Cusack, interview with David Garrow, June 25, 1993, Part II, cassette in DJG, transcript in possession of the author; and Cook, with Chesler, 45.

158 **"But, it didn't"** Cook, with Chesler, 64.

158 **On March 18, 1970** Leichter, with Kornbluh.

158 **"And you know"** Bill Kovach, "Abortion Reform Approved, 31–26, by State Senate," *New York Times*, March 19, 1970: 1+; and Editorial Board, "At Last, Abortion Reform," *New York Times*, March 20, 1970: 46.

158 **"See," she said** Cook, with Chesler, 68.

159 **First, that an** [Smith], "Chronicle of the Activities"; and Nossiff, *Before* Roe, 98.

159 **"I believed in"** Cook, with Chesler, 73.

159 **"It was historic"** Cook, with Chesler, 73.

159 **"essentially says two"** Cisler, "Abortion Law Repeal (Sort Of)," 142. (The phrase "nonsense on sticks" comes from British philosopher Jeremy Bentham, in an influential

critique of rights discourse. See Jeremy Schofield, "Jeremy Bentham's 'Nonsense Upon Sticks,'" n.d., https://www.cambridge.org/core/services/aop-cambridge-core/content/view/S0953820800003745, accessed November 19, 2021.)

160 **"This is not"** Cisler, "Abortion Law Repeal (Sort Of)," 142–43.

160 **"It became obvious"** Schulder and Kennedy, *Abortion Rap*, 178.

160 **St. Patrick's was** Sarah Schulman, *Let the Record Show: A Political History of ACT UP New York, 1987–1993* (New York: Farrar, Straus and Giroux, 2021), 146–49.

160 **Bellevue and other** Alondra Nelson, *Body and Soul: The Black Panther Party and the Fight Against Medical Discrimination* (Minneapolis: University of Minnesota Press, 2011), 59–60 (for background) and see chapter 7.

161 **The third focus** Annelise Orleck, *Common Sense and a Little Fire: Women and Working-Class Politics in the United States, 1900–1965* (Chapel Hill: University of North Carolina Press, 1995), 53–120; Dan Meharg, "Maud Malone—New York City Librarian and Suffrage Powerhouse," July 5, 2019, National Park Service, https://www.nps.gov/articles/maud-malone-the-new-york-city-suffrage-parade-of-1908.htm, accessed November 13, 2021.

161 **"the first time"** Schulder and Kennedy, *Abortion Rap*, 179.

161 **Kennedy herself spoke** Grace Lichtenstein, "Abortion Laws Opposed at Rally," *New York Times*, March 29, 1970: 34.

161 **A sympathizer with** Schulder and Kennedy, *Abortion Rap*, 179.

161 **"Out of the"** Lichtenstein, "Abortion Laws"; and Schulder and Kennedy, *Abortion Rap*, 179.

161 **Symbolizing the way** Lichtenstein, "Abortion Laws"; Schulder and Kennedy, *Abortion Rap*, 179; and Randolph, *Florynce "Flo" Kennedy*, 177–78.

612 **"put the illegal"** Bill Kovach, "Abortion Reform Beaten in the Assembly by 3 Votes," *New York Times*, March 31, 1970: 1.

162 **The tally was** Kovach, "Abortion Reform Beaten"; and Nossiff, *Before Roe*, 99.

162 **"reached the limit"** Cook, with Chesler, 73–74.

162 **Three of Cook's** Nossiff, *Before Roe*, 99.

163 **"a very progressive"** Leichter, with Kornbluh.

163 **"a toss-up"** Kovach, "Assembly Revives Bill on Abortion for 2d Vote Today," *New York Times*, April 9, 1970: 1.

164 **"I never put"** Cook, with Chesler, 29–31.

164 **"his hands trembling"** Kovach, "Abortion Reform Is Voted by the Assembly."

165 **"really a great"** Leichter, with Kornbluh.

166 **"I don't think"** Kovach, "Final Approval of Abortion Bill Voted in Albany," *New York Times*, April 11, 1970: 1.

166 **"wives of the"** Kovach, "Rockefeller, Signing Abortion Bill, Credits Women's Groups," *New York Times*, April 12, 1970: 47.

SEVEN: PALANTE

167 **"a personal matter"** Helen Rodríguez-Trías, Jo Ellen Brainin-Rodríguez, and Laura Brainin-Rodríguez, "A Mother's Story," typescript chapter for *The Conversation Begins:*

Mothers and Daughters Talk About Living Feminism, ed. Christina Looper Baker and Christina Baker Kline , typescript, draft, December 13, 1995, HRT, Box 2, Folder 7.

167 **Lincoln was perhaps** Lincoln Hospital had competition for the title of worst New York City public hospital. Documentary filmmaker Frederick Wiseman chose Metropolitan Hospital in East Harlem to illustrate the deficiencies in the system. See his *Hospital* (WNET, 1970); and Barry Keith Grant, *Hospital*, National Film Registry, Library of Congress, https://www.loc.gov/static/programs/national-film-preservation-board/documents/hospital.pdf, accessed March 9, 2022.

168 **Lincoln Hospital began** Slavery ended officially in New York State in 1827.

169 **"life of accumulated"** *Sketches of the History, Character, and Dying Testimony of BENEFI-CIARIES of the Colored Home, in the City of New-York*, prepared by Mary W. Thompson (New-York: John Trow, Printer, 1851), 5–6, 21, Firestone Library, Princeton University, Stacks.

169 **It moved to** *Lincoln Home and Hospital, Annual Reports*, 1915–1922, American Theological Library, EBSCO Host, African American Serials, via the Firestone Library, Princeton University; and Fitzhugh Mullan, M.D., *White Coat, Clenched Fist: The Political Education of an American Physician* (New York: Macmillan, 1976), 217–18.

169 **It was part** Paul Starr, *The Social Transformation of American Medicine: The Rise of a Sovereign Profession and the Making of a Vast Industry* (New York: Basic Books, 1984), 158 (on the system as a whole).

169 **However, Puerto Rican** Johanna Fernández, *The Young Lords: A Radical History* (Chapel Hill: University of North Carolina Press, 2020), 53.

170 **Community members and** Micky Melendez, *We Took the Streets: Fighting for Latino Rights with the Young Lords* (New York: St. Martin's Press, 2003), 165; Mullan, *White Coat, Clenched Fist*, 212; and "Besieged Hospital Head—Antero Lacot," *New York Times*, August 28, 1970: 24.

170 **"the butcher shop"** Fernández, *Young Lords*, 275, 283; and Mullan, *White Coat, Clenched Fist*, 118, 126.

170 **A cartoon by** Fernández, *Young Lords*, 283; and Daniel Enck-Wanzer, ed., *The Young Lords: A Reader* (New York: NYU Press, 2010), 197.

171 **When my mother** Rickie Solinger, *The Abortionist: A Woman Against the Law* (Berkeley: University of California Press, 2019; originally 1995), argues persuasively that a large number of illegal abortions were performed by skilled practitioners who did not harm their patients.

171 **Lincoln Hospital was** Fernández, *Young Lords*, 276.

171 **In addition to** Mullan, *White Coat, Clenched Fist*, 95–98.

171 **But the embeddedness** Mullan, *White Coat, Clenched Fist*, 98.

171 **One was a** John Dittmer, *The Medical Committee for Human Rights and the Struggle for Social Justice in Health Care* (Jackson: University of Mississippi Press, 2017; originally 2009).

172 **Some of the** *Abramowicz, et al., v. Lefkowitz, et al.*, "Memorandum of Law in Support of Plaintiffs' Motion to Convene a Three-Judge Court and for a Preliminary and Permanent Injunction," Kennedy, Box 10, Folder 10.

172 **Initially, the most** Joshua Bloom and Waldo E. Martin, Jr., *Black Against Empire: The*

History and Politics of the Black Panther Party (Berkeley: University of California Press, 2013), 213–14.

172 **Alongside their military-style** Alondra Nelson, *Body and Soul: The Black Panther Party and the Fight Against Medical Discrimination* (Minneapolis: University of Minnesota Press, 2011); and Bloom and Martin, *Black Against Empire*, 354–55, 368 (on the party's "survival programs").

172 **"like an addiction"** Fernández, *Young Lords*, 32.

172 **Thrown into solitary** Fernández, *Young Lords*, 14–38.

173 **By late 1969** Fernández, *Young Lords*, 48.

173 **"Black red diaper"** Fernández, *Young Lords*, 49.

173 **They called themselves** Antonia Dardar, "Pedro Albizu Campos," *Encyclopedia Britannica*, https://www.britannica.com/biography/Pedro-Albizu-Campos, accessed March 9, 2022.

173 **The Sociedad Albizu** Fernández, *Young Lords*, 87–88.

173 **Juan González, who** Fernández, *Young Lords*, 49.

174 **"Marx, Lenin, Mao"** Melendez, *We Took the Streets*, 95–96.

174 **With Afeni Shakur** Fernández, *Young Lords*, 282–83.

175 **A resolution of** Mike Stivers, "Ocean Hill-Brownsville, Fifty Years Later," *Jacobin*, September 12, 2018, https://jacobinmag.com/2018/09/ocean-hill-brownsville-strikes-1968-united-federation-teachers, accessed November 29, 2021; and Jerald Podair, *The Strike That Changed New York: Blacks, Whites, and the Ocean Hill-Brownsville Crisis* (New Haven, CT: Yale University Press, 2003).

175 **The administration fired** Mullan, *White Coat, Raised Fist*, 139; Fernández, *Young Lords*, 279.

175 **On March 3** Fernández, *Young Lords*, 279–80; Nancy Hicks, "Lincoln Facility in Bronx Reopens," *New York Times*, March 18, 1969: 39.

176 **All the city's** Leon Fink and Brian Greenberg, *Upheaval in the Quiet Zone: A History of Hospital Workers' Union, Local 1199* (Urbana: University of Illinois Press, 1989); and Fernández, *Young Lords*, 276.

176 **"nurse's aides, orderlies"** Fernández, *Young Lords*, 278.

177 **"social and economic"** Silvers quoted in Fernández, *Young Lords*, 279.

177 **And they demanded** Gloria Cruz, Field Worker, Governeur Clinic, Heathy Ministry, Young Lords, "HRUM: Health Workers Organization," *Palante*, vol. 2, no. 3 (May 22, 1970), in Enck-Wanzer, *Young Lords Reader*, 191–92.

177 **Although distinct from** "Gloria González," Young Lords Party, with photographs by Michael Abramson, *Palante: Voices and Photographs of the Young Lords, 1969–1971* (Chicago: Haymarket Books, 2011; originally 1971), 63–64.

177 **By the middle** Fernández, *Young Lords*, 280–81, 283.

178 **"The two are"** New York State Chapter, Young Lords Organization, "Revolutionary Health Care Program for the People," *Young Lords Organization*, vol. I, no. 5 (January 1970), in Enck-Wanzer, *Young Lords Reader*, 188–90.

178 **"door-to-door preventive health"** New York State Chapter, Young Lords Organization, "Ten Point Health Program," *Young Lords Organization*, vol. I, no. 5 (January 1970), in Enck-Wanzer, *Young Lords Reader*, 188–89.

179   **They also let** Fernández, *Young Lords*, 147–49.

179   **"It comes from"** Carl Pastor, Minister of Health, Young Lords Party, "Socialist Medicine," *Palante*, vol. 2, no. 4 (June 5, 1970), in Enck-Wanzer, *Young Lords Reader*, 192.

179   **The action ended** Fernández, *Young Lords*, 273; "Juan Gonzáles," Young Lords Party, *Palante*, 54 (on Ramón Betances).

180   **"hospital to serve"** Cleo Silvers and Danny Argote, "Think Lincoln," *Palante*, vol. 2, no. 6 (July 3, 1970), in Enck-Wanzer, *Young Lords Reader*, 194–95.

180   **"only one doctor"** Carl Pastor, Ministry of Health, Young Lords Party—Bronx Branch, "Patient-Worker Table," *Palante*, vol. 2, no. 7: 3, 20.

180   **"a community-worker board"** Silvers and Argote, "Think Lincoln," 196.

181   **"Care at Jacobi"** Mullan, *White Coat, Clenched Fist*, 78.

181   **Then, he started** Mullan, *White Coat, Clenched Fist*, 81–90.

181   **"It was a poor-sister"** Mullan, *White Coat, Clenched Fist*, 97.

182   **"an authoritarian hand"** Mullan, *White Coat, Clenched Fist*, 100–101.

182   **"thought we were"** Carlos "Carlito" Rivera quoted in Emma Francis Snyder, "Takeover," produced by David Gerber, Luis Miranda, Jr., and Lynn Nottage, published as an op-doc of the *New York Times*, October 12, 2021, https://www.nytimes.com/2021/10/12/opinion/young-lords-nyc-activism-takeover.html, accessed December 8, 2021.

182   **"giant-ass rented U-Haul"** Rivera in Snyder, "Takeover."

183   **"Wake up! The revolution"** Marty Stein quoted in Snyder, "Takeover."

183   **"butcher shop that"** Gloria Cruz quoted in Alfonso A. Narvaez, "Young Lords Seize Lincoln Hospital Building," *New York Times*, July 15, 1970: 34.

183   **"immediate funds"** "7 Demands," in photograph "Rally Outside Lincoln Hospital, Bronx, New York," July 1970, Young Lords Party, *Palante*, 97.

183   **They turned the** Iris Morales quoted in Snyder, "Takeover."

183   **They opened a** Fernández, *Young Lords*, 290.

184   **"The press was"** Mullan, *White Coat, Clenched Fist*, 144.

184   **"We walked out"** Cleo Silvers quoted, and end of the occupation narrated by multiple participants, in Snyder, "Takeover."

185   **Mrs. Carmen Rodríguez** Martin Gansberg, "Abortion Death Reported by City," *New York Times*, July 21, 1970: 32.

185   **The restrictive state** Fernández, *Young Lords*, 293–94.

186   **He chose the** Jennifer Nelson, *Women of Color and the Reproductive Rights Movement* (New York: NYU Press, 2003), 227–28.

186   **"murder"** Gloria Cruz, Health Captain, Young Lords Party National Headquarters, "Murder at Lincoln," *Palante*, vol. 2, no. 8 (July 1970), in Enck-Wanzer, *Young Lords Reader*, 198.

186   **"genocide"** Cruz, "Murder at Lincoln." Compare with Young Lords Party Central Committee, "Young Lords Party Position Paper on Women," *Palante*, vol. 2, no. 12 (September 1970), in Enck-Wanzer, *Young Lords Reader*, 172–73; Denise Oliver, in Young Lords Party, *Palante*, 44.

186   **"Carmen died because"** Cruz, "Murder at Lincoln," 198.

187 "**got people very**" "Gloria González," Young Lords Party, *Palante*, 65; and "History of the Young Lords Party," *Palante*, 14 (on González as activist with the Health Revolutionary Unity Movement and former employee of Gouverneur Hospital).

187 "**The meeting**" Mullan, *White Coat, Clenched Fist*, 148.

187 "**fired by the**" Pablo "Yoruba" Guzmán quoted in Charlayne Hunter, "Community Dispute Cuts Service at City Hospital," *New York Times*, August 26, 1970: 1.

188 "**forced sterilization of**" Olguie Robles quoted in Fernández, *Young Lords*, 254–55.

188 "*machismo* **was never**" "Denise Oliver," Young Lords Party, *Palante*, 46.

188 **And men must** Oliver, *Palante*, 46; and "Richie Pérez," Young Lords Party, *Palante*, 48 (on his experience in the men's caucus).

188 **By September 1970** Health Ministry, Young Lords Party, "Lincoln Hospital Must Serve the People," *Palante*, vol. 2, no. 11 (September 11, 1970), in Enck-Wanzer, *Young Lords Reader*, 199–200.

189 "**On the other**" Central Committee, Young Lords Party, "Young Lords Party Position Paper on Women."

189 "**We have to**" Oliver, *Palante*, 45.

189 **Dr. Helen Rodríguez-Trías applied** Mullan, *White Coat, Clenched Fist*, 169.

189 **An expert in** "Biography: Helen Rodriguez-Trias," *Changing the Face of Medicine*, National Library of Medicine, U.S. National Institutes of Health, https://cfmedicine.nlm .nih.gov/physicians/biography_273.html, accessed March 9, 2022.

189 **By coincidence, that** Michael T. Kaufman, "Lincoln Hospital: Case Study of Dissension That Split Staff," *New York Times*, December 21, 1970: 1, 43.

189 **Einhorn was a** "Ousted Pediatrician—Arnold H. Einhorn," *New York Times*, November 18, 1970: 42.

190 **She then applied** Mullan, *White Coat, Clenched Fist*, 169–70.

190 "**an impertinence**" Mullan, *White Coat, Clenched Fist*, 166.

190 "**impossible to operate**" John Sibley, "Einhorn, 'Reinstated' at Lincoln, Indicates He May Not Go Back," *New York Times*, November 24, 1970: 32.

190 **Finally, in November** Mullan, *White Coat, Clenched Fist*, 170.

190 "**We called her**" Mullan, *White Coat, Clenched Fist*, 170.

190 **Regardless of the** Mark Winston Griffith and Max Freedman, "Third Strike," episode 3 (on racism and antisemitism in Ocean Hill–Brownsville), October 4, 2019, *School Colors*, podcast from Brooklyn Deep, a project of the Brooklyn Movement Center.

191 "**political**" Robert McFadden, "Einhorn Regains Post for 2 Weeks," *New York Times*, November 23, 1970: 1.

191 "**Pediatrics Chief Out**" John Sibley, "Pediatrics Chief Out at Lincoln Hospital; Puerto Rican Named," *New York Times*, November 17, 1970: 1, 37.

191 "**I would do**" "Ousted Pediatrician," *New York Times*.

191 "**simply because he**" ". . . and Lincoln Hospital," editorial, *New York Times*, November 19, 1970: 46.

191 **The New York** Mullan, *White Coat, Clenched Fist*, 172–73.

191 **However, after negotiating** McFadden, "Einhorn Regains Post for 2 Weeks"; and Sibley, "Einhorn 'Reinstated.'"

192　**"one of our"** J. Robert Moskin, "Puerto Rico: Island at a Crossroads," *Look*, March 24, 1964, 32–33, HRT, Box 1, Folder 4.

193　**"In another case"** Helen Rodríguez-Trías, M.D., F.A.A.P., "A Woman Doctor's Perspective on Women and the Health-Care System," *Two Lectures by Helen Rodríguez-Trías, M.D.*, Reid Lectureship, Barnard College, November 10 and 11, 1976 (Barnard College Women's Center, 1977), Stamm-Private, unnamed accordion folder, file titled "Helen Rodriguez-Trias."

193　**"As an intern"** Rodríguez-Trías, Reid Lectureship.

193　**"social inequities reflected"** Rodríguez-Trías, Reid Lectureship.

194　**"He would come"** Notes from author's interview with Jo Ellen Brianin-Rodríguez, August 19, 2019.

194　**"first dared to"** Rodríguez-Trías, Brainin-Rodríguez, and Brainin-Rodríguez, "A Mother's Story."

194　**"He jumped out"** Notes from interview with Jo Ellen Brainin-Rodríguez.

194　**"The man who"** Rodríguez-Trías, Brainin-Rodríguez, and Brainin-Rodríguez, "A Mother's Story."

194　**Rodríguez-Trías's ex-husband** Notes from interview with Jo Ellen Brainin-Rodríguez; and Rodríguez-Trías, Brainin-Rodríguez, and Brainin-Rodríguez, "A Mother's Story."

195　**"felt a surge"** Dr. Helen Rodríguez-Trías, draft foreword to *Our Bodies, Ourselves*, 25th anniversary edition, August 1995, HRT, Box 2, Folder 5.

195　**"Their contents were"** Rodríguez-Trías, draft foreword to *Our Bodies, Ourselves*.

195　**"paradoxical event"** Mullan, *White Coat, Clenched Fist*, 175.

195　**Mullan found it** Mullan, *White Coat, Clenched Fist*, 185.

195　**Rodríguez-Trías felt similarly** N.A., "Historical/Biographical Note," Guide to the Helen Rodríguez-Trías Papers, Archives of the Puerto Rican Diaspora, Centro de Estudios Puertoriquenos, Hunter College, City University of New York, https://centropr.hunter.cuny.edu/sites/default/files/faids/rodriguez_triasb.html, accessed December 11, 2021.

196　**The program continued** Mullan, *White Coat, Raised Fist*, 188.

196　**The city broke** Juan González quoted in Snyder, "Takeover."

196　**The new, seven-hundred-bed** "A Bronx Legacy," NYC Health and Hospitals/Lincoln, https://www.nychealthandhospitals.org/lincoln/about-lincoln-hospital/history/, accessed December 12, 2021; and Mullan, *White Coat, Raised Fist*, 212.

EIGHT: TO THE SUPREME COURT

197　**At 10:08 a.m.** Joshua Prager, "Sarah Weddington's Unexpected Path to *Roe*," *The Atlantic*, January 7, 2022, https://www.theatlantic.com/ideas/archive/2022/01/sarah-weddington-obituary-roe-v-wade/621160/, accessed February 2, 2022.

197　**Blackmun judged her** [Blackmun notes from oral argument], No. 70-18-ATX—*Roe v. Wade*, Argued: December 13, 1971, Blackmun, Box 152, Folder 2.

197　**Thirteen months after** The tally was so high because *Roe v. Wade* invalidated the most restrictive state laws, while its companion case, *Doe v. Bolton*, invalidated all the state "reform" laws inspired by the model legislation circulated by the American

Law Institute. In 1973 only four states—New York, Washington, Hawaii, and Alaska—had revised their laws beyond the point of "reform."

197 **recognized, incompletely but remarkably** *Roe v. Wade* [410 U.S. 154].

197 **The historic rulings** *Doe v. Bolton* [410 U.S. 179] (1973).

198 **Decriminalization in 1970** Susan Edmiston, "A Report on the Abortion Capital of the Country," *New York Times Magazine*, April 11, 1971: 83+.

198 **"the single most"** David J. Garrow, "How *Roe v. Wade* Was Written," *Washington and Lee Law Review*, vol. 71, no. 2 (Spring, 2014): 900.

198 **"that a definitive"** Robert A. Trotter, "Abortion Laws Still in Ferment—States Are Rewriting and Liberalizing Antiquated Abortion Laws, but They Will Be Subject to Attack Until the Supreme Court Rules on Their Constitutionality," *Science News*, January 29, 1972, 75, in Blackmun, Box 152, Folder 3 (marked "the attention of: Justice Blackmun").

199 **The "chaos" and** Lawrence Lader, *Abortion II: Making the Revolution* (Boston: Beacon Press, 1973), 149.

199 **But there was** Arlene Carmen and Howard Moody, *Abortion Counseling and Social Change: From Illegal Act to Medical Practice* (Valley Forge, PA: Judson Press, 1973), 86.

199 **Second was the** Linda Greenhouse, "After July 1, an Abortion Should Be as Easy to Have as a Tonsillectomy, but . . . ," *New York Times*, June 28, 1970: 176.

200 **"fraught with tremendous"** Greenhouse, "After July 1."

200 **A doctor who** Greenhouse, "After July 1."

200 **The Supreme Court** *Whole Women's Health v. Hellerstedt* [579 U.S. 582] (2016); and *June Medical Services v. Russo* [591 U.S. ___] (2020).

201 **For people in** Lael Scott, "Legal Abortions, Ready or Not," *New York Magazine*, May 25, 1970, DJG, Box 5.4, Folder 5.

201 **"A Radical Plan" . . . "Raped by the Medical"** Lader, *Abortion II*, 150–52.

202 **"a woman who"** Carmen and Moody, *Abortion Counseling*, 87.

202 **Chicago's Jane service** Leslie J. Reagan, *When Abortion Was a Crime: Women, Medicine, and Law in the United States, 1867–1973* (Berkeley: University of California Press, 1997), 225.

202 **Practically minded people** Carmen and Moody, *Abortion Counseling*, 67.

203 **"There was no"** Arlene Carmen, interview with Ellen Chesler, FPOHP I, January 1976, 59.

203 **The clinic affiliated** Lader, *Abortion II*, 156.

203 **When the law** Edmiston, "Abortion Capital of the Country."

203 **"it seemed too"** Carmen and Moody, *Abortion Counseling*, 74.

203 **And so Barbara** Edmiston, "Abortion Capital of the Country."

203 **They were ready** Carmen and Moody, *Abortion Counseling*, 75.

203 **"celebrities"** Carmen, with Chesler, 67.

204 **It had a lower** Lader, *Abortion II*, 156.

204 **The patient's body** Edmiston, "Abortion Capital of the Country."

204 **"abortion was not"** Carmen, with Chesler, 63.

204 **Since Women's Services** Carmen and Moody, *Abortion Counseling*, 78–79.

205 **He had never** Carmen, with Chesler, 63.

205   **The city health** Edmiston, "Abortion Capital of the Country."

205   **The *New York Times*** Edmiston, "Abortion Capital of the Country."

205   **Dr. Bernard Nathanson** Lader, *Abortion II*, 156.

205   **The event was** The Nineteenth Amendment did not guarantee all women the vote, since Puerto Ricans and other colonized people were not eligible for the franchise in 1920, and neither were most Black women living under conditions of Jim Crow in the South or many Indigenous Americans.

205   **After a sideswipe** For all her strengths, Friedan was homophobic—literally, in that she was afraid "out" lesbians in the women's movement would ruin its reputation and make progress on its other priorities impossible. She also detested the stance of self-described "radical" feminists who insisted on naming men and masculine power as enemies that had to be confronted and overcome, and argued instead that feminism would liberate men as much as it would liberate women.

205   **"converge the visible"** Betty Friedan, "Call to Women's Strike for Equality, August 26, 1970," n.d. [Spring, 1970], Friedan, Identifier 128-1584.

206   **Although relatively few** Linda Charlton, "Women March down Fifth in Equality Drive," *New York Times*, August 27, 1970: 1.

206   **about fifty thousand** August 26th Women's Strike Coalition, flyer for a meeting after the strike, n.d. [September–October 1970], Friedan, Identifier 103–1187.

206   **"FREE 24-hour child"** N.A., "FREE 24-HOUR CHILD CARE CENTERS— COMMUNITY CONTROLLED," n.d. [August 1970], Friedan, Identifier 128-1584.

206   **"forced sterilization"** August 26th Women's Strike Coalition, flyer for a meeting after the strike.

206   **"comedienne"** Memorandum From: The Women's Strike Committee, To: All Women, August 24, 1970, Friedan, Identifier 103-1187. (These names are all on the group's letterhead.)

207   **"Community Controlled [Health Care]"** N.A., "Abortion: Myth and Reality," n.d. [July–August 1970], Friedan, Identifier 103-Folder 1187.

207   **"with counseling and"** Carmen and Moody, *Abortion Counseling*, 86.

207   **"we had emerged"** Lader, *Abortion II*, 157.

207   **A report in** Edmiston, "Abortion Capital of the Country."

208   **In the six** David Harris, M.D., M.P.H., et al., "Legal Abortion 1970–1971—the New York City Experience," *American Journal of Public Health*, vol. 63, no. 5 (May 1973): 409–18.

208   **Soon, they even** Joseph I. Rovinsky, "Abortion in New York City: Preliminary Experience with a Permissive Abortion Statute," *Obstetrics and Gynecology*, vol. 38, no. 3 (September 1971): 335–36.

208   **"abrupt improvement"** Alan Guttmacher, M.D., "The Genesis of Liberalized Abortion in New York: A Personal Insight," *Case Western Reserve Law Review*, vol. 23, no. 4 (1972): 768.

208   **Women's Services, the** Edmiston, "Abortion Capital of the Country."

209   **At a time** "New York—Two Years Later," *Clergy Consultation Service on Abortion Newsletter*, vol. 3, no. 1, FPOHP 2, Box 1, Folder 7.

209 **Of city residents** "Gordon Chase Cites Success of First Year of New York's New Abortion Law in Twelve Month Report on 165,000 Abortions," press release, Health Services Administration, New York City, RPS, Box 1, Folder 33.

209 **By the following** Johanna Schoen, *Abortion After* Roe (Chapel Hill: University of North Carolina Press, 2015), 35.

209 **"One could assume"** N.A., "New York—Two Years Later."

210 **The model state** New Yorkers for Abortion Law Repeal, "Model Law," October 1970, RPS, Box 1, Folder 33.

210 **The leading sponsors** N.A., "Questions & Answers . . . on repeal of contraception & abortion laws . . . ," New Yorkers for Abortion Law Repeal, n.d., RPS, Box 1, Folder 33.

210 **But the initiative** Lucinda Cisler, "The 1971 Repeal Campaign in New York," October 1971, RPS, Box 1, Folder 33.

211 **"roll up our"** Daniel K. Williams, *Defenders of the Unborn: The Pro-Life Movement Before* Roe v. Wade (New York: Oxford University Press, 2016), 129.

211 **In the 1970** Williams, *Defenders of the Unborn*, 175.

211 **Abortion opponents also** Stacie Taranto, *Kitchen Table Politics: Conservative Women and Family Values in New York* (Philadelphia: University of Pennsylvania Press, 2017), 80–81.

211 **On the day** Robert D. McFadden, "Tenacious Senator-Elect," *New York Times*, November 5, 1970: 31.

211 **He now favored** Ruth Proskauer Smith, President, Abortion Rights Association of New York, New York City, NY, to Governor Nelson Rockefeller, Albany, NY, November 20, 1970, RPS, Box 1, Folder 33.

211 **These covered every** Cisler, "1971 Repeal Campaign in New York."

212 **"an increasingly potent"** Lader, *Abortion II*, 159.

212 **The majority produced** Cisler, "1971 Repeal Campaign in New York."

212 **Governor Rockefeller, who** Constance Cook, interview with Ellen Chesler, January 1976, FPOHP 1, 74.

212 **was reported to** Frank Lynn, "Governor Is Firm on Abortion Law," *New York Times*, April 1971: 54.

212 **But they got** Lader, *Abortion II*, 157–58.

213 **"behavioral choice"** Morris Kaplan, "Says State Rule Denied Equal Protection to Indigent Women," *New York Times*, August 25, 1971: 1.

213 **"affirmative challenge"** Nancy Stearns, interview with Felicia Kornbluh, Part I, October 30, 2019, transcript in possession of the author.

213 **Fordham University law** Headnote to "Plaintiff-Appellant's Brief, *Byrn v. New York City, Health & Hospitals Corporation*" (June 2, 1972), Linda Greenhouse and Reva Siegel, *Before* Roe v. Wade: *Voices That Shaped the Abortion Debate Before the Supreme Court's Ruling* (Creative Commons, 2012), 150.

213 **He asserted that** Judy Klemesrud, "He's the Guardian for the Fetuses About to Be Aborted," *New York Times*, December 17, 1971: 48.

213 **Stearns argued on** Stearns, with Kornbluh, Part II, November 11, 2021, transcript in possession of the author.

213 **"It's virtually the"** Stearns quoted in Greenhouse and Siegel, *Before* Roe v. Wade, 150–51.

214 **Less than two** N.A., "Queens Man Loses Bid to Ban Abortions in City Temporarily," *New York Times*, January 12, 1973: 30.

214 **Backing anti-abortion legislation** Headnote, "Letter from President Richard Nixon to Terence Cardinal Cooke (May 16, 1972)," Greenhouse and Siegel, *Before* Roe v. Wade, 157.

214 **By spring 1972** Williams, *Defenders of the Unborn*, 144.

214 **The movement was** Williams, *Defenders of the Unborn*, 175.

214 **"church ladies"** Taranto, *Kitchen Table Politics*, 82.

214 **With backing from** Williams, *Defenders of the Unborn*, 176.

215 **Governor Rockefeller, with** Williams, *Defenders of the Unborn*, 175–76.

215 **The New York** Taranto, *Kitchen Table Politics*, 84.

215 **"Stop abortion!"** Headnote, "Letter from President Richard Nixon," Greenhouse and Siegel, *Before* Roe v. Wade, 157.

215 **It was a transparent** Robert D. McFadden, "President Supports Repeal of State Law on Abortion," *New York Times*, May 7, 1972: 1.

216 **"admiration, sympathy, and support"** "Letter from President Richard Nixon, to Terence Cardinal Cooke (May 16, 1972)," Greenhouse and Siegel, *Before* Roe v. Wade, 158.

216 **In other words** Williams, *Defenders of the Unborn*, 176.

216 **As it was** Jon Margolis, interview with Felicia Kornbluh, July 29, 2019, transcript in possession of the author.

216 **"frightened, unwed, confused"** "Governor Nelson A. Rockefeller's Veto Message (May 13, 1972)," Greenhouse and Siegel, *Before* Roe v. Wade, 159.

216 **By the eve** Rachel Benson Gold, "Lessons from Before *Roe*: Will Past Be Prologue?—State Abortion Laws Before *Roe*," *Guttmacher Policy Review*, vol. 6, no. 1 (March 1, 2003), https://www.guttmacher.org/gpr/2003/03/lessons-roe-will-past-be-prologue#box, accessed March 10, 2021.

217 **Alaska followed suit** David Garrow, *Liberty and Sexuality: The Right to Privacy and the Making of* Roe v. Wade (Berkeley: University of California Press, 1998; originally 1994), 413–14, 431–32.

217 **"abortion on request"** Garrow, *Liberty and Sexuality*, 411.

217 **The situation was** Dr. Milan Vuitch was effectively free to practice in Washington, D.C. However, he was still under indictment for abortions he performed at his Maryland clinic when the Supreme Court ruled in *Roe v. Wade*.

217 **And permitted individuals** Garrow, *Liberty and Sexuality*, 490.

217 **The last sizable** N.A., "Washington Early-Term Abortion, Referendum 20 (1970)," BallotPedia, https://ballotpedia.org/Washington_Early-term_Abortion,_Referendum_20_(1970), accessed February 12, 2022; and Barbara Winslow, *Revolutionary Feminists: The Women's Liberation Movement in Seattle* (Duke University Press, forthcoming).

218 **In 1971, there** Williams, *Defenders of the Unborn*, 143.

218 **In 1972, the** N.A., "Michigan Abortion Legalization Initiative, Proposal B (1972)," BallotPedia, https://ballotpedia.org/Michigan_Abortion_Legalization_Initiative,_Proposal_B_(1972), accessed February 12, 2022; and Winslow, *Revolutionary Feminists*.

218   **After a wealth** Garrow, "History Lesson for the Judge—What Clinton's Supreme Court Nominee Doesn't Know About *Roe,*" *Washington Post,* June 20, 1993: C3, in Blackmun, Box 152, Folder 2.

218   **"includes the abortion"** *Roe v. Wade* [413 U.S. 155].

218   **Without ruling on** *Roe v. Wade* [413 U.S. 157].

218   **As decriminalization advocates** [Justice Harry A. Blackmun], Memorandum to the Conference, Re: No. 70-18 *Roe v. Wade,* No. 70-040 *Doe v. Bolton,* May 31, 1972, Blackmun, Box 151, Folder 3.

219   *Roe* **and** *Doe* Linda Greenhouse, *Becoming Justice Blackmun: Harry Blackmun's Supreme Court Journey* (New York: Times Books/Henry Holt, 2005), Kindle edition, location 1441.

219   **"The Court does"** [Justice Harry Blackmun, Draft Statement to read from the bench], No. 70-18 *Roe v. Wade,* No. 70-040 *Doe v. Bolton,* [January 16, 1973], Blackmun, Box 151, Folder 3.

219   **"all the way"** Memorandum to the Conference, Re: Abortion Cases, from the Chambers of Harry A. Blackmun, January 16, 1973, Blackmun, Box 151, Folder 3.

219   **an unprecedented move** Garrow, *Liberty and Sexuality,* 587

220   **"to the extent"** *Roe v. Wade* [410 U.S. 164] (1973).

220   **"except when it"** *Roe v. Wade* [410 U.S. 164-65] (1973).

220   **His main source** [Blackmun clerks], "Complete Selected Bibliography, *Legal* Literature," [1972], handwritten, Blackmun, Box 152, Folder 6.

220   **which leading scholars** Melissa Murray and Kristin Luker, *Cases on Reproductive Rights and Justice* (St. Paul, MN: West Academic/Foundation Press, 2015), 661.

220   **The laws became** Cyril Means, Jr., "The Law of New York Concerning Abortion and the Status of the Foetus, 1664–1968: A Case of Cessation of Constitutionality," *New York Law Reform,* vol. 14, no. 3 (Fall 1968): 411–515.

221   **"phoenix of abortional"** Cyril Means, Jr., "The Phoenix of Abortional Freedom: Is a Penumbral or Ninth-Amendment Right About to Rise from the Nineteenth-Century Legislative Ashes of a Fourteenth-Century Common-Law Liberty?," *New York Law Forum,* vol. 17, no. 2 (1971): 331–410.

221   **"legal literature"** [Blackmun clerks], "Complete Selected Bibliography, *Legal* Literature."

221   **As he had** Letter from Justice Blackmun to Thomas E. Keys, c/o The Library, Mayo Clinic, Rochester, MN, December 17, 1971; and Blackmun to Keys, January 24, 1972, Blackmun, Box 152, Folder 2; Greenhouse, *Becoming Justice Blackmun,* location 333.

221   **As journalist Jeffrey** Jeffrey Toobin, "The People's Choice," *New Yorker,* January 28, 2013, https://www.newyorker.com/magazine/2013/01/28/the-peoples-choice-2, accessed February 13, 2022.

221   **One aspect of** Letter from Hadon Carryer, M.D., Allergic Diseases and Internal Medicine, Mayo Clinic, Rochester, MN, to Justice Harry Blackmun, Normandy House, Arlington, VA, September 14, 1972, Blackmun, Box 152, Folder 2.

221   **"For the first"** Richard D. Lyons, "A.M.A. Eases Abortion Rules," *New York Times,* June 26, 1970: 1.

222 **The rapid change** *Roe v. Wade* [410 U.S. 142-45] (1973).

222 **"to perform a"** Excerpts, Deliberations of the American Medical Association House of Delegates, 1970, in [Blackmun clerks], "AMA Stuff, '1969—Resolved that the present policy of the AMA on abortion be rescinded . . .,'" Blackmun, Box 152, Folder 5.

222 **"the logistic and"** Excerpts, Reference Committee Report, American Medical Association Meeting, 1970, "AMA Stuff," Blackmun Box 152, Folder 5, with [Blackmun's] handwritten check marks.

222 **The American Public** Ruth Cusack, interview with David Garrow, June 25, 1993, Part I, cassette recording DJG, transcript in possession of the author.

222 **These standards were** *Roe v. Wade* [410 U.S. 145-47] (1973).

222 **APHA members participated** "Standards for Changing Practice in Abortion," editorial, *American Journal of Public Health*, vol. 61 (February 1971): 215–17, in Blackmun, Box 152, Folder 5.

223 **"a number of"** American Bar Association, "Uniform Abortion Act" (1972), quoted at length in *Roe v. Wade* [410 U.S. 147] (1973), fn. #40.

223 **To be sure** *Griswold v. Connecticut* [381 U.S. 479] (1965); *United States v. Vuitch* [402 U.S. 62] (1971); and *Baird v. Eisenstadt* [405 U.S. 438] (1972).

223 **In preparing his** *People v. Belous* [71 Cal. 2d 954] (1969); *Byrn v. New York City Health and Hospitals Corporation* [31 N.Y. 2d 194] (1972); *Abele v. Markle* [342 F. Supp. 800] (Conn., 1972); and *Abele v. Markle* [351 F. Supp. 224] (Conn., 1972).

223 **Justice Blackmun concluded** *Roe v. Wade* [410 U.S. 155].

223 **In October 1971** Garrow, *Liberty and Sexuality*, 385, 513.

224 **"that the decision"** Jack Rosenthal, "Survey Finds Majority, in Shift, Now Favors Liberalized Laws," *New York Times*, August 25, 1972: 1, in Blackmun, Box 152, Folder 5. The underlining appears to have been Justice Blackmun's, but it may have been the work of a clerk who wanted him to notice the data in Rosenthal's article.

224 **Her first major** Garrow, *Liberty and Sexuality*, 588.

225 **Carol Marsh remembered** Marsh, with Kornbluh; and Stamm, with Kornbluh.

NINE: FIGHTING POPULATION CONTROL IN 1970S NEW YORK CITY

226 **"big, many-windowed room"** Maritza Arrastía, "My Nation Is the Struggle," in *Revolution Around the Corner: Voices from the Puerto Rican Socialist Party in the United States*, ed. José Velázquez, Carmen Rivera, and Andrés Torres (Philadelphia: Temple University Press, 2021), 147.

227 **"Helen was very"** Maritza Arrastía, interview with Felicia Kornbluh, Part I, April 29, 2020. Arrastía tells the same story in "My Nation Is the Struggle," 148–49.

227 **"one of those"** Arrastía, with Kornbluh, Part I.

227 **She helped write** Digna Sánchez, interview with Felicia Kornbluh, March 30, 2020.

227 **It was as** The Young Lords eventually did switch focus from Puerto Rican communities on the U.S. mainland to Puerto Rican independence from the United States.

For the ideology and history of the Puerto Rican Socialist Party, see generally, Velázquez, Rivera, and Torres, *Revolution Around the Corner.*

227   **Via its Women's** Carmen Vivian Rivera, interview with Felicia Kornbluh, May 1, 2020; Carmen Vivian Rivera, "Our Movement: One Woman's Story," in *The Puerto Rican Movement: Voices from the Diaspora,* ed. Andrés Torres and José E. Velázquez (Philadelphia: Temple University Press, 1998), 192–209.

227   **"all but card-carrying"** Sánchez, with Kornbluh.

228   **They were all** Thomas M. Shapiro, *Population Control Politics: Women, Sterilization, and Reproductive Choice* (Philadelphia: Temple University Press, 1985), 58.

228   **Women consented to** Iris López, "Sterilization in Puerto Rico: Coercion or Personal Choice?," in *Genetic Determinism and Children,* ed. Ethel Tobach and Betty Rosoff (New York: Gordian Press, 1980), 66–75.

228   **CESA's founders, like** Keisha N. Blain, *Until I Am Free: Fannie Lou Hamer's Enduring Message to America* (Boston: Beacon Press, 2021), xv, 34.

228   **Marsh could have** Carol Marsh, interview with Felicia Kornbluh, August 6, 2020, transcript in possession of the author.

228   **Stamm had to** Karen Stamm, interview with Felicia Kornbluh, October 25, 2019, transcript in possession of the author.

228   **"package deal"** Helen Rodríguez-Trías, M.D., F.A.A.P, "A Woman Doctor's Perspective on Women and the Health-Care System," *Two Lectures by Helen Rodriguez-Trias, M.D.,* Reid Lectureship, Barnard College, November 10 and 11, 1976 (Barnard College Women's Center, 1977), from Stamm-Private, unnamed accordion folder, file titled "Helen Rodriguez-Trias."

229   **"forced sterilization"** Laurie Johnston, "Nationwide Drive for Abortion Planned in 3-Day Session Here," *New York Times,* July 20, 1971: 30.

229   **"basically individual rich"** Marsh, with Kornbluh.

229   **"kept asking them"** Stamm, with Kornbluh.

229   **"there was something"** Marsh, with Kornbluh; Stamm, with Kornbluh; and Stamm, private communication to the author, December 21, 2021.

230   **In addition to** Marsh, with Kornbluh; Sue Davis, "A Doctor Who Fought Sterilization Abuse," *Workers World,* April 20, 2005, https://www.workers.org/2005/us/rakow-0428/, accessed December 22, 2021 (on Ray Rakow); Davis, interview with Felicia Kornbluh, August 12, 2020 (on her own participation); and Stearns, with Kornbluh.

230   **In 1974, at** Stamm, with Kornbluh; Barbara Caress, "Sterilization Guidelines," from *Health/PAC Bulletin* no. 65 (July-August 1975), Box 2965, folder titled "Sterilization NYC 1975 Regs."

230   **"was really the"** Marsh, with Kornbluh.

231   **"And so a lot of the work"** Arrastía, with Kornbluh, Part I.

231   **"a huge domestic"** Stamm, with Kornbluh.

231   **Rodríguez-Trías's particular genius** Karen Stamm, "Helen Rodriguez-Trias (1929–2001)," *Against the Current* no. 101 (November-December 2002), https://againstthecurrent.org/atc101/p722/, accessed December 26, 2021.

232 **But white, wealthy** Rebecca Kluchin, *Fit to Be Tied: Sterilization and Reproductive Rights in America, 1950–1980* (New Brunswick, NJ: Rutgers University Press, 2011), 22–23.

232 **"It was just"** Stamm, with Kornbluh.

232 **The clinic received** "Suit Says Girls Were Sterilized," *New York Times*, June 27, 1973: 44.

232 **She said later** "Suit Says Girls Were Sterilized," *New York Times*.

233 **In 1970, Congress** "Title X Turns 50," U.S. Department of Health and Human Services, Office of Population Affairs, https://opa.hhs.gov/grant-programs/title-x -service-grants/title-x-turns-50, accessed March 12, 2022.

233 **All twenty-five thousand** Bill Kovach, "Guidelines Found on Sterilization," *New York Times*, July 7, 1973: 53; and Warren Hern, interview with Felicia Kornbluh, December 19, 2019, transcript in possession of the author.

233 **But the guidelines** Press release—HEW News, U.S. Department of Health, Education, and Welfare, July 19, 1973, ACLU, Box 2931, unnumbered folder titled "Compulsory Sterilization" and "Relf v. Weinberger."

234 **He was the** *United States v. Vuitch* [305 F. Supp. 1032] (D.C. Circuit, 1969). As discussed previously, the U.S. Supreme Court overturned Gesell's judgment on the D.C. law but interpreted it generously so that Dr. Vuitch did not have to serve time in jail.

234 **Gesell ruled in** Bruce Lambert, "Judge Gerhard Gesell Dies at 82; Oversaw Big Cases," *New York Times*, February 21, 1993: 39; and Stanley Kutler, *Wars of Watergate: The Last Crisis of Richard Nixon* (New York: Penguin Random House, 2013, originally 1990), 383–414.

234 **"federally assisted family"** *Relf v. Weinberger*, 372 F. Supp. 1196 (D.D.C. 1974), 1202.

234 **"an indefinite number"** *Relf v. Weinberger*, 1200.

234 **"limiting irresponsible reproduction"** *Relf v. Weinberger*, 1205.

235 **"began to understand"** Rodríguez-Trías quoted in Joyce Wilcox, "The Face of Women's Health: Helen Rodriguez-Trias," *American Journal of Public Health*, vol. 92, no. 4 (April 2002): 566–69.

236 **"we set up"** Stamm, with Kornbluh.

236 **"movement support"** Maritza Arrastía, interview with Felicia Kornbluh, Part II, February 28, 2022, notes in possession of the author.

236 **other CESA members** Kluchin, *Fit to Be Tied*, 187; Nelson, *Women of Color and the Reproductive Rights Movement*, 142; Shapiro, *Population Control Politics*, 138; Stearns, with Kornbluh; and Stamm, with Kornbluh.

236 **Stamm credited Rodríguez-Trías** Stamm, with Kornbluh.

237 **Although CESA members** "CESA Statement of Purpose," 1975, Chicago Women's Liberation Union Herstory Project, https://www.cwluherstory.org/health/cesa -statement-of-purpose, accessed December 23, 2021.

237 **The report pointed** Rodríguez-Trías, Reid Lectureship.

237 **"These factors, combined"** [Advisory Committee on Sterilization, New York City Health and Hospitals Corporation], "Position Paper on Sterilization," n.d. [April– May 1975], ACLU, Box 2965, folder titled "Sterilization NYC 1975 Regs."

238   **An early version** Judith Mears, [American Civil Liberties Union], to Dr. Lowell Bellin, President, Health Services, NYC, NY, May 5, 1975, ACLU, Box 2965, folder titled "Sterilization NYC 1975 Regs" (expressing concerns about the regulations from the ACLU perspective).

238   **In the final** New York City Health and Hospitals Corporation, "Guidelines for Female Elective Sterilization," effective November 1, 1975, ACLU, Box 2965, folder titled "Sterilization NYC, 1975 Regulations."

238   **The committee suggested** [Advisory Committee on Sterilization], "Position Paper on Sterilization."

238   **"in at least"** [Advisory Committee on Sterilization], "Position Paper on Sterilization."

238   **"presumed involuntary"** [Advisory Committee on Sterilization], "Position Paper on Sterilization."

238   **"IF YOU DECIDE"** [Advisory Committee on Sterilization], "Position Paper on Sterilization."

239   **"should not be"** New York City Health and Hospitals Corporation, "Female Sterilization Consent, Tubal Procedures," n.d. [November 1975—final draft], ACLU, Box 2965, folder titled "Sterilization NYC, 1975 Regulations."

239   **It had patients** [Advisory Committee on Sterilization], "Position Paper on Sterilization."

239   **"carefully considered all"** New York City Health and Hospitals Corporation, "Female Sterilization Consent."

239   **"tone of distrust"** Copy of letter from Myron Gordon, M.D., Chief of Service, Metropolitan Hospital Center, HHC, NYC and New York Medical College, Department of Obstetrics and Gynecology, to Norman Herzig, M.D., Co-Chairperson Advisory Comm. On Sterilization, Director ObGyn Morrisania Hospital, Bronx, NY, July 29, 1975, ACLU, Box 2965, folder titled "Sterilization NYC, 1975 Regulations"; and Caress, "Sterilization Guidelines," ibid.

240   **In Puerto Rico** Shapiro, *Population Control Politics*, 54.

240   **A study of** Shapiro, *Population Control Politics*, 133.

240   **In hindsight, the** Stamm, with Kornbluh.

240   **"While we find"** *Gonzalez v. Carhart* [550 U.S. 124] (2007).

240   **After months of** Norman Herzig, M.D., FACOG, Bronx, NY, Director of Obstetrics and Gynecology, Montefiore-Morrisania Affiliation, to Ms. Esta Armstrong, Health and Hospitals Corporation, NYC, NY, July 31, 1975, ACLU, Box 2965, folder titled "Sterilization NYC, 1975 Regulations."

240   **The American College** *Belly of the Beast*, directed by Erika Cohn, Public Broadcasting Service (2020).

240   **They argued that** Jennifer Nelson, *Women of Color and the Reproductive Rights Movement* (New York: NYU Press, 2003), 142.

240   **"short answer" to** Stamm, with Kornbluh.

241   **"in sync with"** Stamm, "Helen Rodriguez-Trias (1929–2001)."

241   **The Association for Voluntary** "Historical Note," Inventory of the Papers of the Association for Voluntary Sterilization, Archives and Special Collections, University of Minnesota Libraries, https://archives.lib.umn.edu/repositories/11/resources/2395, accessed December 17, 2021.

242 **On the other** Kluchin, *Fit to Be Tied*, 114–47 (on the whole debate).

242 **"strong support for"** Letter from Judith Mears, Director, Reproductive Freedom Project, American Civil Liberties Union, New York, NY, and Ira Glasser, Executive Director, New York Civil Liberties Union, to Dr. Lowell Bellin, Commissioner, New York City Health Department, June 2, 1975 (on stationery of the Women's Rights Project, ACLU), ACLU, Box 2965, folder titled "Sterilization NYC, 1975 Regulations."

242 **Quiet dissent from** Letter from Kathleen Willert Peratis, Women's Rights Project, ACLU, to Ruth Bader Ginsburg, Columbia Law School, New York City, November 13, 1975, ACLU, Box 2965, folder titled "Sterilization NYC, 1975 Regulations"; letter from Barbara L. Kaiser to Ruth Bader Ginsburg, Esq., General Counsel, Women's Rights Project, American Civil Liberties Union, November 9, 1975, ibid.

243 **"So almost to"** Stamm, with Kornbluh.

243 **"We represent Bellevue"** Armstrong quoted in Shapiro, *Population Control Politics*, 140. (Shapiro spelled the name of the hospital "Belleview.")

243 **"were thinking what"** Stamm, with Kornbluh.

243 **"I said we're"** Stamm, with Kornbluh.

244 **"So we put"** Stamm, with Kornbluh.

244 **The guidelines were** Shapiro, *Population Control Politics*, 142; and Kluchin, *Fit to Be Tied*, 193–99.

244 **New York City's own** "New York City Health Dept. Opposes Measure on Sterilization Control," *New York Times*, March 25, 1977: 23.

244 **The result was** Nelson, *Women of Color and the Reproductive Rights Movement*, 143.

244 **"thousands of people"** N.A. [Karen Stamm], "Lessons of the Campaign for the Guidelines," n.d., Stamm-NYU, Box 2, Folder 4.

244 **By February 1977** N.A. [Karen Stamm?], CESA, "Organizations Endorsing Intro. 1105 [the Burden bill]," February 1, 1977, Stamm-Private, unnumbered box, unmarked accordion file, folder titled "NYC '77."

245 **By the time** Karen Stamm, "NWHN [National Women's Health Network]—Sterilization Report," 1981, Stamm-NYU, Box 4, Folder 17.

245 **CESA members accepted** Nina Martin, "U.S. Bishops Take Aim at Sterilization," ProPublica, December 30, 2014, https://www.propublica.org/article/u.s.-bishops -take-aim-at-sterilization, accessed December 26, 2021.

245 **While this didn't** Stamm, with Kornbluh; Shapiro, *Population Control Politics*, 147.

245 **"'Because I'm poor'"** Stamm, with Kornbluh.

246 **"multi-racial groups of"** Stamm, "NWHN—Sterilization Report."

246 **"advanced fertility management"** Paul Wagman, "To Sterilize Millions," *St. Louis Post-Dispatch*, April 22, 1977: 1, 10. Thanks to Thomas Shapiro for this clipping. For more general background on the project, I rely on Thomas Shapiro, interview with Felicia Kornbluh, June 4, 2020.

247 **Activists around Hartford** Shapiro, *Population Control Politics*, 147–48; Stamm, with Kornbluh.

247 **Barbara Smith of** "Barbara Smith," in *How We Get Free: Black Feminism and the Combahee River Collective*, ed. Keeanga-Yamahtta Taylor (Chicago: Haymarket Books, 2017), 50.

247 **She recalled Dr.** Smith, *How We Get Free*, 51.

247 **Chicanas organized the** Alexandra Minna Stern, *Eugenic Nation: Faults and Frontiers of Better Breeding in Modern America* (Berkeley: University of California Press, 2016), 227.

247 **Ten women sued** Maya Manian, "Coerced Sterilization of Mexican-American Women: The Story of *Madrigal v. Quilligan*," in *Reproductive Rights and Justice Stories*, ed. Melissa Murray, Katherine Shaw, and Reva B. Siegel (St. Paul, MN: West Academic, Foundation Press, 2019), 97–116; and Renee Tajima-Pena, *No Más Bebés*, Independent Lens Documentary, Public Broadcasting Service, premiered February 1, 2016.

248 **"bona fide belief"** "Madrigal v. Quilligan," No. CV 75-2057-JWC (C.D. Cal. 1978), in Melissa Murray and Kristin Luker *Cases on Reproductive Rights and Justice* (St. Paul, Minnesota: Foundation Press, 2015), 882–90.

248 **"womb transplant"** Brianna Theobald, *Reproduction on the Reservation: Pregnancy, Childbirth, and Colonialism in the Long Twentieth Century* (Chapel Hill: University of North Carolina Press, 2019), 156.

248 **Reviewing four of** Theobald, *Reproduction on the Reservation*, 158–59.

249 **The report did** This background and framing appears in Jane Lawrence, "The Indian Health Service and the Sterilization of Native American Women," *American Indian Quarterly*, vol. 24, no. 5 (Summer 2000): 400–19; Brint Dillingham, "Indian Women and IHS Sterilization Practices," *American Indian Journal*, vol. 3, no. 2 (February 1977): 27–28; Meg Devlin O'Sullivan, "Informing Red Power and Transforming the Second Wave: Native American Women and the Struggle Against Coerced Sterilization in the 1970s," *Women's History Review*, vol. 25, no. 6 (2016): 965–82; and Susan Burch, *Committed: Remembering Native Kinship in and Beyond Institutions* (Chapel Hill: University of North Carolina Press, 2021).

249 **"personal sovereignty"** Theobald, *Reproduction on the Reservation*, 161.

249 **"inner cohesion and"** [Stamm], "Lessons of the Campaign."

TEN: TOWARD REPRODUCTIVE FREEDOM

250 **With the Hyde** Marlene Gerber Fried, "Hyde Amendment History," from "The Hyde Amendment: 30 Years of Violating Women's Rights," Center for American Progress, October 6, 2006, https://www.americanprogress.org/article/the-hyde-amendment-30-years-of-violating-womens-rights/, accessed January 1, 2002.

251 **it "was going"** Atina Grossmann, interview with Felicia Kornbluh, July 9, 2020, transcript in possession of the author.

251 **"cool as a"** Karen Stamm, "Helen Rodriguez-Trias (1929–2001)," *Against the Current*, no. 101 (November–December 2002), https://againstthecurrent.org/atc101/p722/, accessed December 26, 2021.

252 **"Come down"** Meredith Tax, interview with Felicia Kornbluh, September 19, 2019, transcript in possession of the author.

252 **"Who are you?"** Tax, with Kornbluh.

253 **"completely freaked out"** Alix Kates Shulman, interview with Felicia Kornbluh, August 11, 2020, transcript in possession of the author.

253 **"And so I was"** Tax, with Kornbluh.

253 **Netsy Firestein, a** Netsy Firestein, interview with Felicia Kornbluh, September 4, 2020, transcript in possession of the author.

253 **"and a whole"** Tax, with Kornbluh.

254 **The word has** Firestein, with Kornbluh.

254 **Fighting the Hyde** Susan Davis, interview with Felicia Kornbluh, August 12, 2020, transcript in possession of the author.

254 **As they were** Stamm, with Kornbluh, October 25, 2019.

255 **"crappy little apartment"** Tax, with Kornbluh.

255 **At the national** Editors, "A Sad Compromise on Abortion," *New York Times*, December 10, 1977: 20.

255 **But a unified** Letter from Alfred F. Moran, Executive Vice President [Planned Parenthood New York City], to Ms. Anne Teicher, Legislative Committee, CARASA, NYC, NY, April 17, 1979, Stamm-Private, unnamed accordion folder, file called "Correspondence"; and "Regarding Positions on Abortion Funds," *New York Times*, October 10, 1982: Section 11, 31 (retrospectively noting no interruption in Medicaid funding for abortion during the early years of the Hyde Amendment).

255 **This was remarkable** Lesley Oelsner, "Strong Impact on Poor Reported from Cut in Medicaid Abortions," *New York Times*, December 26, 1978: 1.

256 **They wanted storefront** Sandra Sullaway, Report on Phone Conversation with Francine Stein, Administrator, Surgical Services, Loan and Technical Assistance Program, International Planned Parenthood Federation, early July 1977, Stamm-Private, unnumbered box, unnamed accordion folder, file titled "General."

256 **The bill they** New York State Assembly, Memorandum in Support of Legislation, n.d., Title of Bill: AN ACT to amend the public health law in relation to the regulation of sterilization procedures, ACLU, Box 2965, unnumbered files, Collection of State Files, Reproductive Freedom Project, folder titled "New York."

256 **"wide loopholes through"** Anne Teicher, CARASA, and Karen Stamm, CESA, to Dear Health Committee Member, Albany, New York, February 11, 1978, Stamm-Private, unnumbered box, unnamed accordion folder, file titled "General."

256 **As in New** CESA and CARASA, primarily Anne Teicher, Committee for Abortion Rights and Against Sterilization Abuse and Karen Stamm, Committee to End Sterilization Abuse, New York, to Dear [New York Senate] Health Committee Member, February 11, 1978, Stamm-Private, unnumbered box, unnamed accordion folder, file titled "Albany/Siegel Bill"; draft sterilization bill, introduced by Senator Mark Allen Siegel, with [Stamm's?] handwritten annotations, ibid.; and Dan Gaines, "Siegel's Sterilization Bill Is Dropped," *East Side Express*, March 16, 1978: 5, in ibid.

257 **"grossly abusive situation"** Karen Stamm, Committee to End Sterilization Abuse, and Anne Teicher, Committee for Abortion Rights and Against Sterilization Abuse, to Mr. Kalev Pehme, Editor, *East Side Express*, NYC, March 24, 1978, ACLU, Box 2965, unnumbered files, Collection of State Files, Reproductive Freedom Project, folder titled "New York."

257 **"they were ready"** Armstrong quoted in Shapiro, *Population Control Politics*, 139–40.

257 **"I would choose"** Judy Klemesrud, "Complacency on Abortion: A Warning to Women," *New York Times*, January 23, 1978: A18.

257 **A delegation from** Shapiro, *Population Control Politics*, 142.

258 **"a federal project"** Stamm, with Kornbluh.

258 **The only catch** Rebecca Kluchin, *Fit to be Tied: Sterilization and Reproductive Rights in America, 1950–1980* (New Brunswick, NJ: Rutgers University Press, 2011), 204.

258 **If Stamm and** Stamm, personal communication with the author, December 30, 2021, notes in possession of the author.

259 **The public had** Memorandum from Pam Horowitz, to John, Kathy, Ellen, and Janet [Benshoof], Reproductive Freedom Project, Re: HEW's Proposed Sterilization Regulations, December 8, 1977, ACLU, Box 2965, unnumbered file titled "HHS-Regulations cont."

259 **One of CARASA's** [Meredith Tax], "New York 1978: A CARASA Demonstration at NYU Law School Against a Speech by Joseph Califano," https://www.meredithtax.org/gallery.php, accessed January 9, 2022. The demonstration was also discussed in Tax, with Kornbluh and Maxine Wolfe, interview with Jim Hubbard, February 19, 2004, ACT UP.

260 **"patient advocacy with"** Testimony of Helen Rodríguez-Trías, M.D., January 17, 1978, On Proposed Rules Governing Federal Financial Participation in Sterilizations Funded the Department of Health, Education, and Welfare, HRT, Box 3, Folder 7.

260 **At the end** National Organization for Women, Transcript, 1978 Issues Conference, NOW, Box 24, Folder 39, Part 2.

260 **"indignant letters from"** Kluchin, *Fit to Be Tied*, 206.

261 **The National Medical** Kluchin, *Fit to Be Tied*, 203–7.

261 **"Your decision at"** Reprint, *Federal Register*, November 8, 1978, Part V, Department of Health, Education, and Welfare, Public Health Service, Health Care Financing Administration, Office of Human Development Services, Sterilizations and Abortions, Federal Financial Participation, ACLU, Box 2965, unnumbered folder titled "Sterilization Abuse—Regulations: HHS Regulations"; "Información para EL HOMBRE—Operación para la esterilización, Información para LA MUJER— Operación para la esterilización, ibid.

261 **The administration left** Copy of letter from Bernard Passer, Director, Division of Health Services Delivery, Department of Health, Education, and Welfare, Division II, New York, NY, to Project Directors, January 25, 1979, ACLU, Box 2965, unnumbered folder titled "Sterilization Abuse—Regulations: HHS Regulations."

261 **"*verklempt*"** Davis, with Kornbluh.

262 **"hundreds of people"** Firestein, with Kornbluh.

262 **"We just met"** Rayna Rapp, interview with Felicia Kornbluh, September 25, 2020, transcript in possession of the author.

262 **"so, so important"** Rapp, with Kornbluh.

263 **"like liberation, women's"** Davis, with Kornbluh.

263 **It encompassed the** Marie-Amélie George, *Becoming Equal: American Law and the Rise of the Gay Family* (Cambridge: Cambridge University Press, forthcoming).

264 **"Because what does"** Rapp, with Kornbluh.

264 **"Child Care: What"** Jennifer Nelson, *Women of Color and the Reproductive Rights Movement* (New York: New York University Press, 2003), 164.

264 **CARASA was one** Nelson, *Women of Color and the Reproductive Rights Movement*, 165.

264 **In 1983, CARASA** Nelson, *Women of Color and the Reproductive Rights Movement*, 166–67.

265 **The U.S. Court of** *Oil, Chemical, and Atomic Workers v. American Cyanamid* [741 F. 2d. 444] (D.C. Circuit, 1984); and Chuck Smith, "The Willow Island Sterilization Case," *The West Virginia Encyclopedia*, June 3, 2020, https://www.wvencyclopedia.org/articles/1283, accessed May 2, 2022.

265 **In remarks she** Nelson, *Women of Color and the Reproductive Rights Movement*, 159–61.

265 **The main author** Rosalind Pollack Petchesky, Rayna Rapp, et al., *Women Under Attack: Abortion, Sterilization, and Reproductive Freedom* (New York: Committee for Abortion Rights and Against Sterilization Abuse, 1979).

265 **Grossmann, a historian** Grossmann, with Kornbluh.

266 **"reproduction control"** Petchesky, Rapp, et al., *Women Under Attack*, 9.

266 **"It must mean"** Petchesky, Rapp, et al., *Women Under Attack*, 11.

266 **"Women have never"** Petchesky, Rapp, et al., *Women Under Attack*, 11.

266 **That was a** Tax, with Kornbluh; Firestein, with Kornbluh; Stamm, with Kornbluh.

267 **Despite an article** Maritza Arrastía, interview with Felicia Kornbluh, April 29, 2020, transcript in possession of the author.

267 **"slaughterhouse"** Deb Kayman, "Dr. Silva's 'Slaughterhouse'," *CARASA News*, vol. IV, no. 10 (December, 1980): 12.

267 **CARASA also included** Sarah Schulman, communication to the author, January 9, 2022; Welfare Action Coalition, "How We Won the Right to Welfare and Other Benefits," *CARASA News*, vol. IV, no. 10 (December, 1980): 9–11.

267 **However, in Tax's** Tax, with Kornbluh.

268 **"almost categorical"** Petchesky, Rapp, et al., *Women Under Attack*, 9–10.

268 **"second in command"** Rapp, with Kornbluh.

268 **"one of the"** Davis, with Kornbluh.

268 **They mentioned the** Susan E. Davis, ed., *Women Under Attack: Victories, Backlash, and the Fight for Reproductive Freedom* (Boston: South End Press, 1988), 5, 30, 65–68.

269 **"Everybody is so"** Tax, with Kornbluh. (Susan Davis, too, remembered the event. Davis, with Kornbluh.)

269 **In the wake** Janet Price, "Lesbian Rights and Reproductive Rights," *CARASA News*, vol VI, no. 6 (July 1982): 6.

269 **"the great disruption"** Stamm, with Kornbluh.

269 **The three were** Katherine Acey, interview with Kelly Anderson, Voices, 34 (Acey had a long-term relationship with Stephanie Roth during this period and was also a member of CARASA); and Sarah Schulman, *Let the Record Show: A Political History of ACT UP New York, 1987-1993* (New York: Farrar, Straus and Giroux, 2021).

270 **Schulman joined the** Schulman communication, January 9, 2022.

270 **Schulman, Roth, and** Schulman communication, January 9, 2022.

270 **"As one man"** Sarah Schulman, "Zaps Off With Fines After Threatening Congress," *My American History: Lesbian and Gay Life During the Reagan and Bush Years* (New York and London: Routledge, 2019, originally Womannews, November, 1983), 69.

270 **She added later** Schulman communication, January 9, 2022.

270 **The judge, who** Schulman, "Zaps Off," 69; and Schulman communication, January 9, 2022.

271 **One member accused** Schulman, with Kornbluh.

271 **"simply another separate"** Nelson, *Women of Color and the Reproductive Rights Movement*, 174.

271 **"may not live"** Alison Colbert, "An Open Letter to CARASA," *CARASA News*, vol. IV, no. I (January, 1980): 20.

272 **Dworkin thanked Schulman** Schulman, with Kornbluh.

272 **"delivered in her"** Schulman communication, January 9, 2022.

272 **They threw things** Wolfe, with Hubbard; and Schulman communication, January 9, 2022.

272 **"As soon as"** Wolfe, with Hubbard.

272 **Although, as Stamm** Karen Stamm, personal communication with the author, December 30, 2021, notes in possession of the author.

273 **"one of the"** Schulman, "Zaps Off."

273 **"demoralized" and "disheartened"** Stamm, with Kornbluh.

273 **"depending on the"** Stamm, with Kornbluh.

273 **"devastating"** Davis, with Kornbluh.

273 **Stamm underlined the** Stamm, with Kornbluh; and Stamm, Memorandum to the Author, Inventory of articles in *CARASA News* on lesbian and gay rights.

273 **"It was scary"** Price, "Lesbian Rights and Reproductive Rights."

274 **"And I wasn't"** Tax, with Kornbluh.

274 **Members of this** Schulman, with Kornbluh.

275 **"really, really, really"** Grossmann, with Kornbluh.

275 **"it might have"** Firestein, with Kornbluh.

275 **"That's all we"** Tax, with Kornbluh.

277 **A single issue** "Members of the Reproductive Rights National Network," *Reproductive Rights Newsletter—Newsletter of the Reproductive Rights National Network*, Spring 1981, in Teicher, unnumbered box, unnamed folder.

277 **"Since NOW wasn't"** Stamm, with Kornbluh.

277 **"a national network"** Sarah Schulman, "Tensions Run High as Reproductive Rights Activists Form Coalitions," *My American History*, originally *off our backs*, January 1982, 28–32.

277 **"pretty white"** Marlene Gerber Fried, interview with Felicia Kornbluh, July 22, 2019, transcript in possession of the author.

277 **Wolfe and Schulman** Wolfe, with Hubbard; Schulman, with Kornbluh.

277 **"and so, we were trying"** Wolfe, with Hubbard.

278 **"fighting for women's"** Wolfe, with Hubbard. Schulman, with Kornbluh, also discussed Wimmin for Womyn.

278   **Although many of** Stephanie Poggi (with input from other white women), "Report from white women on the Reproductive Rights National Network (R2N2) Conference 1984," Teicher, unnumbered box, unnamed folder; Stephanie Roth, Margie Fine, and Marlene Fried, to R2N2 Member Groups, March 9, 1985 (on stationery of the Reproductive Rights National Network), ibid.

278   **R2N2's demise was** Schulman, "The Pro-Family Left," *My American History*, 47–49.

278   **Volunteer people power** Wolfe, with Hubbard.

278   **She, Schulman, and** Schulman, *Let the Record Show.*

278   **It was here** Wolfe, with Hubbard (on local groups not using CARASA paraphernalia on lesbian rights); Schulman, with Kornbluh (on a default in the early 1980s in much of R2N2 to defend abortion rights more than to fight for the rest of the group's agenda).

279   **"We came here"** "Statement from the Women of Color Task Force," 11-11-84, Teicher, unnumbered box, unnamed folder.

279   **"everything we do"** Statement from the Women of Color Task Force.

279   **"affirmed [their] commitment"** Roth, Fine, and Fried, to R2N2 Member Groups.

280   **CARASA opposed the** Memorandum, To: HHC Advisory Committee on Sterilization, From: Esta Armstrong, Co-Chairperson, Sterilization Advisory Committee, Re: HHS Review of Sterilization Guidelines, June 24, 1982, with attached letter from Stanley Brezenoff, President, New York City Health and Hospitals Corporation, New York, NY, to Mr. Robert Streimer, Administrator, Health Care Financing Administration, Department of Health, Education, and Welfare, Baltimore, M.D., June 17, 1982, ACLU, Box 2965, folder titled "HHS Regulations on Sterilization, Reports, Article, Etc. 1982–1983"; Memorandum from CARASA, New York City, to Administrator, Health Care Financing Administration, Comments on Sterilization Regulations, June 21, 1981, ibid.; and Comments on the Renewal of the Federal Sterilization Regulations Submitted by the Center for Constitutional Rights, June 1982, ibid.

280   **"There seemed to"** Stamm, with Kornbluh.

281   **The overall trend** Letter from Brezenoff to Streimer; Memorandum from Sylvia [Law], to Suzanne, Janet B[enshoof], Rhonda [Copelon], Sarah, Anne, Janet G., Nadine [Strossen], Judy, and Nan, August 9, 1983 (on monitoring of sterilization guidelines), ACLU, Box 2965, folder titled "HHS Regulations on Sterilization, Reports, Article, Etc. 1982–1983."

281   **However, Stamm took** Stamm, with Kornbluh; Stamm, personal communication with the author, December 30, 2021, notes in possession of the author.

281   **"technical noncompliance"** Wendy Chavkin, interview with Felicia Kornbluh, September 10, 2020; biography, Wendy Chavkin, Mailman School of Public Health, Columbia University, https://www.publichealth.columbia.edu/people/our-faculty/wc9, accessed January 8, 2022.

281   **"It's part of"** Stamm, with Kornbluh.

282   **The U.S. Supreme** *Harris v. McRae* [448 U.S. 297] (1980) excerpted with explanatory notes, Melissa Murray and Kristin Luker, *Cases on Reproductive Rights and Justice* (St. Paul, MN: West Academic Press, 2015), 677–83.

282   **So was a** *Harris v. McRae.*

283 **The Department of** Rhonda Copelon and Sylvia Law, "'Nearly Allied to Her Right to Be'—Medicaid Funding for Abortion: The Story of *Harris v. McRae*," *Women and the Law Stories*, chapter 6, no page, https://www.law.nyu.edu/sites/default/files/ECM_PRO_075040.pdf, accessed January 9, 2022; Max H. Seigel, "U.S. Court Overturns Curb on Medicaid Abortions," *New York Times*, October 23, 1976: 1; and Seigel, "Federal Judge Again Bids H.E.W. Continue Medicaid for Abortions," *New York Times*, July 29, 1977: 41.

283 **These feminist legal activists** Copelon and Law, "'Nearly Allied to Her Right to Be.'"

283 **Judge Dooling considered** *McRae v. Califano* [491 F. Supp. 630] (EDNY, 1980).

283 **CARASA legislation committee** Karen Stamm and Anne Teicher, private communications with the author (email), December 31, 2021.

283 **"doubly protected when"** *McRae v. Califano.*

284 **"& so ends"** Case Notes, No. 79-1268, *Harris v. McRae*, Blackmun, Box 316, Folder 7 (Supreme Court Case File—October Term 1979).

284 **"constitutional entitlement to"** *Harris v. McRae*, Murray and Luker, *Cases on Reproductive Rights and Justice*, 679–80.

284 **Justice John Paul** Linda Greenhouse, "Limit on Abortions Paid by Medicaid Upheld by Justices," *New York Times*, July 1, 1980: 1, B8.

EPILOGUE: WHAT THEN? WHAT NOW?

286 **It seemed clear** Felicia Kornbluh, "God Save the United States and This Honorable Court," *The American Prospect*, December 6, 2021, https://prospect.org/justice/god-save-the-united-states-and-this-honorable-court/, accessed March 14, 2022.

286 **And then, on** Guttmacher Institute, "Abortion Policy in the Absence of *Roe*," April 4, 2022, https://www.guttmacher.org/state-policy/explore/abortion-policy-absence-roe, accessed May 3, 2022; and Josh Gerstein and Alexander Ward, "Supreme Court Has Voted to Overturn Abortion Rights, Draft Opinion Shows," *Politico*, May 2, 2022, https://www.politico.com/news/2022/05/02/supreme-court-abortion-draft-opinion-00029473, accessed May 3, 2022.

286 **The draft opinion** Mark Joseph Stern, "Alito's Draft Fully Overruling *Roe* is Jaw-Dropping and Unprecedented," *Slate*, May 2, 2022, https://slate.com/news-and-politics/2022/05/supreme-court-draft-abortion-leak-roe-overturned-explained.html, accessed May 3, 2022.

286 **They encapsulated the** Loretta Ross, interview with Felicia Kornbluh, October 11, 2019, transcript in possession of the author.

286 **Reproductive justice expanded** Marlene Gerber Fried, interview with Felicia Kornbluh, July 22, 2019, transcript in possession of the author.

287 **"contraception, comprehensive sex"** SisterSong Women of Color Reproductive Justice Collective, "We Believe That Reproductive Justice Is . . .," n.d., https://www.sistersong.net/reproductive-justice, accessed January 14, 2022.

287 **In August 2020** Scott Neuman, "NOW President Resigns Amid Allegations of Creating Toxic Work Environment," National Public Radio, August 18, 2020, https://www.npr

.org/sections/live-updates-protests-for-racial-justice/2020/08/18/903254443/
now-president-resigns-amid-allegations-of-creating-toxic-work-environment,
accessed January 14, 2022; and Christian Nunes, president, National Organization
for Women, brief biography, https://now.org/staff/christian-f-nunes/, accessed
January 14, 2022.

287 **following Aileen Clarke** "Aileen Clarke Hernandez (1926–2017), 'A Pioneer
for Women and Civil Rights,'" Veteran Feminists of America, https://www
.veteranfeministsofamerica.org/vfa-pioneer-histories-project-aileen-hernandez/
interview-aileen-hernandez/, accessed June 11, 2021; and "Aileen Clarke Hernandez—Biography," based on interviews conducted April 12, 2007, and November 8,
2013, The History Makers, https://www.thehistorymakers.org/biography/aileen
-clarke-hernandez, accessed June 11, 2021.

287 **Spokespeople for Planned** Mary Ziegler, *After* Roe: *The Lost History of the Abortion
Debate* (Cambridge, MA: Harvard University Press, 2015), chapter 3.

288 **"mom, anti-racist, feminist"** Mini Timmaraju, @mintimm, Profile, Twitter, n.d.,
https://twitter.com/mintimm, accessed January 14, 2022.

288 **However, she condemned** "Our History," Planned Parenthood Federation of
America, https://www.plannedparenthood.org/about-us/who-we-are/our-history,
accessed March 14, 2022.

288 **"We will no"** Alexis McGill Johnson, "I'm the Head of Planned Parenthood. We're
Done Making Excuses for Our Founder," *New York Times*, April 17, 2021, https://
www.nytimes.com/2021/04/17/opinion/planned-parenthood-margaret-sanger
.html, accessed January 13, 2022.

288 **The Association for** "Association for Voluntary Sterilization," Social Networks
and Archival Context, from the description of Association for Voluntary Sterilization Records, University of Minnesota, https://snaccooperative.org/ark:/99166/
w6n92q99, accessed March 15, 2022.

289 **Black women demanded** Ross, with Kornbluh; Loretta Ross, interview with Joyce
Follet, transcript of video recording, November 3–5 and December 1–3, 2004,
and February 4, 2005, Voices.

289 **It was even** Byllye Avery, "Breathing Life into Ourselves: The Evolution of the
National Black Women's Health Project," in *The Black Women's Health Book*, ed. Evelyn
C. White (Seattle: Seal Press, 1990), 4–10; and "Our Story," Black Women's Health
Imperative, https://bwhi.org/our-story/, accessed January 12, 2022.

289 **"Whether you die"** Byllye Avery, interview with Felicia Kornbluh, February 11,
2021, transcript in possession of the author.

289 **By 1988, the** Avery, "Breathing Life into Ourselves."

290 **"They do their"** Luz Martinez, interview by Loretta Ross, transcript of video
recording, December 6–7, 2004, Voices, 71, narrator's introduction.

290 **At the same** Ross, with Follet, 185–91.

290 **"all trying to"** Ross, with Follet, 190.

290 **"Just like the"** Ross, with Follet, 191.

291 **"right to safe"** Pamphlet reprinted as illustration to Natalegé Whaley, "Black Women
and the Fight for Abortion Rights: How This Brochure Sparked the Movement

for Reproductive Freedom," NBC News, March 25, 2019, https://www.nbcnews .com/news/nbcblk/black-women-fight-abortion-rights-how-brochure-sparked -movement-reproductive-n983216#:~:text=Largely%2C%20the%20voices%20 of%20black%20women%20had%20been,We%20Remember%3A%20 African-American%20Women%20are%20for%20Reproductive%20 Freedom.%E2%80%9D, accessed January 13, 2022.

291 **"nothing in the Constitution"** *Webster v. Reproductive Services* [492 U.S. 492] (1989).

291 **"undue burden"** *Planned Parenthood of Southeastern Pennsylvania v. Casey* [505 U.S. 833] (1992).

291 **In response, the** Zakiya Luna, *Reproductive Rights as Human Rights: Women of Color and the Fight for Reproductive Justice* (New York: NYU Press, 2020), 59.

291 **"at the first"** Ross, with Kornbluh.

291 **It helped that** Ross, with Follet, narrator's introduction.

292 **its members spoke** Luna, *Reproductive Rights as Human Rights*; and SisterSong, "We Believe That Reproductive Justice Is . . ."

292 **The first global** U.N. Women, "World Conferences on Women," n.d. [2019?], https://www.unwomen.org/en/how-we-work/intergovernmental-support/world -conferences-on-women, accessed January 18, 2022; and United Nations, "World Conference of the International Women's Year 19 June–2 July, Mexico City, Mexico, https://www.un.org/en/conferences/women/mexico-city1975, accessed January 18, 2022.

293 **She helped bring** Ross, with Kornbluh.

293 **The meeting in** Betsy Hartmann, *Reproductive Rights and Wrongs: The Global Politics of Population Control* (Chicago: Haymarket Books, 2016; originally 1987), 121–23, 144–48.

293 **As one sign** Helen Rodríguez-Trías, M.D., FAAP, "Foreword," in *Reproductive Rights and Wrongs*, xxii.

293 **"the full range"** Vanessa Williams, "Why Black Women Issued a Call for 'Reproductive Justice' 25 Years Ago," *Washington Post*, August 16, 2019, https://www.washingtonpost. com/nation/2019/08/16/reproductive-justice-how-women-color-asserted-their -voice-abortion-rights-movement/, accessed January 15, 2022.

293 **After only a** Toni M. Bond Leonard, "Laying the Foundations for a Reproductive Justice Movement," in *Radical Reproductive Justice*, ed. Loretta J. Ross, Lynn Roberts, Erika Derkas, Whitney Peoples, and Pamela Bridgewater Toure (New York: Feminist Press, 2017), 41.

293 **Women of African** Williams, "Why Black Women Issued a Call for 'Reproductive Justice.'" Loretta Ross, in a private communication to the author, January 18, 2022, explained that the title of the statement in those advertisements did not include the phrase "Reproductive Justice," because members of the National Black Women's Health Imperative thought that readers would not understand that phrase.

294 **Rodríguez-Trías attended** Rodríguez-Trías, "Foreword."

294 **"And those babies"** Ross, with Follet, 276.

294 **The Consensus didn't** Rodríguez-Trías, "Foreword"; and Ross, with Follet, 275.

295 **However, their program** United Nations Population Fund, Programme of Action Adopted at the International Conference on Population and Development, Cairo, 5–13

September 1994 (United Nations Population Fund, 2004); Lori Ashford, "What Was Cairo? The Promise and Reality of ICPD," Population Reference Bureau, 2004, https://www.prb.org/resources/what-was-cairo-the-promise-and-reality-of-icpd/, accessed January 16, 2022; and Betsy Hartmann, interview with Felicia Kornbluh, October 3, 2019.

295 **"that yo-yo"** Ross, with Follet, 295–98; and Ross, communication to the author, January 14, 2022.

298 **"and almost everyone"** [Karen Stamm], "Lessons of the Campaign for the Guidelines," n.d., Stamm-NYU, Box 2, Folder 4.

301 **"divergence of thinking"** *Roe v. Wade* [410 U.S. 160] (1973).

301 **In *Harris v. McRae*** *Harris v. McRae* [448 U.S. 297] (1980), excerpted with explanatory notes, Melissa Murray and Kristin Luker, *Cases on Reproductive Rights and Justice* (St. Paul, MN: Foundation Press, 2015), 677–83.

303 **Morgentaler served eighteen** Carol Joffe, *Doctors of Conscience: The Struggle to Provide Abortion Before and After Roe v. Wade* (Boston: Beacon Press, 1995), 105.

303 **Both became subjects** *R v. Morgentaler* (*Dr. Henry Morgentaler, Dr. Leslie Frank and Dr. Robert Scott v. Her Majesty the Queen and The Attorney General of Canada*), 1 S. C. R. 30, 1988 SCC 19556, https://scc-csc.lexum.com/scc-csc/scc-csc/en/item/288/index.do, accessed July 15, 2021; and *United States v. Vuitch* [402 U.S. 62] (1971).

304 **I ditched a** Nixon's own dedication to reproductive rights was inspired by her mother, Anne Nixon, who had an illegal abortion in New York in the years before the law changed.

304 **"We have fundamentally"** Kanyakrit Vongkiatkajorn, "Cynthia Nixon Just Gave a Defiant Concession Speech Following Loss in New York Governor's Primary," *Mother Jones*, September 13, 2018, https://www.motherjones.com/politics/2018/09/cynthia-nixon-just-gave-a-defiant-concession-speech-following-loss-in-new-york-governors-primary-andrew-cuomo/, accessed March 15, 2022.

305 **But the Reproductive** "Facts About the Reproductive Health Act," February 12, 2019, Office of New York State Senator Liz Kreuger, https://www.nysenate.gov/newsroom/articles/2019/liz-krueger/faqs-about-reproductive-health-act, accessed March 15, 2022.

305 **By a vote** N.A., "Vermont House Passes Reproductive Liberty Amendment (Prop 5)," VermontBiz, February 8, 2022, https://vermontbiz.com/news/2022/february/08/vermont-house-passes-reproductive-liberty-amendment-prop-5, accessed March 15, 2022.

305 **"personal reproductive autonomy"** Vermont Reproductive Liberty Amendment Campaign, "What Is the Reproductive Liberty Amendment?," https://reprolibertyvt.org/learn-more/, accessed January 18, 2022.

306 **"to consolidate our"** Dr. Helen Rodríguez-Trías, M.D., F.A.A.P., "Toward a Healthier Outlook for Women of Color," Stanford Conference on the Health of Women of Color, Conference Keynote, n.d., HRT, Box 3, Folder 9.

Bibliography

INTERVIEWS

Acey, Katherine, with Kelly Anderson, Voices, July 19, 2007.
Alumnae of the Committee to End Sterilization Abuse and Committee for Abortion
     Rights and Against Sterilization Abuse, with Felicia Kornbluh (group dialogue
     over Zoom including Harriet Cohen, Susan Davis, Netsy Firestein, Faye Ginsburg,
     Kristin Booth Glen, Harriet Goldberg, Atina Grossmann, Carol Marsh, Janet Price,
     Rayna Rapp, Susan Ritz, Karen Stamm, Alix Kates Shulman, Dale Stark, Meredith
     Tax, Anne Teicher, Sharon Thompson, and Barbara Winslow), August 13, 2020.
Aronowitz, Nona Willis, with Felicia Kornbluh, November 2, 2021.
Arrastía, Maritza, with Felicia Kornbluh, Part I, April 29, 2020.
Arrastía, with Kornbluh, Part II, February 28, 2022.
Avery, Byllye, with Loretta Ross, Voices, July 21, 2005.
Avery, with Felicia Kornbluh, February 11, 2021.
Berman, David, with Felicia Kornbluh, April 27, 2020.
Braun, Beatrice Kornbluh, with Felicia Kornbluh, July 5, 2016.
Brownmiller, Susan, with Felicia Kornbluh, August 10, 2020.
Brainin-Rodríguez, Jo Ellen, with Felicia Kornbluh, August 19, 2019.
Carmen, Arlene, with Ellen Chesler, FPOHP I, January 1976.
Chavkin, Wendy, with Felicia Kornbluh, September 10, 2020.
Cogan, Bruce, with Felicia Kornbluh, May 5, 2020.
Cook, Constance, with Ellen Chesler, FPOHP I, January 1976.
Curet-Rodríguez, Daniel, with Felicia Kornbluh, September 22, 2019.
Cusack, Ruth, with David Garrow, DJG, Part I, June 25, 1993.
Cusack, with Garrow, DJG, Part II, June 25, 1993.
Davis, Susan, with Felicia Kornbluh, August 12, 2020.
Faust, Jean, [with Jacqui Cabellos], Veteran Feminists of America, n.d. [after 2009].
Ferguson, Frances Hand, with James Reed, FPOHP I, June 1974.
Firestein, Netsy, with Felicia Kornbluh, September 4, 2020.
Garrow, David, with Felicia Kornbluh, January 14, 2021.
Gerber Fried, Marlene, with Felicia Kornbluh, July 22, 2019.

Greenhouse, Linda, with Felicia Kornbluh, February 19, 2020.

Grossmann, Atina, with Felicia Kornbluh, July 9, 2020.

Hartmann, Betsy, with Felicia Kornbluh, October 3, 2019.

Hern, Warren, with Felicia Kornbluh, December 9, 2019.

Hernandez, Aileen Clarke, with [Jacqui Cabellos?], Veteran Feminists of America, n.d., published 2014.

Katz, Stanley, with Felicia Kornbluh, October 23, 2020.

Kornbluh, David, with Felicia Kornbluh, September 4, 2017.

Lader, Lawrence, with Ellen Messer and Kathryn E. May, in Messer and May, eds., *Back Rooms: An Oral History of the Illegal Abortion Era* (New York: Touchstone/Simon and Schuster, 1988).

Leichter, Franz, with Felicia Kornbluh, July 14, 2017.

López, Iris, with Felicia Kornbluh, September 18, 2020.

Luhrs, Peggy, with Felicia Kornbluh, August 15, 2019.

Margolis, Jon, with Felicia Kornbluh, July 29, 2019.

Marsh, Carol, with Felicia Kornbluh, August 6, 2020.

Martínez, Luz, with Loretta Ross, Voices, December 1, 2004.

Moll, Judith Kornbluh, with Felicia Kornbluh, May 7, 2020.

Rapp, Rayna, with Felicia Kornbluh, September 25, 2020.

Rivera, Carmen Vivian, with Felicia Kornbluh, May 1, 2020.

Ross, Loretta, with Joyce Follet, Voices, November 3–5 and December 1–3, 2004, and February 4, 2005.

Ross, with Felicia Kornbluh, February 11, 2019.

Sánchez, Digna, with Felicia Kornbluh, March 30, 2020.

Schulman, Sarah, with Felicia Kornbluh, January 6, 2022.

Shapiro, Thomas, with Felicia Kornbluh, June 4, 2020.

Shulman, Alix Kates, with Felicia Kornbluh, August 11, 2020.

Stamm, Karen, with Felicia Kornbluh, October 25, 2019.

Stearns, Nancy, with Felicia Kornbluh, October 30, 2019.

Stearns, with Kornbluh, Part II, November 11, 2021.

Stark, Dale, with Felicia Kornbluh, September 17, 2020.

Steigman, Daria, with Felicia Kornbluh, April 30, 2020.

Steinem, Gloria, with Evelyn White, Voices, September 30, 2007.

Tax, Meredith, with Felicia Kornbluh, September 19, 2019.

Weddington, Sarah, with Jeannette Cheek, FPOHP I, March 1976.

Weinstein, Elayne, with Felicia Kornbluh, May 18, 2020.

Winslow, Barbara, with Felicia Kornbluh, July 28, 2021.

Wolfe, Maxine, with Jim Hubbard, ACT UP, February 19, 2004.

Zadworny, Mickenzie, with Felicia Kornbluh, July 29, 2019.

Court Cases

Abele v. Markle [342 F. Supp. 800] (Conn., 1972).

Abele v. Markle [351 F. Supp. 224] (Conn., 1972).

Baird v. Eisenstadt [405 U.S. 438] (1972).

Buck v. Bell [274 U.S. 200] (1927).

Byrn v. New York City Health & Hospitals Corp. [286 N.E.2d 887] (1972).

Dobbs v. Jackson Women's Health Organization [597 U.S. ___] (2022).

Doe v. Bolton [410 U.S. 149] (1973).

Frontiero v. Richardson [411 U.S. 677] (1973).

Gonzales v. Carhart [550 U.S. 124] (2007).

Griswold v. Connecticut [381 U.S. 479] (1965).

Hall v. Lefkowitz [305 F. Supp. 1030] (S.D.N.Y. 1969).

Harris v. McRae [448 U.S. 297] (1980).

Hoyt v. Florida [368 U.S. 57] (1961).

June Medical Services v. Russo [591 U.S. ___] (2020).

McRae v. Califano [491 F. Supp. 630] (E.D.N.Y. 1980).

People v. Belous [71 Cal. 2d 954] (1969).

Planned Parenthood of Southeastern Pennsylvania v. Casey [505 U.S. 833] (1992).

R v. Morgentaler [1 SCR 30, Canada] (1988).

Relf v. Weinberger [565 F.2d 722] (D.C. Circuit, 1977).

Roe v. Wade [410 U.S. 113] (1973).

Skinner v. Oklahoma ex rel. Williamson [316 U.S. 535] (1942).

United States v. Vuitch [305 F. Supp. 1032] (D.D.C. 1969).

United States v. Vuitch [402 U.S. 62] (1971).

Webster v. Reproductive Health Services [492 U.S. 490] (1989).

Whole Women's Health v. Hellerstedt [579 U.S. ___] (2016).

BOOKS AND SELECTED ARTICLES

This list includes the most important published works consulted for this project. It is not a complete inventory of journalistic or scholarly works that informed my writing or that are referenced in the notes.

Abramson, Michael. *Palante: Young Lords Party*. Chicago: Haymarket Books, 2011.

Alter, Robert. *The Hebrew Bible: A Translation with Commentary*. New York: W.W. Norton, 2019.

Antler, Joyce. *Jewish Radical Feminism: Voices from the Women's Liberation Movement*. New York: New York University Press, 2018.

Aronowitz, Nona Willis, ed. *The Essential Ellen Willis*. Minneapolis: University of Minnesota Press, 2014.

———. "The First Time Women Shouted Their Abortions." *New York Times*, March 23, 2019.

Arrastía, Maritza. "My Nation Is the Struggle: Writing and Resistance." In *Revolution Around the Corner: Voices from the Puerto Rican Socialist Party in the United States*, edited by José E. Velázquez, Carmen V. Rivera, and Andrés Torres, 139–52. Philadelphia: Temple University Press, 2021.

Atkinson, Ti-Grace. *Amazon Odyssey*. New York: Links Press, 1974.

Ayala, César, and Rafael Bernabe. *Puerto Rico in the American Century: A History Since 1898.* Chapel Hill: University of North Carolina Press, 2007.

Balkin, Jack, ed. *What Roe v. Wade Should Have Said: The Nation's Top Legal Experts Rewrite America's Most Controversial Decision.* New York: New York University Press, 2007.

Baxandall, Rosalyn Fraad, and Linda Gordon. *Dear Sisters: Dispatches from the Women's Liberation Movement; Broadsides, Cartoons, Manifestos and Other Documents from the Twentieth Century's Most Influential Movement.* New York: Basic Books, 2000.

Baynton, Douglas C. *Defectives in the Land: Disability and Immigration in the Age of Eugenics.* Chicago: University of Chicago Press, 2016.

Bell, Derrick A. "*Brown v. Board of Education* and the Interest-Convergence Dilemma." In *Critical Race Theory: The Key Writings That Formed the Movement,* edited by Kimberlé Crenshaw, Neal Gotanda, Gary Peller, and Kendall Thomas, 20–29. New York: New Press, 1995; originally *Harvard Law Review,* 1980.

Bernard, Emily. *Black Is the Body: Stories from My Grandmother's Time, My Mother's Time, and Mine.* New York: Vintage, 2019.

Biale, Rachel. *Women and Jewish Law: An Exploration of Women's Issues in Halakhic Sources.* New York: Schocken Press, 1995.

Bloom, Joshua, and Waldo E. Martin, Jr. *Black Against Empire: The History and Politics of the Black Panther Party.* Berkeley: University of California Press, 2013.

Breines, Winifred. *The Trouble Between Us: An Uneasy History of White and Black Women in the Feminist Movement.* New York: Oxford University Press, 2006.

Bridges, Khiara M. "Elision and Erasure: Race, Class, and Gender in *Harris v. McRae.*" In *Reproductive Rights and Justice Stories,* edited by Melissa Murray, Katherine Shaw, and Reva Siegel, 117–35. St. Paul, MN: West Academic Press, 2019.

———. *The Poverty of Privacy Rights.* Palo Alto, CA: Stanford University Press, 2017.

Briggs, Laura. *How All Politics Became Reproductive Politics: From Welfare Reform to Foreclosure to Trump.* Berkeley: University of California Press, 2018.

———. *Reproducing Empire: Race, Sex, Science, and U.S. Imperialism in Puerto Rico.* Berkeley: University of California Press, 2002.

Brodkin, Karen. *How Jews Became White Folks—and What That Says About Race in America.* New Brunswick, NJ: Rutgers University Press, 1998.

Brownmiller, Susan. *In Our Time: A Memoir of Revolution.* New York: Dial Press, 1999.

Burch, Susan. *Committed: Remembering Native Kinship in and Beyond Institutions.* Chapel Hill: University of North Carolina Press, 2021.

Burnett, Christina Duffy, and Burke Marshall, eds. *Foreign in a Domestic Sense: Puerto Rico, American Exceptionalism, and the Constitution.* Durham, NC: Duke University Press, 2001.

Calderone, Mary Steichen. *Abortion in the United States: A Conference Sponsored by the Planned Parenthood Federation of America, Inc., at Arden House and the New York Academy of Medicine.* New York: Paul B. Hoeber, the Medical Book Department of Harper and Brothers, 1958.

Carmen, Arlene, and Howard Moody. *Abortion Counseling and Social Change: From Illegal Act to Medical Practice.* Valley Forge, PA: Judson Press, 1973.

Caro, Robert. *The Power Broker: Robert Moses and the Fall of New York.* New York: W.W. Norton, 1974.

Carroll, Tamar W. *Mobilizing New York: AIDS, Antipoverty, and Feminist Activism*. Chapel Hill: University of North Carolina Press, 2015.

Chang, Jeff. *Can't Stop Won't Stop: A History of the Hip-Hop Generation*. New York: St. Martin's Press, 2005.

Chernin, Kim. *In My Mother's House*. West Lafayette, IN: Purdue University Press, 2019; originally 1983.

Chesler, Ellen. *Woman of Valor: Margaret Sanger and the Birth Control Movement in America*. New York: Simon and Schuster, 2007; originally 1992.

Cohen, Adam. *Imbeciles: The Supreme Court, American Eugenics, and the Sterilization of Carrie Buck*. New York: Penguin, 2016.

Colón, Jesús. *A Puerto Rican in New York and Other Sketches*. New York: Mainstream Publishers, 1961.

Connelly, Matthew James. *Fatal Misconception: The Struggle to Control World Population*. Cambridge, MA: Harvard University Press/Belknap, 2010.

Copelon, Rhonda, and Sylvia Law. "'Nearly Allied to Her Right to Be'—Medicaid Funding for Abortion: The Story of *Harris v. McRae*." In *Women and the Law Stories*, edited by Elizabeth Schneider and Stephanie Wildman, 207–52. New York: Thompson/Reuters Foundation Press, 2011.

Córdova, Isabel M. *Pushing in Silence: Modernizing Puerto Rico and the Medicalization of Childbirth*. Austin: University of Texas Press, 2018.

Crenshaw, Kimberlé. "Demarginalizing the Intersection of Race and Sex: A Black Feminist Critique of Antidiscrimination Doctrine, Feminist Theory and Antiracist Politics." *University of Chicago Legal Forum*, no. 1 (1989): 139–67.

Davis, Susan E. *Love Means Second Chances*. New York: Bread and Roses Collaborative, 2011.

————, ed. *Women Under Attack: Abortion, Sterilization Abuse, and Reproductive Freedom*. Boston: South End Press, 1988.

DeHart, Jane Sherron. *Ruth Bader Ginsburg: A Life*. New York: Alfred A. Knopf, 2018.

DiAngelo, Robin. *White Fragility: Why It's So Hard for White People to Talk About Racism*. Boston: Beacon Press, 2018.

Dirks, Doris Andrea, and Patricia A. Relf. *To Offer Compassion: A History of the Clergy Consultation Service on Abortion*. Madison: University of Wisconsin Press, 2017.

Dittmer, John. *The Good Doctors: The Medical Committee for Human Rights and the Struggle for Social Justice in Health Care*. Jackson: University of Mississippi Press, 2017; originally 2009.

Duany, Jorge. *The Puerto Rican Nation on the Move: Identities on the Island and in the United States*. Chapel Hill: University of North Carolina Press, 2002.

Du Bois, W.E.B. *The Souls of Black Folk: Essays and Sketches*. Project Gutenberg, e-book #408, originally 1903.

Duplessis, Rachel Blau, and Ann Snitow, eds. *The Feminist Memoir Project: Voices from Women's Liberation*. New Brunswick, NJ: Rutgers University Press, 2007.

Dworkin, Andrea. *Pornography: Men Possessing Women*. New York: Putnam, 1981.

Echols, Alice. *Daring to Be Bad: Radical Feminism in America, 1967–1975*. Minneapolis: University of Minnesota Press, 1989.

————. *Shortfall: Family Secrets, Financial Collapse, and a Hidden History of American Banking*. New York: The New Press, 2017.

Enck-Wanzer, Darrel, ed. *The Young Lords: A Reader*. New York: New York University Press, 2010.

Fahs, Branne. "Ti-Grace Atkinson and the Legacy of Radical Feminism." *Feminist Studies*, vol. 37, no. 3 (Fall 2011): 561–90.

Fernández, Johanna. *The Young Lords: A Radical History*. Chapel Hill: University of North Carolina Press, 2020.

Finger, Anne. *Past Due: A Story of Disability, Pregnancy and Birth*. Seattle: Seal Press, 1990.

Firestone, Shulamith. *The Dialectic of Sex: The Case for Feminist Revolution*. New York: Bantam, 1971.

Forbath, William, Hendrik Hartog, and Martha Minow. "Introduction: Legal Histories from Below." *Wisconsin Law Review* (1985): 759–66.

Foster, Diana Greene. *The Turnaway Study: Ten Years, a Thousand Women, and the Consequences of Having—or Being Denied—an Abortion*. New York: Scribner, 2021.

Frankenberg, Ruth. *White Women, Race Matters: The Social Construction of Whiteness*. New York and London: Routledge Press, 1993.

Freeman, Jo. *The Politics of Women's Liberation: A Case Study of an Emerging Social Movement and Its Relation to the Policy Process*. New York: Longman, 1975.

Fried, Marlene Gerber, ed. *From Abortion to Reproductive Freedom: Transforming a Movement*. Boston: South End Press, 1991.

Friedan, Betty. *"It Changed My Life": Writings on the Women's Movement*. Cambridge, MA: Harvard University Press, 1998; originally 1976.

———. *Life So Far*. New York: Simon and Schuster, 2006.

———. *The Feminine Mystique*. New York: W. W. Norton, 1963.

Friedman, Lawrence Meir. *American Law in the 20th Century*. New Haven, CT: Yale University Press, 2002.

Fuentes, Sonia Pressman. *Eat First—You Don't Know What They'll Give You: The Adventures of an Immigrant Family and Their Feminist Daughter*. Philadelphia: Xlibris, 1999.

Gans, Herbert J. *The Levittowners: Ways of Life and Politics in a New Suburban Community*. New York: Knopf, 1967.

Garrow, David J. *Liberty and Sexuality: The Right to Privacy and the Making of Roe v. Wade*. Berkeley: University of California Press, 1998; originally 1994.

Gilmore, Stephanie. *Groundswell: Grassroots Feminist Activism in Postwar America*. New York and London: Routledge Press, 2013.

González, Juan. *Harvest of Empire: A History of Latinos in America*. New York: Penguin, 2011; originally 2000.

Gordon, Linda. *Woman's Body, Woman's Right: Birth Control in America*. New York: Penguin, 1990; originally 1976.

Gornick, Vivian. *Essays in Feminism*. New York: Harper and Row, 1978.

———. *Fierce Attachments: A Memoir*. New York: Farrar, Straus and Giroux, 1987.

Greenhouse, Linda. *Becoming Justice Blackmun: Harry Blackmun's Supreme Court Journey*. New York: Times Books/Henry Holt, 2005.

Greenhouse, Linda, and Reva B. Siegel, eds. *Before Roe v. Wade: Voices That Shaped the Abortion Debate Before the Supreme Court's Ruling*. New York: Kaplan, 2010.

Greenlee, Cynthia. "How Abortion Storytelling Was Born." Rewire News Group, January 22, 2016. https://rewirenewsgroup.com/article/2016/01/22/abortion-storytelling-born/, accessed March 18, 2022.

———. "Percy Sutton's 1966 Abortion Rights Bill: Groundbreaking, but Often Unremembered." Rewire News Group, February 24, 2015. https://rewirenewsgroup.com/article/2015/02/24/percy-suttons-1966-abortion-rights-bill-groundbreaking-often-unremembered/, accessed March 18, 2022.

Grossmann, Atina. *Reforming Sex: The German Movement for Birth Control and Abortion Reform, 1920–50.* New York: Oxford University Press, 1995.

Gurr, Barbara. *Reproductive Justice: The Politics of Health Care for Native American Women.* New Brunswick, NJ: Rutgers University Press, 2015.

Gutiérrez, Elena R. *Fertile Matters: The Politics of Mexican-Origin Women's Reproduction.* Austin: University of Texas Press, 2008.

Halley, Janet, Prabha Kotiswaran, Rachal Rebouche, and Hila Shamir. *Governance Feminism: An Introduction.* Minneapolis: University of Minnesota Press, 2018.

Hansen, Randall, and Desmond King. *Sterilized by the State: Eugenics, Race, and the Population Scare in Twentieth-Century North America.* Cambridge: Cambridge University Press, 2013.

Hardin, Garrett. *Exploring New Ethics for Survival: The Voyage of the Spaceship* Beagle. New York: Viking Press, 1972.

Harris, Cheryl I. "Whiteness as Property." *Harvard Law Review*, vol. 106, no. 8 (June 1993): 1707–993.

Hartmann, Betsy. *Reproductive Rights and Wrongs: The Global Politics of Population Control.* Chicago: Haymarket Books, 2016; originally 1987.

Hartog, Hendrik. *Man and Wife in America: A History.* Cambridge, MA: Harvard University Press, 2000.

Helm, Sarah. *Ravensbruck: Life and Death in Hitler's Concentration Camp for Women.* New York: Anchor Books, 2015.

Hennessee, Judith Adler. *Betty Friedan: Her Life.* New York: Random House, 1999.

Horowitz, Daniel. *Betty Friedan and the Making of "The Feminine Mystique": The American Left, the Cold War, and Modern Feminism.* Amherst: University of Massachusetts Press, 1998.

Immerwahr, Daniel. *How to Hide an Empire: A History of the Greater United States.* New York: Picador, 2019.

Jacobson, Matthew Frye. *Whiteness of a Different Color: European Immigrants and the Alchemy of Race.* Cambridge, MA: Harvard University Press, 1999.

Joffe, Carole. *Doctors of Conscience: The Struggle to Provide Abortion Before and After* Roe v. Wade. Boston: Beacon Press, 1995.

Jones, Martha F. *Vanguard: How Black Women Broke Barriers, Won the Vote, and Insisted on Equality for All.* New York: Basic Books, 2020.

Kamen, Scott. "Rethinking Postwar Liberalism: The Americans for Democratic Action, Social Democracy, and the Struggle for Racial Equality." *The 1960s*, vol. 11, no. 1 (2018): 69–92.

Kaplan, Laura. *The Story of Jane: The Legendary Underground Feminist Abortion Service.* Chicago: University of Chicago Press, 1995.

Kendall, Mikki. *Hood Feminism: Notes from the Women That a Movement Forgot.* New York: Penguin, 2021.

Kennedy, Florynce. *Color Me Flo: My Hard Life and Good Times.* Englewood Cliffs, NJ: Prentice-Hall, 1976.

Kerber, Linda K. *No Constituitonal Right to be Ladies: Women and the Obligations of Citizenship.* New York: Hill and Wang, 1999.

Klarman, Michael J. Brown v. Board of Education *and the Civil Rights Movement.* New York: Oxford University Press, 2007.

Kluchin, Rebecca M. *Fit to Be Tied: Sterilization and Reproductive Rights in America, 1950–1980.* New Brunswick, NJ: Rutgers University Press, 2011.

Kolbert, Katherine, and Julie F. Kay. *Controlling Women: What We Must Do Now to Save Reproductive Freedom.* New York: Hachette Books, 2021.

Kornbluh, Felicia. *The Battle for Welfare Rights: Politics and Poverty in Modern America.* Philadelphia: University of Pennsylvania Press, 2007.

Kornbluh, Felicia, and Gwendolyn Mink. *Ensuring Poverty: Welfare Reform in Feminist Perspective.* Philadelphia: University of Pennsylvania Press, 2019.

Kutler, Stanley I. *The Wars of Watergate: The Last Crisis of Richard Nixon.* New York: W.W. Norton, 2012.

Lader, Lawrence. *Abortion.* New York: Bobbs-Merrill, 1966.

———. *Abortion II: Making the Revolution.* Boston: Beacon Press, 1973.

———. *Breeding Ourselves to Death.* New York: Ballantine, 1971.

Lash, Joseph. *Eleanor Roosevelt: A Friend's Memoir.* New York: Doubleday, 1964.

Lee, Sophia Z. *The Workplace Constitution from the New Deal to the New Right.* Cambridge: Cambridge University Press, 2014.

Levenstein, Lisa. *They Didn't See Us Coming: The Hidden History of Feminism in the Nineties.* New York: Basic Books, 2020.

Linton, Simi. *Claiming Disability: Knowledge and Identity.* New York: New York University Press, 1998.

Lombardo, Paul A. *Three Generations, No Imbeciles: Eugenics, the Supreme Court, and* Buck v. Bell. Baltimore: Johns Hopkins University Press, 2008.

López, Iris Ofelia. *Matters of Choice: Puerto Rican Women's Struggle for Reproductive Freedom.* New Brunswick, NJ: Rutgers University Press, 2008.

———. "Sterilization in Puerto Rico: Coercion or Personal Choice?" In *Genetic Determinism and Children,* edited by Ethel Tobach and Betty Rosoff, 66–75. New York: Gordian Press, 1980.

Lorde, Audre. *The Collected Poems of Audre Lorde.* New York: W.W. Norton, 2017.

Lovett, Laura L. *With Her Fist Raised: Dorothy Pitman Hughes and the Transformative Power of Black Community Activism.* Boston: Beacon Press, 2020.

Loyd, Jenna M. *Health Rights Are Civil Rights: Peace and Justice Activism in Los Angeles, 1963–1978.* Minneapolis: University of Minnesota Press, 2014.

Lucas, Roy. "Federal Constitutional Limitations on the Enforcement and Administration of State Abortion Statutes." *North Carolina Law Review,* vol. 46, no. 4 (June 1968): 730–78.

Luker, Kristin. *Abortion and the Politics of Motherhood.* Berkeley: University of California Press, 1984.

Luna, Zakiya T. *Reproductive Rights as Human Rights: Women of Color and the Fight for Reproductive Justice.* New York: New York University Press, 2020.

MacLean, Nancy. *Freedom Is Not Enough: The Opening of the American Workplace.* Cambridge, MA: Harvard University Press, 2008.

Mahler, Jonathan. *Ladies and Gentlemen, the Bronx Is Burning: 1977, Baseball, Politics, and the Battle for the Soul of a City.* New York: Picador, 2005.

Mamdani, Mahmood. *The Myth of Population Control: Family, Caste, and Class in an Indian Village.* New York: Monthly Review Press, 1973.

Manian, Maya. "Coerced Sterilization of Mexican-American Women: The Story of *Madrigal v. Quilligan.*" In *Reproductive Rights and Justice Stories,* edited by Melissa Murray, Katherine Shaw, and Reva B. Siegel, 1–16. St. Paul, MN: Foundation Press, 2019.

Materson, Lisa. "Gender, Generation, and Women's Independence Organizing in Puerto Rico." *Radical History Review,* vol. 128 (2017): 121–46.

May, Elaine Tyler. *America and the Pill: A History of Promise, Peril, and Liberation.* New York: Basic Books, 2011.

Mayeri, Serena. *Reasoning from Race: Feminism, Law, and the Civil Rights Revolution.* Cambridge, MA: Harvard University Press, 2014.

McCorvey, Norma, and Andy Meisler. *I Am Roe: My Life,* Roe v. Wade, *and Freedom of Choice.* New York: Harper Perennial, 1995.

McIntosh, Peggy. "White Privilege: Unpacking the Invisible Knapsack." *Peace and Freedom Magazine,* July–August 1989: 10–12.

Means, Cyril, Jr. "The Law of New York Concerning Abortion and the Status of the Foetus, 1664–1968: A Case of Cessation of Constitutionality." *New York Law Forum,* vol. 14, no. 3 (1968): 411–515.

———. "The Phoenix of Abortional Freedom: Is a Penumbral or Ninth-Amendment Right About to Arise from the Nineteenth-Century Legislative Ashes of a Four-teenth-Century Common-Law Liberty?" *New York Law Forum,* vol. 17, no. 2 (1971): 335–410.

Melendez, Miguel "Mickey." *We Took the Streets: Fighting for Latino Rights with the Young Lords.* New York: St. Martin's Press, 2003.

Messer, Ellen, and Katherine E. May. *Back Rooms: An Oral History of the Illegal Abortion Era.* New York: Simon and Schuster, 1988.

Millett, Kate. *Sexual Politics.* New York: Doubleday, 1969.

Mintz, Morton. *At Any Cost: Corporate Greed, Women, and the Dalkon Shield.* New York: Pantheon, 1985.

Mohr, James C. *Abortion in America: The Origins and Evolution of National Policy.* New York: Oxford University Press, 1978.

———. *Doctors and the Law: Medical Jurisprudence in Nineteenth-Century America.* New York: Oxford University Press, 1993.

Moore, Deborah Dash, et al. *Jewish New York: The Remarkable Story of a City and a People.* New York: New York University Press, 2017.

Moraga, Cheríe, and Gloria Anzaldúa, eds. *This Bridge Called My Back: Writings by Radical Women of Color.* New York: Kitchen Table: Women of Color Press, 1981.

Morgan, Robin, ed. *Sisterhood Is Powerful.* New York: Vintage Press, 1970.

Moskowitz, Faye, ed. *Her Face in the Mirror: Jewish Women on Mothers and Daughters*. Boston: Beacon Press, 1994.

Mullan, Fitzhugh. *White Coat, Clenched Fist: The Political Education of an American Physician*. New York: MacMillan, 1976.

Murray, Melissa, and Kristin Luker. *Cases on Reproductive Rights and Justice*. St. Paul, MN: Foundation Press, 2015.

NeJaime, Douglas, and Reva Siegel. "Answering the *Lochner* Objection: Substantive Due Process and the Role of Courts in a Democracy." *New York University Law Review*, vol. 96 (2021): 1902–65.

Nelson, Alondra. *Body and Soul: The Black Panther Party and the Fight Against Medical Discrimination*. Minneapolis: University of Minnesota Press, 2011.

Nelson, Jennifer. *More Than Medicine: A History of the Feminist Women's Health Movement*. New York: New York University Press, 2015.

———. *Women of Color and the Reproductive Rights Movement*. New York: New York University Press, 2003.

Nossiff, Rosemary. *Before Roe: Abortion Policy in the States*. Philadelphia: Temple University Press, 2001.

Nourse, Victoria F. *In Reckless Hands: Skinner v. Oklahoma and the Near Triumph of American Eugenics*. New York: W. W. Norton, 2008.

Painter, Nell Irvin. *The History of White People*. New York: W.W. Norton, 2010.

Petchesky, Rosalind Pollack. *Abortion and Woman's Choice: The State, Sexuality, and Reproductive Freedom*. Boston: Northeastern University Press, 1990; originally 1984.

Petchesky, Rosalind, and Rayna Rapp, et al. *Women Under Attack: Abortion, Sterilization, and Reproductive Freedom*. New York: Committee for Abortion Rights and Against Sterilization Abuse, 1979.

Piercy, Marge. *Braided Lives: A Novel*. Oakland, CA: PM Press, 2013.

Pogrebin, Letty Cottin. *Deborah, Golda, and Me: Being Jewish and Female in America*. New York: Anchor Books, 1992.

Pollitt, Katha. *Pro: Reclaiming Abortion Rights*. New York: Picador, 2014.

Prager, Joshua. *The Family Roe: An American Story*. New York: W.W. Norton, 2021.

Randolph, Sherie M. *Florynce "Flo" Kennedy: The Life of a Black Feminist Radical*. Chapel Hill: University of North Carolina Press, 2018.

Reagan, Leslie J. *Dangerous Pregnancies: Mothers, Disabilities, and Abortion in Modern America*. Berkeley: University of California Press, 2012.

———. *When Abortion Was a Crime: Women, Medicine, and Law in the United States, 1880–1973*. Berkeley: University of California Press, 1997.

Reed, James. *From Private Vice to Public Virtue: The Birth Control Movement and American Society Since 1830*. New York: Basic Books, 1978.

Reverby, Susan M. *Examining Tuskegee: The Infamous Syphilis Study and Its Legacy*. Chapel Hill: University of North Carolina Press, 2009.

Rich, Adrienne. *The Dream of a Common Language: Poems, 1974–1977*. New York: W.W. Norton, 1978.

Rivera, Carmen Vivian. "Our Movement: One Woman's Story." In *The Puerto Rican Movement:*

Voices from the Diaspora, edited by Andrés Torres and José E. Velázquez. Philadelphia: Temple University Press, 1998, 192–209.

Roberts, Dorothy. *Killing the Black Body: Race, Reproduction, and the Meaning of Liberty*. New York: Pantheon, 1997.

Rodríguez-Trías, Helen. Foreword to *Reproductive Rights and Wrongs: The Global Politics of Population Control*, by Betsy Hartmann. Chicago: Haymarket Books, 2016.

Romney, Patricia. *We Were There: The Third World Women's Alliance and the Second Wave*. New York: Feminist Press, 2021.

Rosen, Jeffrey. *Conversations with RBG: Ruth Bader Ginsburg on Life, Love, Liberty, and Law*. New York: Henry Holt, 2019.

Ross, Loretta J., Lynn Roberts, Erika Derkas, Whitney Peoples, and Pamela Bridgewater Toure, eds. *Radical Reproductive Justice: Foundation, Theory, Practice, Critique*. New York: Feminist Press, 2017.

Ross, Loretta, and Rickie Solinger. *Reproductive Justice: An Introduction*. Berkeley: University of California Press, 2017.

Rossi, Alice. *The Feminist Papers: From Adams to De Beauvoir*. Boston: Northeastern University Press, 1992.

Roth, Benita. *Separate Roads to Feminism: Black, Chicana, and White Feminist Movements in America's Second Wave*. Cambridge: Cambridge University Press, 2004.

Santiago, Esmeralda. *When I Was Puerto Rican*. New York: Vintage, 1993.

Santiago, Roberto, ed. *Boricuas: Influential Puerto Rican Writings—an Anthology*. New York: One World/Ballantine, 1995.

Satter, Beryl. *Family Properties: Race, Real Estate, and the Exploitation of Black Urban America*. New York: Picador, 2009.

Schiff, Karenna Gore. *Lighting the Way: Nine Women Who Changed Modern America*. New York: Miramax Books, 2005.

Schneir, Miriam, ed. *Feminism in Our Time: The Essential Writings, World War II to the Present*. New York: Vintage Press, 2006.

Schoen, Johanna. *Abortion After Roe*. Chapel Hill: University of North Carolina Press, 2017.

———. *Choice and Coercion: Birth Control, Sterilization, and Abortion in Public Health and Welfare*. Chapel Hill: University of North Carolina Press, 2005.

Schulder, Diane, and Florynce Kennedy. *Abortion Rap*. New York: McGraw-Hill, 1971.

Schulman, Sarah. *Let the Record Show: A Political History of ACT UP New York, 1987–1993*. New York: Picador, 2022.

———. *My American History: Lesbian and Gay Life During the Reagan and Bush Years*. New York and London: Routledge Press, 1994.

———. *The Sophie Horowitz Story*. Tallahassee, FL: Naiad Press, 1984.

Self, Robert. *All in the Family: The Realignment of American Democracy Since the 1960s*. New York: Hill and Wang, 2012.

Sethna, Christabelle, and Steve Hewitt. *Just Watch Us: RCMP Surveillance of the Women's Liberation Movement in Cold War Canada*. Montreal and Kingston, ON: McGill-Queen's University Press, 2018.

Shapiro, Thomas M. *Population Control Politics: Women, Sterilization, and Reproductive Choice*. Philadelphia: Temple University Press, 1985.

Shulman, Alix Kates. *Burning Questions*. New York: Alfred A. Knopf, 1978.

———. *Memoirs of an Ex-Prom Queen*. New York: Alfred A. Knopf, 1972.

Shulman, Alix Kates, and Honor Moore, eds. *Women's Liberation! Feminist Writings That Inspired a Revolution and Still Can*. New York: Library of America, 2021.

Siegel, Reva B. "*Roe's* Roots: The Women's Rights Claims That Engendered *Roe*." *Boston University Law Review*, vol. 90 (2010): 1875–907.

Siegel, Reva B., and Linda Greenhouse. "Before (and After) *Roe v. Wade*: New Questions About Backlash." *Yale Law Journal*, vol. 120, no. 8 (2011): 2028–87.

Silliman, Jael Miriam, Marlene Gerber Fried, Loretta Ross, and Elena R. Gutiérrez, eds. *Undivided Rights: Women of Color Organize for Reproductive Justice*. Chicago: Haymarket Books, 2016.

Simon, Kate. *Bronx Primitive: Portraits in a Childhood*. New York: Perennial Library, 1983.

Snitow, Ann Barr, Christine Stansell, and Sharon Thompson, eds. *Powers of Desire: The Politics of Sexuality*. New York: Monthly Review, 1983.

Solinger, Rickie. *The Abortionist: A Woman Against the Law*. Berkeley: University of California Press, 2019; originally 1995.

———. *Beggars and Choosers: How the Politics of Choice Shapes Adoption, Abortion, and Welfare in the United States*. New York: Hill and Wang, 2002.

Sparrow, Bartholomew H. *The Insular Cases and the Emergence of American Empire*. Lawrence: University Press of Kansas, 2006.

Starr, Paul. *The Social Transformation of American Medicine: The Rise of a Sovereign Profession and the Making of a Vast Industry*. New York: Basic Books, 1984.

Steedman, Carolyn Kay. *Landscape for a Good Woman: A Story of Two Lives*. New Brunswick, NJ: Rutgers University Press, 1987.

Stein, Marc. *Sexual Injustice: Supreme Court Decisions from* Griswold *to* Roe. Chapel Hill: University of North Carolina Press, 2010.

Steinem, Gloria. *Outrageous Acts and Everyday Rebellions*. New York: Picador/Henry Holt, 1983.

Stern, Alexandra Minna. *Eugenic Nation: Faults and Frontiers of Better Breeding in Modern America*. Berkeley: University of California Press, 2016; originally 2005.

Stettner, Shannon, Kristin Burnett, and Travey Hay, eds. *Abortion: History, Politics, and Reproductive Justice After Morgentaler*. Vancouver: University of British Columbia Press, 2017.

Taranto, Stacie. *Kitchen Table Politics: Conservative Women and Family Values in New York*. Philadelphia: University of Pennsylvania Press, 2017.

Tax, Meredith. *The Rising of the Women*. New York: Monthly Review, 1980.

———. *Rivington Street*. New York: Jove, 1983.

———. *Union Square*. New York: William Morrow, 1988.

Taylor, Keeanga-Yamahtta. "How Black Feminists Defined Abortion Rights." *New Yorker*, February 22, 2022.

———. *How We Get Free: Black Feminism and the Combahee River Collective*. Chicago: Haymarket Books, 2017.

Theobald, Brianna. *Reproduction on the Reservation: Pregnancy, Childbirth, and Colonialism in the Long Twentieth Century*. Chapel Hill: University of North Carolina Press, 2019.

Thompson, Heather Ann. *Blood in the Water: The Attica Prison Uprising of 1971 and Its Legacy.* New York: Pantheon, 2016.

Toobin, Jeffrey. "The People's Choice." *New Yorker*, January 20, 2013.

Turk, Katherine. *Equality on Trial: Gender and Rights in the Modern American Workplace.* Philadelphia: University of Pennsylvania Press, 2016.

Tushnet, Mark V. *The NAACP's Legal Strategy Against Segregated Education, 1925–1950.* Chapel Hill: University of North Carolina Press, 1995.

Velázquez, José E., Carmen V. Rivera, and Andrés Torres, eds. *Revolution around the Corner: Voices from the Puerto Rican Socialist Party in the United States.* Philadelphia: Temple University Press, 2021.

Wallace, Deborah, and Rodrick Wallace. *A Plague on Your Houses: How New York Was Burned Down and Public Health Crumbled.* New York and London: Verso Books, 1990.

Wanzer-Serrano, Darrel. *The New York Young Lords and the Struggle for Liberation.* Philadelphia: Temple University Press, 2015.

Washington, Harriet A. *Medical Apartheid: The Dark History of Medical Experimentation on Black Americans from Colonial Times to the Present.* New York: Doubleday, 2006.

Weddington, Sarah. *A Question of Choice.* New York: Penguin Press, 1993.

White, Evelyn C., ed. *The Black Women's Health Book: Speaking for Ourselves.* Seattle: Seal Press, 1990.

Wilkerson, Isabel. *Caste: The Origins of Our Discontents.* New York: Random House, 2020.

Williams, Daniel K. *Defenders of the Unborn: The Pro-Life Movement Before Roe v. Wade.* New York: Oxford University Press, 2016.

Williams, Patricia. *The Alchemy of Race and Rights: Diary of a Law Professor.* Cambridge, MA: Harvard University Press, 1992.

Willis, Ellen. *No More Nice Girls: Countercultural Essays.* Minneapolis: University of Minnesota Press, 2012.

Wollstonecraft, Mary. *Vindication of the Rights of Woman.* London: Penguin, 2005; originally 1792.

Zarnow, Leandra Ruth. *Battling Bella: The Protest Politics of Bella Abzug.* Cambridge, MA: Harvard University Press, 2019.

Ziegler, Mary. *Abortion in America: A Legal History from Roe to the Present.* Cambridge: Cambridge University Press, 2020.

———. *After Roe: The Lost History of the Abortion Debate.* Cambridge, MA: Harvard University Press, 2015.

Acknowledgments

Aᴀ

A FTER MY mother died, my sisters and I spent over a year sift-
ing through her things and preparing to sell the home where
we grew up. She had divided the papers and marked them
up with notes about their contents, as though preparing for their
eventual use by a daughter-historian. In the five years it took to finish
this book, I have been haunted by the sense that it was my mother's
idea all along that I would write a version of this story.

By the time Karen, Rebecca, and I sold apartment 8B, my father
was terminally ill. My grief over the loss of both parents, in a time
of so many losses, is the soil in which this project has grown.

But it has not all been grief. This work has also been nourished by
the generosity of many people. I am grateful first of all to my family: to Karen for asking the question that opened the door on this
project, my mother for her undying commitment to women's rights
and for leaving a paper trail that made me think it was possible, my
late father for distracting us both from his awful diagnosis by talking
to me from a hospital bed about liberal New York City politics in
the 1960s and 1970s, Rebecca for her love and support, Gayla for
a vote of confidence when it mattered most, Judith for being part
of my "pod" and Saturday-night stir-fry team at the height of the
COVID-19 scare, Bruce Cogan, David Berman, Mimi Feinstein, and
Judy Moll for filling me in on family history (and secrets), and my
spouse, Anore, for being my #1 interlocutor and for the example she
provides every day of commitment to creating a better world.

Next on the list of those who enabled this project are the family, friends, and colleagues of Dr. Helen Rodríguez-Trías. I am grateful to the late Eddie Gonzáles for making her papers publicly available and for the willingness of her three children, Jo Ellen Brainin-Rodríguez, Laura Brainin-Rodríguez, and Daniel Curet-Rodríguez, to be partners in this work. Among colleagues, the biggest thanks go to Meredith Tax, Atina Grossmann, and Karen Stamm for organizing the group Zoom of CESA and CARASA alums who taught me so much about Rodríguez-Trías as well as about those two remarkable organizations.

I can never offer deep enough thanks to my agents, Gail Ross, who took me on as a client when I wasn't 100% sure I could write a trade book, and the tireless Dara Kaye, who made me smarter and a better writer each time she worked with me on another draft of the book proposal. The same is true for my editor, Amy Hundley, production director Sal Destro, managing editor Julia Berner-Tobin, and everyone at Grove Atlantic who supported the acquisition of this book and helped birth it. Somewhere in my youth or childhood, I must have done something right, or else I would not have wound up with a brilliant feminist editor who was willing to lose almost as much sleep as I did finishing this project. Thanks to Grove Atlantic for putting the excellent copy editor Maureen Klier on the job, and for remaining an independent publishing house whose mission I believe in as they apparently believe in mine.

Five years might sound like a long time to work on a book, but it would have taken many more years without the exceptional institutional support I received. Thanks a thousand times to everyone at Princeton's Law and Public Affairs Program, my home for the 2019–2020 academic year (until COVID sent me back north in March, 2020), including Director Paul Frymer, Associate Director Leslie Gerwin, my great mentor Hendrik Hartog, revered colleagues Stan Katz and Kim Scheppele, and comrades for the year Robin Lenhardt, Kunal Parker, Cheryl Harris, Sarah Light, and Steve Chanenson. Thanks, too, to mentors Dan Rodgers and Deb Nord at Princeton, colleagues Judith Surkis, George Aumoithe, and Margot Canaday, and members of the Professors' Minyan at the Center for Jewish Life including Beth Bacall and Martha Himmelfarb, for making my time in Princeton a lovely one. Thanks as well to Harvard University's Schlesinger Library and the Mellon Foundation for summer research support and making me a persona grata with extraordinary access to the holdings of the Schlesinger at a time when virtually all of the archives in my field were closed. And the most longstanding thanks to the University of Vermont (UVM), especially as represented by History Department chair Paul Deslandes, College of Arts and Sciences Dean Bill Falls and Associate Dean Abby McGowan, and the leaders of my union, United Academics, AFT/AAUP, who made it possible for me to spend that time in Princeton and enabled both a semester-long sabbatical and course reduction that provided time and energy for writing. Thank you, too, to Luis Vivanco and the UVM Humanities Center for additional course releases and subvention funds.

The number of colleagues who pitched in for aid on this project is almost too large to remember, but I will try: For sharing her thoughts, over and again, about this history, I thank Karen Stamm. For reading portions of the manuscript, I am forever indebted to Ellen Chesler, Stamm, Carol Marsh, Tax, Grossmann, Reva Siegel, Nancy Stearns, Linda Greenhouse, David Garrow, Maritza Arrastía, Digna Sánchez, Carmen Vivian Rivera, Sarah Schulman, Nona Willis Aronowitz, Jo Ellen Brainin-Rodríguez, Laura Brainin-Rodríguez, Daniel Curet-Rodríguez, Iris López, and Loretta Ross. Thanks to Associate Dean Rebecca Zietlow of the University of Toledo Law School for inviting me to give the 2022 Cannon Lecture, which allowed an airing of the book's main arguments before publication, and to Bill Nelson for convening the Virtual Legal History Seminar that gave me an opportunity to discuss chapter 5—and to get edits from the ever-generous Nina Dayton. Thank you, Eileen Boris, Serena Mayeri, Kristin Luker, and Linda Hirshman for early conversations about the project, and

Sonya Michel and Jane DeHart for these and helping me navigate the world of agents and editors; Hartog, Johanna Schoen, Chesler, and Garrow for writing letters to support my fellowship applications; Rickie Solinger and Laura Briggs for stimulating conversations about CARASA; Daniel Horowitz for a last-minute fact check on Betty Friedan; Christabelle Sethna for information on abortion tourism across the U.S.-Canadian border; Susan Burch, Michael Rembis, and Kim Nielsen for answering queries about sterilization and disabled Americans; Mary Ziegler for sharing fragments of her own ongoing research on abortion and U.S. law; Linda Gordon for thinking with me over lunch and sharing vital contacts; and Laura Lovett for appreciating the book's conundrums better than I thought anyone could. Thank you, Sarah Schulman and Maxine Wolfe, for crafting the slogan, "A Woman's Life is a Human Life," and for okay-ing its use in this book's title.

For sharing documents and photographs, I thank Stearns for sending a copy of her remarkable brief in the *Abramowicz* case, Stamm for scans of the *CARASA News*, Stamm and Anne Teicher for access to their manuscripts (at Teicher's apartment, which she gave over gamely to a hurried research blitz) only days before they were deposited in the archives, and Garrow for access to the astounding collection in his basement, without which I would never have learned that my father, occasionally given to tall tales, was telling the truth when he said my mother wrote (the first draft of) the law that decriminalized abortion in New York State.

I am indebted to the staff of the Schlesinger Library, especially Director Jane Kamensky and Research Librarian Jennifer Fauxsmith, whose willingness to scan and send hundreds of pages made the difference between book and no book, and to the staffs of the archives at the Center for Puerto Rican Studies/Centro de Estudios Puertorriquenos, the Seeley G. Mudd Manuscripts Library at Princeton, the Tamiment Library at New York University, the Center for the History of Medicine at the Countway Library of Medicine at Harvard, the

Rockefeller Archives, the New York State Archives in Albany, and the Sophia Smith Collection at Smith College. For additional assistance with photographs, I thank Joan E. Biren (JEB) for research she conducted in her own photo archives, Daniel Rodríguez at Redux pictures for help with photos from the *New York Times* collection, the staff at Getty Images for help accessing their photographs, and photojournalist Bev Grant for help locating images of the Young Lords Party.

For permission to quote from *In My Mother's House*, I thank Purdue University Press, and for permission to reprint Audre Lorde's poem, "Who Said It Was Simple," thanks go to W. W. Norton and Company.

For invaluable assistance with research and everything else, I thank the excellent Meghan Letizia, Mickinzie Zadworny, Fiona McMurrey, Richard Witting, Noah Grey Rosenzweig, Cordelia Brazile, and Tom Anderson-Monterosso.

For teaching me about the hard work of sustaining reproductive rights *and* standing for reproductive justice, I am grateful to my colleagues on the Board of Directors of Planned Parenthood of Northern New England, especially Daryl Fort, Kesha Ram Hinsdale, and Lisa Sockabasin, and my colleagues in the Planned Parenthood of Vermont Action Fund, including Lucy Leriche, Marni Maynard, Melinda Moulton, Randall Perkins, and Allie Stickney. For working with me on "Repro Shabbat" and teaching me about the Jewish dimensions of this story, I owe thanks to Temple Sinai Social Action Committee members Carol Hoffer, David Shiman, and Rabbi David Edleson. For seeing me through thin and thick, deepest thanks to Heather Dune Macadam and Suzannah Lessard of my nonfiction writers' group.

Last but not least, I thank the students at UVM, Duke, and Princeton with whom I have had the privilege of discussing the histories of law and constitutionalism, feminism, the postwar United States, and American Jews for the past two decades-plus. I hope this is a book you can use in what may be tough fights ahead.

About the Author

FELICIA KORNBLUH is a writer, activist, and professor who specializes in the histories of poverty, social welfare, feminism, and reproductive politics. She is Professor of History and of Gender, Sexuality, and Women's Studies at the University of Vermont and the author or coauthor of two books on gender, race, and poverty in the modern United States. She writes regularly for the scholarly and popular press, including in the *Journal of American History*, *American Historical Review*, *Law and Social Inquiry*, *Journal of the History of Sexuality*, *New York Times Book Review*, the *Nation*, *Los Angeles Times* op-ed page, and *Women's Review of Books*. She has published on abortion rights and the federal courts for *The American Prospect*, the *Washington Post*, and *The Forward*. Kornbluh holds a B.A. from Harvard-Radcliffe and an M.A. and Ph.D. from Princeton.

Kornbluh has taught at Princeton, Duke, and the University of Vermont. She has held fellowships from the Law and Public Affairs Program at Princeton, the Mellon Foundation and Schlesinger Library, the Institute for Gender, Sexuality, and Feminist Studies at McGill University, the American Historical Association, the American Bar Foundation, the Woodrow Wilson Foundation (now the Institute for Citizens and Scholars), and New York University Law School, and has been a Visiting Scholar at the Center for the Study of Law and Society at Berkeley Law.

Earlier in her career, Kornbluh served as a staff member of the U.S. House of Representatives Select Committee on Children, Youth, and Families, and as a researcher at both the Institute for Policy Studies and Urban Institute think tanks in Washington, D.C. She has been a reporter and advocate since she was a child in New York City, working with Children's Express News Service. Among many stories she covered, Kornbluh reported on children's fears of nuclear war from Japan and the Soviet Union, and on the impact of war on children from Cambodia.

Kornbluh chairs the Board of Directors of the Planned Parenthood of Vermont Action Fund, the lead organization in the campaign to add a Reproductive Liberty Amendment to the state's constitution. Since moving to Vermont in 2009, she has also served as Director of the Gender, Sexuality, and Women's Studies Program at the University of Vermont, as president of UVM's faculty union, United Academics (AFT/AAUP), as a member of the board of Planned Parenthood of Northern New England, and as a member of the state Commission on Women.

Index